PENGUIN BOOKS

MOVIES

Gilbert Adair is the author of the novels *The Holy Innocents*, which won the Authors' Club First Novel Award, *Love and Death on Long Island*, *The Death of the Author*, *The Key of the Tower* and *A Closed Book*. He also wrote *Hollywood's Vietnam*, which analysed the cinema's treatment of the Vietnam War; *Myths & Memories*, *The Postmodernist Always Rings Twice* and *Surfing the Zietgeist*, three collections of essays on British culture; *Flickers*, a celebration of the cinema's centenary; and two sequels to classics of children's literature, *Alice Through the Needle's Eye* and *Peter Pan and the Only Children*. He lives in London and is frequently published as a journalist.

MOVIES

Edited by
GILBERT ADAIR

PENGUIN BOOKS

PENGUIN BOOKS

Published by the Penguin Group
Penguin Books Ltd, 27 Wrights Lane, London W8 5TZ, England
Penguin Putnam Inc., 375 Hudson Street, New York, New York 10014, USA
Penguin Books Australia Ltd, Ringwood, Victoria, Australia
Penguin Books Canada Ltd, 10 Alcorn Avenue, Toronto, Ontario, Canada M4V 3B2
Penguin Books (NZ) Ltd, Private Bag 102902, NSMC, Auckland, New Zealand

Penguin Books Ltd, Registered Offices: Harmondsworth, Middlesex, England

First published in Penguin Books 1999
10 9 8 7 6 5 4 3 2 1

Acknowledgements on pp. 445–7 constitute an extension of this copyright page

The moral right of the editor has been asserted

Set in 9.5/12.5 pt PostScript Adobe New Caledonia
Typeset by Rowland Phototypesetting Ltd, Bury St Edmunds, Suffolk
Printed in England by Clays Ltd, St Ives plc

Contents

List of Illustrations

Preface

The single most significant fact about the cinema at the turn of the millennium is that everyone now is a film buff. In an era of pandemic imagorrhea there truly does exist a literacy of the filmic image.

Cinephilia, or its crude facsimile, is currently an indispensable item in the thinking person's intellectual baggage. Journalists who know next to nothing of the theory, history and sociology of the cinema toss once-specialized coinages like *auteur*, *noir* and *cinémathèque* into their copy with characteristic hack nonchalance. Advertisers who have never heard of Fritz Lang contrive to get hold of what they suppose is some silly pulp science-fiction melodrama from the 1920s (i.e. *Metropolis*), graft a rock score on to it, colorize its images, chop them up, pop them into the video microwave and – hey presto! – a postmodern commercial for alcohol-free lager. Adolescents for whom Marlon Brando is a fat old slob, and *Rebel Without a Cause* a movie made before they were born, have posters of Brando and James Dean pinned up over their beds. Ordinary once-a-month filmgoers who have been familiar for as long as they can remember with the image of an ecstatic Marilyn Monroe standing astride a Manhattan sidewalk grating, her white dress billowing about her limbs like an outsized orchid, are utterly incapable of identifying the specific film from which it was extracted. (The answer, for the record, is Billy Wilder's *The Seven Year Itch*.) As for the culture industry's sociologists and semiologists, mythologists and stylologists, they skim over the glossy, glassy surface of film like so many semi-intellectual hovercrafts without ever submersing themselves in its depths.

Contemporary metropolitan culture is steeped in what might be called the *metacinematic* – to the point, finally, where it's no longer required of us that we confine our engagement with the medium to two hours or so spent within the discrete and cloistered obscurity of an auditorium. The cinema now comes to us or, at any event, meets us halfway, diffracted through such parasitical media as television, video and advertising.

All roads lead, or can be made to lead, to the cinema. In consequence, the millennial film buff is capable of instantly switching attention and allegiance from the past to the present, from Bogart to De Niro, from *The Seven Samurai* to *The Magnificent Seven*, from a James Dean poster to a *Trainspotting* T-shirt, from the *Movie of the Week* to the *Late, Late Show*. For many buffs, indeed, the dissemination of film history – or, rather, what has come to pass for film history – is now contingent on television in exactly the way that the dissemination of the history of music has long been contingent on the record business.

It is not, however, as simple as that. The above examples were not chosen at random, being neither historically nor geographically innocent. Even the most venerable of the films whose titles I cited, *The Seven Samurai*, is, at least from an uncompromisingly film-cultural viewpoint, of relatively recent provenance, since the cinema is over a hundred years old and Kurosawa's masterpiece dates from only 1954. Nor is it by chance that it is the only one made in a language other than English.

For it is one of the particularities of the postmodern ethos that the relativism which has generally been considered its principal contribution to the ongoing history of ideas and forms is itself a relative concept. Although, in theory, this relativism means that every period, every school, every last 'ism', of film history is equally ripe for recycling, the concomitant absence of any consensual cultural hierarchy – a direct and inevitable repercussion of that relativism – has in fact been responsible for the erosion of the scholarship and erudition which would lend shape and meaning to such a concerted ransacking of the past.

Put baldly, the indiscriminate dissemination of film history to which I refer above tends to focus ever more narrowly on what is still doing the cultural rounds, what is still in the unspecialized public domain, what is more or less *on now* – Brian De Palma's remake of *Scarface* rather than Howard Hawks's musty old black and white original, *Metropolitan* rather than *Metropolis*. There are, to be sure, exceptions to this bias, exceptions which have been co-opted to serve as token representatives of the preceding seven or eight decades, but these are invariably the small cluster of unadventurous Hollywood titles with which everyone is likely to be conversant: *Citizen Kane*, *Casablanca*, *The Wizard of Oz*, *It's a Wonderful Life*, etc.

Hence, even if the movies are everywhere, even if their influence has seeped into virtually every vacant pocket of our lives, even if the qualifier 'filmic' has started to acquire something of the same transcultural connotations as the qualifier 'poetic' (which a long time ago ceased to be the exclusive preserve of commentaries on written verse forms), it would be a serious mistake to equate these movies with 'the movies', of whose incomparably rich and multifarious totality they represent but a tiny and insular sampling – new rather than old, mainstream rather than marginal, in colour rather than in black and white, in English rather than subtitled, with a soundtrack rather than silent.

I may be overly pessimistic here, but, for me, such tunnel vision represents nothing less than the End of Cinema. If I capitalize these two words, however, it's because I use them in the specific sense intended by the American historian Francis Fukayama when he coined the phrase 'the End of History'. Fukayama's theory (posited in his bestselling book *The End of History and the Last Man*) was that, with the disintegration of the communist bloc, and the subsequent disrepute into which every species of Marxist socialism has fallen, it is possible to claim the complete and potentially everlasting victory of liberal, free-market democracy as 'the only coherent political aspiration which spans different regions and cultures around the globe'. Since everyone wants the same thing, and can acquire it only by endorsing the same economic system, then (so Fukayama's argument ran) there will by definition be no more global ideological conflicts, no more world wars.

Naturally, one has merely to scan a newspaper to measure how mistaken he was, how slavishly contingent his speculation was on the exclusion of all non-global sociopolitical agendas (the growth of Islamic fundamentalism, the rise of numerous new nationalisms, and so on). At the same time, however, his basic argument, an intellectually respectable paraphrase of the immemorial prejudice that what America already has the rest of us covet, can certainly be applied to the present state of both filmmaking and filmgoing. What I meant above by the End of Cinema is therefore not that the cinema is either dead or dying – which, notwithstanding the threat of various hypermodern information technologies, is patently untrue – but that one type of cinema (and no prizes are given for guessing which) has triumphed over all its former competitors.

As Marx nearly said, a spectre is haunting Europe – the spectre of Hollywood. Hollywood is a hegemony, a near-monopoly. It has *won*. Everyone now sees the same movies, laughs at the same jokes, sheds the same tears, gasps at the same special effects. Just as in every shopping street in the world there may be found the same few brand name stores, so the same few films are screened in every multiplex in the world, all but a handful of them American. Even intellectuals, who would once have queued up to catch the new Bergman or Buñuel, Fellini or Antonioni, Truffaut or Godard, will now make an unreflecting beeline for the latest big splashy Hollywood entertainment. Movie-wise, what America likes, everyone else wants.

The ambition of this anthology is, on a modest, necessarily very partial level, to offer a corrective to that bias, an antidote to the profound cultural amnesia, the intellectual coma, into which film appreciation has sunk. I have not by any means ignored the American cinema which we all (as they say) know and love: the spell cast by Hollywood over the collective imagination remains one of the incontrovertible facts of the twentieth century and it would be perverse not to acknowledge and celebrate its enduring power and charisma. If, though, in my search for stimulating texts (texts, for the most part, by filmmakers themselves and non-specialist writers rather than critics or scholars), I tried to cast my net wider afield than other anthologists before me, it was in order to demonstrate that the cinema, the quintessential art form of our ebbing century, not only *has* a history but *is* a history – our history.

Gilbert Adair
January 1999

Pioneering

VLADIMIR NABOKOV
from *Speak, Memory*

In recent years, the term 'prehistory', when applied to the cinema, seems to have changed its meaning. For long-standing cinéphiles of an older generation it refers solely to the kinetoscopes, praxinoscopes, mechanical shadowboxes and magic lanterns which, during the ebbing years of the nineteenth century, predated the medium's proper history. For the current generation of movie buffs, weaned on Willis and Scorsese, De Niro and De Palma, it represents, by contrast, practically any film made prior to Mean Streets *or even, in the most extreme cases,* Reservoir Dogs. *It represents, in other words, what a cinéphile would think of as the* history, *not the prehistory, of the cinema; and, for those youthful buffs, of course, the medium's true prehistory belongs to an age now as dim and unknowable as that of the invention of the wheel.*

Yet the cinema's Stone Age, as one might describe it, was in actual fact not all that long ago. And it, too, was possessed of its own cranky charm, as witness this extract from Vladimir Nabokov's sumptuous autobiographical memoir, Speak, Memory.

Sometime during the following winter, Lenski conceived the awful idea of showing, on alternate Sundays, Educational Magic-Lantern Projections at our St Petersburg home. By their means he proposed to illustrate ('abundantly,' as he said with a smack of his thin lips) instructive readings before a group that he fondly believed would consist of entranced boys and girls sharing in a memorable experience. Besides adding to our store of information, it might, he thought, help make my brother and me into good little mixers. Using us as a core, he accumulated around this sullen center several layers of recruits – such coeval cousins of ours as happened to be at hand, various youngsters we met every winter at more or less tedious parties, some of our schoolmates (unusually quiet they were – but, alas, registered every trifle), and the children of the servants. Having been given a completely free hand by my gentle and optimistic mother, he rented an elaborate apparatus and hired a dejected-looking university student to man it; as I see it now, warmhearted Lenski was, among other things, trying to help an impecunious comrade.

Never shall I forget that first reading. Lenski had selected a narrative poem by Lermontov dealing with the adventures of a young monk who left his Caucasian retreat to roam among the mountains. As usual with Lermontov, the poem combined pedestrian statements with marvelous melting fata morgana effects. It was of goodly length, and its seven hundred and fifty rather monotonous lines were generously spread by Lenski over a mere four slides (a fifth I had clumsily broken just before the performance).

Fire-hazard considerations had led one to select for the show an obsolete nursery in a corner of which stood a columnar water heater, painted a bronzy brown, and a webfooted bath, which, for the occasion, had been chastely sheeted. The close-drawn window curtains prevented one from seeing the yard below, the stacks of birch logs, and the yellow walls of the gloomy annex containing the stables (part of which had been converted into a two-car garage). Despite the ejection of an ancient wardrobe and a couple of trunks, this depressing back room, with the magic lantern installed at one end and transverse rows of chairs, hassocks, and settees arranged for a score of spectators (including Lenski's fiancée, and three or four governesses, not counting our own Mademoiselle and Miss Greenwood), looked jammed and felt stuffy. On my left, one of my most fidgety girl cousins, a nebulous little blonde of eleven or so with long, Alice-in-Wonderland hair and a shell-pink complexion, sat so close to me that I felt the slender bone of her hip move against mine every time she shifted in her seat, fingering her locket, or passing the back of her hand between her perfumed hair and the nape of her neck, or knocking her knees together under the rustly silk of her yellow slip, which shone through the lace of her frock. On my right, I had the son of my father's Polish valet, an absolutely motionless boy in a sailor suit; he bore a striking resemblance to the Tsarevich, and by a still more striking coincidence suffered from the same tragic disease – hemophilia – so several times a year a Court carriage would bring a famous physician to our house and wait and wait in the slow, slanting snow, and if one chose the largest of those grayish flakes and kept one's eye upon it as it came down (past the oriel casement through which one peered), one could discern its rather coarse, irregular shape and also its oscillation in flight, making one feel dull and dizzy, dizzy and dull.

The lights went out. Lenski launched upon the opening lines:

> The time – not many years ago;
> The place – a point where meet and flow
> In sisterly embrace the fair
> Aragva and Kurah; right there
> A monastery stood.

The monastery, with its two rivers, dutifully appeared and stayed on, in a lurid trance (if only one swift could have swept over it!), for about two hundred lines, when it was replaced by a Georgian maiden of sorts carrying a pitcher. When the operator withdrew a slide, the picture was whisked off the screen with a peculiar flick, magnification affecting not only the scene displayed, but also the speed of its removal. Otherwise, there was little magic. We were shown conventional peaks instead of Lermontov's romantic mountains, which

> Rose in the glory of the dawn
> Like smoking altars,

and while the young monk was telling a fellow recluse of his struggle with a leopard –

> O, I was awesome to behold!
> Myself a leopard, wild and bold,
> His flaming rage, his yells were mine

– a subdued caterwauling sounded behind me; it might have come from young Rzhevuski, with whom I used to attend dancing classes, or Alec Nitte who was to win some renown a year or two later for poltergeist phenomena, or one of my cousins. Gradually, as Lenski's reedy voice went on and on, I became aware that, with a few exceptions – such as, perhaps, Samuel Rosoff, a sensitive schoolmate of mine – the audience was secretly scoffing at the performance, and that afterward I would have to cope with various insulting remarks. I felt a quiver of acute pity for Lenski – for the meek folds at the back of his shaven head, for his pluck, for the nervous movements of his pointer, over which, in cold, kittenish paw-play, the colors would sometimes slip, when he brought it too close to the screen. Toward the end, the monotony of the proceedings became quite unbearable; the flustered operator could not find the fourth slide, having got it mixed up with the used ones, and while Lenski patiently waited in the dark, some of the spectators started to project the black shadows of their raised hands upon the frightened white screen, and presently, one ribald and agile boy (could it be I after all – the Hyde of my Jekyll?) managed to silhouette his foot, which, of course, started some boisterous competition. When at last the slide was found and flashed onto the screen, I was reminded of a journey, in my early childhood, through the long, dark St Gothard Tunnel, which our train entered during a thunderstorm, but it was all over when we emerged, and then

> Blue, green and orange, wonderstruck
> With its own loveliness and luck,
> Across a crag a rainbow fell
> And captured there a poised gazelle.

I should add that during this and the following, still more crowded, still more awful Sunday afternoon sessions, I was haunted by the reverberations of certainly family tales I had heard. In the early eighties, my maternal grandfather, Ivan Rukavishnikov, not finding for his sons any private school to his liking, had created an academy of his own by hiring a dozen of the finest professors available and assembling a score of boys for several terms of free education in the halls of his St Petersburg house (No. 10, Admiralty Quay). The venture was not a success. Those friends of his whose sons he wanted to consort with his own were not always compliant, and of the boys he did get, many proved disappointing. I formed a singularly displeasing image of him, exploring schools for his obstinate purpose, his sad and strange eyes, so familiar to me from photographs, seeking out the best-looking boys among the best scholars. He is said to have actually paid needy parents in order to muster companions for his two sons. Little as our tutor's naïve lantern-slide shows had to do with Rukavishnikovian extravaganzas, my mental association of the two enterprises did not help me to put up with Lenski's making a fool and a bore of himself, so I was happy when, after three more performances (*The Bronze Horseman* by Pushkin; *Don Quixote*; and *Africa – the Land of Marvels*), my mother acceded to my frantic supplications and the whole business was dropped.

Now that I come to think of it, how tawdry and tumid they looked, those jellylike pictures, projected upon the damp linen screen (moisture was supposed to make them blossom more richly) but, on the other hand, what loveliness the glass slides as such revealed when simply held between finger and thumb and raised to the light – translucent miniatures, pocket wonderlands, neat little worlds of hushed luminous hues! In later years, I rediscovered the same precise and silent beauty at the radiant bottom of a microscope's magic shaft. In the glass of the slide, meant for projection, a landscape was reduced, and this fired one's fancy; under the microscope, an insect's organ was magnified for cool study. There is, it would seem, in the dimensional scale of the world a kind of delicate meeting place between imagination and knowledge, a point, arrived at by diminishing large things and enlarging small ones, that is intrinsically artistic.

ANTOINE LUMIÈRE
Letter to Jules Carpentier

The twentieth century began, not as popular myth would have it, postmaturely, in 1912, with the sinking of the Titanic, *but in 1895, prematurely, with the revelation in Paris of a new art form. For ciné-philes, in consequence, the object illustrated below (a brief note from Antoine, father of the two Lumière brothers) is as precious and miracu-lous as would be an invitation to the* vernissage *of the Lascaux cave drawings.*

Paris, 28 December 1895

Monsieur Carpentier
20 rue Delambre
Paris

Dear Monsieur Carpentier,
I shall make sure that everything is ready by six o'clock. Please come to the Grand Café with as many people as you wish. A handshake.
Lumière

LOUIS AND AUGUSTE LUMIÈRE
L'Arrivée d'un train en gare de La Ciotat

L'Arrivée d'un train en gare de La Ciotat *(the train in question, incidentally, was coming from Marseilles) was one of the earliest of all films to have been shot by the* frères Lumière. *Several decades later, Orson Welles excitedly defined the cinema as 'the biggest electric train set any boy ever had!' Well, why not. What tends to be forgotten, however, by an industry increasingly in thrall to the facile fascinations of special effects, is that the train should have, as the Lumières' did, real passengers in it.*

MAXIM GORKY
The Kingdom of Shadows

No films belong more to an exclusively archivist culture, no films reek more of the cinémathèque, than those of the Lumières, to the point where it has become next to impossible to imagine that they, too, were once 'new films' watched by ordinary paying spectators (just like the latest Pedro Almodóvar or Julia Roberts). Maxim Gorky was not, of course, precisely an ordinary spectator – indeed, to be precise, there was no such thing at the turn of the century as an ordinary spectator of a medium that itself was still extraordinary. He was, however, in 1896, a jobbing journalist who (under the pseudonym I. M. Pacatus) contributed this review, of an early Lumière programme screened at the Nizhni-Novgorod fair, to his local newspaper.

Last night I was in the Kingdom of Shadows.

If you only knew how strange it is to be there. It is a world without sound, without colour. Everything there – the earth, the trees, the people, the water and the air – is dipped in monotonous grey. Grey rays of the sun across the grey sky, grey eyes in grey faces, and the leaves of the trees are ashen grey. It is not life but its shadow, it is not motion but its soundless spectre.

Here I shall try to explain myself, lest I be suspected of madness or indulgence in symbolism. I was at Aumont's and saw Lumière's *cinématographe* – moving photography. The extraordinary impression it creates is so unique and complex that I doubt my ability to describe it with all its nuances. However, I shall try to convey its fundamentals.

When the lights go out in the room in which Lumière's invention is shown, there suddenly appears on the screen a large grey picture, *A Street in Paris* – shadows of a bad engraving. As you gaze at it, you see carriages, buildings and people in various poses, all frozen into immobility. All this is in grey, and the sky above is also grey – you anticipate nothing new in this all too familiar scene, for you have seen pictures of Paris streets more than once. But suddenly a strange flicker passes through the screen and the picture stirs to life. Carriages coming from somewhere in the perspective of the picture are moving straight at you, into the darkness in which you sit; somewhere from afar people appear and loom larger as they come closer to you; in the foreground children are playing with a dog, bicyclists tear along, and pedestrians cross the street picking their way among the carriages. All this moves, teems with life and, upon approaching the edge of the screen, vanishes somewhere beyond it.

And all this in strange silence where no rumble of the wheels is heard, no sound of footsteps or of speech. Nothing. Not a single note of the intricate symphony that always accompanies the movements of people. Noiselessly, the ashen-grey foliage of the trees sways in the wind, and the grey silhouettes of the people, as though condemned to eternal silence and cruelly punished by being deprived of all the colours of life, glide noiselessly along the grey ground.

Their smiles are lifeless, even though their movements are full of living energy and are so swift as to be almost imperceptible. Their laughter is soundless, although you see the muscles contracting in their grey faces. Before you a life is surging, a life deprived of words and shorn of the living spectrum of colours – the grey, the soundless, the bleak and dismal life.

It is terrifying to see, but it is the movement of shadows, only of shadows. Curses and ghosts, the evil spirits that have cast entire cities into eternal sleep, come to mind and you feel as though Merlin's vicious trick is being enacted before you. As though he had bewitched the entire street, he compressed its many-storied buildings from rooftops to foundations to yard-like size. He dwarfed the people in corresponding proportion, robbing them of the power of speech and scraping together all the pigment of earth and sky into a monotonous grey colour.

Under this guise he shoved his grotesque creation into a niche in the dark room of a restaurant. Suddenly something clicks, everything vanishes and a train appears on the screen. It speeds straight at you – watch out! It seems as though it will plunge into the darkness in which you sit, turning you into a ripped sack full of lacerated flesh and splintered bones, and crushing into dust and into broken fragments this hall and this building, so full of women, wine, music and vice.

But this, too, is but a train of shadows.

Noiselessly, the locomotive disappears beyond the edge of the screen. The train comes to a stop, and grey figures silently emerge from the cars, soundlessly greet their friends, laugh, walk, run, bustle, and . . . are gone. And here is another picture. Three men seated at the table, playing cards. Their faces are tense, their hands move swiftly. The cupidity of the players is betrayed by the trembling fingers and by the twitching of their facial muscles. They play . . . Suddenly, they break into laughter, and the waiter who has stopped at their table with beer laughs too. They laugh until their sides split but not a sound is heard. It seems as if these people have died and their shadows have been condemned to play cards in silence unto eternity . . .

This mute, grey life finally begins to disturb and depress you. It seems as though it carries a warning, fraught with a vague but sinister meaning that makes your heart grow faint. You are forgetting where you are. Strange imaginings invade your mind and your consciousness begins to wane and grow dim . . .

But suddenly, alongside of you, a gay chatter and a provoking laughter of a woman is heard . . . and you remember that you are at Aumont's, Charles Aumont's . . . But why of all places should this remarkable invention of Lumière find its way and be demonstrated here, this invention which affirms once again the energy and the curiosity of the human mind, forever striving to solve and grasp all, and – while on the way to the solution of the mystery of life – incidentally builds Aumont's fortune? I do not yet see the scientific importance of Lumière's invention but, no doubt, it is there, and it could probably be applied to the general ends of science, that is, of bettering man's life and the developing of his mind. This is not to be found at Aumont's where vice alone is being encouraged and popularized. Why then at Aumont's, among the 'victims of social needs' and among the loafers who here buy their kisses? Why here, of all places, are they showing this latest achievement of science? And soon probably Lumière's invention will be perfected, but in the spirit of Aumont-Toulon and Company.

Besides those pictures I have already mentioned, is featured *The Family Breakfast*, an idyll of three. A young couple with its chubby firstborn is seated at the breakfast table. The two are so much in love, and are so charming, gay and happy, and the baby is so amusing. The picture creates a fine, felicitous impression. Has this family scene a place at Aumont's?

And here is still another. Women workers, in a thick, gay and laughing crowd, rush out of the factory gates into the street. This too is out of place at Aumont's. Why remind here of the possibility of a clean, toiling

life? This reminder is useless. Under the best of circumstances this
picture will only partially sting the woman who sells her kisses.

I am convinced that these pictures will soon be replaced by others
of a genre more suited to the general tone of the Concert Parisien. For
example, they will show a picture titled: *As She Undresses*, or *Madam
at Her Bath*, or *A Woman in Stockings*. They could also depict a sordid
squabble between a husband and wife and serve it to the public under
the heading of *The Blessings of Family Life*.

Yes, no doubt, this is how it will be done. The bucolic and the idyllic
could not possibly find their place in Russia's markets thirsting for the
piquant and the extravagant. I also could suggest a few themes for development by means of a *cinématographe* and for the amusement of the market
place. For instance: to impale a fashionable parasite upon a picket fence,
as is the way of the Turks, photograph him, then show it.

It is not exactly piquant but quite edifying.

'Tracking shots are a question of morality'

JEAN-LUC GODARD

LEO TOLSTOY
A Conversation on Film

Leo Tolstoy was born in 1828, just seven years after Napoleon's death, and died in 1910, just 15 years after the première not only of a film but of the cinema itself – 15 years after the arrival not only of the Lumières' train in La Ciotat station but also of an entirely new art form in the world. It was, moreover, an art form that would not only exploit his work (film versions have been made of both War and Peace *and* Anna Karenina*) but bequeath to posterity a brief but invaluable trace of his own existence (footage exists of the white-bearded old patriarch sitting in his garden). The following conversation – monologue, rather – was added as an appendix to* Kino, *Jay Leyda's classic history of Soviet cinema. It contains a memorable definition of the cinema as a monumental revolving stage; a hint that one of the greatest of all novelists might once seriously (?) have considered writing the scenario for a film; and a poetic fable that one can only wish were true.*

'Y ou will see that this little clicking contraption with the revolving handle will make a revolution in our life – in the life of writers. It is a direct attack on the old methods of literary art. We shall have to adapt ourselves to the shadowy screen and to the cold machine. A new form of writing will be necessary. I have thought of that and I can feel what is coming.

'But I rather like it. This swift change of scene, this blending of emotion and experience – it is much better than the heavy, long-drawn-out kind of writing to which we are accustomed. It is closer to life. In life, too, changes and transitions flash by before our eyes, and emotions of the soul are like a hurricane. The cinema has divined the mystery of motion. And that is greatness.

'When I was writing "The Living Corpse", I tore my hair and chewed my fingers because I could not give enough scenes, enough pictures, because I could not pass rapidly enough from one event to another. The accursed stage was like a halter choking the throat of the dramatist;

and I had to cut the life and swing of the work according to the dimensions and requirements of the stage. I remember when I was told that some clever person had devised a scheme for a revolving stage, on which a number of scenes could be prepared in advance. I rejoiced like a child, and allowed myself to write ten scenes into my play. Even then I was afraid the play would be killed.

'But the films! They are wonderful! Drr! and a scene is ready! Drr! and we have another! We have the sea, the coast, the city, the palace – and in the palace there is tragedy (there is always tragedy in palaces, as we see in Shakespeare).

'I am seriously thinking of writing a play for the screen. I have a subject for it. It is a terrible and bloody theme. I am not afraid of bloody themes. Take Homer or the Bible, for instance. How many bloodthirsty passages there are in them – murders, wars. And yet these are the sacred books, and they ennoble and uplift the people. It is not the subject itself that is so terrible. It is the propagation of bloodshed, and the justification for it, that is really terrible! Some friends of mine returned from Kursk recently and told me a shocking incident. It is a story for the films. You couldn't write it in fiction or for the stage. But on the screen it would be good. Listen – it may turn out to be a powerful thing!'

And Leo Tolstoy related the story in detail. He was deeply agitated as he spoke. But he never developed the theme in writing. Tolstoy was always like that. When he was inspired by a story he had been thinking of, he would become excited by its possibilities. If someone happened to be nearby, he would unfold the plot in all its details. Then he would forget all about it. Once the gestation was over and his brain-child born, Tolstoy would seldom bother to write about it.

Someone spoke of the domination of the films by businessmen interested only in profits. 'Yes, I know, I've been told about that before,' Tolstoy replied. 'The films have fallen into the clutches of businessmen and art is weeping! But where aren't there businessmen?' And he proceeded to relate one of those delightful little parables for which he is famous.

'A little while ago I was standing on the banks of our pond. It was noon of a hot day, and butterflies of all colours and sizes were circling around, bathing and darting in the sunlight, fluttering among the flowers through their short – their very short – lives, for with the setting of the sun they would die.

'But there on the shore near the reeds I saw an insect with little lavender spots on its wings. It, too, was circling around. It would flutter about, obstinately, and its circles became smaller and smaller. I glanced over there. In among the reeds sat a great green toad with staring eyes on each side of his flat head, breathing quickly with his greenish-white, glistening throat. The toad did not look at the butterfly, but the butterfly kept flying over him as though she wished to be seen. What happened? The toad looked up, opened his mouth wide and – remarkable! – the butterfly flew in of her own accord! The toad snapped his jaws shut quickly, and the butterfly disappeared.

'Then I remembered that thus the insect reaches the stomach of the toad, leaves its seed there to develop and again appear on God's earth, become a larva, a chrysalis. The chrysalis becomes a caterpillar, and out of the caterpillar springs a new butterfly. And then the playing in the sun, the bathing in the light, and the creating of new life, begins all over again.

'Thus it is with the cinema. In the reeds of film art sits the toad – the businessman. Above him hovers the insect – the artist. A glance, and the jaws of the businessman devour the artist. But that doesn't mean destruction. It is only one of the methods of procession, or propagating the race; in the belly of the businessman is carried on the process of impregnation and the development of the seeds of the future. These seeds will come out on God's earth and will begin their beautiful, brilliant lives all over again.'

JAMES AGEE
Comedy's Greatest Era

No great film deserves to be called 'silent', for if such a silent is indeed genuinely great it will always have something to say to us. Nor does any great film deserve to be called 'old', for if there exists a single quality shared by virtually all of the cinema's great old films, it's the virtue, paradoxically, of youth. (It could even be argued that the only truly 'old' films are those being made today.) James Agee, a prizewinning novelist (A Death in the Family) and occasional scenarist (of John Huston's The African Queen), was also one of the very first English-language film critics to celebrate the medium's past – or even to acknowledge the fact that it might have had one.

In the language of screen comedians four of the main grades of laugh are the titter, the yowl, the bellylaugh and the boffo. The titter is just a titter. The yowl is a runaway titter. Anyone who has ever had the pleasure knows all about a bellylaugh. The boffo is the laugh that kills. An ideally good gag, perfectly constructed and played, would bring the victim up this ladder of laughs by cruelly controlled degrees to the top rung, and would then proceed to wobble, shake, wave and brandish the ladder until he groaned for mercy. Then, after the shortest possible time out for recuperation, he would feel the first wicked tickling of the comedian's whip once more and start up a new ladder.

The reader can get a fair enough idea of the current state of screen comedy by asking himself how long it has been since he has had that treatment. The best of comedies these days hand out plenty of titters and once in a while it is possible to achieve a yowl without overstraining. Even those who have never seen anything better must occasionally have the feeling, as they watch the current run or, rather, trickle of screen comedy, that they are having to make a little cause for laughter go an awfully long way. And anyone who has watched screen comedy over the past ten or fifteen years is bound to realize that it has quietly but steadily deteriorated. As for those happy atavists who remember silent comedy in its heyday and the bellylaughs and boffos that went with it, they have something close to an absolute standard by which to measure the deterioration.

When a modern comedian gets hit on the head, for example, the most he is apt to do is look sleepy. When a silent comedian got hit on the head he seldom let it go so flatly. He realized a broad license, and a ruthless discipline within that license. It was his business to be as funny as possible physically, without the help or hindrance of words. So he gave us a figure of speech, or rather of vision, for loss of consciousness. In other words he gave us a poem, a kind of poem, moreover, that everybody understands. The least he might do was to straighten up stiff as a plank and fall over backward with such skill that his whole length seemed to flap the floor at the same instant. Or he might make a cadenza of it – look vague, smile like an angel, roll up his eyes, lace his fingers, thrust his hands palms downward as far as they would go, hunch his shoulders, rise on tiptoe, prance ecstatically in narrowing circles until, with tallow knees, he sank down the vortex of his dizziness to the floor, and there signified nirvana by kicking his heels twice, like a swimming frog.

Startled by a cop, this same comedian might grab his hatbrim with both hands and yank it down over his ears, jump high in the air, come to earth in a split violent enough to telescope his spine, spring thence into a coattail-flattening sprint and dwindle at rocket speed to the size of a gnat along the grand, forlorn perspective of some lazy back boulevard.

Those are fine clichés from the language of silent comedy in its infancy. The man who could handle them properly combined several of the more difficult accomplishments of the acrobat, the dancer, the clown and the mime. Some very gifted comedians, unforgettably Ben Turpin, had an immense vocabulary of these clichés and were in part so lovable because they were deep conservative classicists and never tried to break away from them. The still more gifted men, of course, simplified and invented, finding out new and much deeper uses for the idiom. They learned to show emotion through it, and comic psychology, more eloquently than most language has ever managed to, and they discovered beauties of comic motion which are hopelessly beyond reach of words.

It is hard to find a theater these days where a comedy is playing; in the days of the silents it was equally hard to find a theater which was not showing one. The laughs today are pitifully few, far between, shallow, quiet and short. They almost never build, as they used to, into something combining the jabbering frequency of a machine gun with the delirious momentum of a roller coaster. Saddest of all, there are few comedians now below middle age and there are none who seem to learn much from picture to picture, or to try anything new.

To put it unkindly, the only thing wrong with screen comedy today is that it takes place on a screen which talks. Because it talks, the only comedians who ever mastered the screen cannot work, for they cannot combine their comic style with talk. Because there is a screen, talking comedians are trapped into a continual exhibition of their inadequacy as screen comedians on a surface as big as the side of a barn.

At that moment, as for many years past, the chances to see silent comedy are rare. There is a smattering of it on television – too often treated as something quaintly archaic, to be laughed at, not with. Some two hundred comedies – long and short – can be rented for home projection. And a lucky minority has access to the comedies in the collection of New York's Museum of Modern Art, which is still incomplete but which is probably the best in the world. In the near future, however, something of this lost art will return to regular theaters. A thick straw in the wind is the big business now being done by a series of revivals of W. C. Fields's memorable movies, a kind of comedy more akin to the old silent variety than anything which is being made today. Mack Sennett now is preparing a sort of pot-pourri variety show called *Down Memory Lane* made up out of his old movies, featuring people like Fields and Bing Crosby when they were movie beginners, but including also interludes from silents. Harold Lloyd has re-released *Movie Crazy*, a talkie, and plans to revive four of his best silent comedies (*Grandma's Boy*, *Safety Last*, *Speedy* and *The Freshman*). Buster Keaton hopes to remake at feature length, with a minimum of dialogue, two of the funniest short comedies ever made, one about a porous homemade boat and one about a prefabricated house.

Awaiting these happy events we will discuss here what has gone wrong with screen comedy and what, if anything, can be done about it. But mainly we will try to suggest what it was like in its glory in the years from 1912 to 1930, as practiced by the employees of Mack Sennett, the father of American screen comedy, and by the four most eminent masters: Charlie Chaplin, Harold Lloyd, the late Harry Langdon and Buster Keaton.

Mack Sennett made two kinds of comedy: parody laced with slapstick, and plain slapstick. The parodies were the unceremonious burial of a century of hamming, including the new hamming in serious movies, and nobody who has missed Ben Turpin in *A Small Town Idol*, or kidding Erich von Stroheim in *Three Foolish Weeks* or as *The Shriek of Araby*, can imagine how rough parody can get and still remain subtle and roaringly funny. The plain slapstick, at its best, was even better: a profusion of hearty young women in disconcerting bathing suits, frisking around with a gaggle of insanely incompetent policemen and of equally certifiable male civilians sporting museum-piece mustaches. All these people zipped and caromed about the pristine world of the screen as jazzily as a convention of water bugs. Words can hardly suggest how energetically they collided and bounced apart, meeting in full gallop around the corner of a house; how hard and how often they fell on their backsides; or with what fantastically adroit clumsiness they got themselves fouled up in folding ladders, garden hoses, tethered animals and each other's headlong cross-purposes. The gestures were ferociously emphatic; not a line or motion of the body was wasted or inarticulate. The reader may remember how splendidly upright wandlike old Ben Turpin could stand for a Renunciation Scene, with his lampshade mustache twittering and his sparrowy chest stuck out and his head flung back like Paderewski assaulting a climax and the long babyish back hair trying to look lionlike, while his Adam's apple, an orange in a Christmas stocking, pumped with noble emotion. Or huge Mack Swain, who looked like a hairy mushroom, rolling his eyes in a manner patented by French Romantics and gasping in some dubious ecstasy. Or Louise Fazenda, the perennial farmer's daughter and the perfect low-comedy housemaid, primping her spit curl; and how her hair tightened a good-looking face into the incarnation of rampant gullibility. Or snouty James Finlayson, gleefully foreclosing a mortgage, with his look of eternally tasting a spoiled pickle. Or Chester Conklin, a myopic and inebriated little walrus stumbling around in outsize pants. Or Fatty Arbuckle, with his cold eye and his loose, serene smile, his silky manipulation of his bulk and his satanic marksmanship with pies (he was ambidextrous and could simultaneously blind two people in opposite directions).

The intimate tastes and secret hopes of these poor ineligible dunces were ruthlessly exposed whenever a hot stove, an electric fan or a bulldog took a dislike to their outer garments: agonizingly elaborate drawers, worked up on some lonely evening out of some Godforsaken lace curtain; or men's underpants with big round black spots on them. The Sennett sets – delirious wallpaper, megalomaniacally scrolled iron beds, Grand Rapids *in extremis* – outdid even the underwear. It was their business, after all, to kid the squalid braggadocio which infested the domestic interiors of the period, and that was almost beyond parody. These comedies told their stories to the unaided eye, and by every means possible they screamed to it. That is one reason for the India-ink silhouettes of the cops, and for convicts and prison bars and their shadows in hard sunlight, and for barefooted husbands, in tigerish pajamas, reacting like dervishes to stepped-on tacks.

The early silent comedians never strove for or consciously thought of anything which could be called artistic 'form', but they achieved it. For Sennett's rival, Hal Roach, Leo McCarey once devoted almost the whole of a Laurel and Hardy two-reeler to pie-throwing. The first pies were thrown thoughtfully, almost philosophically. Then innocent bystanders began to get caught into the vortex. At full pitch it was Armageddon. But everything was calculated so nicely that until late in the picture, when havoc took over, every pie made its special kind of point and piled on its special kind of laugh.

Sennett's comedies were just a shade faster and fizzier than life. According to legend (and according to Sennett) he discovered the speed tempo proper to screen comedy when a green cameraman, trying to save money, cranked too slow.[1] Realizing the tremendous drumlike power of mere motion to exhilarate, he gave inanimate objects a mischievous life of their own, broke every law of nature the tricked camera would serve him for and made the screen dance like a witches' Sabbath. The thing one is surest of all to remember is how toward the end of nearly every Sennett comedy, a chase (usually called the 'rally') built up such a majestic trajectory of pure anarchic motion that bathing girls, cops, comics, dogs, cats, babies, automobiles, locomotives, innocent bystanders, sometimes what seemed like a whole city, an entire civilization, were hauled along head over heels in the wake of that energy like dry leaves following an express train.

'Nice' people, who shunned all movies in the early days, condemned the Sennett comedies as vulgar and naive. But millions of less pretentious people loved their sincerity and sweetness, their wild-animal innocence and glorious vitality. They could not put these feelings into words, but they flocked to the silents. The reader who gets back deep enough into that world will probably even remember the theater: the barefaced honkey-tonk and the waltzes by Waldteufel, slammed out on a mechanical piano; the searing redolence of peanuts and demirep perfumery, tobacco and feet and sweat; the laughter of unrespectable people having a hell of a fine time, laughter as violent and steady and deafening as standing under a waterfall.

Sennett wheedled his first financing out of a couple of ex-bookies to whom he was already in debt. He took his comics out of music halls, burlesque, vaudeville, circuses and limbo, and through them he tapped in on that great pipeline of horsing and miming which runs back unbroken through the fairs of the Middle Ages at least to ancient Greece. He added all that he himself had learned about the large and spurious gesture, the late decadence of the Grand Manner, as a stage-struck boy in East Berlin, Connecticut and as a frustrated opera singer and actor. The only thing he claims to have invented is the pie in the face, and he insists, 'Anyone who tells you he has discovered something new is a fool or a liar or both.'

The silent comedy studio was about the best training school the movies have ever known, and the Sennett studio was about as free and easy and as fecund of talent as they came. All the major comedians we will mention worked there, at least briefly. So did some of the major stars of the twenties and since – notably Gloria Swanson, Phyllis Haver, Wallace Beery, Marie Dressler and Carole Lombard. Directors Frank Capra, Leo McCarey and George Stevens also got their start in silent comedy; much that remains most flexible, spontaneous and visually alive in sound movies can be traced, through them and others, to this silent apprenticeship. Everybody did pretty much as he pleased on the Sennett lot, and everybody's ideas were welcome. Sennett posted no rules, and the only thing he strictly forbade was liquor. A Sennett story conference was a most informal affair. During the early years, at least, only the most important scenario might be jotted on the back of an envelope. Mainly Sennett's men thrashed out a few primary ideas and carried them in their heads, sure the better stuff would turn up while they were shooting, in the heat of physical action. This put quite a load on the prop man; he had to have the most improbable apparatus on hand – bombs, trick telephones, what not – to implement whatever idea might suddenly turn up. All kinds of things did – and were recklessly used. Once a low-comedy auto got out of control and killed the cameraman, but he was not visible in the shot, which was thrilling and undamaged; the audience never knew the difference.

Sennett used to hire a 'wild man' to sit in on his gag conferences, whose whole job was to think up 'wildies'. Usually he was an all but brainless, speechless man, scarcely able to communicate his idea; but he had a totally uninhibited imagination. He might say nothing for an hour; then he'd mutter, 'You take . . .' and all the relatively rational others would shut up and wait. 'You take this cloud . . . ,' he would get out, sketching vague shapes in the air. Often he could get no further; but thanks to some kind of thought-transference, saner men would take this cloud and make something of it. The wild man seems in fact to have functioned as the group's subconscious mind, the source of all creative energy. His ideas were so weird and amorphous that Sennett can no longer remember one of them, or even how it turned out after rational processing. But a fair equivalent might be one of the best comic sequences in a Laurel and Hardy picture. It is simple enough – simple and real, in fact, as a nightmare. Laurel and Hardy are trying to move a piano across a narrow suspension bridge. The bridge is slung over a sickening chasm, between a couple of Alps. Midway they meet a gorilla.

Had he done nothing else, Sennett would be remembered for giving a start to three of the four comedians who now began to apply their sharp individual talents to this newborn language. The one whom he did not train (he was on the lot briefly but Sennett barely remembers seeing him around) wore glasses, smiled a great deal and looked like the sort of eager young man who might have quit divinity school to hustle brushes. That was Harold Lloyd. The others were grotesque and poetic in their screen characters in degrees which appear to be impossible when the magic of silence is broken. One, who never smiled, carried a face as still and sad as a daguerreotype through some of the most preposterously ingenious and visually satisfying physical comedy ever invented. That was Buster Keaton. One looked like an elderly baby and, at times, a baby dope fiend; he could do more with less than any other comedian. That was Harry Langdon. One looked like Charlie Chaplin, and he was the first man to give the silent language a soul.

When Charlie Chaplin started to work for Sennett he had chiefly to reckon with Ford Sterling, the reigning comedian. Their first picture together amounted to a duel before the assembled professionals. Sterling, by no means untalented, was a big man with a florid Teutonic style which, under this special pressure, he turned on full blast. Chaplin defeated him within a few minutes with a wink of the mustache, a hitch of the trousers, a quirk of the little finger.

With *Tillie's Punctured Romance*, in 1914, he became a major star. Soon after, he left Sennett when Sennett refused to start a landslide among the other comedians by meeting the raise Chaplin demanded. Sennett is understandably wry about it in retrospect, but he still says, 'I was right at the time.' Of Chaplin he says simply, 'Oh well, he's just the greatest artist that ever lived.' None of Chaplin's former rivals rate him much lower than that; they speak of him no more jealously than they might of God. We will try here only to suggest the essence of his supremacy. Of all comedians he worked most deeply and most shrewdly within a realization of what a human being is, and is up against. The Tramp is as centrally representative of humanity, as many-sided and as mysterious, as Hamlet, and it seems unlikely that any dancer or actor can ever have excelled him in eloquence, variety or poignancy of motion. As for pure motion, even if he had never gone on to make his magnificent feature-length comedies, Chaplin would have made his period in movies a great one singlehanded even if he had made nothing except *The Cure*, or *One A.M.* In the latter, barring one immobile taxi driver, Chaplin plays alone, as a drunk trying to get upstairs and into bed. It is a sort of inspired elaboration on a soft-shoe dance, involving an angry stuffed wildcat, small rugs on slippery floors, a Lazy Susan table, exquisite footwork on a flight of stairs, a contretemps with a huge, ferocious pendulum and the funniest and most perverse Murphy bed in movie history – and, always made physically lucid, the delicately weird mental processes of a man ethereally sozzled.

Before Chaplin came to pictures people were content with a couple of gags per comedy; he got some kind of laugh every second. The minute he began to work he set standards – and continually forced them higher. Anyone who saw Chaplin eating a boiled shoe like brook trout in *The Gold Rush*, or embarrassed by a swallowed whistle in *City Lights*, has seen perfection. Most of the time, however, Chaplin got his laughter less from the gags, or from milking them in any ordinary sense, than through his genius for what may be called *inflection* – the perfect, changeful shading of his physical and emotional attitudes toward the gag. Funny as his bout with the Murphy bed is, the glances of awe, expostulation and helpless, almost whimpering desire for vengeance which he darts at this infernal machine are even better.

A painful and frequent error among tyros is breaking the comic line with a too-big laugh, then a letdown; or with a laugh which is out of key or irrelevant. The masters could ornament the main line beautifully;

they never addled it. In *A Night Out* Chaplin, passed out, is hauled along the sidewalk by the scruff of his coat by staggering Ben Turpin. His toes trail; he is as supine as a sled. Turpin himself is so drunk he can hardly drag him. Chaplin comes quietly to, realizes how well he is being served by his struggling pal, and with a royally delicate gesture plucks and savors a flower.

The finest pantomime, the deepest emotion, the richest and most poignant poetry were in Chaplin's work. He could probably pantomime Bryce's *The American Commonwealth* without ever blurring a syllable and make it paralyzingly funny into the bargain. At the end of *City Lights* the blind girl who has regained her sight, thanks to the Tramp, sees him for the first time. She has imagined and anticipated him as princely, to say the least; and it has never seriously occurred to him that he is inadequate. She recognizes who he must be by his shy, confident, shining joy as he comes silently toward her. And he recognizes himself, for the first time, through the terrible changes in her face. The camera just exchanges a few quiet close-ups of the emotions which shift and intensify in each face. It is enough to shrivel the heart to see, and it is the greatest piece of acting and the highest moment in movies.

Harold Lloyd worked only a little while with Sennett. During most of his career he acted for another major comedy producer, Hal Roach. He tried at first to offset Chaplin's influence and establish his own individuality by playing Chaplin's exact opposite, a character named Lonesome Luke who wore clothes much too small for him and whose gestures were likewise as unChaplinesque as possible. But he soon realized that an opposite in itself was a kind of slavishness. He discovered his own comic identity when he saw a movie about a fighting parson: a hero who wore glasses. He began to think about those glasses day and night. He decided on horn rims because they were youthful, ultravisible on the screen and on the verge of becoming fashionable (he was to make them so). Around these large lensless horn rims he began to develop a new character, nothing grotesque or eccentric, but a fresh, believable young man who could fit into a wide variety of stories.

Lloyd depended more on story and situation than any of the other major comedians (he kept the best stable of gagmen in Hollywood, at one time hiring six); but unlike most 'story' comedians he was also a very funny man from inside. He had, as he has written, 'an unusually large comic vocabulary'. More particularly he had an expertly expressive body and even more expressive teeth, and out of his thesaurus of smiles he could at a moment's notice blend prissiness, breeziness and asininity, and still remain tremendously likable. His movies were more extroverted and closer to ordinary life than any others of the best comedies: the vicissitudes of a New York taxi driver; the unaccepted college boy who, by desperate courage and inspired ineptitude, wins the Big Game. He was especially good at putting a very timid, spoiled or brassy young fellow through devastating embarrassments. He went through one of his most uproarious Gethsemanes as a shy country youth courting the nicest girl in town in *Grandma's Boy*. He arrived dressed 'strictly up to date for the Spring of 1862', as a subtitle observed, and found that the ancient colored butler wore a similar flowered waistcoat and moldering cutaway. He got one wandering, nervous forefinger dreadfully stuck in a fancy little vase. The girl began cheerfully to try to identify that queer smell which dilated from him; Grandpa's best suit was rife with mothballs. A tenacious litter of kittens feasted off the goose grease on his home-shined shoes.

Lloyd was even better at the comedy of thrills. In *Safety Last*, as a rank amateur, he is forced to substitute for a human fly and to climb a medium-sized skyscraper. Dozens of awful things happen to him. He gets fouled up in a tennis net. Popcorn falls on him from a window above, and the local pigeons treat him like a cross between a lunch wagon and St Francis of Assisi. A mouse runs up his britches-leg, and the crowd below salutes his desperate dance on the window ledge with wild applause of the dare-devil. A good deal of this full-length picture hangs thus by its eyelashes along the face of a building. Each new floor is like a new stanza in a poem; and the higher and more horrifying it gets, the funnier it gets.

In this movie Lloyd demonstrates beautifully his ability to do more than merely milk a gag, but to top it. (In an old, simple example of topping, an incredible number of tall men get, one by one, out of a small closed auto. After as many have clambered out as the joke will bear, one more steps out: a midget. That tops the gag. Then the auto collapses. That tops the topper.) In *Safety Last* Lloyd is driven out to the dirty end of a flagpole by a furious dog; the pole breaks and he falls, just managing to grab the minute hand of a huge clock. His weight promptly pulls the hand down from IX to VI. That would be more than enough for any ordinary comedian, but there is further logic in the situation. Now, hideously, the whole clockface pulls loose and slants from its trembling springs above the street. Getting out of difficulty with the clock, he makes still further use of the instrument by getting one foot caught in one of these obstinate springs.

A proper delaying of the ultrapredictable can of course be just as funny as a properly timed explosion of the unexpected. As Lloyd approaches the end of his horrible hegira up the side of the building in *Safety Last*, it becomes clear to the audience, but not to him, that if he raises his head another couple of inches he is going to get murderously conked by one of the four arms of a revolving wind gauge. He delays the evil moment almost interminably, with one distraction and another, and every delay is a suspense-tightening laugh; he also gets his foot nicely entangled in a rope, so that when he does get hit, the payoff of one gag sends him careening head downward through the abyss into another. Lloyd was outstanding even among the master craftsmen at setting up a gag clearly, culminating and getting out of it deftly, and linking it smoothly to the next. Harsh experience also taught him a deep and fundamental rule: never try to get 'above' the audience.

Lloyd tried it in *The Freshman*. He was to wear an unfinished, basted-together tuxedo to a college party, and it would gradually fall apart as he danced. Lloyd decided to skip the pants, a low-comedy cliché, and lose just the coat. His gagmen warned him. A preview proved how right they were. Lloyd had to reshoot the whole expensive sequence, build it around defective pants and climax it with the inevitable. It was one of the funniest things he ever did.

When Lloyd was still a very young man he lost about half his right hand (and nearly lost his sight) when a comedy bomb exploded prematurely. But in spite of his artificially built-out hand he continued to do his own dirty work, like all of the best comedians. The side of the building he climbed in *Safety Last* did not overhang the street, as it appears to. But the nearest landing place was a roof three floors below him, as he approached the top, and he did everything, of course, the hard way, that is, the comic way, keeping his bottom stuck well out, his shoulders hunched, his hands and feet skidding over perdition.

If great comedy must involve something beyond laughter, Lloyd was not a great comedian. If plain laughter is any criterion – and it is a healthy counterbalance to the other – few people have equaled him, and nobody has ever beaten him.

Chaplin and Keaton and Lloyd were all more like each other, in one important way, than Harry Langdon was like any of them. Whatever else the others might be doing, they all used more or less elaborate physical comedy; Langdon showed how little of that one might use and still be a great silent-screen comedian. In his screen character he symbolized something as deeply and centrally human, though by no means so rangily so, as the Tramp. There was, of course, an immense difference in inventiveness and range of virtuosity. It seemed as if Chaplin could do literally anything, on any instrument in the orchestra. Langdon had one queerly toned, unique little reed. But out of it he could get incredible melodies.

Like Chaplin, Langdon wore a coat which buttoned on his wishbone and swung out wide below, but the effect was very different: he seemed like an outsized baby who had begun to outgrow his clothes. The crown of his hat was rounded and the brim was turned up all around, like a little boy's hat, and he looked as if he wore diapers under his pants. His walk was that of a child which has just gotten sure on its feet, and his body and hands fitted that age. His face was kept pale to show off, with the simplicity of a nursery-school drawing, the bright, ignorant, gentle eyes and the little twirling mouth. He had big moon cheeks, with dimples, and a Napoleonic forelock of mousy hair; the round, docile head seemed large in ratio to the cream-puff body. Twitchings of his face were signals of tiny discomforts too slowly registered by a tinier brain; quick, squirty little smiles showed his almost prehuman pleasures, his incurably premature trustfulness. He was a virtuoso of hesitations and of delicately indecisive motions, and he was particularly fine in a high wind, rounding a corner with a kind of skittering toddle, both hands nursing his hatbrim.

He was as remarkable a master as Chaplin of subtle emotional and mental process and operated much more at leisure. He once got a good three hundred feet of continuously bigger laughs out of rubbing his chest, in a crowded vehicle, with Limburger cheese, under the misapprehension that it was a cold salve. In another long scene, watching a brazen showgirl change her clothes, he sat motionless, back to the camera, and registered the whole lexicon of lost innocence, shock, disapproval and disgust, with the back of his neck. His scenes with women were nearly always something special. Once a lady spy did everything in her power (under the Hays Office) to seduce him. Harry was polite, willing, even flirtatious in his little way. The only trouble was that he couldn't imagine what in the world she was leering and pawing at him for, and that he was terribly ticklish. The Mata Hari wound up foaming at the mouth.

There was also a sinister flicker of depravity about the Langdon character, all the more disturbing because babies are premoral. He had an instinct for bringing his actual adulthood and figurative babyishness into frictions as crawley as a fingernail on a slate blackboard, and he wandered into areas of strangeness which were beyond the other comedians. In a nightmare in one movie he was forced to fight a large, muscular young man; the girl Harry loved was the prize. The young man was a good boxer; Harry could scarcely lift his gloves. The contest took place in a fiercely lighted prize ring, in a prodigious pitch-dark arena. The only spectator was the girl, and she was rooting against Harry. As the fight went on, her eyes glittered ever more brightly with blood lust and, with glittering teeth, she tore her big straw hat to shreds.

Langdon came to Sennett from a vaudeville act in which he had fought a losing battle with a recalcitrant automobile. The minute Frank Capra saw him he begged Sennett to let him work with him. Langdon was almost as childlike as the character he played. He had only a vague idea of his story or even of each scene as he played it; each time he went before the camera Capra would brief him on the general situation and then, as this finest of intuitive improvisers once tried to explain his work, 'I'd go into my routine.' The whole tragedy of the coming of dialogue, as far as these comedians were concerned – and one reason for the increasing rigidity of comedy ever since – can be epitomized in the mere thought of Harry Langdon confronted with a script.

Langdon's magic was in his innocence, and Capra took beautiful care not to meddle with it. The key to the proper use of Langdon, Capra always knew, was 'the principle of the brick'. 'If there was a rule for writing Langdon material,' he explains, 'it was this: his only ally was God. Langdon might be saved by the brick falling on the cop, but it was *verboten* that he in any way motivate the brick's fall.' Langdon became quickly and fantastically popular with three pictures, *Tramp, Tramp, Tramp, The Strong Man* and *Long Pants*; from then on he went downhill even faster. 'The trouble was,' Capra says, 'that high-brow critics came around to explain his art to him. Also he developed an interest in dames. It was a pretty high life for such a little fellow.' Langdon made two more pictures with high-brow writers, one of which (*Three's a Crowd*) had some wonderful passages in it, including the prize-ring nightmare; then First National canceled his contract. He was reduced to mediocre roles and two-reelers which were more rehashes of his old gags; this time around they no longer seemed funny. 'He never did really understand what hit him,' says Capra. 'He died broke [in 1944]. And he died of a broken heart. He was the most tragic figure I ever came across in show business.'

Buster Keaton started work at the age of three and one-half with his parents in one of the roughest acts in vaudeville ('The Three Keatons'); Harry Houdini gave the child the name Buster in admiration for a fall he took down a flight of stairs. In his first movies Keaton teamed with Fatty Arbuckle under Sennett. He went on to become one of Metro's biggest stars and earners; a Keaton feature cost about $200,000 to make and reliably grossed $2,000,000. Very early in his movie career friends asked him why he never smiled on the screen. He didn't realize he didn't. He had got the dead pan habit in variety; on the screen he had merely been so hard at work it had never occurred to him there was anything to smile about. Now he tried it just once and never again. He was by his whole style and nature so much the most deeply 'silent' of the silent comedians that even a smile was as deafeningly out of key as a yell. In a way his pictures are like a transcendent juggling act in which it seems that the whole universe is in exquisite flying motion and the one point of repose is the juggler's effortless, uninterested face.

Keaton's face ranked almost with Lincoln's as an early American archetype; it was haunting, handsome, almost beautiful, yet it was irreducibly funny; he improved matters by topping it off with a deadly horizontal hat, as flat and thin as a phonograph record. One can never forget Keaton wearing it, standing erect at the prow as his little boat is being launched. The boat goes grandly down the skids and, just as grandly, straight on to the bottom. Keaton never budges. The last you see of him, the water lifts the hat off the stoic head and it floats away.

No other comedian could do as much with the dead pan. He used this great, sad, motionless face to suggest various related things: a one-track mind near the track's end of pure insanity; mulish imperturbability under the wildest of circumstances; how dead a human being can get and still be alive; an awe-inspiring sort of patience and power to endure, proper to granite but uncanny in flesh and blood. Everything that he was and did bore out this rigid face and played laughs against it. When he moved his eyes, it was like seeing them move in a statue. His short-legged body was all sudden, machinelike angles, governed by a daft aplomb. When he swept a semaphorelike arm to point, you could almost hear the electrical impulse in the signal block. When he ran from a cop his transitions from accelerating walk to easy jogtrot to brisk canter to headlong gallop to flogged-piston sprint – always floating, above this frenzy, the untroubled, untouchable face – were as distinct and as soberly in order as an automatic gearshift.

Keaton was a wonderfully resourceful inventor of mechanistic gags (he still spends much of his time fooling with Erector sets); as he ran afoul of locomotives, steamships, prefabricated and over-electrified houses, he put himself through some of the hardest and cleverest punishment ever designed for laughs. In *Sherlock Jr*, boiling along on the handlebars of a motorcycle quite unaware that he has lost his driver, Keaton whips through city traffic, breaks up a tug-of-war, gets a shovelful of dirt in the face from each of a long line of Rockette-timed ditch-diggers, approaches a log at high speed which is hinged open by dynamite precisely soon enough to let him through and, hitting an obstruction, leaves the handlebars like an arrow leaving a bow, whams through the window of a shack in which the heroine is about to be violated, and hits the heavy feet-first, knocking him through the opposite wall. The whole sequence is as clean in motion as the trajectory of a bullet.

Much of the charm and edge of Keaton's comedy, however, lay in the subtle leverages of expression he could work against his nominal dead pan. Trapped in the side-wheel of a ferryboat, saving himself from drowning only by walking, then desperately running, inside the accelerating wheel like a squirrel in a cage, his only real concern was, obviously, to keep his hat on. Confronted by Love, he was not as dead pan as he was cracked up to be, either; there was an odd, abrupt motion of his head which suggested a horse nipping after a sugar lump.

Keaton worked strictly for laughs, but his work came from so far inside a curious and original spirit that he achieved a great deal besides, especially in his feature-length comedies. (For plain hard laughter his nineteen short comedies – the negatives of which have been lost – were even better.) He was the only major comedian who kept sentiment almost entirely out of his work, and he brought pure physical comedy to its greatest heights. Beneath his lack of emotion he was also uninsistently sardonic; deep below that, giving a disturbing tension and grandeur to the foolishness, for those who sensed it, there was in his comedy a freezing whisper not of pathos but of melancholia. With the humor, the craftsmanship and the action there was often, besides, a fine, still and sometimes dreamlike beauty. Much of his Civil War picture *The General* is within hailing distance of Mathew Brady. And there is a ghostly, unforgettable moment in *The Navigator* when, on a deserted, softly rolling ship, all the pale doors along a deck swing open as one behind

Keaton and, as one, slam shut, in a hair-raising illusion of noise.

Perhaps because 'dry' comedy is so much more rare and odd than 'dry' wit, there are people who never much cared for Keaton. Those who do cannot care mildly.

As soon as the screen began to talk, silent comedy was pretty well finished. The hardy and prolific Mack Sennett made the transfer; he was the first man to put Bing Crosby and W. C. Fields on the screen. But he was essentially a silent-picture man, and by the time the Academy awarded him a special Oscar for his 'lasting contribution to the comedy technique of the screen' (in 1938), he was no longer active. As for the comedians we have spoken of in particular, they were as badly off as fine dancers suddenly required to appear in plays.

Harold Lloyd, whose work was most nearly realistic, naturally coped least unhappily with the added realism of speech; he made several talking comedies. But good as the best were, they were not so good as his silent work, and by the late thirties he quit acting. A few years ago he returned to play the lead (and play it beautifully) in Preston Sturges's *The Sin of Harold Diddlebock*, but this exceptional picture – which opened, brilliantly, with the closing reel of Lloyd's *The Freshman* – has not yet been generally released.

Like Chaplin, Lloyd was careful of his money; he is still rich and active. Last June, in the presence of President Truman, he became Imperial Potentate of the AAONMS (Shriners). Harry Langdon, as we have said, was a broken man when sound came in.

Up to the middle thirties Buster Keaton made several feature-length pictures (with such players as Jimmy Durante, Wallace Beery and Robert Montgomery); he also made a couple of dozen talking shorts. Now and again he managed to get loose into motion, without having to talk, and for a moment or so the screen would start singing again. But his dark, dead voice, though it was in keeping with the visual character, tore his intensely silent style to bits and destroyed the illusion within which he worked. He gallantly and correctly refuses to regard himself as 'retired'. Besides occasional bits, spots and minor roles in Hollywood pictures, he has worked on summer stages, made talking comedies in France and Mexico and clowned in a French circus. This summer he has played the straw hats in *Three Men on a Horse*. He is planning a television program. He also has a working agreement with Metro. One of his jobs there is to construct comedy sequences for Red Skelton.

The only man who really survived the flood was Chaplin, the only one who was rich, proud and popular enough to afford to stay silent. He brought out two of his greatest nontalking comedies, *City Lights* and *Modern Times*, in the middle of an avalanche of talk, spoke gibberish and, in the closing moments, plain English in *The Great Dictator*, and at last made an all-talking picture, *Monsieur Verdoux*, creating for that purpose an entirely new character who might properly talk a blue streak. *Verdoux* is the greatest of talking comedies though so cold and savage that it had to find its public in grimly experienced Europe.

Good comedy, and some that was better than good, outlived silence, but there has been less and less of it. The talkies brought one great comedian, the late, majestically lethargic W. C. Fields, who could not possibly have worked as well in silence; he was the toughest and the most warmly human of all screen comedians, and *It's A Gift* and *The Bank Dick*, fiendishly funny and incisive white-collar comedies, rank high among the best comedies (and best movies) ever made. Laurel and Hardy, the only comedians who managed to preserve much of the large, low style of silence and who began to explore the comedy of sound, have made nothing since 1945. Walt Disney, at his best an inspired comic inventor and teller of fairy stories, lost his stride during the war and has since regained it only at moments. Preston Sturges has made brilliant, satirical comedies, but his pictures are smart, nervous comedy-dramas merely italicized with slapstick. The Marx Brothers were side-splitters but they made their best comedies years ago. Jimmy Durante is mainly a nightclub genius; Abbott and Costello are semiskilled laborers, at best; Bob Hope is a good radio comedian with a pleasing presence, but not much more, on the screen.

There is no hope that screen comedy will get much better than it is without new, gifted young comedians who really belong in movies, and without freedom for their experiments. For everyone who may appear we have one last, invidious comparison to offer as a guidepost.

One of the most popular recent comedies is Bob Hope's *The Paleface*. We take no pleasure in blackening *The Paleface*; we single it out, rather, because it is as good as we've got. Anything that is said of it here could be said, with interest, of other comedies of our time. Most of the laughs in *The Paleface* are verbal. Bob Hope is very droit with his lines and now and then, when the words don't get in the way, he makes a good beginning as a visual comedian. But only the beginning, never the middle or the end. He is funny, for instance, reacting to a shot of violent whisky. But he does not know how to get still funnier (i.e., how to build and milk) or how to be funniest last (i.e., how to top or cap his gag). The camera has to fade out on the same old face he started with.

One sequence is promisingly set up for visual comedy. In it, Hope and a lethal local boy stalk each other all over a cow town through streets which have been emptied in fear of their duel. The gag here is that through accident and stupidity they keep just failing to find each other. Some of it is quite funny. But the fun slackens between laughs like a weak clothesline, and by all the logic of humor (which is ruthlessly logical) the biggest laugh should come at the moment, and through the way, they finally spot each other. The sequence is so weakly thought out that at that crucial moment the camera can't afford to watch them; it switches to Jane Russell.

Now we turn to a masterpiece. In *The Navigator* Buster Keaton works with practically the same gag as Hope's duel. Adrift on a ship which he believes is otherwise empty, he drops a lighted cigarette. A girl finds it. She calls out and he hears her; each then tries to find the other. First each walks purposefully down the long, vacant starboard deck, the girl, then Keaton, turning the corner just in time not to see each other. Next time around each of them is trotting briskly, very much in earnest; going at the same pace, they miss each other just the same. Next time around each of them is going like a bat out of hell. Again they miss. Then the camera withdraws to a point of vantage at the stern, leans its chin in its hand and just watches the whole intricate superstructure of the ship as the protagonists stroll, steal and scuttle from level to level, up, down and sidewise, always managing to miss each other by hair's-breadths, in an enchantingly neat and elaborate piece of timing. There are no subsidiary gags to get laughs in this sequence and there is little loud laughter; merely a quiet and steadily increasing kind of delight. When Keaton has got all he can out of this fine modification of the movie chase he invents a fine device to bring the two together: the girl, thoroughly winded, sits down for a breather, indoors, on a plank which workmen have left across sawhorses. Keaton pauses on an upper deck, equally winded and puzzled. What follows happens in a couple of seconds at most: air suction whips his silk topper backward down a ventilator; grabbing frantically for it, he backs against the lip of the ventilator, jacknifes and falls in backward. Instantly the camera cuts back to the girl. A topper falls through the ceiling and lands tidily, right side up, on the plank beside her. Before she can look more than startled, its owner follows, head between his knees, crushes the topper, breaks the plank with the point of his spine and proceeds to the floor. The breaking of the plank smacks Boy and Girl together.

It is only fair to remember that the silent comedians would have as hard a time playing a talking scene as Hope has playing his visual ones, and that writing and directing are as accountable for the failure as Hope himself. But not even the humblest journeymen of the silent years would have let themselves off so easily. Like the masters, they knew, and sweated to obey, the laws of their craft.

NOTE

1. Silent comedy was shot at 12 to 16 frames per second and was speeded up by being shown at 16 frames per second, the usual rate of theater projectors at that time. Theater projectors today run at 24, which makes modern film taken at the same speed seem smooth and natural. But it makes silent movies fast and jerky.

'Morality is a question of tracking shots'

LUC MOULLET

Moviegoing

RENÉ CLAIR
from *Le Silence est d'or*

René Clair's 1947 comedy Le Silence est d'or *(Silence is Golden), which opens with the following brief exchange, was the director's frilly valentine to the period before the cinema learned to talk. But was silence always so golden? Just as unicorns, in fairytale illustrations, are invariably depicted as superbly idealized specimens of their imaginary genus – even though, as is true of horses, there would logically have had to be stocky unicorns, dumpy unicorns, bandy-legged unicorns, and so on – so the silent cinema has ever been enhaloed, in the cinephilic psyone, by a nostalgic aura of aristocratic purity. In this delightful little scene, however, Clair paints a somewhat less rosy picture. And since it was in those years that his own career as a filmmaker was launched, his revisionist version comes, after all, straight from the horse's – or the unicorn's – mouth.*

W et cobblestones. A puddle. A street. Two little girls, one dressed as Pierrette, the other as an Alsatian, walk in the rain. Near them, the parents in their Sunday best. A soldier crosses the street. A fiacre passes. We're in Paris, a holiday or a Sunday. The year? One of the first of the century. Nineteen hundred and six, perhaps. In the distance, the wooden horses of a merry-go-round.

A running couple stops in front of a showman's stall on the façade of which are the words 'Moving Picture Theater'.

WOMAN: The moving pictures. We went once, do you remember?
MAN: This'll make it twice.
WOMAN: It hurt my eyes.
MAN: Close them. What we want is to get out of the rain.
The couple passes in front of the ticket collector who stands at the entrance to the stall.
TICKET COLLECTOR: Come in, ladies and gentlemen, the moving pictures, the invention of the century. An hour of crazy laughter, an hour of oblivion.

The couple enters the stall. Piano music is heard. The hall is almost empty. A comic film is being shown on the screen. At the foot of the screen are the barker and the lady pianist.

The lady pianist looks alternately at the screen and the ceiling. She stretches out her hand. Is it raining? The barker, as he lugubriously explains the comic film, stretches out his hand in the same way. The projectionist, turning the crank, looks up in the air worried. A pocket of water has formed on the cloth covering the stall and the water trickles through drop by drop.

The couple that has just entered sits down, satisfied to be under cover. The man suddenly looks up in the air anxiously. Is it raining in here too?

'What modern movies lack is the wind in the trees'

D. W. GRIFFITH

PETR KRAL
Time Flies

The cinema, or the synchronization of watches across an abyss of 80 years.

We were watching Feuillade's *Judex*. Insulated both against the cold and the ordinary activities of the town we abandoned ourselves delightedly, there amidst countless panelled enclosures in this little cinema in the sticks, to the all-consuming comfort of another era. Suddenly on the screen there appears a clock set in the centre of the kind of sumptuous salon that epoch, and Feuillade, alone had a taste for; it shows 4.40 p.m. One of us automatically consults his watch: 4.40 to the second. For an instant our present, across the ruins of several decades, has rejoined that of an afternoon in the 1910s.

'The cinema will never be anything more than a sideshow attraction'   **AUGUSTE LUMIÈRE**

JAMES AGEE
from *A Death in the Family*

James Agee's novel A Death in the Family *opens with this vivid vignette
of a father accompanying his son to the cinema. They arrive in the
middle of a (silent) William S. Hart western and duly depart when the
programme has come full circle. 'Well,' says the father, 'reckon this is
where we came in.'*

*This is where we came in. These days it seems unimaginable that
audiences once treated the movies so cavalierly. Who, after all, would
open a novel at the 100th page, start reading from there, then close it
again at the 99th. Yet that's precisely how everyone used to go to the
cinema and it did mean that modest genre movies were never allowed
to get ideas above their station. It's even possible that the medium's
decline as a populist art form can be dated from the exact juncture in
its history, some time in the late 1960s, when such a reprehensible
practice was finally made obsolete.*

At supper that night, as many times before, his father said,
'Well, spose we go to the picture show.'

'Oh, Jay!' his mother said. 'That horrid little man!'

'What's wrong with him?' his father asked, not because he didn't
know what she would say; but so she would say it.

'He's so *nasty*!' she said, as she always did. 'So *vulgar*! With his nasty
little cane; hooking up skirts and things, and that nasty little walk!'

His father laughed, as he always did, and Rufus felt that it had become
rather an empty joke; but as always the laughter also cheered him; he
felt that the laughter enclosed him with his father.

They walked downtown in the light of mother-of-pearl, to the Majestic, and found their way to seats by the light of the screen, in the
exhilarating smell of stale tobacco, rank sweat, perfume and dirty
drawers, while the piano played fast music and galloping horses raised
a grandiose flag of dust. And there was William S. Hart with both guns
blazing and his long, horse face and his long, hard lip, and the great

country rode away behind him as wide as the world. Then he made a
bashful face at a girl and his horse raised its upper lip and everybody
laughed, and then the screen was filled with a city and with the sidewalk
of a side street of a city, a long line of palms and there was Charlie;
everyone laughed the minute they saw him squattily walking with his
toes out and his knees wide apart, as if he were chafed; Rufus' father
laughed, and Rufus laughed too. This time Charlie stole a whole bag of
eggs and when a cop came along he hid them in the seat of his pants.
Then he caught sight of a pretty woman and he began to squat and twirl
his cane and make silly faces. She tossed her head and walked away
with her chin up high and her dark mouth as small as she could make
it and he followed her very busily, doing all sorts of things with his cane
that made everybody laugh, but she paid no attention. Finally she
stopped at a corner to wait for a streetcar, turning her back to him, and
pretending he wasn't even there, and after trying to get her attention
for a while, and not succeeding, he looked out at the audience, shrugged
his shoulders, and acted as if *she* wasn't there. But after tapping his foot
for a little, pretending he didn't care, he became interested again, and
with a charming smile, tipped his derby; but she only stiffened, and
tossed her head again, and everybody laughed. Then he walked back
and forth behind her, looking at her and squatting a little while he
walked very quietly, and everybody laughed again; then he flicked hold
of the straight end of his cane and, with the crooked end, hooked up
her skirt to the knee, in exactly the way that disgusted Mama, looking
very eagerly at her legs, and everybody laughed very loudly; but she
pretended she had not noticed. Then he twirled his cane and suddenly
squatted, bending the cane and hitching up his pants, and again hooked
up her skirt so that you could see the panties she wore, ruffled almost
like the edges of curtains, and everybody whooped with laughter, and
she suddenly turned in rage and gave him a shove in the chest, and he
sat down straight-legged, hard enough to hurt, and everybody whooped
again; and she walked haughtily away up the street, forgetting about
the streetcar, 'mad as a hornet!' as his father exclaimed in delight; and
there was Charlie, flat on his bottom on the sidewalk, and the way he
looked, kind of sickly and disgusted, you could see that he suddenly
remembered those eggs, and suddenly you remembered them too. The
way his face looked, with the lip wrinkled off the teeth and the sickly
little smile, it made you feel just the way those broken eggs must feel
against your seat, as queer and awful as that time in the white pekay

suit, when it ran down out of the pants-legs and showed all over your stockings and you had to walk home that way with people looking; and Rufus' father nearly tore his head off laughing and so did everybody else, and Rufus was sorry for Charlie, having been so recently in a similar predicament, but the contagion of laughter was too much for him, and he laughed too. And then it was even funnier when Charlie very carefully got himself up from the sidewalk, with that sickly look even worse on his face, and put his cane under one arm, and began to pick at his pants, front and back, very carefully, with his little fingers crooked, as if it were too dirty to touch, picking the sticky cloth away from his skin. Then he reached behind him and took out the wet bag of broken eggs and opened it and peered in; and took out a broken egg and pulled the shell disgustedly apart, letting the elastic yolk slump from one half shell into the other, and dropped it, shuddering. Then he peered in again and fished out a whole egg, all slimy with broken yolk, and polished it off carefully on his sleeve, and looked at it, and wrapped it in his dirty handkerchief, and put it carefully into the vest pocket of his little coat. Then he whipped out his cane from under his armpit and took command of it again, and with a final look at everybody, still sickly but at the same time cheerful, shrugged his shoulders and turned his back and scraped backward with his big shoes at the broken shells and the slimy bag, just like a dog, and looked back at the mess (everybody laughed again at that) and started to walk away, bending his cane deep with every shuffle, and squatting deeper, with his knees wider apart, than ever before, constantly picking at the seat of his pants with his left hand, and shaking one foot, then the other, and once gouging deep into his seat and then pausing and shaking his whole body, like a wet dog, and then walking on; while the screen shut over his small image a sudden circle of darkness: then the player-piano changed its tune, and the ads came in motionless color. They sat on into the William S. Hart feature to make sure why he had killed the man with the fancy vest – it was as they had expected by her frightened, pleased face after the killing; he had insulted a girl and cheated her father as well – and Rufus' father said, 'Well, reckon this is where we came in,' but they watched him kill the man all over again; then they walked out.

It was full dark now, but still early; Gay Street was full of absorbed faces; many of the store windows were still alight. Plaster people, in ennobled postures, stiffly wore untouchably new clothes; there was even a little boy, with short, straight pants, bare knees and high socks, obviously a sissy: but he wore a cap, all the same, not a hat like a baby. Rufus' whole insides lifted and sank as he looked at the cap and he looked up at his father; but his father did not notice; his face was wrapped in good humor, the memory of Charlie. Remembering his rebuff of a year ago, even though it had been his mother, Rufus was afraid to speak of it. His father wouldn't mind, but she wouldn't want him to have a cap, yet. If he asked his father now, his father would say no, Charlie Chaplin was enough.

JOE BRAINARD
I Remember . . .

In 1986 I published a book entitled Myths & Memories. *It was in two distinct halves, a centaur of a book, as I defined it, which grafted the head of one beast, a collection of essays in a loosely (Roland) Barthesian style, on to the body of another, a series of brief, often one-sentence memories, all of which started with the two words 'I remember . . .' ('I remember snake-clasp belts', 'I remember* The Flying Enterprise', *etc.) and all of which were inspired by the prior example of a little volume by Georges Perec,* Je me souviens. *The conceit, however, had not originated with Perec. He had heard tell from his friend, the American but Paris-based novelist Harry Mathews, of an American collection, I Remember, by one Joe Brainard. And, just as I would subsequently decide to devise an English version of Perec's, so, several years before me, Perec had devised a French version of Brainard's. Coincidentally, neither Perec nor I had ever read Brainard's original – or not in my case until 1995, when* I Remember *was republished, complete with this endorsement from Paul Auster: 'I Remember is a masterpiece.' He is right.*

The book is composed of around 150 pages of sometimes shared, sometimes wholly personal, memories, not one of them longer than a paragraph. Read narrowly, it represents a fragmented autobiography, one dispensing with tediously time-consuming curricula vitae *and lengthy family genealogies. Read more synoptically, it offers a densely textured evocation of middle-class life and culture in the American hinterland of the early 1950s. In either guise it constitutes the zero degree of nostalgia, since its collection of recollections presents itself on the page as no more than a series of mnemonic seeds planted by the author in order to be cultivated by the reader. These seeds are what might be termed snapshots in print, except that what they arrest is not the present but the past, not a movement but a memory. To borrow from the cinema's terminology, they are close-ups of the past, but close-ups designed less to emphasize closeness than to magnify distance, that distance from the present of which the reader must never lose sight if Brainard's little 'Open Sesames' are to make their full impact. The appeal of* I Remember *is therefore that of seeing in print, without*

any judgement being passed by the writer or required of the reader,
phenomena that 'do not deserve' to be seen in print, phenomena that
novelists have tended to exclude from their field of vision as too 'trivial',
but phenomena that nevertheless knot together the basic connective
tissue of our lives. Thus does Brainard grant an eleventh day to a host
of ten-day wonders.

The following is a selection of his 'I remembers . . .' related to film, of
which he was clearly a buff.

I remember the scandal Jane Russell's costume in *The French Line* caused.

I remember a color foldout pinup picture of Jane Russell lounging in a pile of straw in *Esquire* magazine with one bare shoulder.

I remember that Betty Grable's legs were insured for a million dollars.

I remember a picture of Jayne Mansfield sitting in a pink Cadillac with two enormous pink poodles.

I remember how Long Oscar Levant's piano numbers were.

I remember a *very* chewy kind of candy sold mostly at movie theaters. (Chocolate-covered caramel pieces of candy in a yellow box.) They stuck to your teeth. *So* chewy one box would last for a whole movie.

I remember how boring newsreels were.

I remember a boy named Henry who was said to have poured a mixture of orange pop and popcorn off the balcony of the 'Ritz' movie theater as he made gagging sounds.

I remember that Lana Turner was discovered sipping a soda in a drugstore.

I remember that Rock Hudson was a truck driver.

I remember that Betty Grable didn't smoke or drink or go to Hollywood parties.

I remember the rumor that James Dean got off on bodily cigarette burns.

I remember Belmondo's bare ass (a movie 'first') in a terrible 'art' movie called, I think, *Leda*.

I remember a lot of movie star nose job rumors.

I remember the cherries on Marilyn Monroe's dress playing paddle-ball in *The Misfits*.

I remember, in a musical movie about a fashion designer, a black velvet bat winged suit with a rhinestone cobweb on the back.

I remember slightly 'sissy' pants on Italian boys in art movies.

I remember Maria Schell's very wet eyes in *The Brothers Karamazov*.

I remember a lot of very rowdy goings on in *Seven Brides for Seven Brothers*.

I remember Jane Russell and a lot of muscle men doing a big number around the swimming pool of a luxury liner.

I remember Esther Williams' very large face.

I remember being shown to my seat with a flashlight.

I remember dancing boxes of popcorn and hot dogs singing, 'Let's all go out to the lobby, and get ourselves a treat!'

I remember a fashion newsreel about live bug jewelry on a chain that crawled all over you.

I remember Agnes Gooch.

I remember sending some fashion design drawings to 'Frederick's of

Hollywood' in hopes of being discovered as a child genius fashion designer, but – not a word.

I remember the elephant stampede in *Elephant Walk*.

I remember Elizabeth Taylor in *tons* of white chiffon in – also in *Elephant Walk*, I think it was.

I remember that Rock Hudson 'is still waiting for the right girl to come along'.

I remember, in art movies, two nuns walking by.

I remember pretty women all dressed up in black on witness stands (white hankie in hand) with their legs crossed.

I remember that Lana Turner wore *brown* (ugh) to one of her weddings.

I remember in very scary movies, and in very sad movies, having to keep reminding myself that 'it's only a movie'.

I remember mean prison wardens.

I remember once hearing about something called 'Smell-A-Rama': a movie with associated smells piped into the theater.

I remember the 'casting couch'.

I remember Marilyn Monroe in fuchsia satin, as reflected in many mirrors.

I remember the rumor that the reason Marilyn Monroe and Joe DiMaggio split up was because Marilyn couldn't get turned on without another girl in bed with them, and Joe got fed up with this.

I remember the Marilyn Monroe–John Kennedy affair rumor.

I remember the Gomer Pyle–Rock Hudson affair rumor.

JONAS MEKAS
Warhol's *Sleep*

Andy Warhol's famously minimalist eight-hour-long Sleep, *filmed in 1964, offered the spectator nothing more to chew on than an endless static shot of a man asleep. For its part, Peter Weir's* The Truman Show, *a critical and commercial triumph a quarter of a century later, invited us to believe that a 24-hour-a-day, seven-day-a-week television documentary (or, rather, bogus documentary) which consisted of nothing but a single individual's ordinary quotidian round, presumably including his own eight hours of sleep, would have audiences all over the world glued, as they say, to their sets. This telegraphically pithy account by the avant-gardist filmmaker Jonas Mekas of an early screening of* Sleep *puts Weir's specious little conceit into perspective.*

I received a letter from Mike Getz, manager of the Cinema Theatre in Los Angeles, reporting on the screening of Andy Warhol's movie *Sleep*:

Amazing turnout. 500 people. *Sleep* started at 6.45. First shot, which lasts about 45 minutes, is close-up of man's abdomen. You can see him breathing. People started to walk out at 7, some complaining. People getting more and more restless. Shot finally changes to close-up of man's head. Someone runs up to screen and shouts in sleeping man's ear, 'WAKE UP!!' Audience getting bitter, strained. Movie is silent, runs at silent speed. A few more people ask for money back. Sign on box office says no refunds.

7.45. One man pulls me out into outer lobby, says he doesn't want to make a scene but asks for money back. I say no. He says, 'Be a gentleman.' I say, 'Look, you knew you were going to see something strange, unusual, daring, that lasted six hours.' I turn to walk back to lobby. Lobby full, one red-faced guy very agitated, says I have 30 seconds to give him his money back or he'll run into theater and start a 'lynch riot'. 'We'll all come out here and lynch you, buddy!!' Nobody stopped him when 30 seconds were up; he ran back toward screen. In fact, the guy who had said he didn't want to make a scene now said, 'Come on, I'll go with you!!'

I finally yelled at him to wait a minute. Mario Casetta told crowd to give us a chance to discuss it. Mario and I moved into outer lobby. Thoughts of recent football riot in South America. People angry as hell, a mob on the verge of violence. Red-faced guy stomps toward me: 'Well, what are you going to do?'

'I'll give out passes for another show.' Over two hundred passes given out.

Decided to make an announcement. 'Ladies and gentlemen. I believe that *Sleep* was properly advertised. I said in my ads that it was an unusual six-hour movie. You came here knowing that you were going to see something unusual about sleep and I think you are. I don't know what else I could have said. However – [shout from audience: "Don't cop out!! Don't cop out!!"] – however . . .'

Sleep continued on. Projectionist kept falling asleep. People are not able to take the consequences of their own curiosity. Woman calls at 11 'Are you still there?' 'Sure, why?' 'I was there earlier. Heard people in back of me saying this theater's not going to have a screen very much longer so I left.' Fifty were left at the end. Some people really digging the movie.

'The cinema gives us a substitute world which fits our desires'   ANDRÉ BAZIN

Moviemaking

KARL BROWN
from *Adventures with D. W. Griffith*

Karl Brown was second cameraman under the great Johann Gottlob Wilhelm (known as Billy) Bitzer, one of the most remarkable cinematographers in film history. For 16 years, from 1908 to 1924, Bitzer worked in such close collaboration with the director D. W. Griffith that to this day scholars are incapable of judging to which of the two geniuses ought to be attributed, if not exactly the invention, then the development, refinement and aesthetic maturation of such ground-breaking filmic techniques as the close-up, the fade, the iris and the dolly. For Griffith's supreme masterpiece of masterpieces, Intolerance, *a magnificent monstrosity made in 1916 and still, when inflation is taken into account, the costliest of all superproductions, the film set of all time was built (its construction uniquely became the subject of another film, one made all of 70 years later, the Tavianis'* Good Morning, Babylon), *and this is Brown's own account, from his indispensable memoir* Adventures with D. W. Griffith, *of the problems of shooting in and around it.*

In the meantime, the big set, the really big set, was going up on the lot across the tracks. The building of this set had to wait until we were through with the battle stuff around the walls, because we needed all the room we could get to maneuver our armies and towers and elephants. Now that this was finished, we could clear the land and have room to build. The French set had been struck to make way for the walls and towers. Now the Jerusalem street went the way of all things and so did Golgotha.

As in the case of the big stage, the ground was a gently rolling terrain. Nobody thought of leveling it. It was quicker and easier to build the set on upright timbers, which was just what Huck did.

Naturally enough, it had to be built from the ground up. First the grand stairway, then the flooring. After that, the great swelling columns, designed by Hall after no architectural model I had ever heard of. How he ever managed to hoist those trunk-raised elephants into place was

something I never knew because I was busy elsewhere on about as silly a set of errands as one could imagine.

For some reason I had become known and accepted as a musician, which I was not in the accepted understanding of the term. I couldn't play anything. But I could read music, not only well but easily as you can read the printed words that are before you. Griffith was deep in the rehearsing of the various dances to be done at the great feast of Belshazzar and I was tabbed to find the right kind of authentic Oriental music – on records, mind you – and bring it back to the rehearsal hall so our girls could perfect their dances to the sounds of what had to pass for Babylonian music.

So while Huck was building the great hall of the king of Babylon, I was scouring the music shops for anything that could be played on a phonograph for the girls to use for dancing purposes. Of all the stacks of records I brought to the rehearsal room, only one survived to go into the picture as underscoring: the 'Bacchanale' from Saint-Saëns' *Samson and Delilah*.

Then Griffith sent for some real Oriental musicians, who brought their ancient instruments to the studio and played all the traditional music they could remember. But most of it was dull, reedy, and to our ears, out of tune. It might have done very well as music to charm cobras with, but it did not fit in with Griffith's ideas of lushly luxurious sensuality. Amy Woodford Finden was going great guns at the time with her make-believe Oriental music, mostly set in the idiom of her famous songs, such as 'The Kashmiri Song'. These held his attention for quite some time, because they were so popular, these songs about being less than the dust beneath thy chariot wheel, or those pale hands I loved beside the Shalimar. Griffith's instinct was absolutely correct and he should have followed it. If the people – the audience, not the critics – believed this to be the true feeling of the mystic East, then you'd better concur with their beliefs. But he didn't. After trying everything else, he finally sent for Carl Breil and put him to work on the job of thinking up main themes for the main action of the four different pictures all called *The Mother and the Law*. Breil chose to bite into the Biblical picture first, sent for some gray-bearded Hebrew musicologists, and the sounds of the Hebrew wedding-dance and of 'Mazel Tov' echoed through the studio for days to come, with Breil striving valiantly to adjust his musical thinking from the diatonic scale he was trained to use to the altogether different scale of Orthodox Judaism, which is neither major nor minor but an entity in itself, like the whole-tone scale of the early Greeks, which was also being explored by daring young moderns like Debussy and Satie.

Time passed and the big set was finally ready. There it stood in all its glory, the bulging pillars surmounted by trumpeting elephants, while at one side sat the great goddess Ishtar nursing a figure of a full-grown man at her enormous breasts. The set glittered with gold and glowed with color. Everything everywhere was richly carved, richly decorated, richly draped. It almost cried aloud for a Kinemacolor camera, so much so that I rigged a Pathé with an extra shutter wheel so as to shoot alternate pictures on red and green filters, did the same thing with a projector, and showed Griffith exactly what color would do for his set. It was no go. He was not a man to do anything by half measures. It had to be all color or no color at all, and he couldn't see retaking over a year's work for the addition of color alone. If he had known in time . . . but he hadn't. Too bad. Sorry.

The problem of shooting this enormous set was solved very simply.

A two-level elevator of standard design was built into a tower that rolled on wide-spaced steel mining rails. The track was built at an exact water level, and the flanged steel trucks, four of them, were so exactly fitted and balanced that half a dozen men could push them back and forth without trouble. Dead-end stops were fitted at the ends so this rolling platform could not possibly get out of hand or run off the rails. The elevator permitted any camera height from ground level to fifty feet high. It was a beautiful piece of mechanism constructed by backstage experts who had been 'flying' whole sets for years, building revolving stages, and installing rising and falling orchestra pits as a matter of routine. There was nothing new or difficult about it, not to them. They looked upon it as a simple matter of flying a couple of cameras and six or eight men, merely a matter of a thousand pounds at the very most, while they had flown literally tons of dead weight in the cramped quarters of the limited space of a stage. And besides, having all this open space to work in, without the need for concealing anything from an audience, and with plenty of counterweights to balance everything out, they found it all so easy that they marveled we should think it so marvelous.

The big day came. The dancers were assembled. People by the thousands, all in gorgeous costumes, were packed everywhere people could be placed, even along the top of the great back wall with its winged god and its twin Trees of Life.

We mounted in the elevator. Bitzer and Griffith were on the top level, and I was beside them with my camera. We had visitors with us; DeWolf Hopper and Douglas Fairbanks went along for the ride. On the second, or lower, level was Woodbury with his still camera, along with men to work the elevator. Monte Blue sat on a topmost beam with his pistols and flags.

The idea of a run-through for rehearsal was discussed and discarded. Might as well shoot it. A final checkup with all the various on-the-set costumed directors: Siegmann, von Stroheim, Woody Van Dyke, George Hill, Vic Fleming. They were ready, the dancing girls were ready, the light was brilliantly good.

Griffith nodded to Monte Blue, who fired a blast from one of his .45s. The action began, with the bacchanale in full swing as the tower glided slowly forward and sank at the same time. The action was beautiful. Everything worked to perfection. The scene had started with a full shot of the entire set, and it continued inward and downward, until it ended with a close-up of the king and his Princess Beloved admiring one another to the rhythm of our great crowd of dancing girls, dancing without music but in perfect cadence.

We ran the big rolling platform-elevator back and forth until we had taken all the long shots we could of the big set. I managed to get some fairly close shots of people on the elephant towers by using a six-inch lens that I had had fitted to my camera. With this much-modified camera I was able to range over the whole set, so to speak, with close-ups that nobody knew anything about, especially the characters in the picture. I got one particularly good shot of a group of people on the top platform of one of the big, swelled-out columns, just under one of the elephants. It was just right. Composition, lighting, everything. It was 'very fine', except for one minor detail. One of the gorgeously robed men was having trouble with his underpants, which were too loose or something of the sort. So he hiked up his robe and corrected the trouble with a safety pin. He did this with such earnest concentration that you couldn't see anything else. Which was unfortunate. Not for him, for me. Because the technique of softening, subduing, or even blacking out portions of the printed film was old stuff by now, and it was just another arrow in Griffith's bulging quiver. So that scene became one of the many that I used to find waiting for me at the end of a day's work, carefully numbered as a positive print for me to work over with light box and camera. There were many nights when I regretted ever having thought of that business of reworking the positive release prints. And the fact that I had brought it all upon myself didn't make it one bit easier. That unknown man with his breakaway underbritches could never know how much night work that simple repair cost me.

So we got close-up action, and more and more close-up action. It didn't seem to mean much as far as I could see. A couple of high priests plotted to betray Babylon for reasons of their own. It appeared that Alfred Paget – pardon me, King Belshazzar – should have worshipped the ancient sun god instead of Ishtar, the most female of all possible female goddesses, whose seated image was forever before his eyes and whose precepts he followed with the greatest of pleasure. So the priests plotted, in good old reliable melodramatic whispers, to open the water gate so that Cyrus or Darius could sweep into the city and take it without a struggle.

This was all good plotting of the sort I could understand, but if that was what was to happen, why all that battling at the walls? There was so much about the picture that didn't hang together that I soon stopped trying to understand any of it.

Here we had a set that alone must have cost more than the entire production of *The Clansman*. And what was the big moment of this big set with its big everything? Why, the king sends a message from his side of the table to the princess at the other side, with the equivalent of an early-day greeting card drawn in a tiny golden cart by a pair of harnessed white doves. Talk of the mountain laboring and bringing forth a mouse! Even Woodbury commented on it, saying that it was like piling Pelion on Ossa, only in reverse, whatever he may have meant by that.

Then came what was to me, at that time, the greatest injustice ever to be inflicted upon me at any time in my whole life, absolutely without exception. Let me explain it to you carefully so there can be no mistake: Belshazzar worshipped female flesh, as represented by the huge nude figure of Ishtar, which was forever before his eyes. In doing so he was breaking no new ground; it was right there in the Bible, plain as print could make it, that Solomon had one thousand wives. (One of the favorite pastimes of the back-of-the-camera crew was figuring out his schedule, or how long it took him to get around to wife number one thousand, assuming that he was in good working condition all the time.)

Well, like Solomon, Belshazzar had his wives and lots of them, and they were all beautiful, the best the empire could provide. There had to be a scene in which King B picked out his wife for the night. It was to be like any other beauty contest, with the eligibles draped around the throne but otherwise not draped at all, so he could make an intelligent choice unhampered by concealing clothing.

Our girls, beauties all, were to play the wives. Good! For time had been creeping up on me and I was now eighteen going on nineteen and of the age when I felt it to be a grownup dignity to complain about the nuisance of having to shave all the time. Naturally, I would be right there with Griffith and Bitzer shooting this scene. That goes without saying. And when my mother came home for dinner the night before this scene was to be shot, and complained that she had had a hard day getting the girls – *all* the girls – ready for this scene, and that the credit title would probably have to read 'Razors by Gillette', my anticipation knew no bounds.

Oh sure, I had been taking these girls out to dinner and whatever shows were playing at the Mason Opera House as a matter of natural course. Why not? I had had a couple of the raises called for by the contract and my worn-out old Studebaker had been replaced by a Graham-Paige, advertised as the most beautiful car in America, so my invitations were never refused. I had taken them more or less in rotation because – well, if you must know the truth – I would in all probability consider the matter of marriage in the not-too-distant future, and I felt it not unwise to survey the field and check them out, more or less, before making a final decision. So I never took the same girl out twice for, like Solomon, I had a lot of ground to cover, if that is the phrase.

But now I was to have the finest possible chance to do a bit of, shall we say, window-shopping or perhaps comparison-shopping, all together. How could such an opportunity occur again? I counted myself so blessed that I could hardly sleep that night, thinking of the boom that was to be mine the following day.

And can you guess what happened? They actually barred me from the set. And for the flimsiest of reasons. Said I was too young. Can you imagine any injustice so crass? Bitzer was allowed in, but what possible good could that do him? He was already married. Griffith also was married, or had been. Everybody allowed inside that closely guarded set had nothing to learn, while I, with everything to find out about, was excluded. Injustice, that's what it was.

I managed to dredge up one small bit of comfort for my stricken soul: eventually I'd see that scene on screen.

But it wouldn't be the same at all.

Damnit!

LOUISE BROOKS
Pabst and Lulu

Louise Brooks was simply – simply and, since one cannot resist being categoric, unarguably – the most beautiful woman ever to have graced a screen. So beautiful was she, indeed, that it is for once legitimate to compare her to some mythical creature, a siren or a phoenix, and wonder whether, had the cinema not been around to record and preserve the historical reality of her presence, future generations would refuse to believe that she had existed at all. With Garbo and Dietrich, she was the medium's most sheerly legendary star, her mystique and eroticism far exceeding the confines of her sadly undistinguished filmography (the two Pabst films excepted). Her appeal, still calculated to catch an audience collectively by the throat, was utterly opposed to that of 'the girl next door'. No one, but no one, ever lived next door to Louise Brooks.

She was also, as is testified by the following account of her work with Pabst, a uniquely brilliant chronicler of her own adventures and misadventures in film.

Frank Wedekind's play *Pandora's Box* opens with a prologue. Out of a circus tent steps the Animal Tamer, carrying in his left hand a whip and in his right hand a loaded revolver. 'Walk in,' he says to the audience, 'walk into my menagerie!'

The finest job of casting G. W. Pabst ever did was casting himself as the director, the Animal Tamer of his film adaptation of Wedekind's 'tragedy of monsters'. Never a sentimental trick did this whip hand permit the actors assembled to play his beasts. The revolver he shot straight into the heart of the audience.

As Wedekind wrote and produced *Pandora's Box*, it had been detested, banned and condemned from the 1890s. It was declared to be 'immoral and inartistic'. If, at that time when the sacred pleasures of the ruling class were comparatively private, a play exposing them had called out its dogs of law and censorship feeding on the scraps under the banquet table, how much more savage would be the attack upon a film faithful to Wedekind's text made in 1928 in Berlin, where the ruling class publicly flaunted its pleasures as a symbol of wealth and power. And since nobody truly knows what a director is doing till he is done, nobody connected with the film dreamed that Pabst was risking commercial failure with the story of an 'immoral' prostitute who wasn't crazy about her work, surrounded by the 'inartistic' ugliness of raw bestiality.

Only five years earlier the famous Danish actress Asta Nielsen had condensed Wedekind's play into the moral prostitute film *Loulou*. There was no lesbianism, no incest. Loulou the man-eater devoured her sex victims – Dr Goll, Schwarz and Schoen – and then dropped dead in an acute attack of indigestion. This kind of film, with Pabst improvements, was what audiences were prepared for. Set upon making their disillusionment inescapable, hoping to avoid even my duplication of the straight bob and bangs Nielsen had worn as Loulou, Mr Pabst tested me with my hair curled. But after seeing the test he gave up this point and left me with my shiny black helmet, except for one curled sequence on the gambling ship.

Besides daring to film Wedekind's problem of abnormal psychology – 'this fatal destiny which is the subject of the tragedy – besides daring to show the prostitute as the victim; Mr Pabst went on to the final damning immorality of making his Lulu as 'sweetly innocent' as the flowers which adorned her costumes and filled the scenes of the play. 'Lulu is not a real character,' Wedekind said, 'but the personification of primitive sexuality who inspires evil unaware. She plays a purely passive role.' In the middle of the prologue, dressed in her boy's costume of Pierrot, she is *carried* by a stage hand before the Animal Tamer, who tells her, '. . . Be unaffected, and not pieced out with distorted, artificial folly, even if the critics praise you for it less wholly. And mind – all foolery and making faces, the childish simpleness of vice disgraces.'

This was the Lulu, when the film was released, whom the critics praised not less wholly, but not at all. 'Louise Brooks cannot act. She does not suffer. She does nothing.' So far as they were concerned, Pabst had shot a blank. It was I who was struck down by my failure, although he had done everything possible to protect and strengthen me against this deadly blow. He never again allowed me to be publicly identified with the film after the night during production when we appeared as guests at the opening of an UFA film. Leaving the Gloria Palast, as he hurried me through a crowd of hostile fans, I heard a girl saying something loud and nasty. In the cab I began pounding his knee, insisting, 'What did she say? What did she say?' until he translated: 'That is the American girl who is playing our German Lulu!'

In the studio, with that special, ubiquitous sense penetrating minds and walls alike, Mr Pabst put down all overt acts of contempt. Although I never complained, he substituted another for the assistant who woke me out of my dressing-room naps, beating the door, bellowing, 'Fräulein Brooks! Come!' The subtler forms of my humiliation he assuaged with his own indifference to human regard. Using his strength I learned to block off painful impressions. Sitting on the set day after day, my darling maid Josephine, who had worked for Asta Nielsen and thought she was the greatest actress in the world, came to love me tenderly because I was the world's worst actress. For the same reason, the great actor Fritz Kortner never spoke to me at all. He, like everybody else on the production, thought I had cast some blinding spell over Mr Pabst which allowed me to walk through my part. To them it was a sorry outcome of Pabst's search for Lulu, about which one of his assistants, Paul Falkenberg, said in 1955: 'Preparation for *Pandora's Box* was quite a saga, because Pabst couldn't find a Lulu. He wasn't satisfied with any actress at hand and for months everybody connected with the production went around looking for a Lulu. I talked to girls on the street, on the subway, in railway stations – "Would you mind coming up to our office? I would like to present you to Mr Pabst." He looked all of them over dutifully and turned them all down. And eventually he picked Louise Brooks.'

How Pabst determined that I was his unaffected Lulu with the childish simpleness of vice was part of the mysterious alliance that seemed to exist between us even before we met. He knew nothing more of me than an unimportant part he saw me play in the Howard Hawks film *A Girl in Every Port*. I had never heard of him, and knew nothing of his unsuccessful negotiations to borrow me from Paramount until I was called to the front office on the option day of my contract. Ben Schulberg told me that I could stay on at my old salary or quit. It was the time of the switch-over to talkies and studios were cutting actors' salaries just for the hell of it. And, just for the hell of it, I quit. Then he told me about the Pabst offer, which I was now free to accept. I said I would accept it and he sent off a cable to Pabst. All this took about ten minutes and left Schulberg somewhat dazed by my composure and quick decision.

But if I had not acted at once I would have lost the part of Lulu. At that very hour in Berlin Marlene Dietrich was waiting with Pabst in his office. 'Dietrich was too old and too obvious – one sexy look and the picture would become a burlesque. But I gave her a deadline and the contract was about to be signed when Paramount cabled saying I could have Louise Brooks.' It must be remembered that Pabst was speaking about the pre-von Sternberg Dietrich. She was the Dietrich of *I Kiss Your Hand, Madame*, a film in which, caparisoned variously in beads, brocade, ostrich feathers, chiffon ruffles and white rabbit fur, she galloped from one lascivious stare to another. Years after another trick of fate had made her a top star – for Sternberg's biographer Herman Weinberg told me that it was only because Brigitte Helm was not available that he looked further and found Dietrich for *The Blue Angel* – to Travis Banton, the Paramount dress designer who transformed her spangles and feathers into glittering, shadowed beauty, she said: 'Imagine Pabst choosing Louise Brooks for Lulu when he could have had me!'

So it is that my playing of the tragic Lulu with no sense of sin remains generally unacceptable to this day. Three years ago, after seeing *Pandora's Box* at Eastman House, a priest said to me, 'How did you feel?' playing – *that girl!*' 'Feel? I felt fine! It all seemed perfectly normal to me.' Seeing him start with distaste and disbelief, and unwilling to be mistaken for one of those women who like to shock priests with sensational confessions, I went on to prove the truth of Lulu's world by my own experience in the 1925 *Follies*, when my best friend was a lesbian and I knew two millionaire publishers, much like Schoen in the film, who backed shows to keep themselves well supplied with Lulus. But the priest rejected my reality exactly as Berlin had rejected its reality when we made *Lulu* and sex was the business of the town.

At the Eden Hotel where I lived the café bar was lined with the better priced trollops. The economy girls walked the street outside. On the corner stood the girls in boots advertising flagellation. Actors' agents pimped for the ladies in luxury apartments in the Bavarian Quarter. Racetrack touts at the Hoppegarten arranged orgies for groups of sportsmen. The night club Eldorado displayed an enticing line of homosexuals dressed as women. At the Maly there was a choice of feminine or collar-and-tie lesbians. Collective lust roared unashamed at the theatre. In the revue *Chocolate Kiddies*, when Josephine Baker appeared naked except for a girdle of bananas, it was precisely as Lulu's stage entrance was described. 'They rage there as in a menagerie when the meat appears at the cage.'

*

I revered Pabst for his truthful picture of this world of pleasure which let me play Lulu naturally. The rest of the cast were tempted to rebellion. And perhaps that was his most brilliant directorial achievement – getting a group of actors to play characters without 'sympathy', whose only motivation was sexual gratification. Fritz Kortner as Schoen wanted to be the victim. Franz Lederer as the incestuous son Alva Schoen wanted to be adorable. Carl Goetz wanted to get laughs playing the old pimp Schigolch. Alice Roberts, the Belgian actress who played the screen's first lesbian, the Countess Geschwitz, was prepared to go no farther than repression in mannish suits.

Her first day's work was in the wedding sequence. She came on the set looking chic in her Paris evening dress and aristocratically self-possessed. Then Mr Pabst began explaining the action of the scene in which she was to dance the tango with me. Suddenly she understood that she was to touch, to embrace, to make love to another woman. Her blue eyes bulged and her hands trembled. Anticipating the moment of explosion, Mr Pabst, who proscribed unscripted emotional outbursts, caught her arm and sped her away out of sight behind the set. A half hour later when they returned, he was hissing soothingly to her in French and she was smiling like the star of the picture . . . which she was in all her scenes with me. I was just there obstructing the view. In both two-shots and her close-ups photographed over my shoulder she cheated her look past me to Mr Pabst making love to her off camera. Out of the funny complexity of this design Mr Pabst extracted his tense portrait of sterile lesbian passion and Madame Roberts satisfactorily preserved her reputation. At the time, her conduct struck me as silly. The fact that the public could believe an actress's private life to be like one role in one film did not come home to me till last year when I was visited by a French boy. Explaining why the young people in Paris loved *Lulu*, he put an uneasy thought in my mind. 'You talk as if I were a lesbian in real life,' I said. 'But of course!' he answered in a way that made me laugh to realise I had been living in cinematic perversion for thirty-five years.

Pabst was a short man, broad shouldered and thick chested, looking heavy and wilful in repose. But in action his legs carried him on wings which matched the swiftness of his mind. He always came to the set, fresh as a March wind, going directly to the camera to check the set-up, after which he turned to his cameraman Guenther Krampf, who was the only person on the film to whom he gave a complete account of the scene's action and meaning. Never conducting group discussions with his actors, he then took each separately to be told what he must know about the scene. To Pabst, the carry-over of the acting technique of the theatre, which froze in advance every word, every move, every emotion, was death to realism in films. He wanted the shocks of life which released unpredictable emotions. Proust wrote: 'Our life is at every moment before us like a stranger in the night, and which of us knows what point he will reach on the morrow?' To prevent actors from plotting every point they would make on the morrow, Pabst never quite shot the scenes they prepared for.

On the day we shot Lulu's murder of Schoen, Fritz Kortner came on the set with his death worked out to the last facial contortion; with even his blood, the chocolate syrup which would ooze from his mouth, carefully tested for sweetness lest it might surprise an unrehearsed reaction. Death scenes are dearer than life to the actor, and Kortner's, spectacularly coloured with years of theatrical dying, went unquestioned during rehearsal. Pabst left it to the mechanics of each shot to alter Kortner's performance. The smoke from the firing of the revolver became of first importance, or the exact moment when Kortner pulled my dress off my shoulder, or the photographic consistency of the chocolate syrup – all such technical irritations broke a series of prepared emotions into unhinged fragments of reality.

Dialogue was set by Pabst while he watched the actors during rehearsal. In an effort to be funny, old actors and directors have spread the false belief that any clownish thing coming to mind could be said in front of the camera in silent films. They forget the title writer had to match his work to the actors' speech. I remember late one night wandering into Ralph Spence's suite in Beverly Wilshire, where he sat gloomily amidst cans of film, cartons of stale Chinese food and empty whisky bottles. He was trying to fix up an unfunny Beery and Hatton comedy and no comic line he invented would fit the lip action. Silent film fans were excellent lip readers and often complained at the box-office about the cowboy cussing furiously trying to mount his horse. Besides which, directors like Pabst used exact dialogue to isolate and intensify an emotion. When Lulu was looking down at the dead Schoen, he gave me the line, 'Das Blut!' Not the murder of my husband but the sight of the blood determined the expression on my face.

That I was a dancer, and Pabst essentially a choreographer in his direction, came as a wonderful surprise to both of us on the first day of shooting *Pandora's Box*. The expensive English translation of the script which I had thrown unopened on the floor by my chair, had already been retrieved by an outraged assistant and banished with Mr Pabst's laughter. Consequently I did not know that Lulu was a professional dancer trained in Paris – 'Gypsy, oriental, skirt dance', or that dancing was her mode of expression – 'In my despair I dance the Can-Can!' On the afternoon of that first day Pabst said to me, 'In this scene Schigolch rehearses you in a dance number.' After marking out a small space and giving me a fast tempo, he looked at me curiously. 'You can make up some little steps here – can't you?' I nodded yes and he walked away. It was a typical instance of his care in protecting actors against the blight of failure. If I had been able to do nothing more than the skippity-hops of Asta Nielsen his curious look would never have been amplified to regret, although the intensity of his concern was revealed by his delight when the scene was finished. As I was leaving the set he caught me in his arms, shaking me and laughing as if I had played a joke on him. 'But you are a professional dancer!' It was the moment when he realised all his intuitions about me were right. He felt as if he had created me. I was his Lulu! The bouquet of roses he gave me on my arrival at the Station am Zoo was my first and last experience of the deference he applied to the other actors. From that moment I was firmly put through my tricks with no fish thrown in for a good performance.

Four days later I was less wonderfully surprised when he also subjected my private life to his direction. His delight in Lulu's character belonged exclusively to the film. Off the screen my dancing days came to an end when a friend of mine from Washington, with whom I had been investigating Berlin's night life till three every morning, left for Paris. On the set the next day I had just accepted an invitation to an 'Artists' Ball – Wow!' when Mr Pabst's quiet, penetrating voice sounded behind me. 'Pretzfelder! Loueees does not go out any more at night.' Pretzfelder melted away as I began to howl in protest. 'But Mr Pabst, I have always gone out at night when I worked! I can catch up on my sleep between scenes here at the studio. I always have!' He didn't hear me because he was busy laying down the law to Josephine, who thereafter, when the day's work was done, returned his Eve to the Eden where I was bathed, fed and put to bed till called for next morning at seven. Cross and restless, I was left to fall asleep listening to the complaints of the other poor caged beasts across Stresemann-Strasse in the Zoologischer Garten.

In the matter of my costumes for the picture I put up a better fight, although I never won a decision. My best punches fanned the air because Pabst had always slipped into another position. Arriving in Berlin on Sunday and starting the picture on the following Wednesday, I found he had selected my first costume, leaving me nothing to do but stand still for a final fitting. This I let pass as an expedient, never suspecting it would be the same with everything else I put on or took off, from an ermine coat to my girdle. Not only was it unheard of to allow an actress no part in choosing her clothes, but I had also been disgustingly spoiled by my directors at Paramount. I had played a manicurist in 500 dollar beaded evening dresses; a salesgirl in 300 dollar black satin afternoon dresses; and a schoolgirl in 250 dollar tailored suits. (It tickles me today when people see these old pictures and wonder why I look so well and the other girls such frumps.)

With this gross over-confidence in my rights and power, I defied Mr Pabst at first with arrogance. The morning of the sequence in which I was to go from my bath into a love scene with Franz Lederer, I came on the set wrapped in a gorgeous negligée of painted yellow silk. Carrying the peignoir I refused to wear, Josephine approached Mr Pabst to receive the lash. Hers was the responsibility for seeing that I obeyed his orders, and he answered her excuses with a stern rebuke. Then he turned to me. 'Loueees, you must wear the peignoir!' 'Why? I hate that big old woolly white bathrobe!' 'Because,' he said, 'the audience must know you are naked beneath it.' Stunned by such a reasonable argument, without another word I retired with Josephine to the bathroom set and changed into the piegnoir.

Not to be trapped in this manner again, when I objected to the train of my wedding dress being 'tied on like an apron' and he explained that it had to be so easily discarded because I could not play a long, frantic sequence tripping over my train, I answered that I did not give a damn, tore off the train and went into an elaborate tantrum. The worst audience I ever had, Mr Pabst instructed the dress designer to have the pieces sewn together again and left the fitting room. My final defeat, crying real tears, came at the end of the picture when he went through my trunks to select a dress to be 'aged' for Lulu's murder as a streetwalker in the arms of Jack the Ripper. While his instinctive understanding of my tastes, he decided on the blouse and skirt of my very favourite suit. I was anguished. 'Why can't you *buy* some cheap little dress to be ruined? Why does it have to be *my* dress?' To these questions I got no answer till the next morning, when my once lovely clothes were returned to me in the studio dressing-room. They were torn and foul with grease stains. Not some indifferent rags from the wardrobe department, but my own suit which only last Sunday I had worn to lunch at the Adlon! Josephine hooked up my skirt, I slipped the blouse over my head and went on the set feeling as hopelessly defiled as my clothes.

Dancing for two years with Ruth St Denis and Ted Shawn had taught me much about the magic worked with authentic costuming. Their most popular duet, *Tillers of the Soil*, was costumed in potato sacking. In her *Flower Arrangement*, Miss Ruth's magnificent Japanese robes did most of the dancing. But the next three years of uncontrolled extravagance in films had so corrupted my judgment that I did not realise until I saw *Pandora's Box* in 1956 how marvellously Mr Pabst's perfect costume sense symbolised Lulu's character and her destruction. There is not a single spot of blood on the pure white bridal satin in which she kills her husband. Making love to her wearing the clean white peignoir, Alva asks, 'Do you love me, Lulu?' 'I? Never a soul!' It is in the worn and filthy garments of the streetwalker that she feels passion for the first time – comes to life so that she may die. When she picks up Jack the Ripper on the foggy London street and he tells her he has no money to pay her, she says, 'Never mind, I like you.' It is Christmas Eve and she is about to receive the gift which has been her dream since childhood. Death by a sexual maniac.

'Film is more than the twentieth-century art. It's another part of the twentieth-century mind. It's the world seen from inside. We've come to a certain point in the history of film. If a thing can be filmed, the film is implied in the thing itself. This is where we are. The twentieth century is *on film* . . . You have to ask yourself if there's anything about us more important than the fact that we're constantly on film, constantly watching ourselves.'   DON DELILLO

W. S. VAN DYKE
Tarzan, the Ape Man Story Conference Notes

The following is an internal Metro-Goldwyn Mayer memo dating from 1931 and relating to a story conference held during the preparation of Tarzan, the Ape Man *(Tarzan of the Apes was presumably a working title), the very first Tarzan of the talkies: it starred Johnny Weissmuller and Maureen O'Sullivan and was directed by W. S. Van Dyke, familiarly known at MGM as 'One Take Woody' for the rapidity of his shooting technique. The offhand amateurishness of this conference, the crassness of the proposed dialogue and the nonchalant racist ideology will only confirm the worst suspicions of those naïve spectators (they probably still exist) who believe that writers and directors make up films as they go along and that it takes just about as long to shoot a film as it does to watch it – around two hours. Yet – and this is the fundamental paradox of Hollywood –* Tarzan of the Apes *is a terrific film, lyrical, poetic and utterly absorbing, not much short of a masterpiece.*

It couldn't happen now. We are all too 'sophisticated', both those who see movies and those who make them. Hollywood has cried wolf so often, the MGM lion has roared so often from the screen, that if it were suddenly to leap into the auditorium we would watch it calmly, be astonished calmly, and calmly be devoured.

Story Conference
TARZAN of the APES
October 24, 1931
4:45 P.M. to 5.45 P.M.
Reporter: G. Appleby
MR HYMAN
MR VAN DYKE
MR NOVELLO

VAN DYKE: We open up on the night camp, and the night noises begin coming. The girl recognizes the bell-bird, and then the hyenas, and she says, 'Oh, those sickening things.' And then on top of that she says, 'Isn't Africa grand?' As she speaks we might get a shot up through the majestic trees – we have such shots from [*Trader*] *Horn* [1931]. She says, 'It's marvelous.' Then comes the lion roar – and it's far. She poetizes on that. And then one roar is close at hand. She kinda shivers and says, 'That was close.' Holt says, 'Too damn close.' He tells Riano [Ivory Williams] to light the lanterns and tells him to put a man on the fire and keep it going. He says, 'Night makes the big cats bold.' He says, 'They stopped building the Uganda–Tanganyika railroad once in this country – they [lions] were taking men out of the coaches.' . . . Suddenly there's a boom-boom. Holt says, 'Hello, there's a village near here somewhere.' And then you suddenly hear a cry, and the girl says, 'What animal was that?' Holt says, 'That's not an animal.' It's repeated and it's coming closer. The men get their rifles. Suddenly a poor native bursts in – bleeding – cut and nearly dead. They say, 'What's the matter?' The native says he faced the Mutia Escarpment.

NOVELLO: What he says in essence is that he broke a law of the tribe.

VAN DYKE: That law is that no one can look upon the Mutia Escarpment. Holt says, 'Mutia Escarpment? Where is that?' The black starts to point, 'There,' and then drops. Suddenly they all stop and listen, and there's not a sound anywhere. Holt says, 'Get him under cover, quick.' The girl says, 'What's the matter?' He says, 'They're coming.' She says, 'I can't hear anything.' Holt says, 'But I can.' You show Holt knows what he is doing. They cover the native up and then listen for a moment. Everybody remains still. The men get around the girl in a protective attitude – all quiet, defensive movements – and all of a sudden you hear s-s-s-sh – and the tribe bursts out and stops in front of the fire. Holt calls to the chief. They all talk in Swahili. The chief steps forward. They talk for a moment or two. The girl says, 'What does he say?' It's practically what the native said.

NOVELLO: 'We are looking for a man who has broken a law.'

VAN DYKE: That's right. Holt says, 'No man has passed here.' The chief says, 'All right,' and goes back to the tribe and they melt into the night. It's just s-s-s-sh – and it fades, that's all.

The girl says, 'They're ghostly.' Holt says, 'Those are the Ubangas – they're a courageous tribe.' Porter says, 'Well, maybe if they're afraid of the Mutia Escarpment there's some reason.' Holt says 'Maybe not. You know their superstition about elephants.'

Then they get this native out and – or maybe they uncover him – maybe they have thrown something over him hastily. They uncover him – there's no move. Holt says, 'Get up.' No move – he leans down and the man is dead. They said he'd die . . . It might be a thrill.

NOVELLO: I think it might.

VAN DYKE: It would be a nice gesture if they threw a tarp over this fellow and Holt sits on him. When the tribe comes in, Holt rises and tells the chief he hasn't seen anyone. The guy is dead, but he had pointed 'over there'. Do you like that?

HYMAN: Very good – very good. I like that tremendously.

VAN DYKE: '. . . I didn't know the guy was dead until I uncovered him.' I think there's kind of a somber tone of Africa in it. That sequence is all right . . .

COLETTE
Backstage at the Studio

Aside from her irregular film criticism, the novelist Colette (1873–1954) actually wrote two screenplays: for Marc Allégret's Lac-aux-Dames *in 1933 (it was based on a bestselling novel by Vicki Baum, the once celebrated author of* Grand Hotel*) and Max Ophüls's* Divine *in 1935 (which was adapted from Colette's own* L'Envers du music-hall *or* Backstage at the Music Hall*). The two brief texts that follow reflect her experience of life backstage at the cinema. The first relates to a 1917 version of her novel* La Vagabonde *(starring Colette's close chum Musidora, the unforgettable 'Irma Vep' of* Les Vampires*) and the second to the filming of* Divine.

I

utside, it's Roman spring: a sapless azure in which swallows' wings scythe, a day of clouds hardly moved by a feeble warm breeze, and of roses in the gardens, lilacs, acacias, whitethorn, wisteria, that a single day of heat fades and that exchange above the Via Nomentana their perfume of vanilla fritters and orange flowers.

Inside, under the skylights of a studio without walls, it is already – and will be until the cool September breezes – a furnace. The arid air offends the throat and the bronchi – 'but,' as one of the apprentices of the Società Cinematografica says, indicating the thermometer, 'it doesn't often go above 120°'.

The midday cannon has boomed above Rome. From the caretaker's shack the odor of hot oil and fried fish, followed by the sizzle of onions, has crossed the glass theater. Several minutes later the air wafts the smell of coffee and orange peel. Twelve-thirty – one o'clock – two – and no supple Italian actor, no huge-eyed extra, has yet rushed, first toward the dressing rooms and then to the *trattoria*: this world guarded by transparent gates, ruled by the motion of sun and clouds, has broken with the customs of millennia.

The star will eat her lunch toward 4 p.m.; more fortunate, an actor in a small role stealthily polishes off a *frittata* between two slices of the national bread, mealy and compact. I am hungry. Five hundred yards from here I could find a *fiacre*, an ageless horse, a worm-eaten coachman full of shadowy ill-will . . . It is not my work that keeps me here, it is the work of others. I am only the witness, the meddler, the lazybones: the author of the scenario they are 'shooting'. Never mind, I stay. I am present at this spectacle I have seen a hundred times, that has renewed itself for me a hundred times. The program for the day includes several attractions: a fistfight between two rivals, in a set of a shabby music hall; the discovery of a letter, setting the scene for a goodbye . . . For the moment, the delay prolongs itself, and the stoutest hearts waver. A white and blonde matron, enormously fat, engaged at so much the pound to play the role of the Fat Lady, pants in her sequined tight jacket; one thinks of the sparkling death-agony of a fish in faraway seas.

Stoic, in pearl-gray trousers, the young male lead rests standing up. He has slipped a folded handkerchief between his collar and his neck, and fans himself with a newspaper. He doesn't speak, he doesn't complain; his bull-like face, that of a handsome man of the people, expresses only one thought: 'I may die standing up and suffocated, but let there live after me the crease in these pearl-gray trousers, the crease that in a moment will be bent, one time only, for the action of kneeling in front of this dazzling young woman . . .'

Dazzling, in fact. There is nothing whiter than her white, powdered face, unless it is her naked arms, her bare neck, the white of her eyes. Every time I look at her eyes my memory whispers to me the phrase of Charles-Louis Philippe: 'She had eyes of a great expanse . . .' Black, her hair; black, her eyelashes; her dark mouth is open over her white teeth – she is already just like her cinematic image, and the professionals of Italy and France will compliment her to you in a manner that admits of no reply: 'Anything more photogenic than her you couldn't find!'

This veteran young beauty defies the crushing light. She has trained herself – with what pain! – to have eyelids that don't blink, a motionless forehead; my eyes tear on seeing her lift her statuelike gaze toward the midday sun . . . She sweats only slightly at the roots of her carefully waved hair, and sometimes, without a muscle of her face twitching, a round tear, the fruit of her wounded eyes and tense eyelids, falls from her lashes and runs down her cheek.

This young woman, the star, has been cooking under the glass roof since nine in the morning. Yesterday she made eleven changes of clothes,

stockings, shoes, hats, hairstyles. The day before, half-naked in the
gardens, she shivered under lilacs dripping with rain. Tomorrow at
7 a.m. an automobile will carry her to the still snowy mountains, twenty-
five miles there, twenty-five back, nowhere to stop in between. Last
December, with the temperature at 27° F, she went swimming in the
ocean. For a detective film she was thrown under a train, from which
she emerged blackened and slightly burned with cinders, and then was
seated on the fender of a moving car . . .

A strange destiny, one to think about. Hard work under austere
conditions, deprived of the recompense which triumphs over fatigue
every evening at the theater: the applause, the warm contact with the
public, the comfort of being looked at and being envied . . . Is it only
the hunger for making money that sustains the principal actors and
actresses of the cinema and makes them take daily risks? I can't believe
it . . .

'Rrrrrrrrr . . .' The continuous purring of the camera alerts me that
the work is beginning again. The thermometer registers 91°, but from
the swaying of the clusters of wisteria against the burnt wall, from the
sudden flight of rose petals, I know that the *ponentino*, the west wind,
has risen, spreading its cool wings over the city, presaging the setting
of the sun and the clement Roman night . . .

'*Andiamo!*' cries the director, and he adds an '*Allons-y! Let's go!*'
which is understood by everyone, since – we should blush for it! –
managers of the X-Company speak rapid and easy French, and so does
the director, and so do the actors; the Fat Lady coos in French like a
great fat pigeon, and the diminutive bit-part player whom I asked – in
what mangled Italian! – to animate his mimed song a little, replied:

'I no make more the acting with the hands, I'm *romanzero.*'

'*Ro–?*'

'I don't sing except the stories, at the cafés. The *romanzero*, he don't
make the acting with the hands.'

They film. They film 'fillers', 'transitions', those comings and goings,
shots of open and closed doors, corridors, which, placed like ingenious
sutures between the important scenes, will give the audience the illusion
of truth, of real life, of ubiquity . . .

Attentive to the director's instructions, the beautiful black-and-white
young woman sways into the magnificent light of 3 p.m.

'You come in here, you go out there, in between you stop a moment
and listen uneasily to see if your husband's following you.'

She listens, reflects, poses this Sibylline question:

'How much?'

'Six feet, maybe seven . . .'

A hermetic dialogue, in which the initiated can understand that this 'transition' must be acted at a pace that will allow it to be captured on at most seven feet of film. This filmic argot is spoken in Paris just as it is here, and I would often forget where we were, the distance from the borders, if I were not reminded of it by the languor of the air and the unusually calm attitude toward a job which among us infallibly excites nerves and crying jags. 'Here,' Renan wrote, 'the rhythm of life is a degree slower . . .' A bit too much serenity enfeebles the passion of the great lover, and I give up trying to understand why we used to reproach the Italian actors for excessive movement and expression. How gentle they are, even that one, playing the role of an acerbic comedian – yes, that one, who just now raises to the cameraman his worldly-wise face, creased by an internal grin, and his eyes blanketed under their heavy eyelids . . .

'Presto, presto, Ecce Homo!'

Ecce Homo? It's actually him. It's the man – the man who played *Christus* and is no more than justly proud of it. But his wife, to whom I am praising this easygoing deity, glows with pride.

'Don't you think he was handsome as Christ? Do you think he looked well on the cross? Didn't they have luck finding somebody with a fallen diaphragm! Isn't that right, Your Holiness?'

The irreverent blonde who is speaking like this – without a trace of accent – calls out in passing to a sumptuous footman, laden with years and gold braid, who is bearing a platter on which well-curled fennel sets off leg of lamb and whipped potatoes. He turns toward us an adorable Italian face, long, embellished with noble wrinkles, crowned with silver.

'Your Holiness, come and be introduced . . . He was the one who did the pope in that movie, you know, the one that was so well done that everyone thought they'd filmed the real pope . . . He's seventy-eight years old.'

His Holiness smiles, balances his platter on his trembling left hand, and raising the right, grants us, on the run, the papal benediction . . .

Let us leave these profane jokes; the so-photogenic young lady is going to 'shoot' an important scene of my scenario, for which no one has either asked my advice or consulted me; if they had, I would have given them to understand, reinforcing my advice with diplomatic periphrasis, that pyjamas on a woman, even accompanied by a Hindu turban, go better with vaudeville than drama.

The series of rites unfolds itself in an atmosphere of general sweatiness. In a set representing an actress's dressing room, a three-sided mirror is pulled back, then brought forward, then taken away, then returned; the dressing table waltzes from one side of the set to the other. An old touring trunk is given the honor of being placed in the foreground, until the moment when the director notices that it carries, among some twenty hotel stickers, the very legible words 'Dresden', 'Munich', etc. Exile of the trunk, to the sound of kicking. In prances that strange animal, six-legged and caparisoned in black, made up of the camera and cameraman. Groans from a portion of the animal. Redistribution, in an immobile group, of the photogenic young woman, a frail gentleman, another robust gentleman, the Fat Lady – you can hear her breathing from the other end of the studio! – a white Pierrot, an eccentric fashion-plate of a girl – sixteen years old, the sweetest possible virginal face – and a Calabrian peasant. A shout:

'*Gira!*'

And the purr of the motor: the whole group animates itself without a sound; the frail gentleman holds by the wrists the young woman in pyjamas and mouths silent curses at her. She struggles, twists her slender wrists, opens her mouth for a great groan which we hardly hear, and whispers into the face of her tormentor, her face the mask of a woman screaming: 'I forbid you . . . I forbid you to treat me this way . . . Coward . . . miserable villain . . .'

The robust gentleman says nothing; he restrains himself and clutches at his cane. His whole left leg is thinking of the crease in the pearl-gray trousers . . . The other actors, in the background, murmur and move about in place like a screen of trees blown by a sudden wind . . . A shout:

'*Basta!*'

And the collective expression of the group falls away; the shoulders sag, the eyes lose their momentary fire, the knees relax . . .

'*Basta per oggi! È finito!*'

È finito! Nevertheless, as the adolescent cries of joy of the released resound, the director detains the photogenic young woman, who is listening to the program for tomorrow:

'Tomorrow, little one, we're filming at Nemi and the car leaves at

8 a.m. Bring the costume for the flight, the dress for the garden, the evening dress with the coat, all the accessories. Don't forget anything, all right? Nemi isn't just around the corner . . .'

She listens in hopeless submission, nods 'yes, yes', and recites in a low voice the litany of her baggage:

'The pink dress, the gray stockings, the doeskin slippers, the black tulle robe, the violet coat, the white gloves, the diadem, the kimono, the furred mules, the blue suit . . .'

And as if until this minute, by an effort of will, she had been in command of nature, she suddenly begins to sweat freely and goes off toward her dressing room reciting her psalms:

'The violet coat, the blue suit, the furred mules, the diadem, the gray stockings . . .'

My eye follows this slim silhouette, this body only a moment ago tensed and now soft and swaying in the silk pyjamas, and I ask myself again: 'The thirst for gain, success on the screen, the love of a daily flirtation with danger – could they be enough to draw a young woman to this existence for year after year? There is love of the craft, I know, and also the spirit of rivalry. But what else?'

A snatch of dialogue between two young cinema actresses comes back to me:

'It isn't as good as the theater, and it's back-breaking work,' said the first.

'Maybe,' said the other. 'But in the movies, you can see yourself . . .'

Perhaps this delicate narcissism should also be noted in the way certain stars of the cinema commonly think and express themselves. One of the most notorious and beautiful of the Italian *prima donnas* criticizes, curses, or admires herself on the screen as if she were talking about another person, with a sort of hallucinated candor.

'Did you see *La Piccola Fonte*?' she said to me. 'Didn't you think it was good? In the garden, when *she* drags herself along the wall and the door, *she* has a way of holding herself, a way of moving her arms, that's lovely . . .'

Among the women who consecrate their youth and the perishable flowers of their faces to the screens, might there not be a sort of lovers' fanaticism toward those mysterious 'doubles' in black and white, detached from them by some cinematic miracle, eternally free, complete, surprising, more full of life than they themselves – 'doubles' whose existence they contemplate as humble creators, sometimes delighted, often astonished, and feeling always toward them a certain lack of responsibility.

I I

The more I see them, cloistered in their work, the more I admire cinema actors. For two months I have been seeing a great deal of them – not enough to suit me. I am ready to ask myself once more where they get their energy. The bitter epigram of one of them does not enlighten me, because it is redolent with a kind of perverse pride, a surly modesty.

Worn out, I was leaving the studio at the end of one of those interminable work days that begin at daybreak under false sunlight, fail to take into account lunch and dinner hours, have only contempt for the limits of human endurance, and often end – since the theaters claim their personnel at eight – only to begin again after midnight . . . I was telling X, an actor in both the theater and the cinema, about the diverse feelings toward cinema actors inspired in me by my own weariness and their courage: 'Bah!' he said to me, 'you're never exhausted when you're well paid.'

He affected bravura under his makeup, which had been done over twice since noon, and posed as the avid businessman. But I am no dupe. Although they greatly exceed the honoraria available in the theater, the profits of cinema do not justify the actors' heroism. I am only now beginning to study – reproaching myself for leaving it until so late in the cinematic day – what a cinematic vocation might be, its true essence, its goal and its reward when this goal and this reward become differentiated from rapacity.

Because, for people of my generation, film will always be surrounded by a sort of aura, defensive and not easily penetrable. At twenty-one, my daughter is already a director, fervent, impatient to show what she can do. She gnaws at her leash of 'assistant' and is an example of humility. For four years she has been *inside* the cinema. So long a novitiate has made her unable to comprehend my reasons for astonishment. She shares the impassibility of the screen actors; like them she 'rests' bolt upright, and like them she maintains a lengthy silence because only one man has the right to storm.

She is capable of discussing subtly the afflictions, the infantilism, the wonders of the cinema; but she will not enlighten me about the basic cause, the emotional source, of such a marvelous equanimity in the face of work and silence . . .

One day during the coldest week in February, I was at the Billancourt studios, where fifty young women, half-naked, were filming music-hall scenes. For seven consecutive hours, sheltered under the heavy special makeup, they underwent the temperature extremes of a cloth-covered courtyard, iced by the east wind and then briefly overheated by a catastrophe of Klieg lights. Following Max Ophuls' quick commands, they climbed up and down the raw wood steps unprotected by guard rails, running and turning with inexhaustible graces. A terrible arrow of light pierced in passing Simone Berriau's golden eyes and Gina Manès' phosphorus-blue ones. Phillippe Hériat, nude and chromed, shuddered with cold and refused the robe that would have tarnished his metallic makeup. No starving extra permitted herself to faint. At a cry from Ophuls – 'We can hear the feet on the stairs! Take off your shoes!' – fifty young women, Simone Berriau among them, took off their shoes without a word and ran barefoot over the unfinished wood, among serpentining cables, metal shavings, rubble, and nails.

This was the same day on which the hands of an animal trainer were to drape over Simone Berriau's shoulders a live python, almost as heavy as a man . . .

'What will he do?' I asked the serpent's trainer shortly before this happened.

He shrugged his shoulders, uncertain.

'You can't tell . . . He's young, you see, and intelligent . . . Not bad-tempered, you understand, but he doesn't know the lady . . . The best thing is to let him alone. If there's any trouble, I always have this . . .'

He showed me, very naturally, a heavy, double-edged knife. Then, from a valise that was keeping warm on a radiator, he took three yards of python, draped it around his neck, and taught me to gently scratch 'Joseph's' chin, which was richly marbled, here and there almost pink.

When he laid this formidable silent actor on the shoulders of 'Divine', dressed as a dancing girl, she sagged a moment, then straightened up. Then she was left entirely alone with 'Joseph', and both were covered with pitiless Klieg lights. At first the serpent was at the level of her hips. It circled her waist solidly and sent off its agile head in the direction of her neck and bosom. It explored her whole bust, which it touched gently with its long bifidal tongue. A sort of grin of anguish flitted over the dancing girl's face, cracked open her mouth to show her gleaming teeth. The serpent's head disappeared behind her shoulder, drawing the body after it in indescribable ophidian progression, and I thought that the ordeal was nearing its end . . . But at the top of her gilded headdress, the python's head reappeared, raised itself like a rattler's. A moment more, and it flowed down the temple, stopped at the corner of the eyebrow, licked her cheek . . . Simone Berriau's large eyelids fluttered downward, his her eyes, and Ophuls allowed her to be rescued . . . But I think that he was more moved than she, who was already shaking off the evil spell and inquiring:

'Did it work? Were we all right, Joseph and me?'

Vocation, vocation – a need to touch the emotions of the mass, to appeal to the common judgment . . .

'Photography is truth. The cinema is truth 24 times a second'   JEAN-LUC GODARD

AKIRA KUROSAWA
from *Something Like an Autobiography*

Akira Kurosawa was, at least as far as his reputation in the West is concerned, the most eminent of all Japanese directors, almost all of whose films – notably, the two most renowned, Rashōmon *and* The Seven Samurai *– conform uncannily to everyone's off-the-top-of-the-head notion of what a Japanese film should look like. Here, in a passage from what he called* Something Like an Autobiography, *he writes of the making of* Rashōmon.

During that time the gate was growing larger and larger in my mind's eye. I was location-scouting in the ancient capital of Kyōto for *Rashōmon*, my eleventh-century period film. The Daiei management was not very happy with the project. They said the content was difficult and the title had no appeal. They were reluctant to let the shooting begin. Day by day, as I waited, I walked around Kyōto and the still more ancient capital of Nara a few miles away, studying the classical architecture. The more I saw, the larger the image of the Rashōmon gate became in my mind.

At first I thought my gate should be about the size of the entrance gate to Tōji Temple in Kyōto. Then it became as large as the Tengaimon gate in Nara, and finally as big as the main two-story gates of the Ninnaji and Tōdaiji temples in Nara. This image enlargement occurred not just because I had the opportunity to see real gates dating from that period, but because of what I was learning, from documents and relics, about the long-since-destroyed Rashōmon gate itself.

'Rashōmon' actually refers to the Rajōmon gate; the name was changed in a Noh play written by Kanze Nobumitsu. 'Rajō' indicates the outer precincts of the castle, so 'Rajōmon' means the main gate to the castle's outer grounds. The gate for my film *Rashōmon* was the main gate to the outer precincts of the ancient capital – Kyōto was at that time called 'Heian-Kyō'. If one entered the capital through the Rajōmon gate and continued due north along the main thoroughfare of the metropolis, one came to the Shujakumon gate at the end of it, and the Tōji and Saiji temples to the east and west, respectively. Considering this city plan, it would have been strange had the outer main gate not been the biggest gate of all. There is tangible evidence that it in fact was: The blue roof tiles that survive from the original Rajōmon gate show that it was large. But, no matter how much research we did, we couldn't discover the actual dimensions of the vanished structure.

As a result, we had to construct the *Rashōmon* gate to the city based on what we could learn from looking at extant temple gates, knowing that the original was probably different. What we built as a set was gigantic. It was so immense that a complete roof would have buckled the support pillars. Using the artistic device of dilapidation as an excuse, we constructed only half a roof and were able to get away with our measurements. To be historically accurate, the imperial palace and the Shujakumon gate should have been visible looking north through our gate. But on the Daiei back lot such distances were out of the question, and even if we had been able to find the space, the budget would have made it impossible. We made do with a cut-out mountain to be seen through the gate. Even so, what we built was extraordinarily large for an open set.

When I took this project to Daiei, I told them the only sets I would need were the gate and the tribunal courtyard wall where all the survivors, participants and witnesses of the rape and murder that form the story of the film are questioned. Everything else, I promised them, would be shot on location. Based on this low-budget set estimate, Daiei happily took on the project.

Later Kawaguchi Matsutarō, at that time a Daiei executive, complained that they had really been fed a line. To be sure, only the gate set had to be built, but for the price of that one mammoth set they could have had over a hundred ordinary sets. But, to tell the truth, I hadn't intended so big a set to begin with. It was while I was kept waiting all that time that my research deepened and my image of the gate swelled to its startling proportions.

When I had finished *Scandal* for the Shōchiku studios, Daiei asked if I wouldn't direct one more film for them. As I cast about for what to film, I suddenly remembered a script based on the short story 'Yabu no naka' ('In a Grove') by Akutagawa Ryūnosuke. It had been written by Hashimoto Shinobu, who had been studying under director Itami Mansaku. It was a very well-written piece, but not long enough to make into a feature film. This Hashimoto had visited my home, and I talked with him for hours. He seemed to have substance, and I took a liking to him. He later wrote the screenplays for *Ikiru* (1952) and *Shichinin no samurai* (*Seven Samurai*, 1954) with me. The script I remembered was his Akutagawa adaptation called 'Male–Female'.

Probably my subconscious told me it was not right to have put that script aside; probably I was – without being aware of it – wondering all the while if I couldn't do something with it. At that moment the memory of it jumped out of one of those creases in my brain and told me to give it a chance. At the same time I recalled that 'In a Grove' is made up of three stories, and realized that if I added one more, the whole would be just the right length for a feature film. Then I remembered the Akutagawa story 'Rashōmon'. Like 'In a Grove', it was set in the Heian period (794–1184). The film *Rashōmon* took shape in my mind.

Since the advent of the talkies in the 1930s, I felt, we had misplaced and forgotten what was so wonderful about the old silent movies. I was aware of the esthetic loss as a constant irritation. I sensed a need to go back to the origins of the motion picture to find this peculiar beauty again; I had to go back into the past.

In particular, I believed that there was something to be learned from the spirit of the French avant-garde films of the 1920s. Yet in Japan at this time we had no film library. I had to forage for old films, and try to remember the structure off those I had seen as a boy, ruminating over the esthetics that had made them special.

Rashōmon would be my testing ground, the place where I could apply the ideas and wishes growing out of my silent-film research. To provide the symbolic background atmosphere, I decided to use the Akutagawa 'In a Grove' story, which goes into the depths of the human heart as if with a surgeon's scalpel, laying bare its dark complexities and bizarre twists. These strange impulses of the human heart would be expressed through the use of an elaborately fashioned play of light and shadow. In the film, people going astray in the thicket of their hearts would wander into a wider wilderness, so I moved the setting to a large forest. I selected the virgin forest of the mountains surrounding Nara, and the forest belonging to the Kōmyōji temple outside Kyōto.

There were only eight characters, but the story was both complex and deep. The script was done as straightforwardly and briefly as possible, so I felt I should be able to create a rich and expansive visual image in turning it into a film. Fortunately, I had as cinematographer a man I had long wanted to work with, Miyagawa Kazuo; I had Hayasaka to compose the music and Matsuyama as art director. The cast was Mifune Toshirō, Mori Masayuki, Kyō Machiko, Shimura Takashi, Chiaki Minoru, Ueda Kichijirō, Katō Daisuke and Honma Fumiko; all were actors whose temperaments I knew, and I could not have wished for a better line-up. Moreover, the story was supposed to take place in summer, and we had, ready to hand, the scintillating midsummer heat of Kyōto and Nara. With all these conditions so neatly met, I could ask nothing more. All that was left was to begin the film.

However, one day just before the shooting was to start, the three assistant directors Daiei had assigned me came to see me at the inn where I was staying. I wondered what the problem could be. It turned out that they found the script baffling and wanted me to explain it to them. 'Please read it again more carefully,' I told them. 'If you read it diligently, you should be able to understand it because it was written with the intention of being comprehensible.' But they wouldn't leave. 'We believe we have read it carefully, and we still don't understand it at all; that's why we want you to explain it to us.' For their persistence I gave them this simple explanation:

Human beings are unable to be honest with themselves about themselves. They cannot talk about themselves without embellishing. This script portrays such human beings – the kind who cannot survive without lies to make them feel they are better people than they really are. It even shows this sinful need for flattering falsehood going beyond the grave – even the character who dies cannot give up his lies when he speaks to the living through a medium. Egoism is a sin the human being carries with him from birth; it is the most difficult to redeem. This film is like a strange picture scroll that is unrolled and displayed by the ego. You say that you can't understand this script at all, but that is because the human heart itself is impossible to understand. If you focus on the impossibility of truly understanding human psychology and read the script one more time, I think you will grasp the point of it.

After I finished, two of the three assistant directors nodded and said they would try reading the script again. They got up to leave, but the third, who was the chief, remained unconvinced. He left with an angry look on his face. (As it turned out, this chief assistant director and I never did get along. I still regret that in the end I had to ask for his resignation. But, aside from this, the work went well.)

During the rehearsals before the shooting I was left virtually speechless by Kyō Machiko's dedication. She came in to where I was still sleeping in the morning and sat down with the script in her hand. 'Please teach me what to do,' she requested, and I lay there amazed. The other actors, too, were all in their prime. Their spirit and enthusiasm was obvious in their work, and equally manifest in their eating and drinking habits.

They invented a dish called Sanzoku-yaki, or 'Mountain Bandit Broil', and ate it frequently. It consisted of beef strips sautéed in oil and then dipped in a sauce made of curry powder in melted butter. But while they held their chopsticks in one hand, in the other they'd hold a raw onion. From time to time they'd put a strip of meat on the onion and take a bite out of it. Thoroughly barbaric.

The shooting began at the Nara virgin forest. This forest was infested with mountain leeches. They dropped out of the trees onto us, they crawled up our legs from the ground to suck our blood. Even when they had had their fill, it was no easy task to pull them off, and once you managed to rip a glutted leech out of your flesh, the open sore seemed never to stop bleeding. Our solution was to put a tub of salt in the entry of the inn. Before we left for the location in the morning we would cover our necks, arms and socks with salt. Leeches are like slugs – they avoid salt.

In those days the virgin forest around Nara harbored great numbers of massive cryptomerias and Japanese cypresses, and vines of lush ivy twined from tree to tree like pythons. It had the air of the deepest mountains and hidden glens. Every day I walked in this forest, partly to scout for shooting locations and partly for pleasure. Once a black shadow suddenly darted in front of me: a deer from the Nara park that had returned to the wild. Looking up, I saw a pack of monkeys in the big trees above my head.

The inn we were housed in lay at the foot of Mount Wakakusa. Once a big monkey who seemed to be the leader of the pack came and sat on the roof of the inn to stare at us studiously throughout our boisterous evening meal. Another time the moon rose from behind Mount Wakakusa, and for an instant we saw the silhouette of a deer framed distinctly against its full brightness. Often after supper we climbed up Mount Wakakusa and formed a circle to dance in the moonlight. I was still young and the cast members were even younger and bursting with energy. We carried out our work with enthusiasm.

When the location moved from the Nara Mountains to the Kōmyōji temple forest in Kyōto, it was Gīon Festival time. The sultry summer sun hit with full force, but even though some members of my crew

succumbed to heat stroke, our work pace never flagged. Every afternoon
we pushed through without even stopping for a single swallow of water.
When work was over, on the way back to the inn we stopped at a beer
hall in Kyōto's downtown Shijō-Kawaramachi district. There each of us
downed about four of the biggest mugs of draft beer they had. But we
ate dinner without any alcohol and, upon finishing, split up to go about
our private affairs. Then at ten o'clock we'd gather again and pour
whiskey down our throats with a vengeance. Every morning we were
up bright and clear-headed to do our sweat-drenched work.

Where the Kōmyōji temple forest was too thick to give us the light
we needed for shooting, we cut down trees without a moment's hesitation
or explanation. The abbot of Kōmyōji glared fearfully as he watched us.
But as the days went on, he began to take the initiative, showing us
where he thought trees should be felled.

When our shoot was finished at the Kōmyōji location, I went to pay
my respects to the abbot. He looked at me with grave seriousness and
spoke with deep feeling. 'To be honest with you, at the outset we were
very disturbed when you went about cutting down the temple trees as
if they belonged to you. But in the end we were won over by your
wholehearted enthusiasm. "Show the audience something good." This
was the focus of all your energies, and you forgot yourselves. Until I
had the chance to watch you, I had no idea that the making of a movie
was a crystallization of such effort. I was very deeply impressed.'

The abbot finished and set a folding fan before me. In commemoration
of our filming, he had written on the fan three characters forming a
Chinese poem: 'Benefit All Mankind'. I was left speechless.

We set up a parallel schedule for the use of the Kōmyōji location and
open set of the Rashōmon gate. On sunny days we filmed at Kōmyōji;
on cloudy days we filmed the rain scenes at the gate set. Because the
gate set was so huge, the job of creating rainfall on it was a major
operation. We borrowed fire engines and turned on the studio's fire
hoses to full capacity. But when the camera was aimed upward at the
cloudy sky over the gate, the sprinkle of the rain couldn't be seen against
it, so we made rainfall with black ink on it. Every day we worked in
temperatures of more than 85° Fahrenheit, but when the wind blew
through the wide-open gate with the terrific rainfall pouring down over
it, was enough to chill the skin.

I had to be sure that this huge gate looked huge to the camera. And
I had to figure out how to use the sun itself. This was a major concern

because of the decision to use the light and shadows of the forest as the keynote of the whole film. I determined to solve the problem by actually filming the sun. These days it is not uncommon to point the camera directly at the sun, but at the time *Rashōmon* was being made it was still one of the taboos of cinematography. It was even thought that the sun's rays shining directly into your lens would burn the film in your camera. But my cameraman, Miyagawa Kazuo, boldly defied this convention and created superb images. The introductory section in particular, which leads the viewer through the light and shadow of the forest into a world where the human heart loses its way, was truly magnificent camera work. I feel that this scene, later praised at the Venice International Film Festival as the first instance of a camera entering the heart of a forest, was not only one of Miyagawa's masterpieces but a world-class masterpiece of black-and-white cinematography.

And yet, I don't know what happened to me. Delighted as I was with Miyagawa's work, it seems I forgot to tell him. When I said to myself, 'Wonderful,' I guess I thought I had said 'Wonderful' to him at the same time. I didn't realize I hadn't until one day Miyagawa's old friend Shimura Takashi (who was playing the woodcutter in *Rashōmon*) came to me and said, 'Miyagawa's very concerned about whether his camera work is satisfactory to you.' Recognizing my oversight for the first time, I hurriedly shouted, 'One hundred percent! One hundred for camera work! One hundred plus!'

There is no end to my recollections of *Rashōmon*. If I tried to write about all of them, I'd never finish, so I'd like to end with one incident that left an indelible impression on me. It has to do with the music.

As I was writing the script, I heard the rhythms of a bolero in my head over the episode of the woman's side of the story. I asked Hayasaka to write a bolero kind of music for the scene. When we came to the dubbing of that scene, Hayasaka sat down next to me and said, 'I'll try it with the music.' In his face I saw uneasiness and anticipation. My own nervousness and expectancy gave me a painful sensation in my chest. The screen lit up with the beginning of the scene, and the strains of the bolero music softly counted out the rhythm. As the scene progressed, the music rose, but the image and the sound failed to coincide and seemed to be at odds with each other. 'Damn it,' I thought. The multiplication of sound and image that I had calculated in my head had failed, it seemed. It was enough to make me break out in a cold sweat.

We kept going. The bolero music rose yet again, and suddenly picture and sound fell into perfect unison. The mood created was positively eerie. I felt an icy chill run down my spine, and unwittingly I turned to Hayasaka. He was looking at me. His face was pale, and I saw that he was shuddering with the same eerie emotion I felt. From that point on, sound and image proceeded with incredible speed to surpass even the calculations I had made in my head. The effect was strange and overwhelming.

And that is how *Rashōmon* was made. During the shooting there were two fires at the Daiei studios. But because we had mobilized the fire engines for our filming, they were already primed and drilled, so the studios escaped with very minor damage.

After *Rashōmon* I made a film of Dostoevsky's *The Idiot* (*Hakuchi*, 1951) for the Shōchiku studios. This *Idiot* was ruinous. I clashed directly with the studio heads, and then when the reviews on the completed film came out, it was as if they were a mirror reflection of the studio's attitude toward me. Without exception, they were scathing. On the heels of this disaster, Daiei rescinded its offer for me to do another film with them.

I listened to this cold announcement at the Chōfu studios of Daiei in the Tokyo suburbs. I walked out through the gate in a gloomy daze, and, not having the will even to get on the train, I ruminated over my bleak situation as I walked all the way home to Komae. I concluded that for some time I would have to 'eat cold rice' and resigned myself to this fact. Deciding that it would serve no purpose to get excited about it, I set out to go fishing at the Tamagawa River. I cast my line into the river. It immediately caught on something and snapped in two. Having no replacement with me, I hurriedly put my equipment away. Thinking this was what it was like when bad luck catches up with you, I headed back home.

I arrived home depressed, with barely enough strength to slide open the door to the entry. Suddenly my wife came bounding out. 'Congratulations!' I was unwittingly indignant: 'For what?' '*Rashōmon* has the Grand Prix.' *Rashōmon* had won the Grand Prix at the Venice International Film Festival, and I was spared from having to eat cold rice.

Once again an angel had appeared out of nowhere. I did not even know that *Rashōmon* had been submitted to the Venice Film Festival. The Japan representative of Italiafilm, Giuliana Stramigioli, had seen it and recommended it to Venice. It was like pouring water into the sleeping ears of the Japanese film industry.

Later *Rashōmon* won the American Academy Award for Best Foreign Language Film. Japanese critics insisted that these two prizes were simply reflections of Westerners' curiosity and taste for Oriental exoticism, which struck me then, and now, as terrible. Why is it that Japanese people have no confidence in the worth of Japan? Why do they elevate everything foreign and denigrate everything Japanese? Even the woodblock prints of Utamaro, Hokusai and Sharaku were not appreciated by Japanese until they were first discovered by the West. I don't know how to explain this lack of discernment. I can only despair of the character of my own people.

'A film is difficult to explain because it is easy to understand'   **CHRISTIAN METZ**

SATYAJIT RAY
from *My Years With Apu*

If there is one mainstream cinematic vein which strikes us now, at the end of the century, as more or less exhausted, it's surely that mode of social and emotional humanism that enhanced the medium with a number of films once widely, if not for some decades now, regarded as among its supreme masterpieces. As an Indian friend lamented to me, 'Oh, where are the sort of films we used to enjoy – you know what I mean, the films of De Sica, Kurosawa and Potemkin?' Yes, I did know what he meant, even if the Marxist 'Potemkin' – or, rather, Eisenstein – was never, and even Kurosawa only intermittently, a humanist.

One filmmaker who most definitely was a humanist, however, as well as being Indian himself, was Satyajit Ray. This little text, extracted from My Years With Apu, *a charming memoir of the shooting of his early trilogy,* Pather Panchali, Aparajito *and* The World of Apu, *recounts how he set about the casting of* Aparajito *and demonstrates that not only the films themselves but their very means of production were imbued with a true humanist spirit. He cast his films in and from the street, as one might ask a stranger to help change a tyre.*

8 April

Worked on the script. The opening is a problem, always is. Long shots establishing locale are a cliché. But should one entirely dispense with them in a film that is laid in Benaras? The instinct to do so is strong. As in *Pather Panchali*, I think it helped in not having a very tight script. Working in these circumstances one must leave a lot of room for improvisation within the groundwork of a broad scheme which one must keep in one's head. There were two things about the script of *Aparajito* that gave me cause to ponder – one was the fact that two Apus were required, one for the first half and one for the second.

In David Lean's version of *Great Expectations* there were two Pips, but there was a big difference in age between the two, the first one being about eight and the second well above twenty. Also the elder Pip was on the screen for a much longer time. It was, therefore, possible for Lean to achieve a smooth transition. Here I had to contend with two Apus, the difference in age between whom was only five to six years. Unless there was a close physical resemblance, would the audience accept the change from one Apu to another? The ideal would be to find brothers, but that was too much to hope for. The second problem concerned a character who was in the book and was very popular with the readers. She was the young Calcutta girl Lila whom Apu meets and befriends, while studying in college. I had to decide if she was essential for the narrative, because Apu's classmate Anil is shown as a close friend of Apu and that called for at least a couple of longish scenes to establish the relationship between them. I had to ask myself what function Lila would have. The more I thought the more I felt that the script could do without her. Apu's attachment to the city which made him somewhat indifferent to his mother living alone in the village could be accounted for by his new and exciting urban environment, his newly acquired friend and his absorption in the task of earning a living in a printing press.

The first problem had to wait, it would depend on the similarity of actors for the two Apus. As for the second, I finally decided to retain Lila's character, primarily out of a need to fulfil the expectations of the readers of the book, and they were legion. As I realise more and more, this was a compromise. How I finally got rid of Lila is a story which will be told in its proper place.

We had decided to start shooting in Benaras at this point. I needed only the actors who were required for roles in the first part of the story. This consisted of Harihar, Sarbajaya, the boy Apu, Sarbajaya's uncle, Bhabataran, who offers her shelter when she is working as a cook in a rich household in Benaras after Harihar's death. We also needed someone to play the part of a Brahmin who strikes up an acquaintance with Harihar. We chose for the part a professional actor named Kali Bannerji, who looked exactly right for the part. We decided to use bit players from Benaras to save on the cost of transportation to and from Calcutta.

I had already found on my first trip to Benaras an old man to play Bhabataran. He was listening to a devotional song sung by a group of singers on the ghats. He seemed to have a very interesting face which I felt would be right for the part. I decided to make a direct approach. I, therefore, introduced myself as a film maker.

'Films?' he murmured.

'Bioscope,' I said.

'I have never seen one,' he said. 'Is it like a pala?'

'Pala' is a form of folk theatre where the plays are usually historical or mythological.

'Rather,' I said.

'I see.'

I now came to the point.

'I would very much like to offer you a part in a film I am making. Have you any experience in acting?'

'None, I left home years ago and came here to die. If you die in Benaras, you go straight to heaven.'

'But you don't seem anywhere near death yet. Would you like to act in my film? It's a simple part, all you have to do is learn a few lines of dialogue. You'll be working about a month in all – less than that in fact, altogether about ten days. It will be a new experience for you, for which you'll be paid good money. There is nothing wrong in that, is there?'

'Nothing at all. When do you need me?'

'I'll let you know. Please give me your address. You'll be informed as soon as we get ready.'

'Very well.'

Just that. He didn't talk about money. He didn't ask what role he had to play. All I knew about him was that he was a Bengali with an East Bengal accent. For the boy Apu, it was the same story as with the Apu of *Pather Panchali*. This time we decided to stand outside schools at the time the boys came out after the classes were over. It proved of no avail. And then he turned up suddenly. Bansi and I had been to see a railway station which we needed for the second half of the film. As we were entering the platform, the train pulled up and a group of school boys filed into a compartment with their teacher. They had obviously gone on an outing. One of the boys caught both mine and Bansi's eyes. There was no doubt that he looked exactly right for the role and he was the right age too.

We soon arrived in Calcutta. The boys got off the train, while we tagged along behind our target. He broke away from the group and made for a waiting train. We followed him into it and sat down beside him. Till then the boy had paid no attention to us. I asked him his name.

'Pinaki,' he said, 'Pinaki Sen Gupta.'

'Do you go to the cinema?'

'Only to those to which my mother takes me.'

'Did your mother take you to see *Pather Panchali*?'

'Yes.'

'Did you like it?'

'Very much.'

'If there was another film about Apu, would you like to play his role?'

'Yes, I would.'

'You think your mother would let you act?'

'I think so.'

'What about your father?'

'My father is dead.'

We took the boy's address and asked him to talk to his mother. We would call at his house in a day or two.

Pinaki was right. His mother, an extremely good looking young widow whom we met within a week, said she was very happy that we had chosen her son to play Apu in *Aparajito*. The news had already come out in the papers and she was aware of the project. We then told her that her son would be shooting in Benaras to start with and then in the studio in Calcutta. She said there would be no problem in managing his leave from school and that Pinaki's uncle would accompany him.

JOHN GREGORY DUNNE
from *The Studio*

In The Studio, *his amusingly trenchant chronicle of a single year, 1967, in the production schedule of Twentieth Century-Fox, the novelist John Gregory Dunne tells with sadistic relish the following anecdote concerning a* mauvais quart d'heure *endured by the director Henry Koster at the end of his career.*

First, though, who precisely was Henry Koster (he died in 1988)? In fact, whether on a cinema or a television screen, everyone is likely to have seen a Koster film at one time or another: he was that kind of director. It might have been one of his several musicals (notably, a cycle of Deanna Durbin vehicles which in the 1930s rescued Universal from virtual bankruptcy) or his equally numerous light comedies (Harvey, for example, in which James Stewart was partnered by an invisible six-foot white rabbit) or else one of the historical and pseudo-Biblical melodramas in which he began to specialize in the 1950s (e.g. The Robe, *a film assured of its own tiny footnote in cinema history by virtue of having been the very first to be released in CinemaScope). In his heyday, then, having been responsible for one commercial hit after another, having amiably pandered to some of the less fastidious appetites of the moviegoing public, Koster might be said to have represented the filmmaker not as artist or even craftsman but as* caterer.

Then came the 1960s, and along with them the great metamorphosis of the American cinema, and Koster's moment, like that of so many directors, writers and performers of the old school, had passed. Fashion had changed and hearts were no longer worn on sleeves.

Mary Ann McGowan, Richard Zanuck's secretary, came into his office and announced that director Henry Koster, producer Robert Buckner and three William Morris agents were waiting outside.

'What's Buckner's first name?' Zanuck asked.

'Robert,' Mary Ann McGowan said, as she disappeared out the door. 'They call him Bob.'

The five visitors filed into Zanuck's office. Zanuck rose and shook the hand of each. 'Hello, Bob,' he said to Buckner.

Koster, Buckner and two of the agents arranged themselves in chairs in front of Zanuck's desk. The third agent slid onto a couch in the corner of the office. Koster cleared his throat and wiped his forehead with a handkerchief. He is a portly man with thinning hair slicked down on the top of his head and a thick middle-European accent. At one time he had directed a number of pictures for the Studio. 'I have a story for you, Dick,' he said.

Zanuck nodded. No one spoke for a moment. Koster wiped his forehead again and mashed the handkerchief in his hand.

'I have wanted to bring to the screen a story of great music,' he said, 'ever since I first came to this country and made *A Hundred Men and a Girl*.' He looked to Zanuck for encouragement. 'With Deanna Durbin,' he added.

Zanuck picked up the bronzed baby shoe behind his desk and began to turn it around in his hands. His eyes did not catch Koster's.

'We fade in on Moscow,' Koster said. 'Behind the credits, we hear one of the world's great symphony orchestras playing – Shostakovich would be good for Moscow. The orchestra has a flamboyant, tempestuous conductor – I think Lenny Bernstein will love this idea. As we finish the credits, we come on on the orchestra and then we close on the cymbals. It is obvious that the cymbal player is sick. The orchestra is supposed to leave Moscow that night for a charity concert in New York.' Koster paused for effect. He was sweating profusely. 'For crippled children.'

One of the Morris agents was examining his fingernails. The head of the agent on the couch began to nod.

'When the concert is over, we find that the cymbal player has a contagious disease,' Koster said. He wound the handkerchief around his palms. 'We can work out the disease later. The orchestra must be quarantined in Moscow. All except the Lenny Bernstein character. I think we can work out that he had the right shots. Anyway we can get Lenny out of Moscow and back to New York. Now here is your problem, Dick. The charity concert must be canceled.'

The agent on the couch had now fallen asleep. An abortive snore jolted him awake.

'Unless,' Koster continued. He smiled benignly. 'There is a youth orchestra in New York and they can take the place of the symphony at the concert. We have, of course, tried to get the Philadelphia and the

Cleveland and Ormandy and George Szell would love to do it, but they have commitments. So the Lenny Bernstein character goes to hear the youth symphony and he says, "No, I cannot conduct them, they are not good enough." He will not yield, the concert must be canceled, there will be no money for the crippled children.' Koster's voice softened. 'But then the president of the charity comes to plead with him against cancellation.' Koster's head swiveled around, taking in everyone in the room. 'In his arms, he is carrying a small boy – with braces on his legs.'

Buckner seemed to sense that Zanuck's attention was wavering. 'We have a love story, too, Dick,' he said.

Koster picked up the cue. 'Yes, we have a love story,' he said. 'There is a beautiful Chinese cellist who does not speak a word of English and a beatnik kook who plays the violin.' The words rolled over his tongue. 'They communicate through the international language of music.'

'Don't forget the jazz,' Buckner said.

'We can get jazz into our story, Dick,' Koster said. 'You see, the concert is only five days away and there are not enough players in the youth orchestra, so the conductor – the Lenny Bernstein character – goes out and hunts them up in a bunch of weird joints.'

'Jazz joints,' Buckner said.

The top of Koster's head was slick with perspiration. His voice began to quicken. 'Working day and night, the conductor molds these untutored players into a symphony orchestra. In just five days.' Koster's face grew somber. 'Then we get word from Moscow. The quarantine has been lifted. The orchestra can get back to New York in time for the concert.'

Zanuck gazed evenly, unblinkingly at Koster.

'Here is the crux of our story, Dick,' Koster said. 'Will our conductor use the youth symphony, or will he use his own orchestra, thus destroying by his lack of faith this beautiful instrument' – Koster's hands moved up and down slowly – 'he has created in just five days?'

Koster sighed and leaned back, gripping both the arms on his chair. There was silence in the office. Zanuck cleared his throat.

'Very nicely worked out,' he said carefully. 'Very nicely.' His jaw muscles began to work as he considered his thoughts. 'But I'm afraid it's not for us at the moment.' He squared the bronzed baby shoe against the edge of his desk. 'We've got a lot of musical things on the schedule right now – *The Sound of Music* is still doing great business, just great, we've got *Dr Dolittle* and we're working on *Hello, Dolly!* – and I don't think we should take on another.' He paused, seeking the right words.

'And quite frankly, I'm just a little afraid of this kind of music. You'll get the music lovers, no doubt about that, none at all. But how about the Beatles fans?'

Koster made a perfunctory objection, but the meeting was over. As if on cue, the dozing agent awoke, and after an exchange of small talk, agents and clients departed Zanuck's office, hurling pleasantries over their shoulders. For a long time, Zanuck sat chewing on a fingernail, saying nothing.

'Jesus,' he said finally.

PETER BERLING
The Making of *Whity*

*Although producer Peter Berling's description of its shambolic shoot
makes* Whity, *made in 1971, sound as if it must have been the director
Rainer Werner Fassbinder's very first, semi-amateur (and totally amateurish) film, it was in fact his seventh, the seventh of 28 – not including
work destined exclusively for television. And although Berling's zestful
account may not be completely free of hyperbole – hyperbole of the
complacent 'Isn't show business just* crazy!' *and 'Dontcha just love it!'
variety – this is still how many low-budget European films get made.
Or don't get made, as the case too often is.*

The telephone rang. Seldom in my life could I resist this sound.
I rolled over in my bed in the Tel Aviv Hilton Hotel. I was sweating
and angry. I had just come back from looking for locations at the Dead
Sea. The prospect of having to spend the next three months in a rocky
wilderness was hardly exciting, not even the thought that the salt lake
would support my three hundred pounds without my splashing. People
were giving me trouble, and I was in a mood to quit.

The telephone rang again. 'Who is disturbing me?' I shouted into the
mouthpiece.

It was Ulli Lommel. 'Listen,' he said, 'I'm making a western and you
have to produce it for me.'

At the word 'western' I became weaker than when tempted with
Lindt Edelbitter chocolate. 'Do you have the money?'

'I'll be at the airport with the check.'

I quit. I flew to Munich. The check didn't bounce. In front of the
bank, I asked for the details. 'Who's the director?'

'Rainer Werner Fassbinder. And the whole Antitheater group. Hanna,
too.'

Hanna had left me two years before. She had called me a capitalist,
and had ridden off on her bicycle, the way she had come. 'Rainer and
Hanna will refuse me,' I said now. 'They all will.'

'I don't believe it,' said Ulli.

'Well, find out for yourself.'

In the afternoon, Ulli came back from his confrontation with the group. 'You're right,' he told me. 'They don't want to make a movie with you. But I said, "No film without Berling!" So they accepted you, but they won't speak to you.'

'This could be fun!'

Lommel and I flew to Madrid on the night plane to meet the Spanish coproducer. Early the next morning, under my interrogation, he turned out to be a crook. Give up the project? 'No,' I said, 'off to Almería!'

Almería, a provincial port in southern Andalusia, had become one of the favorite 'backlots' of Europe in the sixties. The stable good weather guaranteed uninterrupted shooting. The landscape was varied, some-times bizarre, and it included a real desert (see *Lawrence of Arabia*). There were often more productions on the go there than in the film capitals of the Continent. The Los Angeles Hotel was on the road to Almería's airport, which was used only twice weekly when a Convair from Barcelona arrived and departed. It had the advantage of keeping the cast and crew together, making after-hours excursions difficult. In addition, I managed to push the price down to the level of a youth hostel, and since the only capital at the moment was Ulli's Diners Club card, I also convinced the Los Angeles to join the club.

Within five days everything was organized. A 'village' left over from a spaghetti western was rented on the cheap, and horses, stuntmen, and an American B-picture movie star were engaged, if not always on the Diners Club, then on promises of good fortune in the wind. Finally, when Ulli found a raw-film supplier who would take plastic, the green light was given to Munich and the entire Antitheater rolled across Europe, Rainer and Günther in the maestro's 230 SL and the others on lesser wheels. Hanna flew.

On arrival, Rainer said he had come only to announce that he had no intention of making the film and that he would leave immediately, and he stormed off, which is when Harry said that Rainer was merely unhappy with his room, that he was eager to make a western, and that there was nothing to worry about. 'You just have to get used to him.'

I had resolved not to let Fassbinder get to me. The more provocative and unexpected his demands, the more I would let them bounce off my belly, so to speak. I would take all difficulties in my stride, soothe whatever grated, and none of the director's desires would remain unfulfilled.

But the tension didn't subside, it grew. Harry, the go-between, went between Fassbinder and me at shorter and shorter intervals. Fassbinder would start the day demanding ten Cuba libres – rum and Coca-Cola. He would drink nine and throw the tenth at the cameraman. I proceeded stubbornly according to the shooting plan. Fassbinder did, too.

The explosion came on the third day.

A crowd scene had been planned, activity in front of the saloon. I sat on the steps in the sun, observing the arrangements approvingly. Extras, directed by Harry and outfitted by Kurt, strolled over the sandy square. Wagons rolled. The sheriff rocked on the porch. Horses reared. Chickens and pigs abounded.

The only one missing was Fassbinder. Harry brought the news. Rainer has changed his mind. He refuses to shoot the scene and he wants to leave again.

I raised my voice: 'Tell him I said he's shitting in his pants because there are more than three people in the scene.'

Harry smarted but was delighted to report the insubordination. I sat on the porch, not knowing what to expect when Fassbinder came growling around the corner.

'I'm going to bash your fucking face in!' he shouted, coming at me like an angry bull. I had no time to get to my feet, but I used one of them, inserting it between his legs and sending him diving into the dust. He gathered himself together and charged again, but I was standing now and I literally let him bounce off my belly, adding a swift karate chop to the back of his neck. This time, flying over the steps, he landed on the porch. He got up with difficulty, lowered his head, and attacked once more. Feeling a lot more sure of myself now, I let him come, but he threw his arms around my neck and whispered in my ear: 'I love you! Now I know I can finish this film!' Dropping his voice still more, he added, 'Ulli doesn't have a pfennig, you know, only the credit card!'

I was both touched and not a little piqued, touched by the flood of emotion and piqued because Rainer had realized that there was no money to finish the movie before I had.

I got Ulli to lay his cards on the table, and the first thing I learned was that the Diners was no longer among them, the club having ousted him in the meantime. While the search for new credit went on, we kept to the shooting schedule. The staging of the film gave Rainer ample opportunity to vent his implacable rage, particularly at Ulli. There was a character in the script who was a nymphomaniac not averse to beating her grown, mentally retarded stepson. So Rainer cast Ulli's wife, Katrin, as the nympho-sadist and Ulli as the half-wit, and in one scene Rainer made her strike Ulli so many times that they both dropped to the ground weeping for mercy.

Even Hanna fell into disfavor, though her punishment wore kid gloves. The female lead, she played a chattel barmaid at the beck and call of the sexual fancies of a big landowner, our American B-picture star, Ron Randall, and when she began to double in the same role off-camera, Rainer, who viewed her as his creation – an immaculate conception – went bananas. He costumed her as whorishly as his fertile mind could imagine, turned the part into a saloon hooker who sings for her supper, and when the shooting called for a barroom rowdy to louse up her act, Rainer played the bit himself, sporting a whip.

Harry and Kurti, who had had the leads in the last two pictures respectively, were, on general principles, I suppose, demoted drastically. Kurt played a pianist, Harry another idiot stepson, and much to his surprise and humiliation – since Rainer had him made-up blindfolded – he played it as an albino.

But Rainer reserved the most poisonous arrows of his ire for Günther. Günther played 'Whity', a half-caste who works as the dastardly Nicholson family's personal nigger. 'Hanna' – played by Hanna – the sexually exploited barmaid, raises Whity's consciousness and incites him to murder his white masters. But just as Whity in the script is somehow unable to bring himself to act, Günther had the same problem in playing the part. Rainer was merciless. Günther was indifferent. There was a wicked game of dominance going on, ill-defined in my mind back then, but no one, myself included, was immune.

The example that springs to my recall sounds funny today, but at the time blood boiled, particularly my own. In one of the night scenes, which had required meticulous and costly arrangements, Whity has to climb a long rope ladder into Hanna's room on the top floor of the saloon. Günther rehearsed one climb, but not all the way to the top. He was saving his courage, such as it was, for the actual scene, which called for him to swing over the ledge at the top and make for a doorway, through which he was to disappear. End of take.

When everything was ready and Rainer signaled for action, Günther set off intrepidly, clambering upward, and sailing almost gracefully over the ledge toward the doorway. But when he got there, much as he struggled with the handle, the door wouldn't open.

Rainer had a fit. He screamed for Kurti, who was doubling as propman. Kurti declared that there was absolutely nothing wrong with the handle. The trouble lay with the 'door'. It was painted on the wall. Rainer had a second fit. I suggested, to save time and money, that the scene be shifted to an adjoining room that had a real door. Rainer said that the door had to be where he wanted it to be, and he demanded a carpenter. I had a fit. I started to walk off the set, but Rainer said that if I took one more step he would quit. Kurti brought him a tray of Cuba libres, and while the painted door was sawn away to make room for a real one, Rainer drank, I fumed, and Günther was indifferent.

Now it was my turn for punishment. Rainer, who, if he was great, it was because he had a thousand eyes, had evidently noticed that I had more than a business relationship with my secretary, Barbara. She was a beautiful young widow of an American Formula One racing-car driver. I had put her in the room next to mine, but the territory, I suspected, was not my domain alone. I professed to be free of all jealousy, which was chic in those days, but I suppose I protested too much, and Rainer must have seen that.

In any case, late one night the phone by my bedside rang, and Barbara was on the other end of the line.

'I'm lying here in bed with Rainer,' she said, 'and we're naked and making love.'

Rainer got on the phone. 'Are you hurt?'

Sure, I was hurt. But I pretended to be more hurt than I really was, or thought I was, and that was pleasure enough for him to throw her out of his room. I understood, or imagined, that Barbara had been merely used, sacrificed on the altar of my auto-da-fé. I could bounce him off my belly any day, but he was the Force.

By now I felt I had paid my dues, but the same group that had refused to speak to me had lately gone on to protest against having to 'take orders' from me, a nonmember. I had tried to impose traditional film-production discipline, but we were living in the Age of Communes, and Rainer, Great Democrat that he was, summoned everyone together for a hearing.

'This Mr Berling,' I heard anticapitalist Hanna say, 'treats us as though we are the underlings in his privately owned company.'

No one dissented, and finally Rainer with Solomonic wisdom passed judgment. He dubbed me Group Mother – Mutti in German.

'Listen, everybody,' he said. 'What Mutti says, will be done.'

How clever he was to characterize me in that time and circumstance not as a boss but as an all-caring mother, and it worked. 'Mutti,' I was shortly to hear again and again from then on, 'what time do we have to get up tomorrow?' 'Mutti, can I go to the john?' 'Mutti, can I have some money?' Although my answer to the last question was almost always no, the name has stuck with me through all these years.

The production money dried up completely. Salaries had already been frozen, and now the per diem allowances were cut off. We became prisoners of the Los Angeles Hotel, which was suddenly the only place within a thousand miles any of us could still sleep with a roof over his head and get a meal, and only because the owner was too far in the red to throw us out. Now everybody *but* Rainer was threatening to quit. Ulli was constantly on the phone to Germany, selling percentage points in the film by the hundreds for financing that never arrived. Suddenly, Rainer learned that he had won a huge State cash prize for a previous film, but when ever-faithful Irm Hermann arrived from Munich with the cash, it was only a small first installment, the rest to be paid over a period that was too long to do us any good.

Rainer unleashed his fury not at the State but at Irm. He slapped her in front of us all. 'Where's my money?' he wailed. 'Everyone's betraying me. They're sucking my blood!'

Irm burst into tears. 'You promised to marry me,' were the words that came out of her mouth. 'You promised to have children with me. Why don't you marry me?'

She was supposed to have played a part in the film, but Rainer banned her from the set and sent her home. The situation turned desperate when we began to run out of raw stock. The cameraman and I were the only ones who knew, and we kept it secret from Rainer. At first he was astonished and then he began to grow suspicious because the cameraman, Michael Ballhaus, didn't complain when he shot scenes in one take. Normally, a cameraman doesn't feel covered without at least a second take for insurance.

Then the day came when Ballhaus's assistant trudged into the production office and announced that there was no more film for the next day's shooting. I looked at Ulli. Ulli looked at the floor. But my own assistant said he had a possible solution. We all looked at him the way you sometimes look to heaven. All he could do, however, was hem and haw, and he even blushed, until I sensed what it might be. I left the room for his sake, but more so for mine. The truth was that my secretary, Barbara, the apple of my eye, was having an affair with one of the camera-crew members on an American production making a Jack Palance film nearby. They of course were loaded, staying at the luxury hotel Aguadulce, and Barbara's paramour had the key to where they kept their film supply.

Rainer throughout had expressed a desire to meet Palance, whom he had admired in *Panic in the Streets* and *Shane*, so late one night, a whole group of us set off for the Aguadulce. Rainer was annoyed and perhaps a little embarrassed by the size of the entourage, but he was not privy to the caper. We came in several cars and with our prettiest girls, including, of course, my peripatetic secretary Barbara.

The great encounter between Palance and Fassbinder took place in the otherwise empty lobby of the hotel while the girls fanned out and disappeared. Palance, looking like a fugitive from a Beverly Hills men's shop window, seemed lonely and drunk. Rainer, who after a recent press conference had been described by a journalist as 'almost idiotically inarticulate', was just that. We all sat in a half-light. Rainer in leather was lost in the leather upholstery. I remember the dialogue well enough, but what I remember most were the interminable skin-crawling pauses between each exchange. It went something like this:

'You're from Germany?'

'Yeah, from Bavaria.'

A long silence.

'East or west?'

A long silence.

'It's west, but more east.' A long silence. 'Your family is from Russia?'

'No. Kiev.' Silence. 'You want a drink?'

'Vodka?'

'Whisky.'

A long silence.

'I like Cuba libre.'

'What's that?'

'Fidel Castro.'

'Fucking communist.'

'No, rum and Coke.'

'And you drink that shit?'

Silence.

'Yeah, a lot.'

'If there's not a lot of whisky, I drink vodka, a lot.'

Silence.

'I see.'

This took one hour. I know because the girls suddenly showed up and they had drunk a lot of something, about an hour's worth of steady drinking whatever it was. We gathered ourselves together.

'It was a pleasure to meet you, Mr Palance,' said Rainer, in one of the longest English sentences I would ever hear him utter.

'Same to you,' said Palance. 'What's your business?'

'Making movies.'

'Oh, I see. Well, have a good time.'

'Same to you.'

Back at the Los Angeles, when Rainer was serenely tucked in bed with Günther, we opened the trunks of our cars. They were filled to the rubber seal with shiny metal cans of 35-mm Kodak movie film. What a great day!

The shooting schedule was twenty days long, which was a third of what it should have been, but that was part of the Fassbinder phenomenon, and I was as dogged as he was in wanting to keep it to the day. But in the last week the pressure became enormous and it began to take its toll. We were filming fourteen, fifteen, sometimes even eighteen hours a day, and we would get back to the hotel at three or four in the morning, too worked up to go to bed. A stereo system had been set up in the lobby and at that hour it would be going full volume, bouncing the hotel owner off his mattress and driving him clinically mad. In vain would he try in his pajamas to impose a legal prohibition against serving drinks after hours, pulling fuses and padlocking the liquor cabinet, and when it was more than once broken open, he threatened us with the police. But in the end he simply cowered night after night behind the bar, serving Cuba libres on the cuff and standing witness to alcoholic orgies that grew wilder with each passing day.

We were his only guests, all others having long since departed, and when occasionally unsuspecting tourists wandered in, they invariably left no later than the next morning, weary and cursing under, or more often over, their breath. Even without the intimidated owner's complaint, the police appeared more and more frequently. Rainer had fired the interpreter (the last vestige of the Spanish coproduction) and she had taken her revenge by giving fanciful and not so fanciful descriptions to the authorities of the troupe's drinking and unconventional sex life.

Moreover, Günther had run his Lamborghini into a store window, and though we had settled the matter with the shopkeeper, we were unable to pay the settlement, and he too had gone to the police. The local extras filed complaints about being scandalously underpaid, which was true, and some members of the crew were continually brawling at the airport bar, expressing in fisticuffs what we were all feeling mentally: being fed up with one another and the Great Democrat's tsarist rule.

Violence broke out on our own territory, on the terrace of the Los Angeles. Rainer, drunk and stood-up by Günther, kicked the scriptgirl in the shins for no better reason. Two hefty stuntmen seized the moment and him as well and beat him to the ground. Luckily I wasn't present, so I didn't have to take a stand, but most of the rest of the troupe were, and nobody lifted a finger to come to his rescue. Rainer got up and slinked away in silence, and the incident was never spoken of again.

Emotional violence, too, the kind that ends in bleeding hearts and tears, erupted more and more, and one reason was that Rainer suspected that Günther was being unfaithful in the biblical sense. His suspicion was confirmed when either his spies or the view from his bedroom window revealed that Günther at dawn was taking long walks on the beach with Kurti. That was proof enough for Rainer, who knew how to put two and two together better than anybody else I ever knew, but Kurti, who had a sievelike capacity for keeping a secret, eventually told all, the following being the words of his own published confession: 'I felt the sweet feeling of revenge when I took a walk a couple of times with Kaufmann on the beach at dawn. That was wonderful in itself, but the best thing was the secret now in my possession. I had only to think about Fassbinder waiting longingly for Kaufmann while he was giving a few moments of priority to me, and I couldn't ask for anything more!'

When the 'secret' got out, one of the few scenes left to be shot called for Whity to be flogged naked by his master in rage. Everyone was convinced that Günther's marvelously muscular back would be thrashed to shreds, and mischievous Harry, as assistant director, acquired a cat-o'-nine-tails and a tarred towline from a boat for Rainer to choose from. Kurti, as propman, however, had been given other instructions from Rainer, and though the whip as seen in the film looks like a cat-o'-nine-tails, the knotted cords are made of the softest woolen yarn Kurti could find. The scene is not very effective, but some things for Rainer, such as his Bavarian Negro's flesh, had built-in immunity.

Thus, with Whity and Hanna dancing into a metaphorical sunset –

the very last scene shortly afterward safe in the can – the shooting of *Whity* ended (on schedule) almost Christianly, though the long aftermath was more of the same. Some of the bunch went back to Munich. Rainer and Günther crashed the Mercedes in Alicante. Harry followed Juan Carlos to Madrid. Ulli and his wife, Katrin, were held hostage by the Los Angeles until the bills were paid, following which his company went bankrupt. *Whity* premiered at the Berlin Film Festival the following year. It received mixed reviews, but I did fine; I got a call from a friend in the middle of the night telling me that the film opens with the words 'To Peter Berling'. Coming from Rainer, this made me feel as if I'd won an Oscar. Of course he wielded it like a battle-ax over my head in the years to come. That's the way he was.

'In good films, there is always a directness that entirely frees us from the itch to interpret'

SUSAN SONTAG

SARAH MALDOROR
To Make a Film Means to Take a Position

The arrestingly surnamed Sarah Maldoror, of Guadeloupan parentage,
was born in the southern French town of Candou in 1939. By the 1960s
she was working in Algeria, where she made her first film, a short, Monan-
gambee. *Then in 1972 she made the feature-length* Sambizanga, *a fiction*
film relating the experience of the Angolan liberation struggle against
Portugal during the previous decade, a film whose narrative was con-
ceived as a study of the gradual politicization of ordinary people, of ordi-
nary women, rather than as a historical chronicle of the war itself. This
is Maldoror's own account of how and why she made such a film.

I am one of those modern women who try to combine work and
family life, and, just as it is for all the others, this is a problem for me.
Children need a home and a mother. That is why I try to prepare and
edit my films in Paris during the long summer vacation when the children
are free and can come along. My situation is a very difficult one. I
make films about liberation movements. But the money for such film
production is to be found not in Africa but in Europe. For that reason,
I have to live where the money is to be raised, and then do my work in
Africa.

To begin, *Sambizanga* is a story taken from reality: a liberation fighter,
one of the many, dies from severe torture. But my chief concern with
this film was to make Europeans, who hardly know anything about
Africa, conscious of the forgotten wars in Angola, Mozambique and
Guinea-Bissau. And when I address myself to Europeans that is because
it is the French distribution companies who determine whether the
people in Africa will get to see a certain film or not. After twelve years
of independence, it is your companies – UGC, Nef, Claude Nedjar,
and Vincent Malle – which hold in their hands the fate of a possible
African distribution for *Sambizanga*.

At any rate, I don't want to make a 'good little Negro' film. People
often reproach me for that. They also blame me for making a technically

perfect film as any European could. But technology belongs to everyone. 'A talented Negro' – you can relegate that concept to my French past.

In this film I tell the story of a woman. It could be any woman, in any country, who takes off to find her husband. The year is 1961. The political consciousness of the people has not yet matured. I'm sorry if this situation is not seen as a 'good one', and if this doesn't lead to a heightened consciousness among the audience of what the struggle in Africa is all about. I have no time for films filled with political rhetoric.

In the village where Maria lives, the people have no idea at all what 'independence' means. The Portuguese prevent the spread of any information and a debate on the subject is impossible. They even prevent the people from living according to their own traditional culture.

If you feel that this film can be interpreted as being negative, then you're falling into the same trap as many of my Arab brothers did when they reproached me for not showing any Portuguese bombs or helicopters in the film. However, the bombs only began to rain down on us when we became conscious; the helicopters have only recently appeared – you sell them to the Portuguese and they buy them precisely because of our consciousness. For, not long ago, people here believed that all that was happening in Angola was a minor tribal war. They didn't reckon with our will to become an independent nation: could it be true that we Angolese were like them, the Portuguese? No, that wouldn't be possible!

I'm against all forms of nationalism. What does it in fact mean to be French, Swedish, Senegalese, or Guadeloupian? Nationalities and borders between countries have to disappear. Besides this, the colour of a person's skin is of no interest to me. What is important is what the person is doing. I'm no adherent of the concept of the Third World. I make films so that people – no matter what race or colour they are – can understand them. For me there are only exploiters and the exploited, that's all. To make a film means to take a position, and when I take a position I am educating people. The audience has a need to know that there's a war going on in Angola, and I address myself to those among them who want to know more about it. In my films, I show them a people who are busy preparing themselves for a fight and all that that entails in Africa: that continent where everything is extreme – the distances, nature, and so on. Liberation fighters are, for example, forced to wait until the elephants have passed them by. Only then can they cross the countryside and transport their arms and ammunition. Here, in the West, the resistance used to wait until dark. We wait for the elephants. You have radios, information. We have nothing.

Some say that they don't see any oppression in the film. If I wanted to film the brutality of the Portuguese, then I'd shoot my films in the bush. What I wanted to show in *Sambizanga* is the aloneness of a woman and the time it takes to march.

I'm only interested in women who struggle. These are the women I want to have in my films, not the others. I also offer work to as many women as possible during the time I'm shooting my films. You have to support those women who want to work with film. Up until now, we are still few in number, but if you support those women in film who are around, then slowly our numbers will grow. That's the way the men do it, as we all know. Women can work in whatever field they want. That means in film, too. The main thing is that they themselves want to do it. Men aren't likely to help women do that. Both in Africa and in Europe woman remains the slave of man. That's why she has to liberate herself.

No African country, with the exception of Algeria, has its own distribution company. In the French-speaking areas of Africa, distribution is handled by a monopoly that is in French hands. There is not one cinématheque nor even a so-called art cinema. All too often, you hear that there is no African film, or that if there is it's just Jean Rouch. That's to make it easy for those who say such things. One day, we'll come to France and shoot a film, then we'll show the African people our view of France. That will be an entertaining film.

Swedish films, Italian films and the films of other countries did not sprout up like mushrooms from the earth. In Africa there are several young people who are really talented film-makers. We have to put an end to the lack of knowledge and the utter ignorance that people have about the special problem of Africa.

Personally, I feel that Ousmane Sembène is the most talented of our directors. He's often reproached for financing his films with French capital. So what! The most important thing is that we have to develop a cultural policy that can help us – show to the world that such a thing as African film does exist. We have to teach ourselves to sell our films ourselves and then get them distributed. Today we are like small sardines surrounded by sharks. But the sardines will grow up. They'll learn how to resist the sharks.

TERRY SOUTHERN
from *Blue Movie*

The novelist Terry Southern, author of The Magic Christian, Flash &
Filigree *and the infamous* Candy, *was also a celebrated screenwriter of
rather hit-and-miss achievement (*Easy Rider, The Cincinnati Kid *and
the equally infamous film version of* Candy), *but with at least one truly
great script to his name, that for Stanley Kubrick's* Dr Strangelove or
How I Learned to Stop Worrying and Love the Bomb, *still the only
wholly successful encounter of those two otherwise incompatible terms,
'cinema' and 'satire'.* Blue Movie, *from which the following three short
chapters have been extracted, relates the determination of its hero, one
King B., to make – in Liechtenstein, of all unlikely places – the filthiest
but also most expensive pornographic film in cinema history.*

4

They met at six that evening at the Polo Lounge, at a table
on the side which, through an arrangement with the maître d', was
permanently reserved for Sid at this hour. The arrangement, incidentally,
was that Sid would lay starlet cooze on the maître d' by letting him
come to the studio on his day off and introducing him to the girl at
hand as an Italian film director 'who will probably use you if he gets to
know you better', lascivious wink, 'know what I mean? One hand washes
the other. Hee hee hee.' By the same token he had run up a bar bill of
about five hundred dollars.

Sid was already there, drinking a Ramos gin fizz ('keeps my weight
up'), when Boris arrived. They were both wearing shades, which made
B look even more weary and brooding than usual, and big Sid, in his
white linen suit and green silk shirt, just plain sinister.

'Two questions,' he said tersely, 'one: What do you know about
Liechtenstein?'

'Roy Lichtenstein?' asked B absently, nodding to acknowledge a
greeting from across the room.

Sid grimaced in pain. 'No, *mishugenah*, the *country* for Chrissake! *Liechtenstein!*'

Boris shrugged. 'I drove through it once, if that's what you mean – I don't recall stopping for anything.'

'So you didn't *stop*,' said Sid, 'big deal – it's still a *country*, right?'

'It's a country,' Boris agreed. 'Actually it's a principality. It's run by a prince. I met him once, as a matter of fact – at the Cannes Film Festival.'

'Right, right, right,' said Sid, 'it's a *sovereign principality*. Now let me give you a little run-down on the *sovereign principality* of Liechtenstein: situated in the colorful Alps Mountains, between Switzerland and Austria, occupying an area of sixty-four square miles, population of seventeen thou – one half-hour by twin jet from Paris, Rome, Berlin, Vienna, you name it –'

'What the hell are you talking about?' Boris interrupted.

'Will you please just this once listen to your own Sid Krassman,' he pleaded, but was momentarily distracted by a passing miniskirt. 'Hey, I forgot to ask, did you get into that little chickie's pants last night?'

Boris sighed. 'Yes, yes, yes,' as though it were all too futile.

'How was it?'

'What do you mean "how was it"? Haven't you ever been laid, for Chrissake?'

'She give good head?'

'Not especially.'

Sid nodded agreement. 'Young kids like that never seem to give good head. What was she, about eighteen?'

'Seventeen.'

'Seventeen, huh? She had a great ass.'

Boris nodded. 'Yeah, a great ass.'

'You suck her pussy?'

'Ha. That would be kiss-and-tell, wouldn't it?'

'Aw come on, fer Chrissake, did you suck her pussy or didn't you?'

'No. Well, not much anyway, just sort of at the beginning.'

'How many times did you fuck her?'

'Uh, let's see . . . four.'

'*Four?!?* Jeez, she must've been great ass! You fucked her *four times*, for Chrissake?'

'Yeah, well, you know, twice when we went to bed, and twice when we woke up.'

Sid seemed greatly relieved. 'Oh, when you *woke up*. I thought you *meant four times in a row*, for Chrissake! Did she come?'

Boris shrugged. 'Yeah, I guess so. She said she did.'

'Couldn't you *tell*, for Chrissake?'

'Yeah, she came.'

'What, every time?'

'Christ, I don't know if she came every time.' He regarded Sid curiously. 'Have you gone nuts or something? What was all that goofy talk about Liechtenstein?'

'I said I'd ask two questions, right? Okay, second question: You know Al Weintraub? He's Joey Schwartzman's cousin, right? Strictly legit. Now, are you ready for this? Al Weintraub is a *very close friend of the Minister of Finance in Liechtenstein.*'

'Uh-huh,' said B. He looked like he was about to fall asleep.

'Al knows *everything* about that country. We were up all night, we got a call in right now to his friend, the minister . . .'

'Listen, Sid,' Boris began, glancing at his watch, but Sid implored him, 'please, B, just this once listen to Sid Krassman.'

'Well, I don't know what the hell you're talking about.'

'Listen, B, before I go any further, can you let me take a thou until Thursday?'

'What?'

'A thousand bucks – just until Thursday.'

'Sure, I guess so.'

'You'll never regret it, B, believe you me!'

5

Liechtenstein, as it turned out, had the lowest per capita income of any country in Western Europe. Although of Alpine splendor scenic-wise, its relatively inaccessible location had simply not put it on the map, so to speak. The tourists – who, for generations, the country had tried desperately to attract – never came. And yet it had the requisites: inns (picturesque), saline baths (piping hot), ski slopes (mediocre), casino and opera house (closed). It seemed there was something missing – something perhaps even intangible, but a trifle more conveniently at hand . . . in St Moritz, Klosters, Kitzbühel, Innsbruck, etc.

The plan devised by Sid and Al Weintraub (friend of the Liechtenstein

Minister of Finance) was simplicity itself – the movie would be financed by the government of Liechtenstein, in return for which it would be *filmed* in Liechtenstein, and *exhibited there exclusively*. People from London, Paris, Rome, Vienna, Geneva, Zurich, anywhere, would jet in on special charter flights – to the only place where they could see the latest film by the world's greatest director. They would stay overnight, perhaps longer, at the picturesque inns, with eiderdown *pouffe* and the cozy hearth; they would go to the opera, the casino, the ski slopes, the health baths, and the shops, both quaint and smart; they would revel in the scenic Alpine beauty of the place. Perhaps they would fall in love with Liechtenstein – its simple charm, its majestic grandeur – it might even become a *habit*.

6

'They want a ten-year exclusive on the picture,' Sid was saying, about a week later.

Boris nodded. He didn't care where the picture was shown, he just wanted to make it.

'And let me tell you something else,' Sid added slyly. 'Know who I was talking to today? – Abe Becker. Bet you don't know who Abe Becker is, right?'

'That film cutter at Metro?' suggested B.

'*Abe Becker*,' said Sid, almost tersely, 'is the brother-in-law of Nicky Hilton. Know what he said? He said if this goes through, Connie will put up a *LiechtenHilton* like that!' Sharp snap of fingers. 'Shops too, the whole arcade bit. They'll clean up – and Abe *knows* it, believe you me!' Adding this last with a note of resentment, as if he felt they should cut him in for a piece of the action.

The waitress arrived, and Sid was momentarily distracted by the fact that she was topless. They were having a late lunch – about four p.m. – at a restaurant on the Strip called the Shangri-la Tropicana, whose specialty was spareribs and barbequed chicken, and waitresses with names like Honey Pot, Fancy Box, Charity Ball, etc. Sid went there often, and it was no news to him that they were topless, but it was a sometime source of distraction nonetheless.

'Hey,' he said to the girl – a rather heavy Scandinavian type, who maintained a steady frown of suspicious consternation – 'you met my friend, the internationally famous film director, Mr Boris Adrian? I been telling him about you.'

'Boris Adrian?' She was impressed, but then her brow clouded a bit more. 'Oh yeah? Listen, I know *you*'re in show business, Mr Kratzman, I checked that out already, but some of these guys you bring in, what do I know, maybe they're creeps or something. I mean, that's some sense of humor you got there, Mr Kratzman.'

'Yeah, well, the thing is,' said Sid, 'we're doing these commercials, and I been telling Mr Adrian here you might be just the girl for the job. What we've got to be sure of though is *nipple distention*.'

'Huh?'

'There's going to be a very tight close-shot, you see, and we've got to make sure that the line is just right. It's a public-service spot for CBS, it's for, uh, let's see, yeah, *it's for breast feeding of infants*, you know, to encourage breast feeding among young mothers. Some very harmful additives have recently been discovered in the, uh, you know, formula mixtures. It's a thirty-second spot – wouldn't show your face, of course, just the line of the, uh, bosom. Pays seven-fifty.'

'Seven fifty? Seven hundred and fifty?'

'Give or take a few bucks – union dues, that kind of thing.'

The girl looked from one to the other. 'Thirty seconds, seven hundred and fifty dollars? Wow.'

'Uh, yes, well, the thing is,' said Sid gravely, 'we have to be sure about the *line*. Just step over here, will you, dear.'

'Huh?' said the girl, obeying immediately, '*what* line?'

'The nipple,' he said, 'is a very important part of the breast line. Now just relax.' He put one hand on her right hip, placed his other over her bare (left) breast and fingered it gingerly. 'Now, let's just see . . .'

'Hey, wait a minute,' said the girl, glancing about anxiously.

'No, it's all right,' Sid reassured her, releasing the nipple but still holding her hip. 'Here, this is better,' and he took a half-melted ice cube from his drink and began massaging the nipple with it.

The girl tried to draw away, discreetly but somewhat wildly, looking right and left. 'Listen, the manager will flip if he sees this!'

Sid ignored her remark, turned to Boris. 'Yes, you see, Mr Adrian, there's quite a satisfactory distention there, don't you agree?' And even the girl then looked down in curiosity at the nipple, which was perking out like a tiny top hat. And a number of nearby guests, ordinarily blasé, were shooting uneasy looks at the odd spectacle.

'Okay,' said Sid, 'let's try the other one.'

'Hey, listen,' she said, really quite apprehensive now, 'can't we do this later?'

'Okay,' said Sid abruptly, and returned his attention to the menu at once. 'How's your deep-dish Beaver Pie today?'

'Huh?' She stared at him dumbly for a moment, mouth half-open. 'Say, that's some sense of humor you got there, Mr Kratzman, you know that?'

Boris sighed and smiled sadly. 'Oh, he knows that all right. Yes indeed.'

In a town and an industry where the tasteless quip is rife and men of *mauvaise foi* are legion – even here was Sid Krassman notorious for his obsessively aggressive wit and chicanery, always with a slight compulsion toward the grotesquely banal. Getting into a cab, for example, he would sometimes wait for the driver to ask 'Where to?' and he would reply, 'What the hell, let's go to *your* place!' And guffaw raucously. Or, stepping into a crowded elevator, he might intone with tremendous authority: 'I suppose you're all wondering why I've called you together.'

'Okay, King, are you ready for this?' he asked now, still at the Shangri-la Tropicana, opening an attaché case which he had taken from beneath his chair. He extracted a large white folio, untied its ribbon, and began passing eleven by fourteen color prints across the table to Boris. Most of the photographs were of places, rather than persons, and featured town squares, cobblestone streets, country lanes, meadows, forest glades, streams, lakes, cottages, churches, castles – all of obvious European motif, and most against an overwhelming backdrop of snow-covered mountains. Boris went through them in silence, with a slightly bemused smile.

'Well, there's our locations, baby!' exclaimed Sid, with a glee he prayed would be contagious.

'Where'd you get these?' asked Boris, turning one over to look at the back. On it was stamped: 'Property of Krassman Enterprises, Ltd – Unauthorized Reproduction Strictly Prohibited.'

Sid flicked his cigar, caught the waitress's eye and signaled for another cognac.

'Flew Morty Kanowitz over to scout it,' he said easily.

Boris returned his attention to the photographs. 'Didn't you tell me the other night you were *broke*?'

Sid coughed and glanced about the room uneasily, tried a diversionary tactic: 'Say, I think I just saw Dick Zanuck, going into the other room –'

Boris smiled wearily and continued to look at the pictures. 'My thou?'

Sid was greatly relieved that the deception was finally out in the open, and that Boris did not seem too bugged by it. He leaned back in his chair, rolled the cigar from one side of his mouth to the other. 'Well, B,' he said with a grin, 'it *takes* money to *make* money – am I right?'

'Nice pictures,' said Boris, handing them back.

'*Perfect* locations, am I right?'

'Locations for what? I don't even have a story yet.'

'But that'll *come* to you, B baby,' Sid reassured in his most imploring tones, 'that'll *come* to you – from the Blue Fairy of Inspiration!'

It was common knowledge that his last two winners had been shot from 'scripts' about as substantial as a couple of matchcovers.

'And the money?' asked B dryly. 'Blue Fairy too?'

Sid reached into his breast pocket, and produced with a flourish what appeared to be a folded cablegram. 'Three big ones, baby! *And* final cut!'

'Three million? You're kidding.'

'Nope,' he shook his head solemnly, 'talked to Al last night – he's done one helluva promo-job on this, you know – told him to get me a cable confirmation of the deal. Here it is.' He held the cable up in front of his face, gesturing with it as he spoke.

'Well, that's terrific, Sid,' said Boris, and reached out for it.

'One thing, B,' said Sid, not relinquishing it, 'one thing I want to explain – a technicality, you'll see it yourself in the cable, but I wanted to tell you about it first, so it don't take the edge off. Know what I mean?'

Boris, whose hand was still extended for the cable, gazed at Sid without expression, and slowly lowered his hand. 'Nope,' he said softly, 'I'm afraid not.'

'The government of Liechtenstein,' Sid proclaimed in serious measured tones, 'is prepared to advance us – in the form of both credit and cash – up to the amount of *three million dollars* . . .'

Here his voice faltered, and Boris reached out impatiently and snatched the cable from him. Unfolding it, he began to read, muttering the words half aloud, almost verbatim as Sid had described, until near the end, reading this part, quite distinctly: '. . . "in combined accreditation and national currency, to a maximum equivalent of three, repeat three, million dollars (US) – providing that such an amount as to be agreed upon is duly and equally matched by an investor or investors of the second party. Stop. Letter detailing proposal follows. Regards, Max von Dankin, Minister of Finance, Leichtenstein.'"

Boris carefully folded the cable and placed it on the table. 'Where's my thou?'

'Now wait a minute, B,' said Sid with real earnestness. 'I *swear* to you I know how to get the match money. Just *please* give me the chance to explain.'

Boris sighed. 'Go,' he said.

'Well, let's get out of here first,' said Sid. 'I don't want anybody to know about this.' He looked anxiously around the room. 'Place is crawling with fuckin' lip-readers.'

Boris laughed at this, Sid's feigned or real paranoia, and they started for the door.

Things seemed to be going Sid's way again, and his spirits were rising. In the foyer they encountered their waitress.

'What's the matter, darling,' asked Sid in concern, 'do you have a cold?'

'A cold?' said the girl, frowning in surprise. 'What made you think *that*, Mr Kratzman?'

'Oh, I don't know,' said Sid ingenuously, 'your *chest* looks all swollen.' And he reached out to proffer comfort to the afflicted area, guffawing raucously.

'Film music should have the same relationship to the film drama that somebody's piano playing in my living room has to the book I am reading'

IGOR STRAVINSKY

Specializing

MANNY FARBER
Underground Films

Manny Farber, a superlatively good American critic, coined the term 'termite movies' for the sort of cheap 'n' cheerful productions that have aged very much better than the dear 'n' cheerless main features they were originally designed to support – features, that is, by such once-adulated, subsequently more or less discredited Hollywood 'intellectuals' as William Wyler, Fred Zinnemann, Stanley Kramer, Edward Dmytryk and others of that self-important ilk. Farber's quicksilver intelligence, generosity and alertness need no editorial defence. But a question imposes itself. If he was, along with the French critics of Cahiers du Cinéma, *a precocious advocate of the now widely accepted rehabilitation of American populist cinema, and if the low-grade movies he championed (unrepentantly genre movies for the most part) have only belatedly received the enthusiastic approval of the international film-critical Establishment, can it then be claimed of them that, like the avant-gardist art films to which they otherwise bear no resemblance, they were 'ahead of their time'?*

The saddest thing in current films is watching the long-neglected action directors fade away as the less talented De Sicas and Zinnemanns continue to fascinate the critics. Because they played an anti-art role in Hollywood, the true masters of the male action film – such soldier-cowboy-gangster directors as Raoul Walsh, Howard Hawks, William Wellman, William Keighley, the early, pre-*Stagecoach* John Ford, Anthony Mann – have turned out a huge amount of unprized, second-gear celluloid. Their neglect becomes more painful to behold now that the action directors are in decline, many of them having abandoned the dry, economic, life-worn movie style that made their observations of the American he-man so rewarding. Americans seem to have a special aptitude for allowing History to bury the toughest, most authentic native talents. The same tide that has swept away Otis Ferguson, Walker Evans, Val Lewton, Clarence Williams, and J. R. Williams into near oblivion is now in the process of burying a group that kept an endless flow of interesting roughneck film passing through the theaters from the depression onward. The tragedy of these film-makers lies in their having been consigned to a Sargasso Sea of unmentioned talent by film reviewers whose sole concern is not continuous flow of quality but the momentary novelties of the particular film they are reviewing.

Howard Hawks is the key figure in the male action film because he shows a maximum speed, inner life, and view, with the least amount of flat foot. His best films, which have the swallowed-up intricacy of a good soft-shoe dance, are *Scarface*, *Only Angels Have Wings*, *His Girl Friday*, and *The Big Sleep*. Raoul Walsh's films are melancholy masterpieces of flexibility and detailing inside a lower-middle-class locale. Walsh's victories, which make use of tense, broken-field journeys and nostalgic background detail, include *They Drive by Night*, *White Heat*, and *Roaring Twenties*. In any Bill Wellman operation, there are at least four directors – a sentimentalist, deep thinker, hooey vaudevillian, and an expedient short-cut artist whose special love is for mulish toughs expressing themselves in drop-kicking heads and somber standing around. Wellman is at his best in stiff, vulgar, low-pulp material. In that setup, he has a low-budget ingenuity, which creates flashes of ferocious brassiness, an authentic practical-joke violence (as in the frenzied inadequacy of Ben Blue in *Roxie Hart*), and a brainless hell-raising. Anthony Mann's inhumanity to man, in which cold mortal intentness is the trademark effect, can be studied best in *The Tall Target*, *Winchester 73*, *Border Incident*, and *Railroaded*. The films of this tin-can de Sade have a Germanic rigor, caterpillar intimacy, and an original dictionary of ways in which to punish the human body. Mann has done interesting work with scissors, a cigarette lighter, and steam, but his most bizarre effect takes place in a taxidermist's shop. By intricate manipulation of athletes' bodies, Mann tries to ram the eyes of his combatants on the horns of a stuffed deer stuck on the wall.

The film directors mentioned above did their best work in the late 1940s, when it was possible to be a factory of unpretentious picture-making without frightening the front office. During the same period and later, less prolific directors also appear in the uncompromising action film. Of these, the most important is John Farrow, an urbane vaudevillian whose forte, in films like *The Big Clock* and *His Kind of Woman*, is putting a fine motoring system beneath the veering slapstick of his eccentric characterizations. Though he has tangled with such

heavyweights as Book of the Month and Hemingway, Zoltan Korda is
an authentic, hard-grain cheapster telling his stories through unscrubbed
action, masculine characterization, and violent explorations inside a
fascinating locale. Korda's best films – *Sahara, Counterattack, Cry the
Beloved Country* – are strangely active films in which terrain, jobs, and
people get curiously interwoven in a ravening tactility. William Keighley,
in *G-Men* and *Each Dawn I Die*, is the least sentimental director
of gangster careers. After the bloated philosophical safe-crackers in
Huston's *Asphalt Jungle*, the smallish cops and robbers in Keighley's
work seem life-size. Keighley's handling is so right in emphasis, timing,
and shrewdness that there is no feeling of the director breathing, gasping,
snoring over the film.

The tight-lipped creators whose films are mentioned above comprise
the most interesting group to appear in American culture since the
various groupings that made the 1920s an explosive era in jazz, literature,
silent films. Hawks and his group are perfect examples of the anonymous
artist, who is seemingly afraid of the polishing, hypocrisy, bragging, fake
educating that goes on in serious art. To go at his most expedient gait,
the Hawks type must take a withdrawn, almost hidden stance in the
industry. Thus, his films seem to come from the most neutral, humdrum,
monotonous corner of the movie lot. The fascinating thing about these
veiled operators is that they are able to spring the leanest, shrewdest,
sprightliest notes from material that looks like junk, and from a creative
position that, on the surface, seems totally uncommitted and disinterested. With striking photography, a good ear for natural dialogue, an
eye for realistic detail, a skilled inside-action approach to composition,
and the most politic hand in the movie field, the action directors have
done a forbidding stenography on the hard-boiled American handyman
as he progresses through the years.

It is not too remarkable that the underground films, with their twelve-
year-old's adventure-story plot and endless palpitating movement, have
lost out in the film system. Their dismissal has been caused by the
construction of solid confidence built by daily and weekly reviewers.
Operating with this wall, the critic can pick and discard without the
slightest worry about looking silly. His choice of best salami is a picture
backed by studio build-up, agreement amongst his colleagues, a layout
in *Life* mag (which makes it officially reasonable for an American award),
and a list of ingredients that anyone's unsophisticated aunt in Oakland
can spot as comprising a distinguished film. This prize picture, which

has philosophical undertones, pan-fried domestic sights, risqué crevices, sporty actors and actresses, circuslike gymnastics, a bit of tragedy like the main fall at Niagara, has every reason to be successful. It has been made for that purpose. Thus, the year's winner is a perfect film made up solely of holes and evasions, covered up by all types of padding and plush. The cavity-filling varies from one prize work to another, from *High Noon* (cross-eyed artistic views of a clock, silhouettes against a vaulting sky, legend-toned walking, a big song), through *From Here to Eternity* (Sinatra's private scene-chewing, pretty trumpeting, tense shots in the dark and at twilight, necking near the water, a threatening hand with a broken bottle) to next year's winner, which will probably be a huge ball of cotton candy containing either Audrey Hepburn's cavernous grin and stiff behind or more of Zinnemann's glacéed picture-making. In terms of imaginative photography, honest acting, and insight into American life, there is no comparison between average underground triumph (*Phenix City Story*) and the trivia that causes a critical salaam across the land. The trouble is that no one asks the critics' alliance to look straight backward at its 'choices', for example, a horse-drawn truckload of liberal schmaltz called *The Best Years of Our Lives*. These ridiculously maltreated films sustain their place in the halls of fame simply because they bear the label of ART in every inch of their reelage. Praising these solemn goiters has produced a climate in which the underground picture-maker, with his modest entry and soft-shoe approach, can barely survive.

However, any day now, Americans may realize that scrambling after the obvious in art is a losing game. The sharpest work of the last thirty years is to be found by studying the most unlikely, self-destroying, uncompromising, roundabout artists. When the day comes for praising infamous men of art, some great talent will be shown in true light: people like Weldon Kees, the rangy Margie Israel, James Agee, Isaac Rosenfeld, Otis Ferguson, Val Lewton, a dozen comic-strip geniuses like the creator of 'Harold Teen', and finally a half-dozen directors such as the master of the ambulance, speedboat, flying-saucer movie: Howard Hawks.

The films of the Hawks–Wellman group are *underground* for more reasons than the fact that the director hides out in subsurface reaches of his work. The hard-bitten action film finds its natural home in caves: the murky, congested theaters, looking like glorified tattoo parlors on the outside and located near bus terminals in bit cities. These theaters roll action films in what, at first, seems like a nightmarish atmosphere of shabby transience, prints that seem overgrown with jungle moss, soundtracks infected with hiccups. The spectator watches two or three action films go by and leaves feeling as though he were a pirate discharged from a giant sponge.

The cutthroat atmosphere in the itch house is reproduced in the movies shown there. Hawks's *The Big Sleep* not only has a slightly gaseous, subsurface, Baghdadish background, but its gangster action is engineered with a suave, cutting efficacy. Walsh's *Roaring Twenties* is a jangling barrel-house film, which starts with a top gun bouncing downhill, and, at the end, he is seen slowly pushing his way through a lot of Campbell's scotch broth. Wellman's favorite scene is a group of hard-visaged ball bearings standing around – for no damned reason and with no indication of how long or for what reason they have been standing. His worst pictures are made up simply of this moody, wooden standing around. All that saves the films are the little flurries of bulletlike acting that give the men an inner look of credible orneriness and somewhat stupid mulishness. Mann likes to stretch his victims in crucifix poses against the wall or ground and then to peer intently at their demise with an icy surgeon's eye. Just as the harrowing machine is about to run over the wetback on a moonlit night, the camera catches him sprawled out in a harrowing image. At heart, the best action films are slicing journeys into the lower depths of American life: dregs, outcasts, lonely hard wanderers caught in a buzzsaw of niggardly, intricate, devious movement.

The projects of the underground directors are neither experimental, liberal, slick, spectacular, low-budget, epical, improving, or flagrantly commercial like Sam Katzman two-bitters. They are faceless movies, taken from a type of half-polished trash writing, that seem like a mixture of Burt L. Standish, Max Brand, and Raymond Chandler. Tight, cliché-ridden melodramas about stock musclemen. A stool pigeon gurgling with scissors in his back; a fat, nasal-voiced gang leader; escaped convicts; power-mad ranch owners with vengeful siblings; a mean gun with an Oedipus complex and migraine headaches; a crooked gambler trading guns to the redskins; exhausted GIs; an incompetent kid hoodlum hiding out in an East Side building; a sickly elegant Italian barber in a plot to kill Lincoln; an under-paid shamus signing up to stop the blackmailing of a tough millionaire's depraved thumb-sucking daughter.

The action directors accept the role of hack so that they can involve themselves with expedience and tough-guy insight in all types of action:

barnstorming, driving, bulldogging. The important thing is not so much the banal-seeming journeys to nowhere that make up the stories, but the tunnelling that goes on inside the classic Western-gangster incidents and stock hoodlum-dogface-cowboy types. For instance, Wellman's lean, elliptical talents for creating brassy cheapsters and making gloved references to death, patriotism, masturbation, suggest that he uses private runways to the truth, while more famous directors take a slow, embalming surface route.

The virtues of action films expand as the pictures take on the outer appearance of junk jewelry. The underground's greatest mishaps have occurred in art-infected projects where there is unlimited cash, studio freedom, an expansive story, message, heart, and a lot of prestige to be gained. Their flattest, most sentimental works are incidentally the only ones that have attained the almond-paste-flavored eminence of the Museum of Modern Art's film library, i.e., *GI Joe*, *Public Enemy*. Both Hawks and Wellman, who made these overweighted mistakes, are like basketball's corner man: their best shooting is done from the deepest, worst angle. With material that is hopelessly worn out and childish (*Only Angels Have Wings*), the underground director becomes beautifully graphic and modestly human in his flexible detailing. When the material is like drab concrete, these directors become great on-the-spot inventors, using their curiously niggling, reaming style for adding background detail (Walsh); suave grace (Hawks); crawling, mechanized tension (Mann); veiled gravity (Wellman); svelte semicaricature (John Farrow); modern Gothic vehemence (Phil Karlson); and dark, modish vaudeville (Robert Aldrich).

In the films of these hard-edged directors can be found the unheralded ripple of physical experience, the tiny morbidly life-worn detail which the visitor to a strange city finds springing out at every step. The Hawks film is as good as the mellifluous grace of the impudent American hard rock as can be found in any art work; the Mann films use American objects and terrain – guns, cliffs, boulders, an 1865 locomotive, telephone wires – with more cruel intimacy than any other film-maker; the Wellman film is the only clear shot at the mean, brassy, clawlike soul of the lone American wolf that has been taken in films. In other words, these actioneers – Mann and Hawks and Keighley and, in recent times, Aldrich and Karlson – go completely underground before proving themselves more honest and subtle than the water buffaloes of film art: George Stevens, Billy Wilder, Vittorio De Sica, Georges Clouzot. (Clouzot's most successful work, *Wages of Fear*, is a wholesale steal of the mean physicality and acrid highway inventions in such Walsh–Wellman films as *They Drive by Night*. Also, the latter film is a more flexible, adroitly ad-libbed, worked-in creation than Clouzot's eclectic money-maker.)

Unfortunately, the action directors suffer from presentation problems. Their work is now seen repeatedly on the blurred, chopped, worn, darkened, commercial-ridden movie programs on TV. Even in the impossible conditions of the 'Late Show', where the lighting is four shades too dark and the porthole-shaped screen defeats the movie's action, the deep skill of Hawks and his tribe shows itself. Time has dated and thinned out the story excitement, but the ability to capture the exact homely-manly character of forgotten locales and misanthropic figures is still in the pictures along with pictorial compositions (Ford's *Drums Along the Mohawk*) that occasionally seem as lovely as anything that came out of the camera box of Billy Bitzer and Matthew Brady. The conditions in the outcast theaters – the Lyric on Times Square, the Liberty on Market Street, the Victory on Chestnut – are not as bad as TV, but bad enough. The screen image is often out of plumb, the house lights are half left on during the picture, the broken seats are only a minor annoyance in the unpredictable terrain. Yet, these action-film homes are the places to study Hawks, Wellman, Mann, as well as their near and distant cousins.

The underground directors have been saving the American male on the screen for three decades without receiving the slightest credit from critics and prize committees. The hard, exact defining of male action, completely lacking in acting fat, is a common item *only* in underground films. The cream on the top of a *Framed* or *Appointment with Danger* (directed by two first cousins of the Hawks–Walsh strain) is the eye-flicking action that shows the American body – arms, elbows, legs, mouths, the tension profile line – being used expediently, with grace and the suggestion of jolting hardness. Otherwise, the Hollywood talkie seems to have been invented to give an embarrassingly phony impression of the virile action man. The performance is always fattened either by coyness (early Robert Taylor), unction (Anthony Quinn), historic conceit (Gene Kelly), liberal knowingness (Brando), angelic stylishness (Mel Ferrer), oily hamming (José Ferrer), Mother's Boy passivity (Rock Hudson), or languor (Montgomery Clift). Unless the actor lands in the hands of an underground director, he causes a candy-coated effect that is misery for any spectator who likes a bit of male truth in films.

After a steady diet of undergrounders, the spectator realizes that these are the only films that show the tension of an individual intelligence posing itself against the possibilities of monotony, bathos, or sheer cliché. Though the action film is filled with heroism or its absence, the real hero is the small detail which has arisen from a stormy competition between lively color and credibility. The hardness of these films arises from the esthetic give-and-go with banality. Thus, the philosophical idea in underground films seems to be that nothing is easy in life or the making of films. Jobs are difficult, even the act of watching a humdrum bookstore scene from across the street has to be done with care and modesty to evade the type of butter-slicing glibness that rots the Zinnemann films. In the Walsh film, a gangster walks through a saloon with so much tight-roped ad-libbing and muscularity that he seems to be walking backward through the situation. Hawks's achievement of moderate toughness in *Red River*, using Clift's delicate languor and Wayne's claylike acting, is remarkable. As usual, he steers Clift through a series of cornball fetishes (like the Barney Google Ozark hat and the trick handling of same) and graceful, semicollegiate business: stances and kneelings and snake-quick gunmanship. The beauty of the job is the way the cliché business is kneaded, strained against without breaking the naturalistic surface. One feels that this is the first and last hard, clamped-down, imaginative job Clift does in Hollywood – his one nonmush performance. Afterward, he goes to work for Zinnemann, Stevens, Hitchcock.

The small buried attempt to pierce the banal pulp of underground stories with fanciful grace notes is one of the important feats of the underground director. Usually, the piercing consists in renovating a cheap rusty trick that has been slumbering in the 'thriller' director's handbook – pushing a 'color' effect against the most resistant type of unshowy, hard-bitten direction. A mean butterball flicks a gunman's ear with a cigarette lighter. A night-frozen cowboy shudders over a swig of whisky. A gorilla gang leader makes a cannonaded exit from a barber chair. All these bits of congestion are like the lines of a hand to a good gun movie; they are the tracings of difficulty that make the films seem uniquely hard and formful. In each case, the director is taking a great chance with clichés and forcing them into a hard natural shape.

People don't notice the absence of this hard combat with low, commonplace ideas in the Zinnemann and Huston epics, wherein the action is a game in which the stars take part with confidence and glee as though nothing can stop them. They roll in parts of drug addicts, tortured sheriffs; success depending on how much sentimental bloop and artistic japery can be packed in without encountering the demands of a natural act or character. Looking back on a Sinatra film, one has the feeling of a private whirligig performance in the center of a frame rather than a picture. On the other hand, a Cagney performance under the hands of a Keighley is ingrained in a tight, malignant story. One remembers it as a sinewy, life-marred exactness that is as quietly laid down as the smaller jobs played by the Barton MacLanes and Frankie Darros.

A constant attendance at the Lyric-Pix-Victory theaters soon impresses the spectator with the coverage of locales in action films. The average gun film travels like a shamus who knows his city and likes his private knowledges. Instead of the picture-postcard sights, the underground film finds the most idiosyncratic spot of a city and then locates the niceties within the large nicety. The California Street hill in San Francisco (*Woman in Hiding*) with its old-style mansions played in perfect night photography against a deadened domestic bitching. A YMCA scene that emphasizes the wonderful fat-waisted, middle-aged physicality of people putting on tennis shoes and playing handball (*Appointment with Danger*). The terrorizing of a dowdy middle-aged, frog-faced woman (*Born to Kill*) that starts in a decrepit hotel and ends in a bumbling, screeching, crawling murder at midnight on the shore. For his big shock effect, director Robert Wise (a sometime member of the underground) uses the angle going down to the water to create a middle-class mediocrity that out-horrors anything Graham Greene attempted in his early books on small-time gunsels.

Another fine thing about the coverage is its topographic grimness, the fact that the terrain looks worked over. From Walsh's *What Price Glory?* to Mann's *Men in War*, the terrain is special in that it is used, kicked, grappled, worried, sweated up, burrowed into, stomped on. The land is marched across in dark, threading lines at twilight, or the effect is reversed with foot soldiers in white parkas (*Fixed Bayonets*) curving along a snowed-in battleground as they watch troops moving back – in either case, the cliché effect is worked credibly inward until it creates a haunting note like the army diagonals in *Birth of a Nation*. Rooms are boxed, crossed, opened up as they are in few other films. The spectator gets to know these rooms as well as his own hand. Years after seeing the film, he remembers the way a dulled waitress sat on the edge of a hotel bed, the weird elongated adobe in which ranch hands

congregate before a Chisholm Trail drive. The rooms in big-shot directors' films look curiously bulbous, as though inflated with hot air and
turned toward the audience, like the high school operetta of the 1920s.

Of all these poet-builders, Wellman is the most interesting, particularly with Hopper-type scenery. It is a matter of drawing store fronts,
heavy bedroom boudoirs, the heisting of a lonely service station, with
light, furious strokes. Also, in mixing jolting vulgarity (Mae Clarke's face
being smashed with a grapefruit) with a space composition dance in
which the scene seems to be constructed before your eyes. It may be
a minor achievement, but, when Wellman finishes with a service station
or the wooden stairs in front of an ancient saloon, there is no reason
for any movie realist to handle the subject again. The scene is kept light,
textural, and as though it is being built from the outside in. There is no
sentiment of the type that spreads lugubrious shadows (Kazan), builds
tensions of perspective (Huston), or inflates with golden sunlight and
finicky hot air (Stevens).

Easily the best part of underground films are the excavations of
exciting–familiar scenery. The opening up of a scene is more concerted
in these films than in other Hollywood efforts, but the most important
thing is that the opening is done by road-mapped strategies that play
movement against space in a cunning way, building the environment
and event before your eyes. In every underground film, these vigorous
ramifications within a sharply seen terrain are the big attraction, the
main tent. No one does this anatomization of action and scene better
than Hawks, who probably invented it – at least, the smooth version –
in such 1930s gunblasts as *The Crowd Roars*. The control of Hawks's
strategies is so ingenious that, when a person kneels or walks down the
hallway, the movement seems to click into a predetermined slot. It is
an uncanny accomplishment that carries the spectator across the very
ground of a giant ranch, into rooms and out again, over to the wall to
look at some faded fight pictures on a hotel wall – as though he were
in the grip of a spectacular, mobile 'eye'. When Hawks landscapes action
– the cutting between light tower and storm-caught plane in *Ceiling
Zero*, the vegetalizing in *The Thing*, the shamus sweating in a greenhouse
in *The Big Sleep* – the feeling is of a clever human tunneling just under
the surface of terrain. It is as though the film has a life of its own that
goes on beneath the story action.

However, there have been many great examples of such veining by
human interactions over a wide plane. One of the special shockers, in

Each Dawn I Die, has to do with the scissoring of a stooly during the movie shown at the penitentiary. This Keighley–Cagney effort is a wonder of excitement as it moves in great leaps from screen to the rear of a crowded auditorium: crossing contrasts of movement in three points of the hall, all of it done in a sinking gloom. One of the more ironic crisscrossings has to do with the coughings of the stuck victim played against the screen image of zooming airplanes over the Pacific.

In the great virtuoso films, there is something vaguely resembling this underground maneuvering, only it goes on above the story. Egocentric padding that builds a great bonfire of pyrotechnics over a gapingly empty film. The perfect example is a pumped-up fist fight that almost closes the three-hour *Giant* film. This ballroom shuffle between a reforming rancher and a Mexican-hating luncheonette owner is an entertaining creation in spectacular tumbling, swinging, back arching, bending. However, the endless masturbatory 'building' of excitement – beautiful haymakers, room-covering falls, thunderous sounds – is more than slightly silly. Even if the room were valid, which it isn't (a studio-built chromium horror plopped too close to the edge of a lonely highway), the room goes unexplored because of the jumbled timing. The excess that is so noticeable in Stevens's brawl is absent in the least serious undergrounder, which attains most of its crisp, angular character from the modesty of a director working skilfully far within the earthworks of the story.

Underground films have almost ceased to be a part of the movie scene. The founders of the action film have gone into awkward, big-scaled productions involving pyramid-building, a passenger plane in trouble over the Pacific, and postcard Westerns with Jimmy Stewart and his harassed Adam's apple approach to gutty acting. The last drainings of the underground film show a tendency toward moving from the plain guttural approach of *Stool Helmet* to a Germanically splashed type of film. Of these newcomers, Robert Aldrich is certainly the most exciting – a lurid, psychiatric stormer who gets an overflow of vitality and sheer love for movie-making into the film. This enthusiasm is the rarest item in a dried, decayed-lemon type of movie period. Aldrich makes viciously anti-Something movies – *Attack* stomps on Southern racialism and the officer sect in war, *The Big Knife* impales the Zanuck–Goldwyn big shot in Hollywood. The Aldrich films are filled with exciting characterizations – by Lee Marvin, Rod Steiger, Jack Palance – of highly psyched-up, marred, and bothered men. Phil Karlson has done some surprising

Gothic treatments of the Brinks hold-up (*Kansas City Confidential*) and the vice-ridden Southern town (*The Phenix City Story*). His movies are remarkable for their endless outlay of scary cheapness in detailing the modern underworld. Also, Karlson's work has a chilling documentary exactness and an exciting shot-scattering belligerence.

There is no longer a literate audience for the masculine picture-making that Hawks and Wellman exploited, as there was in the 1930s. In those exciting movie years, a smart audience waited around each week for the next Hawks, Preston Sturges, or Ford film – shoe-stringers that were far to the side of the expensive Hollywood film. That underground audience, with its expert voice in Otis Ferguson and its ability to choose between perceptive trash and the Thalberg pepsin-flavored sloshing with Tracy and Gable, has now oozed away. It seems ridiculous, but the Fergusonite went into fast decline during the mid-1940s when the movie market was flooded with fake underground films – plushy thrillers with neo-Chandler scripts and a romantic style that seemed to pour the gore, histrionics, decor out of a giant catsup bottle. The nadir of these films: an item called *Singapore* with Fred MacMurray and Ava Gardner.

The straw that finally breaks the back of the underground film tradition is the dilettante behavior of intellectuals on the subject of oaters. Esthetes and upper bohemians now favor horse operas almost as wildly as they like the cute, little-guy worshipings of De Sica and the pedantic, interpretive reading of Alec Guinness. This fad for Western films shows itself in the inevitable little-magazine review, which finds an affinity between the subject matter of cowboy films and the inner esthetics of Cinemah. The Hawks–Wellman tradition, which is basically a subterranean delight that looks like a cheap penny candy on the outside, hasn't a chance of reviving when intellectuals enthuse in equal amounts over Westerns by Ford, Nunnally Johnson, J. Sturges, Stevens, Delmer Daves. In Ferguson's day, the intellectual could differentiate between a solid genre painter (Ford), a long-winded cuteness expert with a rotogravure movie scene (Johnson), a scene-painter with a notions-counter eye and a primly naïve manner with sun-hardened bruisers (John Sturges), and a *Boy's Life* nature lover who intelligently half-prettifies adolescents and backwoods primitives (Daves). Today, the audience for Westerns and gangster careers is a sickeningly frivolous one that does little more than play the garbage collector or make a night court of films. With this high-brow audience that loves banality and pomp more than the tourists at Radio City Music Hall, there is little reason to expect any stray director to try for a hidden meager-looking work that is directly against the serious art grain.

'Much of Hitchcock's limitations, I think, but also his greatness within them, are to be found in his heavy body. His way of always working in the studio, using a static camera, not moving about, he has erected it all into a system, using long scenes where he won't have to give himself the trouble of having to move about.'

INGMAR BERGMAN

MANNY FARBER
Short and Happy

Just like ordinary human beings, just like you and me, movie stars had pets: by which I mean, all those talking, squawking, quacking, wisecracking ducks, mice, rabbits, dogs, birds and 'puddy tats' that would trot alongside them, faithfully accompanying the 'big film' from city to city, from cinema to cinema. Here, on those countless 'little films' which were once indelibly linked to the moviegoing experience, is Manny Farber again.

Some of the best movies of the year are seven-minute cartoons called by names like *All This and Rabbit Stew* or *The Fighting 69th 1/2*, which comes on as unheralded transitions in the double bill and feature the notorious Bugs Bunny, a rabbit that not only performs physical feats of a Paul Bunyan magnitude but is equally sharp with his mind. They come from Warner Brothers, are produced by Leon Schlesinger, made by Chuck Jones, Friz Freling, Bob McKimson, and called *Merrie Melodies*; ten of them are being reissued this fall still as *Merrie Melodies* but with the addition of a Blue Ribbon.

One reason for the brightness of *Merrie Melodies* and for their superiority over Disney's product is that Jones is out to make you laugh, bluntly, and, as it turns out, cold-bloodedly. This runs him against the grain of the several well-worked grooves down which the animated cartoon has traveled under the belief these grooves will never wear through. However, it no longer seems funny to see animals who talk and act like human beings, who do all sorts of ingenious tricks – most of them superhuman – who go through lives of the highest excitement and reward, but have no inner, or mental, life. The complex emotional life and three-dimensional nature of Jones–McKimson characters allow their makers to poke fun at everything in sight, or out of sight – especially if it is something familiar and well loved, like McKimson's *Hiawatha*, a kind person, or any bad actress's great moments. It is an illusion of most cartoon-makers that they must have a moral, or do good, if it means only killing the villain; Warner's crew isn't under this illusion. The masterpiece, *Inki and the Lion*, is also a masterpiece of amorality – so far the other side of goodness that it is a parody of *Bambi*. In this version of forest life, man is the likable spear-thrower, preyed on by animals, and the king of the forest is a supernatural horror called the Myna bird, who hates man and beast alike.

The artistic method in Warner cartoons is neither in Disney's top drawer (at his best) nor Popeye's bottom one, but, even so, it has gone off at a tangent lately that may open up new paths to the cartoon method. It is a change from the straight, insipid realism to a sophisticated shorthand, made up of flat, stylized, posterlike representations, using a sort of Persian color of fancy tones like dusty pink. It is a much simpler style of cartoon drawing, the animation is less profuse, the details fewer, and it allows for reaching the joke and accenting it much more quickly and directly: it also gets the form out of the impossible dilemma between realism and the wacky humor.

The goal in heroes is a comic figure with a temperament and behavior as peculiarly his own as those of a Chaplin or Fields, which goal is never achieved; but it leads to several rewards, like the Myna bird, who appears in the *Inki* (little African boy) series. The Myna bird is like a toucan, shaped like an acorn, coal black, who moves inscrutably in an atmosphere of overwhelming supernaturalism, to the tune of Mendelssohn's overture to *Fingal's Cave*. At the end of each musical phrase, he gives one prodigious, syncopated hop, thereafter moving forward indomitably. The Myna bird is inevitably followed by a passive three-year-old individual named Inki, who loves to throw spears, and by a lion (the lion is Jones's least successful creation – he looks like Robinson Crusoe). The famous Bugs Bunny is an Avery–Jones one-animal advertisement of the moral that unadulterated torturing of your fellow men pays off.

Despite the various positions on humor (Tex Avery is a visual surrealist proving nothing is permanent, McKimson is a show-biz satirist with throw away gags and celebrity spoofs, Friz Freling is the least contorting, while Jones's speciality, comic character, is unusual for the chopping up of motion and the surrealistic imposition: a Robin Hood duck, whose flattened beak springs out with each repeated faux pas as a reminder of the importance of his primary ineptness), the Warner cartoonists are refreshing iconoclasts because they concentrate on so many other humor antecedents besides brutal mishaps, cultural punning, balletlike sadism. One of Jones's key inventions is the animal who is a totally invulnerable, can't-possibly-be-stopped adversary, a mysterious force like rain that is always surrounded by a hush that is a mixture of the awe, revelation, instinctive reverence of a soon-to-be-victim just before he is maneuvered off the cliff or into a distant puff of smoke miles away in the desert. Ridiculousness is behind every Jones gag, but it is labyrinthine in effect because of how much gentleness is mixed in along with an infinite response to one animal's brass, hunger, manipulative power, or blinding speed. Disney's boredom-encased drawing, Barbera's cat–mouse drag, and the smugly 'mature' Hubley works are incapable of this Warner's lightness: that there should be no end in defining the human quality of hunger (an animal fated from birth to be a scrawny piece of meat trying to eat tin cans, blindly grabbing at flies in a hostile environment of doomful rocks) as long as the metaphorical elaboration is kept within lighter-than-air feats of quick, fractional wit. The never-stop, pushing-on insistence in Warner's cartoons is important: having eaten some Earthquake Pills from a little bottle, the effect on the victim's body is a tremor that has the insistence and unsolvable disaster of hiccups.

Because of the twenty-six-issues-per-year rate at which they are thought up, the *Merrie Melodies* are bound to vary greatly in quality. The surprising facts about them are that the good ones are masterpieces and the bad ones aren't a total loss. For instance, the poor *Rabbit Who Came to Dinner* (Freling) is given a tremendous lift when, in the midst of the inevitable and tedious chase of the rabbit by Elmer, the clock strikes twelve and Bugs breaks into one of his typical emotional upsets, roaring out *Auld Lang Syne*, kissing Elmer, flinging confetti in the age-old tradition of New Year's Eve – Elmer being as easily diverted in July as in any other mouth.

Jones–McKimson–Freling are in the Sennett tradition, which uses the whole sphere of man's emotion and behavior simply as a butt for humor, no matter what it leads to. The aim is purely and simply laughter. Schlesinger's men are rich and inventive humorists, and their smart-alecky freshness has turned what is meant to be an interval on the program into the moment when the whole audience brightens up.

ANDREW SARRIS
Beatitudes of B Pictures

The term is familiarly bandied about by journalists too young ever to have seen a real one, but what exactly was a B-movie?

It was during the heyday of the American studio system, from the early 1930s to the late 1950s, that B-movies flourished. Because the Hollywood studios themselves owned the nationwide cinema chains in which their films were exhibited (until all such monopolies were outlawed by an antitrust law in 1948), they were responsible for furnishing those cinemas with entire evening-length programmes – programmes which, apart from the package's big picture backbone, included cartoons, shorts, newsreels, trailers and, of course Bs. That, simplifying grossly, is the socio-economic history of the B-movie.

And it's also, in a sense, its aesthetic history. For these were films which neither disowned their inherently unpromising narrative material nor sought, as we say, to 'transcend' the generic limitations which had been imposed upon them. Instead, they unflinchingly assumed and even revelled in both, clichés and all. Obliged to wind up their stories in under 70 minutes, saddled with small-time, penny-ante actors and actresses playing small-time, penny-ante mobsters and molls, their directors had no time to be arty or academic or pretentious.

One is reminded of a comment made by the great physicist Heinrich Hertz on the extraordinary power and resonance of certain apparently elementary mathematical theorems. 'One cannot escape the feeling,' he mused, 'that these formulas have an independent existence and intelligence of their own, that they are wiser than we are, wiser even than their discoverers, that we get more out of them than was originally put into them.'

Let us now praise the B picture. But what is it exactly? Or, rather, what was it? In this age of inflation and instant insights, there is nothing on the screen that we can point to and say: This is a B picture. A Z movie, perhaps, but not a B picture. There is too much ambition at one end, too little craftsmanship at the other, and the bottom has fallen out of the middle. Nor is there today any genre lowly enough to be dismissed out of hand by the critical establishment. Kung-fu, porn (soft-core and hard-core), Damon and Pythias squad-car serenades, revisionist Westerns, regressive Disneys, black-power fantasies: all have their sociological and even stylistic rationales. The snobberies that afflicted supposedly serious film criticism in the 1930s, 1940s, and 1950s have now been superseded by an open-mindedness that errs on the side of credulity. Another problem today in finding a B picture is that the notion of the A picture is more nebulous than ever, and you can't have B pictures without A pictures. Indeed, with the predetermined double feature's disappearance, it is less and less often that one hears the once familiar refrain: 'I liked the second feature better than the main one.' Nowadays a double feature is more likely to consist of two failed A pictures, with the older one on the bottom of the bill.

Still, we are beginning to define the conditions that bred the B picture even as we bemoan the absence of these conditions. The B picture trudged out from Hollywood in the 1930s, 1940s, and 1950s. Silent movies tended to be major and minor rather than A or B, and comedy shorts and pulp Westerns didn't really count at any time as Bs. From the point of view of the American moviegoer, the cheapest, tawdriest, silliest foreign-language film was still too exotic to qualify as a B movie. The B picture was thus almost by definition a product of the Hollywood studio system. The B picture was usually in black and white, the feeling being that color was both too expensive and too immodest for a true B. Of course, color became so commonplace in the 1950s and 1960s that the black-and-white requirement went by the board. So much so, in fact, that the black and white used for *The Last Picture Show* (1971) seemed pretentiously archaic and A-pictureish all the way.

There are at least two ways of looking fondly at any given B picture. One is the way of the trivia hound, and the other is the way of the treasure hunter. Whereas the trivia hound loves all B pictures simply because they are B pictures, the treasure hunter loves only certain B pictures because they have somehow overcome the onus of having started out as B pictures. Thus, the trivia hound tends to be encyclopedic, and the treasure hunter tends to be selective. By necessity, the treasure hunter must share some of the zeal of the trivia hound, but the trivia hound need not recognize the aesthetic restrictions of the treasure hunter. I would tend to classify myself as a treasure hunter with a touch of the trivia hound. Hence, I cannot embrace all the B-ness of B pictures. Nor do I consider all genres equal.

Musicals and comedies, for example, seldom surmount the ritualized format of the Bs. Indeed, the big curse of the Bs as a class of movies is a dreary tendency toward facetiousness without wit or humor. Nothing is more depressing about a bad movie than its bad jokes or its failed musical numbers or its unimaginative slapstick. Thus, a disproportionate number of fondly remembered B pictures fall into the general category of the *film noir*. Somehow even mediocrity can become majestic when it is coupled with death, which is to say that if only good movies can teach us how to live, even bad movies can teach us how to die.

But are we talking about really good movies, or merely good moments in bad movies? Even *King Kong* (1933) isn't much good until the last half hour; and it isn't great until the last ten minutes. Not that *King Kong* qualifies as a B picture, *Son of Kong* (1933) qualifies, but not *Kong* itself. One might say that *King Kong* is the heroic night before, and *Son of Kong* the hung over morning after. But I've always had a soft spot in my heart for the ratty fatalism of *Son of Kong*. In its depressing way, the last tramp-steamer two-shot of Robert Armstrong and Helen Mack on their way to no place in particular is every bit as memorable as Kong's last anguished expression atop the Empire State Building. Still, we can stipulate that the progression from an original to a sequel is often from A to B, not always, but almost always. *Dead End* (1937) is an A, but the Dead End Kids and East Side Kids series run from B to Z. The Warner Oland Charlie Chans are either A or high B, the Sidney Toler Chans are all B. *What a Life!* (1930) with Jackie Cooper as Henry Aldrich (and a Brackett and Wilder screenplay) is not only an A, but also one of the most sadistic studies of American adolescence in any medium. Andy Hardy was always A, and Blondie was always B, although both were fantastically profitable. *The Bride of Frankenstein* (1935) and *The Son of Frankenstein* (1939), however, were every bit as ambitious as the original *Frankenstein* (1931). *The Curse of the Cat People* (1944) was even more literary although less mythic than *The Cat People* (1942). Not so the sequels to *Tarzan, the Ape Man* (the 1931 version with Johnny Weissmuller and Maureen O'Sullivan) and *Planet of the Apes* (1968). There sequelitis was more interesting sociologically than stylistically.

If, as the late Robert Warshow once suggested, the faces, bodies, and personalities of players constitute the linguistic tropes of the cinema, then Helen Chandler's mere presence in a Mayfair special entitled *Alimony Madness* (1933) is its own justification. Mayfair, Tiffany, Republic, Monogram, PRC, Eagle-Lion: these are corporate names to conjure with in any discussion of B pictures. Almost everything they turned out was B or lower. Republic is a spectacular case in point. From 1941 to 1958, a Miss Vera Hruba Ralston, the wife and perennial protégée of Republic's President, Herbert Yates, made twenty-six indescribably inane pictures, all for Republic, a feat of conjugal devotion (on her husband's part) romantically credited with dispatching Republic into receivership. Paradoxically, Republic participated during this period in several very arty (though inexpensive) auteurist productions: John Ford's *Rio Grande* (1950), *The Quiet Man* (1952), and *The Sun Shines Bright* (1954); Ben Hecht's *Spectre of the Rose* (1946); Fritz Lang's *House by the River* (1950); Nicholas Ray's *Johnny Guitar* (1954); and Orson Welles's *Macbeth* (1948); none of which fits into the campy category of Vera Hruba Ralston, and none of which qualifies as a B picture.

Nor is the ideal B picture simply a 'sleeper' that catches on with audiences. *It Happened One Night* (1934), *Casablanca* (1942), *Going My Way* (1944), *Sitting Pretty* (1933), *A Letter to Three Wives* (1949), and even *Easy Rider* (1969) were all authentic sleepers in their time, but either their casts were too prominent, or their aspirations were too fully articulated, or both. The late James Agee described *Double Indemnity* (1944) as 'trash', but that didn't make it a B picture. In New York and other cosmopolitan centers in America, the run and ruck of Westerns tend to be so unfashionable that they seem to qualify as Bs in retrospect. Nonetheless it is difficult to consider an expansive spectacle on a wide screen and in color as a B picture no matter how unfashionable it may be otherwise. Even a black-and-white, wide-screen Western like Sam Fuller's *Forty Guns* (1957) seems somewhat too elaborate to be considered a B, despite Barbara Stanwyck's working at a lower salary, not to mention the mere presence of Barry Sullivan in the lead role. Barry Sullivan was a born B picture actor, and a damned good one, so good, in fact, that he usually lifts up Bs in quality, if not in prestige. *The Gangster* (1947) is his greatest vehicle, and it is worth watching just for the pleasure of his understated authority setting up the histrionics of Akim Tamiroff and Joan Lorring. In A pictures, Barry Sullivan could never have been anything more than a leading man, and usually a secondary leading man. But in Bs Barry Sullivan could be a tragic hero.

The last thing I want to do, however, is to restrict the range of the B picture. Nor do I wish to dictate the conditions under which it can be discussed. It's much more fun, and perhaps more useful too, to throw out some recollections of a lifetime of moviegoing. One can never say the last word on this haunting subject. Not only are there too many memories to begin with, but also more and more are being reconstructed each day through revivals.

Black Angel (1946): Dan Duryea falls in love with June Vincent, who is obsessed with saving her unfaithful dullard of a husband from the electric chair. A very erotic movie for the 1940s. Peter Lorre and Freddie Steele are especially fascinating as underworld characters, Lorre lecherously and Steele sadistically, and the girl voluptuously masochistic in their midst. Roy William Neill, who directed the best of the Basil Rathbone–Nigel Bruce Sherlock Holmes pictures, may have had something to do with the edgy elegance of the production, and Cornell Woolrich (the literary source of Hitchcock's *Rear Window*) supplied the original story. But mainly, I think, it is Duryea, who takes the opportunity in a B picture to pull a switch on the ratty villains he played in the As.

Wicked Woman (1953): This B comes closer to camp than almost anything else I can think of in a favorable way, but its sordidness is somehow delicious. I don't remember anymore whether the girl was Beverly Michaels or Cleo Moore, but she was one of these two Hugo-Haas-type blonde floozies of the 1950s, and the movie's one indelible image is that of porcine Percy Helton's kissing his way desperately up her arm, all the while squeaking out expressions of endearment. There is something so marvelously indefatigable about Helton as an actor that he makes most left-wing movies about underdogs seem about as egalitarian as the novels of Disraeli.

Detour (1946): Edgar G. Ulmer directed Tom Neal and Ann Savage in this most despairing and most claustrophobic of all B pictures. *Detour* is not so much an example of a B that rises unexpectedly in class (like *Blondie's Blessed Event* (1942) in the Blondie series) as of a poetic conceit from Poverty Row. Unfortunately, since Ulmer's canonization as a cult favorite, his legitimate successes – *The Black Cat* (1934), *Bluebeard* (1944), *Ruthless* (1948), and *The Naked Dawn* (1955) – make him too prominent for this article. Similarly, Joseph H. Lewis, lately the subject of directorial retrospectives, can no longer be cited solely for *Gun Crazy* (1950), a lyrical meditation on a gun-crazed couple several years before *Bonnie and Clyde* (1967), and several years more before *Badlands* (1974).

Rendezvous with Annie (1946): I liked this movie long before I ever knew it was directed by Allan Dwan, or even who Allan Dwan was supposed to be. What I remember most vividly is Eddie Albert's sharing a cake during the London blitz with Sir C. Aubrey Smith. I enjoyed *Brewster's Millions* (1945), which Dwan also directed, and which looms as large in his later legend as the anti-McCarthy Western *Silver Lode* (1954), which he directed, with Dan Duryea as a villain.

When Strangers Marry (1944): Kim Hunter, Dean Jagger, and Robert Mitchum in a not-bad William Castle imitation of Alfred Hitchcock. The three leads give the film an A gloss, but the most memorable sound in the film is the rollicking, yet rasping laugh of a small, rotund, cherubic character actor named Dick Elliott. His laugh is one of the most explosively distinctive expressions of mirth on the edge of malignancy in the entire history of the sound film, and yet I doubt that there are any more than a handful of moviegoers and trivia hounds who can identify the name with the face, or even recall the face. No matter. He shall serve as my personal proxy for all the other unsung and unremembered favorites of other moviegoers. Dick Elliott has a small part in *Mr Smith Goes to Washington* (1939), but I would never have noticed him if it hadn't been for his extraordinary eruptions in *Vogues of 1938* and *So This Is New York* (1948). In the latter film, Elliott heckles Dona Drake's hapless first-night performance as a maid in an atrocious play written by Bill Williams. Elliott's gusto in reading fairly ordinary insult lines transforms these lines into the roaring sounds of comic opera. But it is in *Vogues of 1938* that Elliott's unique gift serves to fashion one of the most imaginative jokes in the history of the cinema. We first see Elliott at an out-of-town tryout box-office window. Twirling an outsize cigar, he asks for his usual house seats. The show's producer (Warner Baxter) asks the ticket seller about the freeloader with the big cigar and he is told that Elliott is notorious in New Haven for always guessing wrong on shows that later open on Broadway. If he likes a show, it is bound to be a flop. At the intermission, Baxter nervously follows Elliott into the lobby. At first Elliott chuckles quietly to himself, but the bubbling merriment is beginning to spill over his face like lava from a live volcano, and the explosion is not long in coming. As the relatively grim members of the audience look on disapprovingly, Elliott begins to go into convulsions. The last damning peals of laughter occur off screen as Baxter goes to the telephone to make arrangements to close the show out of town. The sound of Elliott's laughter is one of the comic coups of the 1930s, and an example of the many unrecorded glories of the movies from A to B. I could go on and on, but you get the picture. It is my hope that books like this will help illuminate the still-dark corners of the medium. Perhaps if we all pool our memories without shame or snobbery, we can see to it yet that nothing of merit in the movies is ever completely forgotten or completely undiscovered.

'My film is born first in my head; dies on paper; is resuscitated by the living persons and real objects I use, which are killed on film but, placed in a certain order and projected on to a screen, come to life again like flowers in water'

ROBERT BRESSON

J. HOBERMAN
Bad Movies

Hollywood, or the unimportance of being earnest. Can one listen to a bad piano concerto? Or admire a feebly painted still-life? Or find it impossible to put down an atrociously written novel? No, no and no again. Yet, as every cinéphile well knows, and as the critic J. Hoberman explains below – in a chapter excerpted from Vulgar Modernism, *a selection of articles originally published in* Film Comment *and the* Village Voice *– the irresistibility of the cinema, of the American cinema in particular, cannot be separated from the irresistibility of its magnificent duds.*

There are a number of reasons to consider bad movies. The most obvious is that tastes change; that many, if not most, of the films we admire were once dismissed as inconsequential trash; and that trash itself is not without certain socio-aesthetic charms. Then too, bad movies have a pedagogic use value – the evolution of film form has largely been based upon mistakes. A third reason is that movies, to a certain degree, have a life of their own. They mix the documentary with the fictional, and the worst inadvertancies of one can easily overwhelm the best intentions of the other. That is, it is possible for a movie to succeed *because* it has failed.

With their perverse, pioneering affection for the detritus of industrial civilization, the Surrealists were the first to cultivate an appreciation for bad movies. 'The best and most exciting films [are] the films shown in local fleapits, films which seem to have no place in the history of the cinema,' advises Ado Kyrou in *Le Surréalisme au Cinéma*. 'Learn to go see the "worst" films; they are sometimes sublime.' This taste for Elixir of Potboiler – junky spectacles, cheap horror flicks, anonymous pornography, juvenile swashbucklers, movies 'scorned by critics, charged with cretinism or infantilism by the old defenders of rationality' – was based on the innate capacity of such films to produce (if only in random moments) that 'crux of Surrealism', *le merveilleux*.

The Surrealists courted disorientation: A film had a dreamlike latent content – and this could be precipitated by deranging or bypassing the manifest content of its storyline. During World War I, the young André Breton used to wander from movie-house to movie-house, entering mid-film, leaving for the next once the plot became apparent. By the time Breton became Surrealism's Black Pope, this practice had been elevated and refined into the principle of synthetic criticism. The ideal Surrealist spectator habitually broke open a film's continuity to liberate individual images from the prison of the narrative. Thus the American para-Surrealistic Joseph Cornell created his 1936 masterpiece *Rose Hobart* by distilling a studio adventure film, *East of Borneo* (Columbia, 1931), into twenty-four non-linear minutes and projecting it at silent speed through a piece of blue glass to the accompaniment of the song 'Holiday in Brazil'.

For all their admiration for the 'worst' films, and despite their propensity for deconstructing movies inside their heads, the Surrealists developed no canon of films so incoherent that *they unmade themselves* – films that transcend taste and might be termed *objectively bad*. Surrealist bad movies are lurid, oneiric, delirious. An objectively bad movie is all this and more.

'A bad actor,' wrote the underground cinéaste Jack Smith, 'is rich, unique, idiosyncratic, revealing.' The same may be said for the objectively bad film, and for similar reasons. Smith, who began experimenting with bad acting in *Flaming Creatures* (1962), was undoubtedly thinking of his favorite star, the paradigmatic Camp icon Maria Montez. In part, his appreciation for her vehicles is a Surrealist taste. Infantile fantasies like *White Savage*, *Ali Baba and the Forty Thieves*, and *Sudan* are founts of inane, voluptuously exotic imagery. Smith was moved by their poetry.

But there is another aspect as well. It was precisely because Montez was so unconvincing an actress that Smith valued her performances: 'One of her atrocious acting sighs suffused a thousand tons of dead plaster with imaginative life and a truth.' The truth is that Montez is always herself. Montez vehicles are unintended documentaries of a romantic, narcissistic young woman dressing up in pasty jewels, striking fantastic poses, queening it over an all-too-obviously make-believe world. For Smith, her inept portrayals of Scheherezade, the Cobra Woman, and the Siren of Atlantis hyperbolized the actual situation of a Hollywood glamour goddess. Montez's transparent role-playing, and her unconcealed delight at being the center of attention, were more authentic to him than the naturalism achieved by *successfully* phony actresses. The often poignant, heightened realism induced by such a failure to convince is the key to the objectively bad film.

The conventional narrative film does not demand anything so gross as a suspension of disbelief; it only asks an indulgent acceptance of its own diegetic, or fictive, space. The badly made, unconvincing film confounds this minimal requirement by ignoring or (more often) bungling the most rudimentary precepts of screen naturalism. I once saw a porn film set in Outer Space that used a suburban kitchen as the set for its rocket control room. The bluntness with which this profilmic reality disrupted the diegetic web produced a more vivid sense of science fiction than anything in *2001*.

The theoretician Noel Burch has identified a-conventional narrative films (exceptions to what he calls the 'institutional mode of representation') in pre-1905 and non-Western cinema. An early Japanese talkie like *Wife! Be Like a Rose* (1935) may not fully subscribe to the institutionalized codes, but it cannot be considered badly made: the unorthodox eyeline-matches in reverse-angle sequences, odd cutaways and sound bridges, and impossible point-of-view shots are only subtly jarring. An objectively bad film, on the other hand, casually promotes perceptual havoc – as casually as the 3-D cheapster *Robot Monster* (1953) incorporated special effects lifted without modification from the two-dimensional *One Million B.C.*

Objectively bad movies are usually made against all odds in a handful of days on a breathtakingly low budget. Such extreme austerity enforces a delirious pragmatism: homemade sets, no retakes, tacky special effects, heavy reliance on stock footage. The objectively bad film attempts to reproduce the institutional mode of representation, but its failure to do so deforms the simplest formulae and clichés so absolutely that you barely recognize them. They must be actively decoded. In Edward D. Wood, Jr's *Bride of the Monster* (1956), a film that employs so many inappropriate reaction shots that it suggests a combined Kuleshov–Rorschach test, a secretary abruptly picks up a phone and starts talking. Did the director overlook the necessity of dialing? Did he forget to post-dub the sound of the ring? An actress in Oscar Micheaux's *God's Stepchildren* (1937) shakes her head and declares, 'No . . . emphatically . . . no.' Belatedly, one realizes she has incorporated the script's stage direction into her lines.

Poor acting and ludicrous dialogue – though axiomatic to bad filmmaking – do not in themselves make an objectively bad movie. Neither does an absurd plot; if it did, D. W. Griffith, Josef von Sternberg, and Samuel Fuller would all be bad filmmakers. In fact to be objectively bad, a film must relentlessly draw one's attention away from its absurd plot. For Walter Benjamin (and even André Bazin), the seamless 'equipment-free aspect of reality' that movies presented on screen was actually the 'height of artifice'. The objectively bad film acknowledges this: the lie of 'chronology' is confounded by imperfect continuity; 'invisible' editing is ruptured by mismatched cuts; *mise en scène* is foregrounded by cloddish bits of business. A good bad movie is a philosopher's stone that converts the incompetent mistakes of naïve dross into modernist gold. Such movies are unstable objects. They ping-pong back and forth from diegetic intent to profilmic event (or to their own jerry-built construction) the way a Cézanne oscillates between a representational landscape and a paint-gopped canvas.

Objectively bad films are almost always targeted at the most exploitable or *lumpen* sections of the movie audience (ethnic minorities, teenagers, sub-literates, 42nd Street derelicts). Like every other sort of movie, however, the best bad films are personal, even obsessive works. Some guy had a story to tell and he was going to punch it across by whatever impoverished means were at hand. 'For the budget, and for the time, I felt I had achieved greatness,' said Phil Tucker of his $16,000 *Robot Monster*. The best bad movies add nutty ambition and auteurist signatures to their already-heady atmosphere of free-floating *meshugas*. 'There is a very short distance between high art and trash,' observed Douglas Sirk. (Who would know better than he?) 'And trash that contains the element of craziness is by this very quality nearer to art.' A supremely bad movie – an anti-masterpiece – projects a stupidity as awesome as genius.

These thoughts were prompted in part by the World's Worst Film Festival, held at the Beacon Theatre in Manhattan. The series was itself inspired by *The Fifty Worst Films of All Time* and *The Golden Turkey Awards*, a pair of humorous non-books researched by teenaged Harry Medved and written by his older brother Michael. The Medved position – if we discount its patina of *Mad* magazine masochism and resolve to stomach its facetious tone – also suggests that the best bad movies are akin to masterpieces.

'In both cases,' according to the Medveds, 'the viewer marvels at the range of human imagination and creativity.' Another way to put it is that anti-masterpieces break the rules with such exhilaration as to expand our definition of what a movie can be. *They Saved Hitler's Brain* (1958? 1964?), the most structurally inventive film shown at the World's Worst Film Festival, surpasses the temporal complexity of *Muriel* by intercutting two radically different movies. The first is elaborately lighted and was filmed on studio sets by Stanley Cortez; the second, involving a completely distinct set of actors, was shot *vérité*-style in 16mm some six years later. These two strands are densely interwoven, sometimes even within a single scene. Watching it, your head bursts with ideas.

Peter Bogdanovich once produced a similar, if less bewildering exercise in creative geography when Roger Corman commissioned him to add shots of Mamie Van Doren and other Venusian cuties to a womanless Soviet sci-fi film whose rights AIP had acquired. But whereas Bogdanovich's *Voyage to the Planet of the Prehistoric Women* is wittily schematic, *TSHB* (as its fans in the Beacon lobby were heard to refer to it) is unpredictable and irrational. The logic it entails is so unfathomable, the shifts in its action so abrupt, that you have to pinch yourself to make sure it isn't a hallucination.

The Medveds' most sincere defense of bad movies, stated in the prefaces to both their books, is that 'people show greater enthusiasm in laughing together over films they despise than trying to praise films they admire'. There's a self-serving aspect to this questionable observation, but its implications are not without interest. By their unintentional 'success', bad movies deflate the claims of more serious works – and they are leveling in other ways. It's reassuring, the Medveds suggest, to discover that the 'larger-than-life demigods' of Hollywood are also fallible, even clumsy. Beneath the Medveds' glibness is an inchoate protest against the colonization of the imagination by ready-made, seamless dreams.

Obviously, the Medveds' appreciation of badness differs from that of the Surrealists, or of Jack Smith. While the former valorized bad movies for their 'beauty', and the latter prized bad acting for its 'truth', the Medved aesthetic is an affirmation of the American Way: 'Absolutely anyone can recognize a lousy film when he sees one.'

This democratic assertion raises hopes that the Medved books will be treasuries of objectively bad films. But although many of their 'Fifty Worst' are bad to the degree that they are laughable, few are bad enough to be pleasurable, let alone radical. The book – from which aspiring screenwriter Michael prudently withheld his name – is mainly a collection of ponderous mediocrities (*Valley of the Dolls*, *Northwest Mounted Police*), famous flops (Ross Hunter's *Lost Horizon*, *Myra Breckinridge*), and lame performances by well-known stars (John Wayne as The Conqueror, Clarke Gable as Parnell).

The Medveds are alive to the qualities of a *Robot Monster*, but they haven't the imagination to distinguish between purely conceptual (hence, unwatchable) absurdities like the all-midget *Terror of Tiny Town* or the Ronald Reagan–Shirley Temple match-up in *That Hagen Girl* and *films maudits* like *Bring Me the Head of Alfredo Garcia* or *Exorcist II: The Heretic*. This is not so much a factor of their petulant philistinism (they include *Last Year at Marienbad* and *Ivan the Terrible* among the Fifty Worst) as it is of the ingrained literary bias which has them habitually judging films by their bad dialogue and humorously negative reviews.

The Golden Turkey Awards, *The Fifty Worst Films*'s more sleekly packaged sequel (it gives prizes in thirty categories from 'The Worst Two-Headed Transplant Movie Ever Made' to 'The Most Inane and Unwelcome "Technical Advance" in Hollywood History'), is something of a corrective. Having solicited suggestions from readers of the first book, the Medveds shift the emphasis of their second away from punishing star vehicles to horror and sci-fi cheapsters – films which labor under the double burden of having to make the supernatural, as well as their own fictive space, appear convincing. Indicative of this reorientation is the canonization of the previously unmentioned *Plan Nine from Outer Space* (1959) and its director Edward D. Wood, Jr as, respectively, 'The Worst Film of All Time' and 'The Worst Director of All Time'.

Not surprisingly, the Worst Director of All Time was well represented at the World's Worst Film Festival with *Plan Nine*, *Bride of the Monster*, and the 1952 *I Changed My Sex* (also known as *Glen or Glenda?*). Writer-director-editor Wood featured Bela Lugosi in all three: and the presence of this broken-down star (in some respects a tragic male counterpart to Maria Montez) contributes to their atmosphere of rancid glitz. A sense of Hollywood Boulevard Babylon pervades Wood's universe. It's not surprising to learn that he ended up directing hard-core porn, and that his last opus was an 8mm 'home study' segment of *The Encyclopedia of Sex*.

Wood evidently played Svengali to an entourage of *Day of the Locust* weirdos. His movies are less the products of Hollywood's Poverty Row than the fantasies of a parallel Skid Row populated by show biz oddities (Criswell, the TV prophet; Tor Johnson, the 400-pound Swedish wrestler; Vampira, the beatnik ghoul-girl), haggard has-beens (Lugosi, Lyle Bettger), and the talentless progeny of the money-men who bankrolled him. The pitifully emaciated Lugosi gives a particularly painful performance in *Bride of the Monster*, playing a mad scientist with a spare lightstand as the centerpiece to his art *povera* laboratory. Against all odds, Lugosi clings to shreds of his professionalism. One watches in horrified admiration as he shifts gears from enraged ranting to bathetic wimpering to insane cackling in a single, brutally endless take, or when he gamely pretends to struggle in the outstretched tentacles of an unmoving rubber octopus.

A casual *mise en scène* of half-dressed sets and visible Klieg lights is Wood's hallmark, and everywhere in his oeuvre one finds a naive faith in the power of montage. Wood was left with only two minutes of Lugosi footage when the star died early in the production of what became *Plan Nine from Outer Space*. His solution was to hire a stand-in, have him wrap his face in a cape, and use the Lugosi material anyway. Wood's action montages are so perfunctory as to be a slap in the face of public taste. *Plan Nine* features a shameless lackadaisical battle sequence fashioned out of scratchy World War II newsreels, inserts of wobbly tinfoil space ships, and a uniformed actor peering through fieldglasses, a white backdrop behind him. The 'monster' in *Bride of the Monster* is a squid filmed through the glass of an aquarium tank; the bargain basement apocalypse (and utter non-sequitur) that ends the movie is a single shot of an atomic mushroom cloud. With a similar economy of means, every significant moment – and there are many – in *I Changed My Sex* is punctuated with the identical flash of stock-footage lightning. Wood's fondness for dramatic inserts is balanced by a startling refusal to use cross-cutting to create tension. Characters chase each other around the frame instead.

Plan Nine begins with the psychic Criswell shrilly wondering if our nerves can stand the 'idea of grave-robbers from outer space', and ends with his declaration that what we have just seen was based on sworn testimony. ('Can you prove it didn't happen?' he asks in a phrase that might have served Wood as his motto.) Sandwiched between Criswell's two appearances are sequences of people knocked out of their lawn chairs by the 'death-ray' of an off-screen flashlight; Vampira haunting a cardboard cemetery that, no matter the time of day in contiguous shots, exists as a zone of perpetual night; extras grinning at the camera and pointing overhead to where a flotilla of flying saucers is supposedly strafing their car.

Plan Nine is Wood's most enjoyable movie; but it is the didactic, exploitational *I Changed My Sex* that offers the key to his work. The structure and thesis of this remarkable film are far too convoluted to summarize briefly. Suffice to say that its parallel 'case histories' (one a screwball explanation of transvestism; the other a ponderous depiction of a transsexual operation) are set within a thicket of multiple narratives and framed by cutaways to an omniscient Bela Lugosi surrounded by human skeletons and shrieking, 'The story must be told.'

The story must be told indeed. *I Changed My Sex* is a possible psychodrama and, at least, a partial autobiography. According to the Medveds, the mustachioed Wood affected women's pantsuits, pantyhose, and angora sweaters, and bragged he had worn a brassière beneath his World War II combat fatigues. Low budgets and heavy drinking may account for the spectacular lapses of Wood's *mise en scène*, but his artistic personality (a subject surely for further research) was obviously bound up in this most primitive form of make-believe. The unconvincing magic, crackpot logic, and decomposing glamour of Wood's films are in fact a mirror of his own life. Dressed like a tacky transvestite out of *Flaming Creatures*, he played at being a megaphone-brandishing director with the demented conviction of Maria Montez impersonating a movie star. His films, like hers, intimate the full lunacy and pathos of Southern California. He deserves the title of World's Worst Director.

And yet, there is another filmmaker whose anti-masterpieces are so profoundly troubling and whose *weltanschauung* is so devastating that neither the Medveds nor the World's Worst Film Festival are equipped to deal with him. In fact, five decades after their release, his films still have no place in the history of cinema. I refer to the work of Oscar Micheaux.

I think of Micheaux as the Black Pioneer of American film – not just because he was a black man, or because in his youth he pioneered the West, or because he was the greatest figure in 'race' movies and an unjustly ignored force in early American cinema. Micheaux is America's Black Pioneer in the way that André Breton was Surrealism's Black

Pope. His movies throw our history and movies into an alien and startling disarray.

Micheaux's last film, aptly titled *The Betrayal*, opened in New York in 1948. 'There is simply no point in trying to apply normal critical standards . . . or in trying to describe its monumental incompetence as movie-making,' wrote *PM*, while the *Times* reported that it contained 'sequences so gauche as to provoke embarrassed laughter'. The *Herald-Tribune* was bluntest: 'A preposterous, inept bore . . . Acting that is worse than amateurish but this is not even its worst flaw. Micheaux's dialogue is even worse, with senseless and unmouthable lines; his concept of human beings is absurd and his direction somewhat less artful than one would expect of home-movies. The fact that Micheaux expects one to watch this [trash] for more than three hours is a monstrous piece of miscalculation.' Were the above reviews to greet a film opening tomorrow, one might rush to see it on the assumption that only a powerful originality could goad the jaded reviewers of the daily press to such fury. Edward Wood may be the Worst, but Oscar Micheaux (1884–1951) is the Baddest – with all that that implies.

Only the barest facts of Micheaux's life are in the record. He was a native of Illinois who, after several years of work as a Pullman porter, purchased a homestead for himself on the sparsely settled South Dakota plains. Inspired by Booker T. Washington, he began writing a series of thinly novelized autobiographical tracts, which he published and distributed himself. In 1919 his third novel, *The Homesteader*, attracted the attention of one of the several black-owned movie studios that had sprung up in response to the segregated policies of American movie theaters (as well as to counter *The Birth of a Nation*). Micheaux stipulated in the sale of the screen rights that he would direct the film. When the deal fell through, he raised capital among his public and made *The Homesteader* himself.

After this audacious start, Micheaux went on to be one of the most tenacious filmmakers who ever lived. Against all odds, over the next twenty-one years (with *The Betrayal* in 1948), he wrote, directed, and produced some thirty features. His method of distribution was an elaboration of the set-up he'd used to sell his novels. He would drive across the country, stop at each ghetto theater, show the owner his new script, hype his performers ('the Black Valentino', 'the Sepia Mae West'), and ask for an advance against the gate. When he had accumulated sufficient capital, he returned to New York and shot the film. Micheaux's silent pictures were more topical, more lurid, and more critical than those of other black filmmakers.

The painful ambivalence of Micheaux's racial attitudes is one reason why his films are rarely screened and less frequently written about. There seems to be a tacit agreement among scholars of black cinema to avoid discussing this aspect of his work – particularly as he is sometimes offered as a role-model for black directors and his name has been appropriated for the award given those artists inducted into the Black Filmmakers Hall of Fame. Donald Bogle, the only black critic to my knowledge who discusses Micheaux's talkies at length, describes them as depicting 'a fantasy world where blacks were just as affluent, just as educated, just as "cultured," just as well-mannered – in short, just as white – as white America'.

But Micheaux's never-never land is underscored with an almost unbearable bitterness. Despite their fantasy overlay, his films are frought with fury and despair. When the madam of a Chicago brothel in *The Exile* (1931) is reproached by her Abyssinian lover for vamping him away from his studies, she contemptuously replies that 'there are enough Negro doctors and lawyers already' and that he'd only end up as a shyster or abortionist. 'Colored men will sell out anyone for fifty cents' is a typically blunt comment made in the suggestively titled *Lyin' Lips* (1939); and the Harlem chapter of the Communist Party succeeded in temporarily driving *God's Stepchildren* (1937) off the screen, in part because of its hero's contention that 'only one Negro in a thousand tries to think'.

One suspects that Micheaux never reconciled himself to the ugly fact that, in a segregated white society, his options were severely limited. After all, in his cultivation of the West and in his success as a self-made entrepreneur, he was as American as anyone – if not more so. Trapped in a ghetto, but unwilling or unable to directly confront America's racism, Micheaux displaced his rage on his own people. In other words, part of the price that he paid for his American-ness was the internalization of American racial attitudes. Hence his horrified fascination with mis- cegenation and 'passing', his heedless blaming of the victim, his cruel baiting of fellow blacks. *God's Stepchildren*, the imitation *Imitation of Life* which epitomizes Micheaux's complex, contradictory mixture of self-hatred and remorse, forms an essential triptych with *The Birth of a Nation* and *The Searchers*. They are the three richest, most harrowing delineations of American social psychology to be found on celluloid.

Micheaux's films were willed into existence with such strenuous single-mindedness, with so massive a determination to make them tell a story no matter what that, both in form and content, they open up a chasm between intent and actualization almost unprecedented in the history of film. Intricate narratives were based around two or three reshuffled sets (usually the homes of friends), and entire – often violent – scenes were shot in a single take.

Micheaux's films define objective badness. His camera ground relentlessly on while the key light wandered, traffic noise obliterated the dialogue, or a soundman's arm intruded upon the frame. Actors blew their cues, recovered, and continued. Wasting nothing, he re-used footage with impunity, carried the post-dubbing of his soundtracks to the outer limits of possibility, saved up his out-takes and fashioned them into second films. Micheaux films seize every opportunity to announce themselves as constructs. They are embellished with gratuitous cheesecake, tricked out with 'red herring' mystery music, padded with obscurely dangling parallel action, and rife with lengthy cabaret sequences which cut his costs by providing the performers he recruited with 'free advertising' in lieu of pay.

As Micheaux's distanciation evokes Brecht, his continuity surpasses Resnais. Time stops short in an avalanche of unnecessary titles and reaction shots, accelerates suddenly through the elliptical omission of an expected action, doubles back on itself in an unannounced flashback prompted by the use of earlier footage in a new context. Scenes climax in a cubist explosion of herky-jerky jump cuts wherein an actor delivering his lines appears in a succession of slightly askew angles. Micheaux's sense of timing recalls Thelonious Monk or Earl Monroe, and his narrative strategies beggar one's imagination. Actors play multiple roles, some characters seem blessed with precognitive abilities while others get marooned in alternate universes. The extensively post-dubbed *Ten Minutes to Live* (1932) makes elaborate use of telegrams and deaf-mutes to narrate the two separate stories that intermittently supercede the lava flow of entertainment erupting out of the single set called 'Club Libya'. *The Notorious Elinor Lee* (1939) reveals a surprise murder in a courtroom denouement that calls a parrot to testify on the witness stand.

'Every picture he made was mortgaged up to the nose,' a Micheaux associate remembered. It's as though Micheaux directed his films while looking over his shoulder. His actors, their heads precipitously low in the frame, converge breathlessly at the center of the screen as a shot begins. Lines are delivered in unison, there are awkwardly failed attempts at overlapping dialogue, some actors appear to be reciting their parts by rote or reading cue cards. In *The Girl from Chicago* (1932) an off-camera voice prompts an actor to 'give it to her', and his response is to mechanically repeat the phrase.

That Micheaux lacked either the time or the proclivity to invent any but the most obvious bits of business heightens the Kabuki-like quality of the performances. The non-speaking actor in a two-shot is frequently restricted to a single exaggerated tic. Thirty years before Warhol, Micheaux approached *mise en scène* Degree Zero. Left stranded in scenes that are grossly overextended, his performers strike fantastic poses, stare affectingly into space, or gaze casually off-camera.

Edward Wood was a toadstool at the edge of Hollywood, nourished by the movie industry's compost; Micheaux constructed an anti-Hollywood out of rags and bones on some barely imaginable psychic tundra. The spectacles he fashioned of blacks playing whites (which they sometimes did literally, in white-face) constitute a ruthless burlesque of the dominant culture. The collapse of bourgeois 'niceness' that Luis Buñuel's *The Exterminating Angel* or Eugene Ionesco's plays depict, Micheaux's films actually are. Micheaux took the 'institutional mode of representation', up-ended it, and turned it inside out. He demystified movies as no one has ever done and performed this negative magic for an audience that, infinitely more than the Medved boys, was victimized by Hollywood's mechanical dreams. The key to Micheaux's originality is that the social criticism that appears with such painful ambivalence in his scripts was triumphantly sublimated onto the level of form. Regardless of his intentions, Micheaux's films are so devastatingly bad that he can only be considered alongside Georges Méliès, D. W. Griffith, Dziga Vertov, Stan Brakhage, and Jean-Luc Godard as one of the medium's major formal innovators.

Three more things: 1) In *The Exile*, Micheaux uses titan of industry Charles Schwab's Riverside Drive mansion to represent the exterior of a Chicago whore-house; 2) It's been said that Micheaux deliberately left mistakes in his finished films 'to give the audience a laugh'; 3) The longer Micheaux made films, the badder they got. I'm haunted by these facts because they suggest that Micheaux knew what he was doing. And if Oscar Micheaux was a fully conscious artist, he was the greatest genius the cinema ever produced.

'The cinema is not a craft. It is an art. It does not mean teamwork. One is always alone; on the set as before the blank page'

JEAN-LUC GODARD

UMBERTO ECO
How to Play Indians

The Western, it has tirelessly been said, is the quintessential genre of
the American cinema. (Who would ever wish to read a Western novel?
Or see a Western play?) In this essay, 'How to Play Indians', from his
light-fingered collection How to Travel with a Salmon and Other Essays,
Umberto Eco satirizes the genre's most dog-eared clichés and conven-
tions, but unmaliciously, with affection. For he is patently conscious
that, the very finest apart, that was what a Western was: a clan-gathering
of clichés, a convention of conventions. Its action would tend to unfold
in a humble one-street township whose topography was as immutable
as its iconography. There was the sheriff's office (with its easily escapable-
from jailhouse). The telegraph office. The livery stable. The saloon,
naturally. The schoolhouse. The schoolmarm's house (with its white
picket fence). The funeral parlour (from out of which, after a ritual
shoot-out, the local undertaker would scamper with a tape measure).
The plots, too, were more or less immutable, about vengeance, mostly,
and often noirish in tone. It's hardly by chance that, when Howard
Hawks's Rio Bravo, *one of the genre's masterpieces, was remade, it was*
as a thriller, John Carpenter's Assault on Precinct 13.

'Urban' is the word generally used for this type of Western, the type
without Indians and without pretensions. Considering its respect for
the unities of time, place and action, it might equally be thought of as
'Aristotelian'. Considering, finally, the toytown artifice of its décors, the
most accurate word, paradoxically, is 'theatrical'.

Since the future of Native American culture at present seems
dire, the sole possibility for the young brave bent on improving his social
position is to appear in a Western movie. To assist him in this endeavor,
we offer some essential guidelines, tips on correct behavior in both war
and peace situations, to help him qualify as a 'movie Indian', thus
providing as well a solution to the problem of underemployment among
members of this beleaguered minority.

Before Attacking

1. Never attack immediately: make yourself visible at a distance a few days ahead of time, producing easily observed smoke signals, thus giving the stagecoach or the fort ample time to send word to the Seventh Cavalry.

2. If possible, appear prominently in small groups on the surrounding hills. Set up sentinels on totally isolated peaks.

3. Leave clear traces of your progress: hoofprints, smoldering campfires, feathers, and amulets allowing identification of tribe.

Attacking the Stagecoach

4. In any attack on a stagecoach, always follow the vehicle at a short distance or, better still, ride alongside it, to facilitate your being shot.

5. Restrain your mustangs, notoriously faster than coach horses, so you won't outstrip the vehicle.

6. Try to stop the coach single-handed, flinging yourself on the harness, so you can be whipped by the driver and then run over by the vehicle.

7. Never block the coach's advance in a large body. The driver would stop at once.

Attacking an Isolated Farm or a Circle of Covered Wagons

8. Never attack at night when the settlers might not be expecting you. Respect the tradition that Indians attack only in daytime.

9. Insist on making your presence known by giving the coyote cry, thus revealing your position.

10. If a white man gives the coyote cry, raise your head immediately to offer him an easy target.

11. Attack by circling the wagons, but never narrow your circle, so that you and your companions can be picked off one by one.

12. Never employ all your men in a circle, but progressively replace those that fall.

13. As you lack stirrups, manage somehow to entangle your feet in the reins, so that, when you are shot, you are dragged after your mount.

14. Use rifles, bought illegally, whose operation is unfamiliar to you. Take a considerable amount of time loading them.

15. Don't stop circling the wagons when the good guys arrive. Wait for the cavalry without riding out to confront it, then scatter at the first impact in total disorder to allow individual pursuit.

16. In preparing to attack an isolated farm, send only one man to spy on it at night. Approaching a lighted window, he must observe at length a white woman inside, until she has become aware of the Indian face pressed against the pane. Await the woman's cry and the exit of the men before attempting to escape.

Attacking the Fort

17. First of all, turn the horses loose at night. Do not steal them. Encourage them to disperse over the prairie.

18. In using a ladder during the assault, climb up it one man at a time. First allow your weapon to appear, then your head, slowly, and emerge only after the white woman has indicated your presence to a marksman. Never fall forward, inside the fort, but always backward, toward the exterior.

19. In shooting from a distance, assume a clearly visible position on the top of a peak, so that you can fall forward, to be shattered on the rocks below.

20. In the event of a face-to-face confrontation, wait before taking aim.

21. In the same situation, never use a pistol, which would resolve the confrontation at once. Only naked steel.

22. In the case of a sortie on the part of the whites, never steal the weapons of the slain enemy, only his watch. Wait in wonderment, listening to its tick, until another enemy arrives.

23. On capturing an enemy, do not kill him immediately. Tie him to a stake or confine him to a tent, awaiting the new moon, by which time others will come to free him.

24. In any event, you can be certain that the enemy bugler will be killed the moment the signal of the Seventh Cavalry is heard from afar. At this point the bugler inside the fort always stands up and returns the signal from the highest turret of the fort.

Further Instructions

25. In the event that the Indian village is attacked, rush from the tents in total confusion. Run around every which way, trying to collect weapons previously left in places of difficult access.

26. Check the quality of the firewater being sold by the peddlers: the sulfuric acid-to-whisky ratio must be three to one.

27. In the event of a train's passing, make sure there is an Indian

hunter on board and ride alongside the train brandishing rifles and emitting cries of greeting.

28. In leaping from a roof to seize a white man from behind, always hold your knife in such a way that he is not immediately wounded but is allowed to engage in hand-to-hand struggle. Wait until the white man turns around.

UMBERTO ECO
How to Recognize a Porn Movie

This essay is also from How to Travel with a Salmon. *Its title is self-explanatory.*

I don't know if you've ever happened to see a pornographic movie. I don't mean movies with some erotic content, a movie like *Last Tango in Paris*, for example, though even that, I realize, for many people might be offensive. No, what I mean is genuine pornoflicks, whose true and sole aim is to stimulate the spectator's desire, from beginning to end, and in such a way that, while this desire is stimulated by scenes of various and varied copulations, the rest of the story counts for less than nothing.

Magistrates are often required to decide whether a film is purely pornographic or whether it has artistic value. I am not one of those who insist that artistic value excuses everything; sometimes true works of art have been more dangerous, to faith, to behavior, to current opinion, than works of lesser value. But I believe that consenting adults have the right to consume pornographic material, at least for want of anything better. I recognize, however, that on occasion a court must decide whether a film has been produced for the purpose of expressing certain concepts or aesthetic ideals (even through scenes that offend the accepted moral view), or whether it was made for the sole purpose of arousing the spectator's instincts.

Well, there is a criterion for deciding whether a film is pornographic or not, and it is based on the calculation of wasted time. A great, universal film masterpiece, *Stagecoach*, takes place solely and entirely (except for the beginning, a few brief intervals, and the finale) on a stagecoach. But without this journey the film would have no meaning. Antonioni's *L'avventura* is made up solely of wasted time: people come and go, talk, get lost and are found, without anything happening. This wasted time may or may not be enjoyable, but it is exactly what the film is about.

A pornographic movie, in contrast, to justify the price of the ticket or the purchase of the cassette, tells us that certain people couple sexually, men with women, men with men, women with women, women with dogs or stallions (I might point out that there are no pornographic films in which men couple with mares and bitches: why not?). And this would still be all right: but it is full of wasted time.

If Gilbert, in order to rape Gilbertina, has to go from Lincoln Center to Sheridan Square, the film shows you Gilbert, in his car, throughout the whole journey, stoplight by stoplight.

Pornographic movies are full of people who climb into cars and drive for miles and miles, couples who waste incredible amounts of time signing in at hotel desks, gentlemen who spend many minutes in elevators before reaching their rooms, girls who sip various drinks and who fiddle interminably with laces and blouses before confessing to each other that they prefer Sappho to Don Juan. To put it simply, crudely, in porn movies, before you can see a healthy screw you have to put up with a documentary that could be sponsored by the Traffic Bureau.

There are obvious reasons. A movie in which Gilbert did nothing but rape Gilbertina, front, back, and sideways, would be intolerable. Physically, for the actors, and economically, for the producer. And it would also be, psychologically, intolerable for the spectator: for the transgression to work, it must be played out against a background of normality. To depict normality is one of the most difficult things for any artist – whereas portraying deviation, crime, rape, torture, is very easy.

Therefore the pornographic movie must present normality – essential if the transgression is to have interest – in the way that every spectator conceives it. Therefore, if Gilbert has to take the bus and go from A to B, we will see Gilbert taking the bus and then the bus proceeding from A to B.

This often irritates the spectators, because they think they would like the unspeakable scenes to be continuous. But this is an illusion on their part. They couldn't bear a full hour and a half of unspeakable scenes. So the passages of wasted time are essential.

I repeat. Go into a movie theater. If, to go from A to B, the characters take longer than you would like, then the film you are seeing is pornographic.

WIM WENDERS
Re: *Bad Day at Black Rock*

In this essay, from the beautifully titled collection Emotion Pictures, *on
a good if far from great movie of the 1950s, John Sturges's* Bad Day at
Black Rock, *Wim Wenders infallibly hones in on the essential – the
essential not merely of the movie itself but of the (often unwittingly)
surreal charm of the postwar American cinema. 'Unwittingly', because
it was a charm which was cast irrespective of a filmmaker's thematic
preoccupations or stylistic trademarks, if any, and irrespective of
whether he was a true* auteur *or just a good studio man (as we refer to
'a good company man') filming as competently as he knew how a
screenplay to which he had been assigned, even if the success or failure
of the finished movie had already been determined (by the intelligence
of the script, for example, or the quality of the cast) before he turned
up on the set. Film critics are loath to admit it but, as Wenders understood, the charm of the classic American cinema was essentially that of
America itself, its energy, its vulgarity, its generosity, all its sometimes
shiny, sometimes grungy materiality. In other words, you didn't have
to be a good director to make a good American film. All you had to do
was stride on to the set and let the genius of America itself flow through
you.*

A dusty American colour film by John Sturges where everything's so right and correct that it is almost unbearable.

You could say of a James Hadley Chase novel that it reads more like
the description of a film than like a story.

It began on a summer afternoon in July, a month of intense heat, rainless
skies and scorching, dust-laden winds.

At the junction of the Fort Scott and Nevada roads that cuts Highway
54, the trunk road from Pittsburgh to Kansas City, there stands a gas
station and lunchroom bar; a shabby wooden structure with one gas
pump, run by an elderly widower and his fat blonde daughter.

> A dusty Packard pulled up by the lunchroom a few minutes after one
> o'clock. There were two men in the car: one of them was asleep.
>
> The driver, Bailey, a short thickset man with a fleshy brutal face,
> restless, uneasy black eyes and a thin white scar along the side of his jaw,
> got out of the car. His dusty, shabby suit was threadbare. His dirty shirt
> was frayed at the cuffs.
>
> (The beginning of No Orchids for Miss Blandish)

You could say of this John Sturges film that it doesn't show a succession
of images, but of sentences. A whole dozen of these sentences are
written up in the display cases of the theatres showing *Bad Day at Black
Rock*.

Stills of old colour films have a peculiar charm, because they seem
completely detached from the film and tend to look more like old
hand-coloured postcards than the actual scenes in the film. You can
recognize, though, with surprise, the stills from *Bad Day at Black Rock*
when you're watching the actual film; you can even spot the precise
moment they captured. The film retains the impression that the coloured
photographs have left behind. All the way through it looks *hand-painted*.

The backdrops of the landscape that constantly show through windows
or doors have more in common with paintings by Magritte than with
the real landscape shown in the outdoor scenes. But even these look
much more like a mile-wide, sky-high stage-set built in a gigantic studio.

This endless artificiality confused me a lot at the beginning of the
film, because I could only trace it back to the colours. It was only after
a while that I suddenly discovered what was really happening in this
film, when I saw the worn-out seats in the foyer of the hotel in Black
Rock: these seats didn't simply stand around there, they stood around
as precisely the chairs that had to be there, the ashtray beside them was
the only possible ashtray for these seats, the one-armed bandit was the
only conceivable slot-machine for a hotel like that in a town in the
Mid-West. Every thing in this film, by itself, was the most exact and
the most right and the most suitable that could be. Every object was so
right that it could form a completely self-contained sentence, it could
be distinguished from all the others around it, but for precisely this
reason it suited everything else perfectly. In this film all details were
really details!

The ventilator! The broken-down car!
The gas pump! The ketchup bottle!
Every image was full to bursting-point with details and harmony.
The sheriff's office! It's overflowing!
Sam's grill! It's bursting at the seams!
The faces! Lee Marvin is going up the stairs!
Walter Brennan is cursing!
Spencer Tracy is getting more and more frightened!
Ernest Borgnine is getting furious!
Robert Ryan is grinning arrogantly!
Spencer Tracy has only one arm!
Anne Francis is getting cheeky! It's already dark!
The doctor's surgery!
Robert Ryan's on fire. The Southern Pacific is 'radio-equipped'.

ARCH OBOLER
Three-Dementia

The gimmicky output of the producer, director and screenwriter Arch Oboler belongs to a period, the mid-1950s, when the American cinema, in thrall to a manly, not to say macho, obsession with sheer size, deluded itself that its most effective weapons against television were enormous, often outlandishly named, screen formats. The most enduring of these (so much so that its name has become a generic term for all widescreen processes) was CinemaScope, but there was also MetroScope (specific to MGM), WarnerScope (specific, naturally, to Warner Bros.), Super-Scope, VistaVision (with its two mammoth Churchillian Vs), Panavision, Technirama, Cinerama, Todd-AO and, of course, Oboler's own baby, 3-D.

The fad for these formats eventually waned when it became clear that they offered no lasting threat to television. Ruthlessly squeezed on to the smaller screen as into a bulging suitcase, there is not one of the so-called blockbusters, from South Pacific *to* 2001, *which has not regularly turned up in the TV schedules.*

Prophecy is an easy art, since generally the prophet, at the date of accounting, is much too dead to be called to task.

However, since the prophecies of which I speak are going to happen in a very near tomorrow, I don't particularly expect to be supporting a tombstone, hence, gentlemen call me to account!

First, I foresee that the first 3-D motion picture to follow *Bwana Devil* into the theaters, will be jumping with what I call 'three-dementia'. Everything will be leaping madly off the screen. This is a great temptation in making a three-dimensional picture, having objects, from bosoms to zombies, sticking out of the screen into space.

But, gentlemen of production, this is a false path. False because if audiences begin to look upon three-dimensional pictures simply as a circus, the law of diminishing returns can quickly catch up with the entire advance. For circuses are not a weekly habit; the trick once seen suffices for a year!

I do not mean to say that these excitement devices of bringing action off the screen should be completely deleted from forthcoming three-dimensional motion pictures; I simply mean that there is a great danger in overdoing the spectacular. For the spectacular becomes the ordinary very quickly once it has become familiar.

I am reminded of horror plays on radio; we quickly found that the law of diminishing returns caught up with us when we tried to compound horror on horror. The audiences simply began to turn the dials. Not that they were frightened. Simply bored.

All of you are familiar with similar experiences in the horror motion pictures; at first it was Frankenstein alone, then Dracula, then Frankenstein and Dracula, then Frankenstein, Dracula and the Wolfman. And soon there wasn't room enough on the screen for all the horror men, but there was plenty of room in the empty theater seats.

Three dimension, as ideally used, then, is a frame through which the audience looks into reality. Hyperstereo, that is stereo photography, carried to an extreme, with objects poking through the frame of the screen in a distorted manner, is a special effects touch to be used with discretion.

I underline this because I believe that three dimensions in motion pictures can be more than today's bonanza at the box office; it can be a bright financial stabilizer tomorrow and tomorrow to the business.

But there must be self-policing in the industry re. 3-D; above all a sense of personal responsibility.

For example, I do not believe that it helps the industry or the future of three dimension at the box office to lead an audience to believe that it is seeing a full feature 3-D picture when actually all that is screening are bits and pieces of three-dimension experiments. I do not believe it helps the industry to take amateur type 3-D movies and show them in the professional theater at regular prices. This sort of quick dollar not only harms the particular exhibitor, but it ruins the taste of the ticket buyer for future three-dimensional pictures.

I am told that at a recent showing, for full admission prices, of a collected group of three-dimensional shorts, an irate ticket buyer, after seeing that he had been shortchanged by less than a full feature picture, walked up and down in front of the theater shouting to the passersby to stay out of this gyp theater.

Let not the motion picture industry gyp itself out of a three-dimensional financial future.

SUSAN SONTAG
The Imagination of Disaster

Like that cute mascot of quantum physics, Schrödinger's cat, both alive and dead inside its sealed box, supernatural phenomena inhabit a limbo of unknowingness, of agnosticism, their enduring power over us residing in the fact that the material evidence in their favour never becomes sufficiently 'definitive' to confound the doubters and lay speculation to rest once and for all. Even something that ought to be as demonstrably real or not as a robot (of the humanoid type) continues to lurk on the edge of the supernatural, since most of us are incapable to this day of making up our minds with complete confidence whether it's a product of science-fiction or scientific fact.

Science-fiction, precisely. A point made in virtually every review of the recent Independence Day *was that, considering its reputation as one of the most expensive films ever made, its ubiquitous special effects, supposedly the secret of its success, were in fact unexpectedly scrappy. The 'joins' were occasionally perceptible, the hardware appreciably less than state-of-the-art: the 'biggest-budget B-movie in the world', one critic called it. It's possible, though, notably where cinematic science-fiction is concerned, to regard such carping as a compliment (like a blessing) in disguise. I myself once wrote of having been disappointed by the special effects of Steven Spielberg's* Jurassic Park *because they were 'so extraordinarily seamless that they quite fail to register as effects', because they rendered the film's dinosaurs 'so real it's exactly like watching marauding elephants in a dreary Tarzan movie'.* Independence Day *is a truly terrible film, but its effects struck me as subtly superior to those of Spielberg's for the simple reason that they, too, like the phenomena they portray, respect that crucial interstice between expectation and realization, between wishfulness and reality, through which the imagination is able to squeeze. The imagination of disaster, as the critic, novelist and filmmaker Susan Sontag defines it in this essay.*

The typical science fiction film has a form as predictable as a Western, and is made up of elements which, to a practiced eye, are as classic as the saloon brawl, the blonde schoolteacher from the East, and the gun duel on the deserted main street.

One model scenario proceeds through five phases.

(1) The arrival of the thing. (Emergence of the monsters, landing of the alien spaceship, etc.) This is usually witnessed or suspected by just one person, a young scientist on a field trip. Nobody, neither his neighbors nor his colleagues, will believe him for some time. The hero is not married, but has a sympathetic though also incredulous girl friend.

(2) Confirmation of the hero's report by a host of witnesses to a great act of destruction. (If the invaders are beings from another planet, a fruitless attempt to parley with them and get them to leave peacefully.) The local police are summoned to deal with the situation and massacred.

(3) In the capital of the country, conferences between scientists and the military take place, with the hero lecturing before a chart, map, or blackboard. A national emergency is declared. Reports of further destruction. Authorities from other countries arrive in black limousines. All international tensions are suspended in view of the planetary emergency. This stage often includes a rapid montage of news broadcasts in various languages, a meeting at the U N, and more conferences between the military and the scientists. Plans are made for destroying the enemy.

(4) Further atrocities. At some point the hero's girl friend is in grave danger. Massive counter-attacks by international forces, with brilliant displays of rocketry, rays, and other advanced weapons, are all unsuccessful. Enormous military casualties, usually by incineration. Cities are destroyed and/or evacuated. There is an obligatory scene here of panicked crowds stampeding along a highway or a big bridge, being waved on by numerous policemen who, if the film is Japanese, are immaculately white-gloved, preternaturally calm, and call out in dubbed English, 'Keep moving. There is no need to be alarmed.'

(5) More conferences, whose motif is: 'They must be vulnerable to something'. Throughout the hero has been working in his lab to this end. The final strategy, upon which all hopes depend, is drawn up; the ultimate weapon – often a super-powerful, as yet untested, nuclear device – is mounted. Countdown. Final repulse of the monster or invaders. Mutual congratulations, while the hero and girl friend embrace

cheek to cheek and scan the skies sturdily. 'But have we seen the last of them?'

The film I have just described should be in color and on a wide screen. Another typical scenario, which follows, is simpler and suited to black-and-white films with a lower budget. It has four phases.

(1) The hero (usually, but not always, a scientist) and his girl friend, or his wife and two children, are disporting themselves in some innocent ultra-normal middle-class surroundings – their house in a small town, or on vacation (camping, boating). Suddenly, someone starts behaving strangely; or some innocent form of vegetation becomes monstrously enlarged and ambulatory. If a character is pictured driving an auto-mobile, something gruesome looms up in the middle of the road. If it is night, strange lights hurtle across the sky.

(2) After following the thing's tracks, or determining that It is radio-active, or poking around a huge crater – in short, conducting some sort of crude investigation – the hero tries to warn the local authorities, without effect; nobody believes anything is amiss. The hero knows better. If the thing is tangible, the house is elaborately barricaded. If the invading alien is an invisible parasite, a doctor or friend is called in, who is himself rather quickly killed or 'taken possession of' by the thing.

(3) The advice of whoever further is consulted proves useless. Meanwhile, It continues to claim other victims in the town, which remains implausibly isolated from the rest of the world. General help-lessness.

(4) One of two possibilities. Either the hero prepares to do battle alone, accidentally discovers the thing's one vulnerable point, and destroys it. Or, he somehow manages to get out of town and succeeds in laying his case before competent authorities. They, along the lines of the first script but abridged, deploy a complex technology which (after initial setbacks) finally prevails against the invaders.

Another version of the second script opens with the scientist-hero in his laboratory, which is located in the basement or on the grounds of his tasteful, prosperous house. Through his experiments, he unwittingly causes a frightful metamorphosis in some class of plants or animals which turn carnivorous and go on a rampage. Or else, his experiments have caused him to be injured (sometimes irrevocably) or 'invaded' himself. Perhaps he has been experimenting with radiation, or has built a machine to communicate with beings from other planets or transport him to other places or times.

Another version of the first script involves the discovery of some fundamental alteration in the conditions of existence of our planet, brought about by nuclear testing, which will lead to the extinction in a few months of all human life. For example: the temperature of the earth is becoming too high or too low to support life, or the earth is cracking in two, or it is gradually being blanketed by lethal fallout.

A third script, somewhat but not altogether different from the first two, continues a journey through space – to the moon, or some other planet. What the young voyagers discover commonly is that the alien terrain is in a state of dire urgency, itself threatened by extra-planetary invaders or nearing extinction through the practice of nuclear warfare. The terminal dramas of the first and second scripts are played out there, to which is added the problem of getting away from the doomed and/ or hostile planet and back to Earth.

I am aware, of course, that there are thousands of science fiction novels (their heyday was the late 1940s), not to mention the transcriptions of science fiction themes which, more and more, provide the principal subject-matter of comic books. But I propose to discuss science fiction films (the present period began in 1950 and continues, considerably abated, to this day) as an independent subject, without reference to other media – and, most particularly, without reference to the novels from which, in many cases, they were adapted. For, while a novel and film may share the same plot, the fundamental difference between the sources of the novel and the film makes them quite dissimilar.

Certainly, compared with the science fiction novels, their film counterparts have unique strengths, one of which is the immediate representation of the extraordinary: physical deformity and mutation, missile and rocket combat, toppling skyscrapers. The movies are, naturally, weak just where the science fiction novels (some of them) are strong – on science. But in place of an intellectual workout, they can supply something the novels can never provide – sensuous elaboration. In the films it is by means of images and sounds, not words that have to be translated by the imagination, that one can participate in the fantasy of living through one's own death and more, the death of cities, the destruction of humanity itself.

Science fiction films are not about science. They are about disaster, which is one of the oldest subjects of art. In science fiction films disaster is rarely viewed intensively; it is always extensive. It is a matter of quantity and ingenuity. If you will, it is a question of scale. But the scale, particularly in the wide-screen color films (of which the ones by the Japanese director Inoshiro Honda and the American director George Pal are technically the most convincing and visually the most exciting), does raise the matter to another level.

Thus, the science fiction film (like that of a very different contemporary genre, the Happening) is concerned with the aesthetics of destruction, with the peculiar beauties to be found in wreaking havoc, making a mess. And it is in the imagery of destruction that the core of a good science fiction film lies. Hence, the disadvantage of the cheap film – in which the monster appears or the rocket lands in a small dull-looking town. (Hollywood budget needs usually dictate that the town be in the Arizona or California desert. In *The Thing from Another World* (1951) the rather sleazy and confined set is supposed to be an encampment near the North Pole.) Still, good black-and-white science fiction films have been made. But a bigger budget, which usually means color, allows a much greater play back and forth among several model environments. There is the populous city. There is the lavish but ascetic interior of the spaceship – either the invaders' or ours – replete with streamlined chromium fixtures and dials and machines whose complexity is indicated by the number of colored lights they flash and strange noises they emit. There is the laboratory crowded with formidable boxes and scientific apparatus. There is a comparatively old-fashioned-looking conference room, where the scientists unfurl charts to explain the desperate state of things to the military. And each of these standard locales or backgrounds is subject to two modalities – intact and destroyed. We may, if we are lucky, be treated to a panorama of melting tanks, flying bodies, crashing walls, awesome craters and fissures in the earth, plummeting spacecraft, colorful deadly rays; and to a symphony of screams, weird electronic signals, the noisiest military hardware going, and the leaden tones of the laconic denizens of alien planets and their subjugated earthlings.

Certain of the primitive gratifications of science fiction films – for instance, the depiction of urban disaster on a colossally magnified scale – are shared with other types of films. Visually there is little difference between mass havoc as represented in the old horror and monster films and what we find in science fiction films, except (again) scale. In the old monster films, the monster always headed for the great city, where he had to do a fair bit of rampaging, hurling busses off bridges, crumpling trains in his bare hands, toppling buildings, and so forth. The archetype is King Kong, in Schoedsack and Cooper's great film of 1933, running amok, first in the native village (trampling babies, a bit of footage excised from most prints), then in New York. This is really no different in spirit from the scene in Inoshiro Honda's *Rodan* (1957) in which two giant reptiles – with a wingspan of 500 feet and supersonic speeds – by flapping their wings whip up a cyclone that blows most of Tokyo to smithereens. Or the destruction of half of Japan by the gigantic robot with the great incinerating ray that shoots forth from his eyes, at the beginning of Honda's *The Mysterians* (1959). Or, the devastation by the rays from a fleet of flying saucers of New York, Paris, and Tokyo, in *Battle in Outer Space* (1960). Or, the inundation of New York in *When Worlds Collide* (1951). Or, the end of London in 1966 depicted in George Pal's *The Time Machine* (1960). Neither do these sequences differ in aesthetic intention from the destruction scenes in the big sword, sandal, and orgy color spectaculars set in Biblical and Roman times – the end of Sodom in Aldrich's *Sodom and Gomorrah*, of Gaza in De Mille's *Samson and Delilah*, of Rhodes in *The Colossus of Rhodes*, and of Rome in a dozen Nero movies. Griffith began it with the Babylon sequence in *Intolerance*, and to this day there is nothing like the thrill of watching all those expensive sets come tumbling down.

In other respects as well, the science fiction films of the 1950s take up familiar themes. The famous 1930s movie serials and comics of the adventures of Flash Gordon and Buck Rogers, as well as the more recent spate of comic book super-heroes with extraterrestrial origins (the most famous is Superman, a foundling from the planet Krypton, currently described as having been exploded by a nuclear blast), share motifs with more recent science fiction movies. But there is an important difference. The old science fiction films, and most of the comics, still have an essentially innocent relation to disaster. Mainly they offer new versions of the oldest romance of all – of the strong invulnerable hero with a mysterious lineage come to do battle on behalf of good and against evil. Recent science fiction films have a decided grimness, bolstered by their much greater degree of visual credibility, which contrasts strongly with the older films. Modern historical reality has greatly enlarged the imagination of disaster, and the protagonists –

perhaps by the very nature of what is visited upon them – no longer seem wholly innocent.

The lure of such generalized disaster as a fantasy is that it releases one from normal obligations. The trump card of the end-of-the-world movies – like *The Day the Earth Caught Fire* (1962) – is that great scene with New York or London or Tokyo discovered empty, its entire population annihilated. Or, as in *The World, the Flesh, and the Devil* (1957), the whole movie can be devoted to the fantasy of occupying the deserted metropolis and starting all over again, a world Robinson Crusoe.

Another kind of satisfaction these films supply is extreme moral simplification – that is to say, a morally acceptable fantasy where one can give outlet to cruel or at least amoral feelings. In this respect, science fiction films partly overlap with horror films. This is the undeniable pleasure we derive from looking at freaks, being excluded from the category of the human. The sense of superiority over the freak conjoined in varying proportions with the titillation of fear and aversion makes it possible for moral scruples to be lifted, for cruelty to be enjoyed. The same thing happens in science fiction films. In the figure of the monster from outer space, the freakish, the ugly, and the predatory all converge – and provide a fantasy target for righteous bellicosity to discharge itself, and for the aesthetic enjoyment of suffering and disaster. Science fiction films are one of the purest forms of spectacle; that is, we are rarely inside anyone's feelings. (An exception is Jack Arnold's *The Incredible Shrinking Man* (1957).) We are merely spectators; we watch.

But in science fiction films, unlike horror films, there is not much horror. Suspense, shocks, surprises are mostly abjured in favor of a steady, inexorable plot. Science fiction films invite a dispassionate, aesthetic view of destruction and violence – a *technological* view. Things, objects, machinery play a major role in these films. A greater range of ethical values is embodied in the décor of these films than in the people. Things, rather than the helpless humans, are the locus of values because we experience them, rather than people, as the sources of power. According to science fiction films, man is naked without his artifacts. *They* stand for different values, they are potent, they are what get destroyed, and they are the indispensable tools for the repulse of the alien invaders or the repair of the damaged environment.

The science fiction films are strongly moralistic. The standard message is the one about the proper, or humane, use of science, versus the mad, obsessional use of science. This message the science fiction films share in common with the classic horror films of the 1930s, like *Frankenstein, The Mummy, Island of Lost Souls, Dr Jekyll and Mr Hyde.* (George Franju's brilliant *Les Yeux sans Visage* (1959), called here *The Horror Chamber of Doctor Faustus,* is a more recent example.) In the horror films, we have the mad or obsessed or misguided scientist who pursues his experiments against good advice to the contrary, creates a monster or monsters, and is himself destroyed – often recognizing his folly himself, and dying in the successful effort to destroy his own creation. One science fiction equivalent of this is the scientist, usually a member of a team, who defects to the planetary invaders because 'their' science is more advanced than 'ours'.

This is the case in *The Mysterians*, and, true to form, the renegade sees his error in the end, and from within the Mysterian space ship destroys it and himself. In *This Island Earth* (1955), the inhabitants of the beleaguered planet Metaluna propose to conquer earth, but their project is foiled by a Metalunan scientist named Exeter who, having lived on earth a while and learned to love Mozart, cannot abide such viciousness. Exeter plunges his spaceship into the ocean after returning a glamorous pair (male and female) of American physicists to earth. Metaluna dies. In *The Fly* (1958), the hero, engrossed in his basement-laboratory experiments on a matter-transmitting machine, uses himself as a subject, exchanges head and one arm with a housefly which had accidentally gotten into the machine, becomes a monster, and with his last shred of human will destroys his laboratory and orders his wife to kill him. His discovery, for the good of mankind, is lost.

Being a clearly labeled species of intellectual, scientists in science fiction films are always liable to crack up or go off the deep end. In *Conquest of Space* (1955), the scientist-commander of an international expedition to Mars suddenly acquires scruples about the blasphemy involved in the undertaking, and begins reading the Bible mid-journey instead of attending to his duties. The commander's son, who is his junior officer and always addresses his father as 'General', is forced to kill the old man when he tries to prevent the ship from landing on Mars. In this film, both sides of the ambivalence toward scientists are given voice. Generally, for a scientific enterprise to be treated entirely sympathetically in these films, it needs the certificate of utility. Science, viewed without ambivalence, means an efficacious response to danger. Disinterested intellectual curiosity rarely appears in any form other than caricature, as a maniacal dementia that cuts one off from normal human relations. But this suspicion is usually directed at the scientist rather than his work. The creative scientist may become a martyr to his own discovery, through an accident or by pushing things too far. But the implication remains that other men, less imaginative – in short, technicians – could have administered the same discovery better and more safely. The most ingrained contemporary mistrust of the intellect is visited, in these movies, upon the scientist-as-intellectual.

The message that the scientist is one who releases forces which, if not controlled for good, could destroy man himself seems innocuous enough. One of the oldest images of the scientist is Shakespeare's Prospero, the overdetached scholar forcibly retired from society to a desert island, only partly in control of the magic forces in which he dabbles. Equally classic is the figure of the scientist as satanist (*Doctor Faustus*, and stories of Poe and Hawthorne). Science is magic, and man has always known that there is black magic as well as white. But it is not enough to remark that contemporary attitudes – as reflected in science fiction films – remain ambivalent, that the scientist is treated as both satanist and savior. The proportions have changed, because of the new context in which the old admiration and fear of the scientist are located. For his sphere of influence is no longer local, himself or his immediate community. It is planetary, cosmic.

One gets the feeling, particularly in the Japanese films but not only there, that a mass trauma exists over the use of nuclear weapons and the possibility of future nuclear wars. Most of the science fiction films bear witness to this trauma, and, in a way, attempt to exorcise it.

The accidental awakening of the super-destructive monster who has slept in the earth since prehistory is, often, an obvious metaphor for the Bomb. But there are many explicit references as well. In *The Mysterians*, a probe ship from the planet Mysteroid has landed on earth, near Tokyo. Nuclear warfare having been practiced on Mysteroid for centuries (their civilization is 'more advanced than ours'), ninety percent of those now born on the planet have to be destroyed at birth, because of defects caused by the huge amounts of Strontium 90 in their diet. The Mysterians have come to earth to marry earth women, and possibly to take over our relatively uncontaminated planet . . . In *The Incredible Shrinking Man*, the John Doe hero is the victim of a gust of radiation which blows over the water, while he is out boating with his wife; the radiation causes him to grow smaller and smaller, until at the end of the movie he steps through the fine mesh of a window screen to become 'the infinitely small.' . . . In *Rodan*, a horde of monstrous carnivorous prehistoric insects, and finally a pair of giant flying reptiles (the prehistoric Archeopteryx), are hatched from dormant eggs in the depths of a mine shaft by the impact of nuclear test explosions, and go on to destroy a good part of the world before they are felled by the molten lava of a volcanic eruption . . . In the English film, *The Day the Earth Caught Fire*, two simultaneous hydrogen bomb tests by the United States and Russia change by 11 degrees the tilt of the earth on its axis and alter the earth's orbit so that it begins to approach the sun.

Radiation casualties – ultimately, the conception of the whole world as a casualty of nuclear testing and nuclear warfare – is the most ominous of all the notions with which science fiction films deal. Universes become expendable. Worlds become contaminated, burnt out, exhausted, obsolete. In *Rocketship X-M* (1950) explorers from the earth land on Mars, where they learn that atomic warfare has destroyed Martian civilization. In George Pal's *The War of the Worlds* (1953), reddish spindly alligator-skinned creatures from Mars invade the earth because their planet is becoming too cold to be inhabitable. In *This Island Earth*, also American, the planet Metaluna, whose population has long ago been driven underground by warfare, is dying under the missile attacks of an enemy planet. Stocks of uranium, which power the force field shielding Metaluna, have been used up; and an unsuccessful expedition is sent to earth to enlist earth scientists to devise new sources for nuclear power. In Joseph Losey's *The Damned* (1961), nine icy-cold radioactive children are being reared by a fanatical scientist in a dark cave on the English coast to be the only survivors of the inevitable nuclear Armageddon.

There is a vast amount of wishful thinking in science fiction films, some of it touching, some of it depressing. Again and again, one detects the hunger for a 'good war', which poses no moral problems, admits of no moral qualifications. The imagery of science fiction films will satisfy the most bellicose addict of war films, for a lot of the satisfaction of war films pass, untransformed, into science fiction films. Examples: the dogfights between earth 'fighter rockets' and alien spacecraft in the *Battle in Outer Space* (1960); the escalating firepower in the successive assaults upon the invaders in *The Mysterians*, which Dan Talbot correctly described as a non-stop holocaust; the spectacular bombardment of the underground fortress of Metaluna in *This Island Earth*.

Yet at the same time the bellicosity of science fiction films is neatly channeled into the yearning for peace, or for at least peaceful coexistence. Some scientist generally takes sententious note of the fact that it took the planetary invasion to make the warring nations of the earth come to their senses and suspend their own conflicts. One of the main themes of many science fiction films – the color ones usually, because they have the budget and resources to develop the military spectacle – is this UN fantasy, a fantasy of united warfare. (The same wishful UN theme cropped up in a recent spectacular which is not science fiction, *Fifty-Five Days in Peking* (1963). There, topically enough, the Chinese, the Boxers, play the role of Martian invaders who unite the earthmen, in this case the United States, England, Russia, France, Germany, Italy, and Japan.) A great enough disaster cancels all enmities and calls upon the utmost concentration of earth resources.

Science – technology – is conceived of as the great unifier. Thus the science fiction films also project a Utopian fantasy. In the classic models of Utopian thinking – Plato's Republic, Campanella's City of the Sun, More's Utopia, Swift's land of the Houyhnhnms, Voltaire's Eldorado – society had worked out a perfect consensus. In these societies reasonableness had achieved an unbreakable supremacy over the emotions. Since no disagreement or social conflict was intellectually plausible, none was possible. As in Melville's *Typee*, 'they all think the same'. The universal rule of reason meant universal agreement. It is interesting, too, that societies in which reason was pictured as totally ascendant were also traditionally pictured as having an ascetic or materially frugal and economically simple mode of life. But in the Utopian world community projected by science fiction films, totally pacified and ruled by scientific consensus, the demand for simplicity of material existence would be absurd.

Yet alongside the hopeful fantasy of moral simplification and international unity embodied in the science fiction films lurk the deepest anxieties about contemporary existence. I don't mean only the very real trauma of the Bomb – that it has been used, that there are enough now to kill everyone on earth many times over, that those new bombs may very well be used. Besides these new anxieties about physical disaster, the prospect of universal mutilation and even annihilation, the science fiction films reflect powerful anxieties about the condition of the individual psyche.

For science fiction films may also be described as a popular mythology for the contemporary *negative* imagination about the impersonal. The other-world creatures that seek to take 'us' over are an 'it', not a 'they'. The planetary invaders are usually zombielike. Their movements are either cool, mechanical, or lumbering, blobby. But it amounts to the same thing. If they are non-human in form, they proceed with an absolutely regular, unalterable movement (unalterable save by destruction). If they are human in form – dressed in space suits, etc. – then they obey the most rigid military discipline, and display no personal characteristics whatsoever. And it is this regime of emotionlessness, of impersonality, of regimentation, which they will impose on the earth if they are successful. 'No more love, no more beauty, no more pain,' boasts a converted earthling in *The Invasion of the Body Snatchers* (1956). The half-earthling, half-alien children in *The Children of the Damned* (1960) are absolutely emotionless, move as a group and understand each others' thoughts, and are all prodigious intellects. They are the wave of the future, man in his next stage of development.

These alien invaders practice a crime which is worse than murder. They do not simply kill the person. They obliterate him. In *The War of the Worlds*, the ray which issues from the rocket ship disintegrates all persons and objects in its path, leaving no trace of them but a light ash. In Honda's *The H-Man* (1959), the creeping blob melts all flesh with which it comes in contact. If the blob, which looks like a huge hunk of red Jello and can crawl across floors and up and down walls, so much as touches your bare foot, all that is left of you is a heap of clothes on the floor. (A more articulated, size-multiplying blob is the villain in the English film *The Creeping Unknown* (1956).) In another version of this fantasy, the body is preserved but the person is entirely reconstituted as the automatized servant or agent of the alien powers. This is, of course, the vampire fantasy in new dress. The person is really dead, but he doesn't know it. He is 'undead', he has become an 'unperson'. It happens to a whole California town in *The Invasion of the Body Snatchers*, to several earth scientists in *This Island Earth*, and to assorted innocents in *It Came from Outer Space*, *Attack of the Puppet People* (1958), and *The Brain Eaters* (1958). As the victim always backs away from the vampire's horrifying embrace, so in science fiction films the person always fights being 'taken over'; he wants to retain his humanity.

But once the deed has been done, the victim is eminently satisfied with his condition. He has not been converted from human amiability to monstrous 'animal' bloodlust (a metaphoric exaggeration of sexual desire), as in the old vampire fantasy. No, he has simply become far more efficient – the very model of technocratic man, purged of emotions, volitionless, tranquil, obedient to all orders. (The dark secret behind human nature used to be the upsurge of the animal – as in *King Kong*. The threat to man, his availability to dehumanization, lay in his own animality. Now the danger is understood as residing in man's ability to be turned into a machine.)

The rule, of course, is that this horrible and irremediable form of murder can strike anyone in the film except the hero. The hero and his family, while greatly threatened, always escape this fate and by the end of the film the invaders have been repulsed or destroyed. I know of only one exception, *The Day That Mars Invaded Earth* (1963), in which after all the standard struggles the scientist-hero, his wife, and their two children are 'taken over' by the alien invaders – and that's that. (The last minutes of the film show them being incinerated by the Martians' rays and their ash silhouettes flushed down their empty swimming pool, while their simulacra drive off in the family car.) Another variant but upbeat switch on the rule occurs in *The Creation of the Humanoids* (1964), where the hero discovers at the end of the film that he, too, has been turned into a metal robot, complete with highly efficient and virtually indestructible mechanical insides, although he didn't know it and detected no difference in himself. He learns, however, that he will shortly be upgraded into a 'humanoid' having all the properties of a real man.

Of all the standard motifs of science fiction films, this theme of dehumanization is perhaps the most fascinating. For, as I have indicated, it is scarcely a black-and-white situation, as in the old vampire films. The attitude of the science fiction films toward depersonalization is mixed. On the one hand, they deplore it as the ultimate horror. On the other hand, certain characteristics of the dehumanized invaders, modulated and disguised – such as the ascendancy of reason over feelings, the idealization of teamwork and the consensus-creating activities of science, a marked degree of moral simplification – are precisely traits of the savior-scientist. It is interesting that when the scientist in these films is treated negatively, it is usually done through the portrayal of an individual scientist who holes up in his laboratory and neglects his fiancée or his loving wife and children, obsessed by his daring and dangerous experiments. The scientist as a loyal member of a team, and therefore considerably less individualized, is treated quite respectfully.

There is absolutely no social criticism, of even the most implicit kind, in science fiction films. No criticism, for example, of the conditions of our society which create the impersonality and dehumanization which science fiction fantasies displace onto the influence of an alien It. Also, the notion of science as a social activity, interlocking with social and political interests, is unacknowledged. Science is simply either adventure (for good or evil) or a technical response to danger. And, typically, when the fear of science is paramount – when science is conceived of as black magic rather than white – the evil has no attribution beyond that of the perverse will of an individual scientist. In science fiction films the antithesis of black magic and white is drawn as a split between technology, which is beneficent, and the errant individual will of a lone intellectual.

Thus, science fiction films can be looked at as a thematically central allegory, replete with standard modern attitudes. The theme of depersonalization (being 'taken over') which I have been talking about is a new allegory reflecting the age-old awareness of man that, sane, he is always perilously close to insanity and unreason. But there is something more here than just a recent, popular image which expresses man's perennial, but largely unconscious, anxiety about his sanity. The image derives most of its power from a supplementary and historical anxiety, also not experienced *consciously* by most people, about the depersonalizing conditions of modern urban life. Similarly, it is not enough to note that science fiction allegories are one of the new myths about – that is, one of the ways of accommodating to and negating – the perennial human anxiety about death. (Myths of heaven and hell, and of ghosts, had the same function.) For, again, there is a historically specifiable twist which intensifies the anxiety. I mean, the trauma suffered by everyone in the middle of the 20th century when it became clear that, from now on to the end of human history, every person would spend his individual life under the threat not only of individual death, which is certain, but of something almost insupportable psychologically – collective incineration and extinction which could come at any time, virtually without warning.

From a psychological point of view, the imagination of disaster does not greatly differ from one period in history to another. But from a political and moral point of view, it does. The expectation of the apocalypse may be the occasion for a radical disaffiliation from society, as when thousands of Eastern European Jews in the 17th century, hearing that Sabbatai Zevi had been proclaimed the Messiah and that the end of the world was imminent, gave up their homes and businesses and began the trek to Palestine. But people take the news of their doom in diverse ways. It is reported that in 1945 the populace of Berlin received without great agitation the news that Hitler had decided to kill them all, before the Allies arrived, because they had not been worthy enough to win the war. We are, alas, more in the position of the Berliners of 1945 than of the Jews of 17th century Eastern Europe; and our response is closer to theirs, too. What I am suggesting is that the imagery of disaster in science fiction is above all the emblem of an *inadequate response*. I don't mean to bear down on the films for this. They themselves are only a sampling, stripped of sophistication, of the inadequacy of most people's response to the unassimilable terrors that infect their consciousness. The interest of the films, aside from their considerable amount of cinematic charm, consists in this intersection between a naïve and largely debased commercial art product and the most profound dilemmas of the contemporary situation.

Ours is indeed an age of extremity. For we live under continual threat of two equally fearful, but seemingly opposed, destinies: unremitting banality and inconceivable terror. It is fantasy, served out in large rations by the popular arts, which allows most people to cope with these twin specters. For one job that fantasy can do is to lift us out of the unbearably humdrum and to distract us from terrors – real or anticipated – by an escape into exotic, dangerous situations which have last-minute happy endings. But another of the things that fantasy can do is to normalize what is psychologically unbearable, thereby inuring us to it. In one case, fantasy beautifies the world. In the other, it neutralizes it.

The fantasy in science fiction films does both jobs. The films reflect worldwide anxieties, and they serve to allay them. They inculcate a strange apathy concerning the processes of radiation, contamination, and destruction which I for one find haunting and depressing. The naïve level of the films neatly tempers the sense of otherness, of alien-ness, with the grossly familiar. In particular, the dialogue of most science fiction films, which is of a monumental but often touching banality, makes them wonderfully, unintentionally funny. Lines like, 'Come quickly, there's a monster in my bathtub', 'We must do something about this', 'Wait, Professor. There's someone on the telephone', 'But that's incredible', and the old American stand-by, 'I hope it works!' are hilarious in the context of picturesque and deafening holocaust. Yet the films also contain something that is painful and in deadly earnest.

There is a sense in which all these movies are in complicity with the abhorrent. They neutralize it, as I have said. It is no more, perhaps, than the way all art draws its audience into a circle of complicity with the thing represented. But in these films we have to do with things which are (quite literally) unthinkable. Here, 'thinking about the unthinkable' – not in the way of Herman Kahn, as a subject for calculation, but as a subject for fantasy – becomes, however inadvertently, itself a somewhat questionable act from a moral point of view. The films perpetrate clichés about identity, volition, power, knowledge, happiness, social consensus, guilt, responsibility which are, to say the least, not serviceable in our present extremity. But collective nightmares cannot be banished by demonstrating that they are, intellectually and morally, fallacious. This nightmare – the one reflected, in various registers, in the science fiction films – is too close to our reality.

'Confront a man in his office with a nuclear alarm, and you have a documentary. If the news reaches him in his living room, you have a drama. If it catches him in the lavatory, the result is comedy.' **STANLEY KUBRICK**

JONATHAN ROMNEY
Million-Dollar Graffiti: Notes from the Digital Domain

Since special effects henceforth constitute an indispensable component of what the cinema is and how it is destined to evolve in the new millennium, it would be absurd, in such an anthology, not to address the implications of that fact, as the English critic Jonathan Romney does in this essay from his collection Short Orders.

Pigs have yet to fly on screen; cows already have, carried aloft by a computer-generated tornado in *Twister*. Over the short period covered by the reviews in this book, audiences have very quickly become used to miraculous imagery that less than a decade ago would have been unimaginable on film: melting men, sentient strands of water, stampedes of giant chicken creatures through prehistoric landscapes, or of elephants through libraries. We've seen the human body wrenched out of shape, stretched and liquefied, and actors cloned into multiples of themselves. We've seen the Earth all but destroyed by spaceships a quarter of the size of the Moon, and then reprieved as if – in fantasy film's perennial get-out clause – it was *all a dream*. And, as yet, we haven't fully taken stock of how our eyes and imaginations are adapting to this onslaught of marvels – these fantasy objects laden with the irresistible gravity of the real, and at the same time with the elusive weightlessness of dream.

The rapid development of digital imaging technology, which had its first timid stirrings in the 1982 Disney experiment *Tron* and came of age in the late 1980s with *The Abyss* and *Terminator 2*, means that, social taboos apart, there are no longer many practical reasons why anything at all should not be represented on screen.[1] Computer-generated imagery (CGI) covers the whole material range, from the huge, numinous, unarguably solid presence of dinosaurs in *Jurassic Park* to the miniature, seemingly banal and, above all, weightless – like the feather that floats over the opening credits of *Forrest Gump*. It's

the very immateriality and weightlessness of the digital image, its independence of either physical or imaginative gravity, that makes it so
versatile.

The aspirations of digital imagery are nothing short of Promethean.
CGI is not simply used for effects that would otherwise be too expensive
or arduous to achieve – the traditional role of special-effects technology
– but specialises in feats that are impossible, unnatural. George Lucas
knew what he was doing when he called his effects company Industrial
Light and *Magic*. CGI aspires to master all those aspects of nature that
are traditionally beyond control. It tames the animal kingdom, which
has always been notoriously intractable for film-makers, causing pigs
to speak (*Babe*) or summoning up whole cavalcades of jungle beasts
(*Jumanji*). It can harness the extremes of the weather, most grandiosely
in *Twister*, although even a demurely naturalistic film like *Sense and
Sensibility* has benefited from its rain effects. And in *Independence
Day*, it can create a vision of the apocalyptic sublime, as clouds of fire
billow over Earth's cities.

CGI can also recreate, transform, mutilate the human body, as in
the extravagant perforation of Goldie Hawn's midriff in *Death Becomes
Her*; the woman-into-monster transformation in *Species*; the blubbery
metamorphoses of *The Nutty Professor*, in which two versions of Eddie
Murphy slug it out within one body. Digitals already offer the possibility
of recreating the dead: *The Crow* and *Wagons East!* were both completed
after the untimely deaths of their respective stars, Brandon Lee and
John Candy, whose living images were digitally integrated into the film.
More radically, virtual versions of Marilyn Monroe, Bruce Lee and
George Burns are in development – and may yet break the ultimate
Promethean barrier by creating from scratch convincing simulacra of
human life: James Cameron has announced a hundred-million-dollar
film called *Avatar*, which will feature fully digitised actors, or, in *Variety*-
speak, 'synthespians'.[2]

It's easy to see why imagery of such enormity and ambition has caught
on with film-makers, despite the still considerable cost of the technology.
It's not just that such images raise the stakes of what can be represented,
but that they are, to use the cliché, more real than the real. They are
certainly more dynamic than the real – in purely visual terms, at once
more precise and more plastic than physical matter can be. Their
hyper-real presence brings reality into question, and makes it look a
little half-hearted. *Jumanji*'s rhinos seem not merely as good as real

ones but better, enhanced for dramatic effect; one of them even turns and winks at the camera. They are certainly more charismatic than the film's nominal star Robin Williams, who plays second fiddle to their destructive energy. It's no accident that the big effects films (*Jurassic Park*, *Twister*, *Independence Day*, *Species*) tend to favour second-rank or faceless stars; actors look like disposable, inanimate attractions next to these dynamic marvels. (The only star whose charisma has actually benefited from CGI is Jim Carrey in *The Mask*, who successfully rides the phenomenon by using his body as a vehicle for its effects, thereby making CGI into his own personalised prosthesis.)

It's too early to say for sure whether, as its most fervent adepts might claim, digitisation really is bringing about a Copernican revolution in cinema. It's hard to imagine quite what that revolution might consist of – a radical change in the type of images we see on screen, a change in the very way we perceive them, or simply a constant upgrading of the technology by which film images are created? What is certain is that we have become used to CGI remarkably quickly. Cinema's capacity for representing the unrepresentable seemed to have turned a corner only a few years ago, when we were first dazzled, indeed mystified, by apparitions like the watery tentacle of *The Abyss* (1989), the protean, mercury-sleek android of *Terminator 2* (1991) and, above all, the dinosaurs of *Jurassic Park* (1993), those quintessential images of impossible life miraculously fished out of the stream of history. But already we are so used to these marvels that we tend to be disappointed by any new Hollywood blockbuster that doesn't feature digital manipulation to a spectacular degree. This process of domestication is already at work within *Jurassic Park* itself: it begins with the genuinely awe-inspiring sight of placid giants grazing in the hazy distance, and ends with the menacing velociraptors, which are no more than run-of-the-mill super-lizards, crocodile-plated Freddy Kruegers.

We can't yet gauge what substantial effect this sudden glut of miracle is having on the film-goer's perception or imagination. But we can say that it represents a sudden and drastic change in the kind of illusion that film offers us. The tradition of cinematic *trompe-l'œil* since the work of silent pioneer Georges Méliès is based on the assumption that every illusion created on the screen has its ontological origins in some real event enacted in front of the camera – the magicianly stagecraft of Méliès's work, say, or the actual work of ink drawing in traditional cel animation. Méliès was one of the first to explore the possibilities of trickery within the camera, but, in the first instance, his films invoke and actually record a tradition of stage mechanics – of cardboard rockets, or actors cloaked in black to give the impression of disembodied heads and limbs. As late as the 1970s and early 1980s, the *Star Wars* trilogy, though it ushered in the age of digital illusion with the founding of effects house Industrial Light and Magic, was one of the last major projects to use the full array of traditional reality-based illusion, from matte painting to models.

In this tradition – let's call it 'analogue' filming, in parallel with the tape-and-vinyl technology that preceded digital sound recording – the act of filming disguises the original material nature of the event. It offers us a record of the event encoded in such a way that it provides a cue for our eyes and brain to participate in the work of illusion-making. Computer-generated imagery, on the other hand, may invoke the existence of a real object, but there is no guarantee that such an object ever existed; in fact, because CGI tends to specialise in the spectacular and fantastic, its use is practically a guarantee that the object *never* existed. The computer-generated image is purely the visual translation of a series of algorithms, by which the appearance of a solid object is conjured out of thin air – or rather, thin light – and then embedded in the texture of the film, compressed into the two-dimensional space of the celluloid frame.

Consider how far this takes us from the formulations of André Bazin, who in his 1945 essay 'The Ontology of the Photographic Image' argued that the power of photography, and therefore of film, was its ability to capture reality directly, with no other mediation than that of the photographic apparatus. Bazin locates photography in the tradition of art conceived as 'the preservation of life by a representation of life':[3] 'For the first time, an image of the world is formed automatically, without the creative intervention of man.' He goes on to say, 'Photography affects us like a phenomenon of nature.'[4]

Bazin's arguments have been much contested, both theoretically and practically; whole schools of cinema exist that challenge the blithe assumption of cinema's realistic function. But digital imagery seems to shatter the primacy of the real entirely. No longer does a real object need to stand in front of a camera; in the digital world, we can sever as many attachments to the real as technology and our imaginations will allow. From a medium in which the human factor supposedly plays no part at all – or at least, takes a back seat to the laws of chemistry and optics that govern the photographic process – we arrive at one in which human creative invention is at its maximum, in which every aspect of the image is expressly fabricated.

Rather than being a simple 'preservation' of life, digital imagery aspires to be something more – its crystallisation, its liquefaction. It has the mystique of an alchemical process in which all matter, transmogrified through the medium of light, can become other matter: in which flesh becomes unstable, or passes through variously liquid, metallic or crystalline avatars. Digital imagery may as a rule incline to hyper-realism, but to hyper-realism at its most unstable. Any form, however complete, can morph into another; there's no reason why the most convincingly solid object, or indeed the whole screen, shouldn't suddenly dissolve into a shower of its constituent pixels (as it does in, say, *Super Mario Bros.* or the *Lawnmower Man* films, which explicitly if ineptly invoke the constructed, decorative nature of arcade-game or virtual-reality imagery). Little wonder that such images strike us as uncanny. Even more than Bazin's photography, CGI affects us as 'a force of nature' that can't easily be accounted for. In fact, one of the problems of CGI is that it unsettles the notion of authorship: we are no longer entirely sure where images come from. Should we attribute them to the director of a film (can we honestly talk about *Spielberg*'s dinosaurs or *Jan De Bont*'s twisters?), or are the real authors the effects houses that generated them – ILM, Digital Domain, Pixar? Or perhaps we should attribute them to the technology itself, as if to an invisible god, the ghost in the movie-machine?

Because these uncanny 'made objects' are so tightly integrated into the rest of the celluloid image as to be indivisible from it, there is no longer any firm distinction in the film frame between the real and the artificially generated – as there is, say, in *Who Framed Roger Rabbit*, where live action and animation coexist in the same space, interacting yet manifestly separate. In that film, we can easily read one set of images as being photographic and the other as simply graphic. But because hyper-realistic digital illusionism tends to level out all images to the same status within the frame, it does not invite us to play the same active part that earlier illusionism does. The trick is already performed for us. We can 'read' Méliès's beheadings as stage play, Mary Poppins's levitations as the wire-powered flight of Peter Pan panto, or Jessica Rabbit's sinuous sashaying as 'just the way she's drawn'. But with CGI at its most sophisticated, it's hard to read the digital object as anything *but* an object. We see the final sum but not the calculations, the product of the computing but not the computing itself; our eye can't read the programming, or even decompose the image into its original pixels, in the way that we might once have been able to decode a matte painting as painting.

Fred Raimondi, Visual Effects Supervisor at Digital Domain, makes the stakes perfectly clear: 'My goal is to do completely photo-real computer-generated scenes that are completely and totally believable – where the viewer would look at it and not be able to identify the technique, not be able to say, "Was that photographed, or was that computer-generated?" '[5] The aim, in other words, is to bypass the eye's critical faculty, so that the viewer will not only be unable to resolve the question of the distinction between reality and illusion, but will not even ask it in the first place.

Rather than engage in the making of the image, we're held spellbound by it, as in a car's headlights; the extreme precision of the object imposes on us a surfeit of data which our cognitive capacities, short-circuited, simply aren't up to analysing. Given enough information about the 'real' status of a dinosaur – the way it moves, the way its scales catch the light, the fact that its foot can apparently reduce a Land Rover to scrap metal – we are persuaded to ignore the obvious fact that such a monster cannot exist, and to accept it as 'perceptually realistic', to use Stephen Prince's term.[6]

Stunned, glutted and seduced into perceptual passivity, audiences are left with new appetites that constantly demand stimulation. The sudden onslaught of the new imagery, and the speed with which the studios have latched onto digitals as the ultimate commercial weapon, recalls a similar explosion a century ago, the rapid world-wide proliferation of cinema in the years following the unveiling of the Lumière brothers' cinematograph. The history of Hollywood over the last five years is a rush towards constant improvement (you could say 're-armament'): towards bigger, more elaborately defined images; and towards more sophisticated technologies that can infiltrate the celluloid image more seamlessly. In fact, not to underrate audiences entirely, we are already learning to spot digital imagery, to detect it as a technique without necessarily ceasing to believe in the reality of what it shows us. There are some uses of CGI too coarsely integrated into a film to be plausible (*Eraser* and *Multiplicity* offer particularly rough examples); while the technique of morphing, the smooth slide from one form to another, is by nature too flagrant not to draw attention to itself.

But seasoned film-goers are already attuned to sniffing out CGI even in its more subtle incarnations.

As CGI's shock effect wears off, it must be constantly renewed, leading to an inflation of imagery, to what has been called 'impact aesthetics', a visual culture in thrall to the shock of the new.[7] Occasionally, CGI does indeed come up with a spectacular novelty, and the shock waves duly hit the box-office. *Twister* – after *Independence Day*, the second most successful film in North America in 1996[8] – is a perfect emblem of the digital image at its most spectacular: its whirlwinds are nothing but swirling air, embodied in a two-dimensional construction of pure light, but they also remind us, against all expectation, how aggressively weighty such immateriality can be. Short of recapturing the awe evoked in those first few shots of *Jurassic Park*, CGI can at least find new ways to knock us off our feet; the digital arsenal is in the service of an increasingly warlike cinema of attrition.

As digitals rush towards ever more efficient magic, more dazzling apocalypses, the fabric of reality, as we're used to seeing it represented in cinema, is changing. It's hard to say what the overall change will have been over a decade of digital imagery, but already a diagnosis – admittedly, a somewhat alarmist one – is beginning to take shape. It seems as if the representable world were being invaded. We can trace three stages of digital encroachment into the cinematic image of the world; they are conceptual rather than strictly historical, since the types of imaging they represent overlap in different films, but taken together they provide a schema of the way in which the digital domain seems to be slowly becoming more like a digital dominion.

Let the first stage be represented by *Jurassic Park* – the first film to build its entire appeal on the shocking introduction of discrete digital entities into a recognisable real world, through the technique of compositing. The film's dinosaurs are fully integrated into the fictional world of the film as autonomous three-dimensional beings, but their existence does not threaten the coherence of that world. These digital beings are entirely believable creatures possessed of their own reality but, in a sense, safely contained within it; they are like marvels on display in a zoo or a theme park, *in* the world yet somehow suspended from it. It's this state that *Jurassic Park* explicitly dramatises: these creatures have come from an unimaginable elsewhere to make their logic-defying appearance in our world. In the film, the Park's dinosaurs have been created by technocrat-entrepreneur John Hammond

(Richard Attenborough), who has had them cloned out of the minimal unit material of DNA, just as the images of them have been generated by Industrial Light and Magic from the minimal unit of the pixel. In the story, the dinosaurs are contained in a theme-park environment; similarly, their terrifying image – a digital chimera with an amplified roar that is nevertheless capable of shaking rows of cinema seats – is safely contained within the narrow parameters of the two-dimensional film frame.

Arguably, this question of containment is the real theme of *Jurassic Park*. The film teases us with a speculation on what might happen if these apparently real images were to tear loose from the containing screen, just as Hammond's creatures threaten to break out of his Park.[9] What, *Jurassic Park* implicitly asks, would happen to the structure of visible reality if digital imagery were to break free from the bounds of the discrete object? The film has the familiar conservative thrust of much 'What if?' sci-fi; *Jurassic Park* glories in the computer's creations, only to conclude that information technology is ultimately an unpredictable ally, to be reined in to the maximum.

But what if the digital were to infiltrate reality, seep into it like a transforming virus? This is the possibility envisioned in the second stage of digitisation, embodied in *Forrest Gump*. The film's rewriting of the visible world is problematic, not so much in those virtuoso sequences that stitch Tom Hanks into period newsreel footage (simply a refinement of similar effects in Woody Allen's *Zelig*), but at those moments where the digital treatment is so discreet as to be clandestine, where it whittles away at represented reality, doctors it cosmetically. Most notoriously, digitals allow the film-makers to amputate the legs of actor Gary Sinise, playing at Vietnam war veteran – an assault on the body all the more devastating because it is undetectable. There is no dotted line at the knee, none of that fuzzy bordering we associate with traditional blue-screen work; and because most viewers are unfamiliar with Sinise as an actor, the incongruity of the effect can go unperceived in a way it would not have done if Tom Hanks had been the amputee.

This bloodless, scarless operation is one of the more drastic instances of digitals as an art not of creation but of erasure. The most common application of the digital cut-and-paste process is the 'painting-out' of safety wires in stunt scenes; it can also remove unwanted actors from shot, restore decorum to the cut of a swimsuit (*My Father the Hero*), or modify a bit of background product placement (*Demolition Man*).[10]

Forrest Gump doctors reality in more spectacular but equally imperceptible ways. The thousands of people that fill a baseball stadium in one of the film's more grandiose shots are in fact a crowd of extras photographed in one section of the stadium then digitally reproduced and re-applied to the image, pasted on like wallpaper. Unlike the obviously impossible images of *Jurassic Park*, nothing in this shot is impossible *per se* – there's no reason to think that a prestigious filmmaker like Robert Zemeckis couldn't have afforded this many extras for the scene (or indeed, that he couldn't have managed some unusually complex airborne close-up tracking shots of the falling feather in the credit sequence). But digitals allow him to create all these images with unprecedented clarity and expediency, and, above all, to create them undetected.

In *Forrest Gump*, we can never entirely be sure what we're seeing. Where CGI's more ostentatious mirages flaunt their distance from familiar reality, the images of *Forrest Gump* seep into the real and merge with it. Clearly the film, as a comic-strip rewriting of recent American history, raises a new set of ethical questions about what aspects of visible reality it is appropriate for cinema to forge. These questions may be no different in kind to those that have always been asked about photography's power to falsify, but, at the very least, the stakes are raised immeasurably by the traceless nature of digital manipulation.

The third phrase of digitisation might be legitimate cause for paranoia if it weren't, so far at least, a unique case. John Lasseter's *Toy Story* – made for Walt Disney by the digital production company Pixar – is the first feature film in which a digitally generated, convincingly three-dimensional world entirely supplants photographic reality. *Toy Story* was marketed simply as a de luxe upgrade of the traditional animation feature, perhaps for fear of the hi-tech angle scaring off the mainstream audience. But it represents rather more than that. In *Toy Story*, not only are the toy heroes digitally generated, but so are the backgrounds they move in; Lasseter and his team elaborate an entirely dynamic world in which objects and backgrounds are imbued with life, and the imaginary camera constantly shifts position, causing everything we see to somersault through a dizzying choreography of perspectives.

The eye so easily accepts *Toy Story* as being simply 'like' a cartoon, but more real, that once we start thinking about the film *as* a digital construction we become aware of something quite alarming – we realise it takes some considerable perceptual effort for the eye to read it consistently as such. The film's universe looks too perfect to be anything but autonomous, as if it had simply generated itself; it oppresses us with its plenitude, the suavity of its textures, its self-sufficiency – above all, with its coherence. Its objects both look real and obey real physical laws – they don't morph or dissolve, but interact as solids with the entirely constructed universe they inhabit. This is no small matter: one of the great problems of such animation is to ensure that planes don't intersect where they shouldn't, that these mathematical abstractions in the guise of solids actually behave like solids. The film's most extraordinary phenomenon is its simplest: the fact that when astronaut Buzz Lightyear lands on the floor he actually comes to a stop instead of passing through it like a ghost.

Toy Story presents us with a world designed from scratch, from its most basic physical laws up. It's a world indistinguishable from the real in one respect only: although it seems to obey the laws of the known universe, it is nevertheless stylised to resemble a two-dimensional cartoon miraculously pumped up to three dimensions, so that there is no chance of any viewer over five years old mistaking it for reality. After all, its inhabitants are toys. There's a simple, genre-driven reason for this: *Toy Story* is a Disney film, and audiences need to be reassured they are still in the familiar corporate domain of Disney animation. But perhaps the film's benign nursery-idyll tone also serves to reassure us that there's nothing to fear, just yet – that the real is not yet being supplanted by this uncanny virtual universe. However, now that *Toy Story* has established a genre, it remains to be seen whether its successors will jettison the cartoon style and head towards more defined, and perhaps more alienating, simulacra. Viewer-friendly though it is, *Toy Story* already induces an uncanny malaise – the feeling of being shut inside a parallel, entirely hermetic reality.

Only the most paranoid speculation would suggest that *Toy Story*'s caricatural realism could ever supplant the real world photographed on film, but that's only because, for the foreseeable future, it will remain easier and cheaper to place real objects in front of a camera than to construct simulacra from scratch. And yet ... Digital researchers continue to fine-tune existing technologies in the hope of conquering all those areas that CGI does not yet have a purchase on. In doing so, they close the gap between the real and the digital worlds.

Toy Story already unsettles the distinction between reality and artifice.

It makes the world of toys more true to life than the world of humans: the geometric domain of the nursery is scrupulously mapped out, textured and finished; the toys themselves, their musculature, movements, expressions, the textures of their wood, plastic and paper surfaces, are minutely defined and calibrated. But the film's human universe is markedly less convincing, almost shoddy. The scrubby back garden looks half-formed, sketchy, like an afterthought; humans are bulbous, robotic, excessively cartoonish. It's only the natural universe that looks as if it was knocked up on a computer.

Here, the film is primarily making witty capital out of a specific limitation of computer imagery. Digitals still don't quite have the measure of organic material. Forms that can be reduced to geometric planes and curves are manageable: it's relatively easy to gather data about them, assemble composites of relevant shapes and then wrap textures around them. Organic forms (flesh, hair, vegetable matter) are much more complex and elusive than the inorganic (plastic or metal). Nevertheless CGI continues its assault on unconquered terrain. For the lion's mane alone in *Jumanji*, it took three months for ILM to create the appropriate software and then another five to generate the hair itself. Never mind that the result looks entirely unconvincing; what is impressive is its sheer tactile abstraction, like a mass of optical-fibre tentacles swaying underwater. Again, as with *Toy Story*, the film's narrative provides its own alibi for this artificial appearance. This doesn't look like a real lion, because it isn't: it is pure manifestation, a demon sprung fully formed out of a satanic board game. Still, it does suggest that the technology's limitations might supply a new strain of kitsch: if it can't always rival the real, digitisation might at least aim at the aesthetic of the lava lamp.

Such serendipitous misfires apart, CGI continues to colonise every field of visual expertise in which there remain objects to be quantified. It's as if everything needs to be duplicated and represented, as if no object will have taken its place in the visible universe until all its available data have been logged and its parameters reproduced. There's an encyclopaedic thrust here, as if the sum of objects in the world were gradually being inventoried and added to the digital repertoire. This emphasis on the replicable and the visible has its history; James Roberts points out that CGI is the latest stage in a project of visual research that began with Renaissance theory of perspective, and the culmination of a visual ideology in which 'the equation of what something is with what it means allows very little scope for any other reality than the optical'.[11]

The problem becomes apparent in the ontology of the digital as opposed to the photographic object. A traditional approach to the status of the object in film stresses the immediacy of its photographic capture, as if, to echo Bazin's terms, the object were simply embalmed in celluloid. The object appears to have soaked directly into the grain of the image, preserving its autonomy in the process. Consequently, the celluloid image always retains a degree of arbitrariness, each shot being obliged to cope with objects *as they are*. The film-maker's job is to control the extent of this arbitrariness, through framing, lighting, camera position, use of colour – all of which limit the object's tendency to be what it happens to be, and coerce it into being what the film-maker wants it to be.

But the object refuses to be brought to heel; once it is incorporated into the image, certain aspects of it will always be beyond the camera's control. A thing always carries an unquantifiable surplus of meaning beyond the primary meaning for which it is destined. This surplus can include an actor's look and all the intangibles that comprise 'charisma', including associations carried over from his or her other films, which a viewer is free to read into the image. It can include the tendency of objects and people to be in not quite the right place at the right time, or contingencies such as the self-evident rubberiness of a rubber octopus; the films of Edward D. Wood Jr, in fact, provide a primer of the ways in which the intransigent object-ness of an object can eclipse the symbolic service into which a film-maker tries to press it.

Digitisation would seem to provide a foolproof method of disciplining the rebelliousness of things. The cut-and-paste function can edit out accidents entirely. No more of those unpredictable passing dogs that enlivened Italian neo-realism, or striking faces in crowds, as in *Les Enfants du Paradis*; in the new school of French costume drama, exemplified by Jean-Paul Rappeneau's *The Horseman on the Roof* (*Le Hussard sur le toit*), obtrusive extras are mercilessly excised. In this ruthless new world, only the strictly relevant objects are there for our attention. But by reducing the field of our attention, digitals also reduce the potential resonance of the image. In a film entirely controlled by the principle of relevance, it would be futile to look for the *something extra* that viewers thrive on sniffing out; we'd find nothing except what we're given. What we see really would be what we get: no reality other than the optical.

Meaning is even more harshly constrained in those objects that are entirely digitally generated. Such an object can't get into the frame in the first place except as the result of a rigorously conceived set of calculations that determine its action and appearance down to the last detail. A digital image of the simplest natural object – a chunk of rock, say – is not simple at all, but a complex set of planes and curves that has had to be exhaustively analysed before it can have any objective existence, any 'perceptual reality'. For the rock to exist at all, digital artists have to use procedures such as ray tracing, reflection mapping, texture mapping; have to analyse its light properties, the way it would move, its degree of flexibility. The digital object is absolutely intended, determined; its only properties are those that are deemed essential. You could say that CGI implies a theological perspective, in which every object is the creation of a deity entirely in control of its faculties and which leaves nothing to chance – which mercilessly suppresses chance, in fact.

But what space do such creations leave for vagaries of the viewer's eye? Images that come to the screen charged with some degree of indeterminacy allow for idiosyncrasies of critical perception. When certain real objects in the frame distract our attention from others, or when an object's peripheral properties seem more striking than those that are supposedly its principal ones, we know that we have a certain scope for reading the image. We may choose to read the marginalia rather than the main text, or to ignore the distinction between text and marginalia altogether. We may be transfixed by the passer-by in the background rather than the star making the big speech; in fact, Robert Altman has developed a whole style out of our tendency to watch the 'wrong' person, listen to the 'wrong' conversation.

Within the limits determined by a film's discourse (narrative or non-narrative, realist or anti-realist), an object on screen is normally free to signify in whatever way the viewer is prepared to allow. In pre-digital representation (alarming but true: we can already talk about the 'pre-digital'), an object can literally represent itself, but it can also represent other things, depending on the rules of interpretation set by the context. The sea in Fellini's *Casanova* is clearly an expanse of plastic sheeting, but it is also a sea; the ambivalence does not have to be resolved.

But such ambivalence is foreign to the digital realm. A computer-generated object is caught within the strict bounds of its own appearance, simply because so much rigorous calculation has gone into constructing that appearance; the digital object is not perfected but *sur-fected*, saturated with its own tautological being. It is what it is; it can't be anything else. Except in such cases as *Jumanji*'s cartoonish lion, which makes a virtue of their imperfection, the digital object cannot be anything other than literal and integral; its every aspect is required to cohere unequivocally with the whole, and the whole to cohere with the larger picture it is incorporated into.

We are not required as viewers to take stock of such an object as potential material for metaphor; in fact, we're discouraged from doing so. We're simply asked to acknowledge the fact that the object has been made to exist. Any ambivalence, any symbolic or metaphoric potential in an object, is ruled out from the start. This goes side by side with another development: since there is no longer anything that technology cannot represent, there is no longer any need to allude to the unrepresentable, and so no need for symbolism, which developed in cinema both as a way of addressing the unspeakable and as a way round physical or financial restraints.

Hence the extraordinary lack of resonance that makes the new digital epics so frustrating. How is it, for example, that a film like *Twister* moves us so little? It is, after all, a classic example of what used to be called 'the cinema of wonder'; it does, after all, depict a series of extraordinary natural phenomena, the grandest of which is referred to by one character as 'the finger of God'. After such a metaphysical hard sell, how is it that *Twister*'s giant whirlwinds produce so little sublime awe? Certainly, there are obvious flaws in such films' economy – the technology is so expensive that the effects need to be cost-effective, that is, as visible as possible. Too bad if that means sidelining all the things that once might have been considered the backbone of such a film: plot, character, suspense. This is a comparatively new development – consider the extraordinarily slow-burning build up of *Close Encounters of the Third Kind*, then compare the prosaic on-with-the-show pacing of *Jurassic Park*.

It might be said that the fault with the new spectacle lies in the way it is mobilised – *Independence Day* might conceivably have achieved some sense of holy terror if only the film hadn't been pitched at such a hysterical level of flag-waving crassness. But the deeper reason for the hollowness is in the nature of the images themselves. There is no longer any sense of trepidation in the prospect of seeing 'the finger of God', because we know that if Jan De Bont wants to show us that finger he can. The sublime comes pre-programmed, at a price, and that price is only partly financial; symbolic resonance is the first casualty. The very idea of representing a massive intergalactic nemesis seems to lead inexorably to transcendental bathos – *unless*, perhaps, we can be persuaded that some extraordinarily brazen feat of Mélièsesque gimcrackery is being pulled off before our eyes. I suspect it's in the nature of cinema that Moses parting the Red Sea with divine powers will always be less impressive than Cecil B. DeMille doing it with smoke and mirrors and a lot of audience goodwill.[12]

It's plausible to imagine that, over the next few years, the inflation of hyper-real illusion will result in audiences so jaded that there will be a massive backlash against digital fantasy; viewers will want guarantees that they are seeing reality itself, with a minimum of mediation and adulteration, and the more extreme the better. There are already signs that this is beginning to happen. The 1996 US box-office hit *Rumble in the Bronx*, a vehicle for Hong Kong's Jackie Chan, was prominently advertised as featuring 'the action star who does all his own stunts'. You can see the appeal of such a star when Hollywood's leading muscle-men increasingly palm off their audiences with feats that were clearly performed on computer consoles in Burbank.

If real action, why not real sex, and real pain too – no longer the contortions of digital morphing, but the body itself explored to its physical limits. Cases of actors putting on weight and taking the punches, like De Niro in *Raging Bull*, will no longer be Method anomalies but the norm; acting will become a form of brutal body art. It will no longer be enough to see an actor's legs digitally severed; he'll have to do it for real, or, at the very least, simulate amputation as torturously as Lon Chaney would have done in his day.

This new cult of the real will be pornographic, in fact – pornography being the form of cinema that most fetishises the real, or at least the promise of it. Post-digital pornographic realism will value performance over simulation, insist on real taboo-breaking, real come-shots, or, in the case of that apocryphal *maudit* sub-genre the snuff movie, real death. There's no reason, indeed, why any of these extremes shouldn't eventually become mainstream, just as figures of physicality and mortality have begun to enter the mainstream of art debate from the performance margins – from the health-threatening, body-stretching art of performers like Stelarc, Ron Athey, Orlan, who respectively use prosthetics, blood-letting and surgery in ways we couldn't yet easily tolerate if we saw them on a cinema screen.

Such nightmare hyper-literalism would certainly provide that material weight that computer-generated imagery promises but so frustratingly denies us. Still, before we take that route of muscle and blood, perhaps there's room to salvage the immateriality of digitals for more fruitful use. At the risk of invoking some vaporous idealist code of aesthetics, I'd say there's still every possibility for CGI to be used in the service of poetry – by which I mean, simply, to create images that are not shackled to the sensationalist hyper-real but have some consciousness of their own texture and constructedness. Some directors working outside mainstream realism have tried, and it hasn't always worked: morphing has been used by Peter Jackson in his psychosexual drama *Heavenly Creatures* and by Terence Davies in *The Neon Bible*, and in both cases the effect was less to startle you with the images than to impress on you that the directors had suddenly acquired an effects budget.

A more successful 'invisible' use of digitals was the creation of snowfall in the Coen Brothers' *The Hudsucker Proxy* – it at once looked like real snow and at the same time tended to a Christmas-card abstraction in keeping with the film's stylisation. Another avenue was the densely unreal vision of Jeunet and Caro's *The City of Lost Children*, which uses the full range of digital effects – morphing, cloning, entirely created objects – to create an entirely self-enclosed picture-book universe. A residue of visual literalism may undermine the film's aspirations to the texture of dream, but nearly all its images are charged with some cultural allusion or other – Gustave Doré's engravings, Marcel Carné's films, *Tintin* comics and, above all, the Méliès tradition. What the film loses in being too concrete, it gains by placing CGI within a cultural history, and by drawing attention to itself as a performance of illusion making, rather than just illusion provided ready-made.

There is also the option – practically unexplored in the mainstream, for obvious reasons – of using computer effects to loosen the hold of realism altogether and explode the economy of the film frame. In *Prospero's Books* and *The Pillow Book*, Peter Greenaway fragments the image, critically measuring the signifying power of the screen against other readable surfaces – painting, books, the human body. The latter film, in particular, consciously offers itself as a provocative if overly aesthetic manifesto for a new digital cinema, being as close as film has

come to the multi-dimensional density of text and image offered by
CD-ROM.

Such examples may seem to point towards a strain of art cinema that
is becoming increasingly unfashionable, and which may soon be quite
unfeasible in commercial terms, unless some massive change occurs in
the cost of CGI, or some radically new funding system comes into
effect world-wide. To be realistic, the signs are that digital research will
continue to lead us into the questionable utopia of the theme-park ride.
But even in the mainstream, there's scope for more imagination. In
most respects, the Jim Carrey comic-book adaptation *The Mask* is
commercial spectacle at its most pedestrian, yet there's a mercurial
quality to its use of digitals that almost redeems the film. *The Mask*
exceeds its entirely ordinary brief in the way that the colour green
becomes its central fixation, almost its protagonist – the colour of
the Mask's demonic face, and of the whirlwind he whips up in his
transformation scenes. The film shamelessly recycles gags from old Tex
Avery cartoons like *Red Hot Riding Hood* – the lolling tongue, the eyes
popping out and remaining suspended in mid-air – and applies them
in three dimensions to a human figure. In *Roger Rabbit*, cartoon was
simply integrated into the real world; here it has escaped its restraints
and formed a hybrid with the real, neither drawn nor photographic, but
formed from the elasticity of light and colour.

A more thorough infiltration of the real by cartoonish CGI is accomplished by Tim Burton's *Mars Attacks!* Its hordes of little green men
are ostentatiously impossible figures, whose cartoon nature is derived
from a series of early 1960s trading cards. They belong neither on
Planet Earth nor in the stable terrestrial reality that we expect from
earth-invasion sci-fi, and which we find in the film's bullish counterpart,
Independence Day. Inside their spacecraft, Burton's Martians inhabit
a digital realm that is clearly made of sculpted light, the same material
that comprises the nursery of *Toy Story*. But as soon as they arrive on
Earth, the encroachment begins: their presence makes the known world
and all the actors in it, from Jack Nicholson down, look like an extension
of the cartoon universe. The recognisable real becomes simply a screen
for Burton's little green vandals to deface: their zap-guns, erasing and
redrawing human bodies as blazing green skeletons, are a joyously
macabre figure of the explosive power of the pixel, which need show
no respect for the real.

Anthony Lane once characterised CGI at its worst as 'million-dollar graffiti, scrawled across a crumbling film in the hope of keeping it upright'.[13] I'd argue that the state of graffiti is *exactly* what computer imagery should aspire to, and both *The Mask* and *Mars Attacks!* represent tentative mainstream moves in that direction. It's time we saw the realism of both CGI and analogue photography being flawed, scratched, riddled with graffiti – not just scrawled across a film's surface, but stitched into its workings, distressing it from the inside. The appeal of such a prospect is that you can't yet imagine quite where that aesthetic might eventually lead; you can only imagine something more vibrant and disorderly than we've yet seen, and, with any luck, closer to the reckless cartoonery of Tex Avery than to the technocratic dullness of *Twister* or *Independence Day*. In his famous challenge to what would become the French New Wave, Alexandre Astruc called for the *caméra-stylo*, the camera as the film-maker's pen for writing in a new visual language. Digital technology can take us far beyond the pen – it can be word processor, airbrush, spray gun, even a blowtorch to combust the real entirely. It's up to film-makers to invent new kinds of writing that meet the challenge of this new tool – or perhaps just reinvent the pleasures of the graffiti scrawl.

NOTES

1. So far, for example, we have not yet seen a digital erection, although director Paul Verhoeven claims he offered to provide one to a bashful Kyle MacLachlan in *Showgirls*.

2. The term has been copyrighted by the effects company Kleiser-Walczak Construction Co.; see 'H'wood cyber dweebs are raising the dead', *Variety*, 4–10 November 1996. See also Pat Kane, 'How to remake a star', *Guardian* Friday Review, 17 January 1997.

3. Andre Bazin, *What is Cinema?* trans. Hugh Gray (University of California Press, Berkeley, 1967), p. 10.

4. Ibid., p. 13.

5. Interviewed in *Electric Passions*, Channel Four Television, 1996.

6. Stephen Prince, 'True Lies: Perceptual Realism, Digital Images and Film Theory', *Film Quarterly*, Spring 1996, pp. 27–37.

7. Philip Hayward, quoted in Robin Baker, 'Computer Technology and Special Effects in Contemporary Cinema', *Future Vision: New*

Technologies of the Screen, ed. Philip Hayward, Tana Wollen (BFI, London, 1993), p. 41.

8. *Variety*, 13–19 January 1997.

9. This is a scenario made even more concrete in the three-dimensional illusionism of the *Back to the Future* ride in the Universal Studios' theme parks in Hollywood and Florida; the public, 'flying' in a De Lorean car, experience the alarmingly vivid hallucination of being swallowed by a giant dinosaur. Digital Domain's *Terminator 2: 3D* show takes the audience's disorientation a stage further by mixing three-dimensional projection with live actors on stage, so that screen space and actual space merge unpredictably.

10. See *Premiere* (US), January 1996.

11. 'The Story of the Eye', *Frieze* 29, June–August 1996.

12. To be fair, *Independence Day* does indeed use such gimcrackery; it mixes CGI with more traditional forms of sci-fi special effect, including matte painting and models, and its technical aspects were publicised as being a return to the *Star Wars* tradition of artisanship. In fact, some reviewers, discerning an opaque creakiness to some of the effects, saw the film as an overtly camp pastiche of 1950s sci-fi B-movies. I personally couldn't see that any of the film's other effects fell short of CGI's standard of seamlessness, and felt that all its effects, digital or not, elicited that passive perceptual response I have described here. I'd argue that any film prominently featuring digital spectacle tends to put us into that passive mode of perception. CGI's effect is so persuasive that it engulfs a film; we see it even when it isn't there.

13. *Independent on Sunday*, 21 September 1991, quoted by Baker 1993, p. 45.

'I went out there for a thousand a week, and I worked Monday, and I got fired Wednesday. The guy that hired me was out of town Tuesday'

NELSON ALGREN

Theorizing

ABEL GANCE
The Era of the Image Has Arrived

Abel Gance, Abel Extravagance! And he was just as extravagant in his (rare) writings on the cinema as in his films. When, as is nowadays the case, the image has become almost as omnipresent as the word, when cinematic images are fashioned no longer to resemble the extra-cinematic world but, rather, to resemble other, pre-existent cinematic images, it's a salutary experience to read, from 1927, Gance's exalted hymn to the supremacy of a purely visual cinema.

The image only exists as a representation of the power of the person who creates it, but this representation may be more or less apparent and yet function in the same way; which means that if I create an image and someone else creates exactly the same image, the impression on the spectator will not be of the same essence, although the quality of the image is absolutely identical. The image has two different lives according to the animating potential. This is the secret that I don't think any critic has understood. And this is the admirable 'psychological' side of cinema that is now coming to life.

The process of creating a screenplay is the opposite of that of creating a novel or a theatrical drama. There everything comes from the outside. First of all, there is floating mist, then an atmosphere is established which seizes you and from which the drama will come; the earth is created, human beings are not yet created. Kaleidoscopes form: from them a selection is made and the details remain, bad, golden, gentle or perfidious, and bearing the seeds or the triggers of the drama.

Antitheses form: a snow-covered landscape will contrast with a landscape of soot or of railway lines; complimentary factors are linked; from then on the drama is born in the atmosphere. It takes place on a peak or in a torrent, in a cheap saloon or in a desert, on a boat or in the Pacific. All we have to do is to create the human machines that will live in it.

People pass, necessary inhabitants of these chosen climates. In fact, they are fluid and so barely distinguishable from their background that one doesn't know whether it is they or the objects who will speak the best. They have the color, perfume, voice of the milieu.

Now the attention, the poetry, the creative suffering forms itself around them, sweeps them up, stops them, and here while I watch them, they exist, and they exist even more strongly because they are the threads of the things on which they are going to rest.

The drama takes form, psychology finds its places, little by little the heart beats, the human machines are ready. The Art of cinema is beginning.

Cinema will impart a new sense to man. He will listen with his eyes. 'Wecol naam roum eth nacoloss' ('They have seen the voices'), says the Talmud. He will be as sensitive to the versifications of light as he was to the measures of poetry. He will see birds talk to the wind. A railway line will become musical. A wheel will be as beautiful as a Greek temple. A new form of opera will be born. Singers will be heard without being seen, such joy!

The Ride of the Valkyries will become a possibility: Shakespeare, Rembrandt, Beethoven will make films, because their realms will be both one and vaster. A mad and tumultuous upheaval of artistic values, a sudden and magnificent blossoming of dreams larger than all that went before. Not only printing, but 'manufacture of dreams', exquisite water, sunflower tincture, changing at will all psychology.

The era of the image has arrived!

There is an initial mistake: thinking that only the blind cannot see clearly. A large part of the audience still keeps a white film over its eyes, which we will not now endeavor to analyze psychologically, so as not to reveal this illness to those of my readers who wrongly would like to believe that they themselves suffer from it.

And we put all our strength, all our enthusiasm in front of our images, and we put all our weakness or our desperate unhappiness behind them. We make them the least transparent possible so that only the strength can be seen, but experienced eyes are often able to see us kneeling behind them . . .

Truly, the era of the image has arrived!

All legends, all mythology, and all myths, all the founders of religions and all religions themselves, all the great figures of history, all the objective reflections of the imagination of people for thousands of years, each and every one, await their shining resurrection, and the heroes are jostling each other to enter our doors. All the life of dreams and all the dreams of life are ready to run along the sensitive ribbon, and it's not a Victor Hugo-like whim to think that Homer would have used it to print the *Iliad*, or better still the *Odyssey*.

The era of the image has arrived!

Explain? Comment? What is the use? Some of us are walking quickly toward cloud horses, and when we fight, it is with reality, to force reality to become a dream . . .

A great film?

Music: from the crystal of souls that clash and search for themselves, from the harmony of visual return, from the very quality of silence;

Painting and sculpture through composition;

Architecture through construction and order;

Poetry through puffs of dream stolen from the souls of beings and of things;

And dance through the inner rhythm which speaks to the soul, which brings it out of you and makes it mingle with the actors of the drama.

Everything joins in.

A great film. Crossroads of the arts that do not recognize one another once out of the crucible of light, and that in vain deny their origins.

A great film? The gospel of tomorrow. Bridge of dreams from one era to another; alchemists' art, philosophers' stone for the eyes.

The era of the image has arrived!

So the cinema gives to the most frozen appearance of things and people the great gift before death: life. And this life is given through its highest aspect: personality.

Personality surpasses intelligence. Personality is the visible soul of things and of people, their outward heredity; their past becomes unforgettable, their future already present. All the aspects of the world, brought to life by the cinema, have only been chosen on the condition that they have their own personality. That is the second precision we can bring, as of now, to the rules of *photogénie*. I suggest, therefore: only the mobile and personal aspects of things, of beings, and of souls can be photogenic, that is to say, acquire a superior moral value through cinematographic reproduction.

A close-up of an eye is no longer the eye, it's *an* eye: that is to say, the mimetic decor where suddenly appears the character of the look . . . I very much enjoyed a recent competition organized by a film paper. It asked for the names of forty screen actors, more or less well known, whose pictures were reproduced in the paper in truncated form, only showing the eyes. It meant identifying forty personalities by their look. Here was a strange, unconscious attempt to train spectators to study and to recognize a personality by his eyes.

And a close-up of a revolver is no longer a revolver, it's the character-revolver, that is to say, the desire or the remorse for the crime, the bankruptcy, the suicide. It is as dark as the temptations of the night, as bright as the reflection of coveted gold, as taciturn as passion, brutal, heavy, cold, suspicious, threatening. It has a nature, morals, memories, a will, a soul.

Mechanically, only the lens sometimes manages to divulge the intimacy of things.

'Americans don't like sexual movies – they like sexy movies'   JACK NICHOLSON

JEAN VIGO
Speech at the première of *À propos de Nice*

Jean Vigo died in 1934 of leukemia at the age of 29, leaving behind him a body of work – two shorts, one medium-length production and just one feature – so meagre that the combined running times of all his films amount to less than that of Titanic, *yet also so consistently sublime that it contrives to include two of the very greatest of all films,* Zéro de conduite *(1932) and* L'Atalante *(1934). His short documentary about the French Riviera,* À propos de Nice, *was defined by one critic, George Morrison of the magazine* Sequence, *as 'one of the most unconventional documentaries ever made. With a bitterness and irony comparable to Stroheim's, the camera explores this centre of middle-class decadence, the monstrous hotels with their armies of servants, the baroque casinos, the amorous elderly women with their ruthless gigolos, the stinking alleys and grimy bistros filled with tramps, ponces, fences: a scathing contrast of the idle poor and the idle rich.' The film was premièred in 1930 at the Vieux Colombier theatre in Paris, to an invited audience composed mostly of something called the* Groupement des spectateurs d'avant-garde *(those were the days!), and was preceded by this brief introductory speech by Vigo himself.*

'I would like to talk about a more defined form of social cinema, something to which I am closest: the social documentary – or, more precisely, *point de vue documenté.*

'In this area of endeavor, I affirm, the camera is King – or at least President of the Republic.

'I don't know whether the result will be a work of art, but I am sure it will be cinema. Cinema, in the sense that no other art, no science, can take its place.

'The maker of social documentaries is a man thin enough to squeeze through a Rumanian keyhole and shoot Prince Carol getting up in his nightshirt – assuming that were a spectacle worthy of interest. He is a

Fantasy sequence from À *Propos de Nice*

fellow small enough to squat under the chair of the croupier – the Great God of the casino at Monte Carlo – and that, as you may well imagine, is no easy thing.

'Social documentary is distinct from the ordinary short film and the weekly newsreel in that its creator will establish his own point of view: he will dot his own "i"s.

'If it doesn't involve an artist, it at least involves a man . . . Conscious behaviour cannot be tolerated, character must be surprised by the camera if the whole "documentary" value of this kind of cinema is to be achieved.

'We shall achieve our end if we can reveal the hidden reason for a gesture, if we can extract from an ordinary person his interior beauty – or a caricature of him – quite by chance, if we can reveal his complete inner spirit through his purely external manifestations.

'À *Propos de Nice* is only a rough draft . . . In this film, the description of a whole town begging from sheer laziness, we are spectators at the trial of a particular world. After indicating this life and atmosphere of Nice – and, alas, elsewhere – the film proceeds to a generalized impression of gross pleasures, to different signs of a grotesque existence, of flesh and of death. These are the last twitchings of a society that neglects its own responsibilities to the point of giving you nausea and making you an accomplice in a revolutionary solution.'

JORGE LUIS BORGES
An Overwhelming Film

Jorge Luis Borges, one of the great writers of the century, was, on and off from 1931 to 1944, the official film critic of the Argentinian literary magazine Sur. *He was, rather, its reviewer, since he seldom extended himself beyond 500 or 600 words and never committed himself to what could be described as even a vaguely theoretical text. Naturally, a fair amount of rubbish fell to his, as to every workaday reviewer's, lot: to his comrade-in-literature and occasional collaborator, Adolfo Bioy Casares, he compared himself as a filmgoer to 'a reader of Madame Delly' (whose English equivalent would be Ethel M. Dell). Confronted by trashy albeit sometimes entertaining thrillers and melodramas, he would turn his reviews into précis of films his readers were then dispensed from bothering to see, just as his short stories were so many précis of novels he never felt like writing.*

Borges did, however, encounter the odd masterpiece, and this review, from the awkwardly titled collection Borges in/and/on Film, *edited by Edgardo Coszarinsky, is interesting if for no other reason than that it illustrates the far from unanimous press that even the most apparently incontrovertible of classics is liable to meet with on its original release.*

*C*itizen Kane (called *The Citizen* in Argentina) has at least two plots. The first, of an almost banal imbecility, tries to milk applause from the very unobservant. It may be formulated in this way: a vain millionaire accumulates statues, orchards, palaces, swimming pools, diamonds, cars, libraries, men and women. Like an earlier collector (whose observations are traditionally attributed to the Holy Ghost), he discovers that these miscellanies and plethoras are vanity of vanities, all is vanity. At the moment of his death, he yearns for a single thing in the universe: a fittingly humble sled that he played with as a child! The second plot is far superior. It links Koheleth to the memory of another nihilist: Franz Kafka. The theme (at once metaphysical and detective-fictional, at once psychological and allegorical) is the investigation of a man's secret soul by means of the works he has made, the words he has spoken, the many destinies he has destroyed. The procedure is the same as in Joseph Conrad's *Chance* (1914) and the beautiful film *The Power and the Glory*: a rhapsody of heterogeneous scenes, out of chronological order. Overwhelmingly, endlessly, Orson Welles shows fragments of the life of the man, Charles Foster Kane, and invites us to combine them and to reconstruct him. The film teems with forms of multiplicity, of incongruity: the first scenes record the treasures amassed by Kane; in one of the last, a poor woman, sumptuous and suffering, plays with an enormous jigsaw puzzle on the floor of a palace that is also a museum. At the end, we realize that the fragments are not governed by any secret unity: the detested Charles Foster Kane is a simulacrum, a chaos of appearances. (A possible corollary, foreseen by David Hume, Ernst Mach, and our own Macedonio Fernández: no man knows who he is, no man is anyone.) In one of Chesterton's stories – 'The Head of Caesar', I think – the hero observes that nothing is so frightening as a labyrinth with no center. This film is precisely that labyrinth.

We all know that a party, a palace, a great undertaking, a lunch for writers and journalists, an atmosphere of light-hearted and spontaneous camaraderie are essentially horrible. *Citizen Kane* is the first film that shows these things with some awareness of this truth.

In general, the film's execution is worthy of its vast subject. There are shots with admirable depth, shots whose farthest planes (as in the paintings by the Pre-Raphaelites) are no less precise and detailed than the closest.

Nevertheless, I venture to guess that *Citizen Kane* will endure as certain of Griffith's or Pudovkin's films have 'endured' – films whose historical value no one denies, films no one especially wants to see again. *Citizen Kane* suffers from gigantism, from pedantry, from tediousness. It is not intelligent, it is a work of *genius* – in the most nocturnal and Germanic sense of that bad word.

JORGE LUIS BORGES
On Dubbing

This second essay by the Argentinian fabulist not only offers a peculiarly Borgesian 'take' on one of the scourges of international film distribution, but also anticipates the still incompletely tapped potential of morphing.

The possibilities for the art of combination are not infinite, but they are apt to be frightening. The Greeks engendered the chimera, a monster with the head of a lion, the head of a dragon, and the head of a goat; the theologians of the second century, the Trinity, in which the Father, the Son, and the Holy Ghost are inextricably linked; the Chinese zoologists, the *ti-yiang*, a bright red, supernatural bird equipped with six feet and six wings but with neither face nor eyes; the geometrists of the nineteenth century, the hypercube, a four-dimensional figure that encloses an infinite number of cubes and is bounded by eight cubes and twenty-four squares. Hollywood has just enriched this frivolous, teratological museum: by means of a perverse artifice they call dubbing, they offer monsters that combine the well-known features of Greta Garbo with the voice of Aldonza Lorenzo. How can we fail to proclaim our admiration for this distressing prodigy, for these ingenious audio-visual anomalies?

Those who defend dubbing will reason (perhaps) that the objections to it can be brought, similarly, against any other example of translation. This argument ignores, or avoids, the central fault: the arbitrary grafting of another voice and another language. The voice of Hepburn or Garbo is not accidental; it is, for the whole world, one of their defining attributes. Similarly, it is worth remembering that miming is different in English and Spanish.[1]

I have heard that they enjoy dubbing in the provinces. That is a simple argument from authority, and so long as they do not publish the syllogisms of the connoisseurs from Chilecito and Chivilcoy, I, at least, shall not let myself be intimidated. I also hear that people who do not know English find dubbing delightful, or tolerable. My comprehension of English is less perfect than my incomprehension of Russian; nevertheless, I would never resign myself to seeing *Alexander Nevsky* again in any language other than the original, and I would see it eagerly, for the ninth or tenth time, if they showed it in the original version or one that I believed to be the original. This last point is important: worse than dubbing, worse than the substitution that dubbing implies, is the widespread awareness of a substitution, of a deception.

There is no advocate of dubbing who does not wind up invoking predestination and determinism. They swear that this expedient is the result of an inevitable evolution and that soon we will have to choose between seeing dubbed films and not seeing films at all. Given the world-wide decadence of motion pictures – hardly reformed by any single exception such as *The Mask of Demetrios* – the second of these alternatives is not painful. Recent bad pictures – I am thinking of Moscow's *The Diary of a Nazi* and Hollywood's *The Story of Dr Wassell* – prompt us to judge movies as a kind of negative paradise. 'Sightseeing is the art of disappointment,' Stevenson noted. The definition applies to films and, with sad frequency, to that continuous, unavoidable exercise called life.

NOTE

1. More than one spectator asks himself: Since there is usurpation of voices, why not of faces as well? When will the system be perfect? When will we see Juana González directly, in the role of Greta Garbo, in the role of Queen Christina of Sweden?

COLETTE
Black and White

When inventories are drawn up of the century's greatest writers – or even of the century's greatest women writers – the name of Colette tends almost always to be omitted. Charming, chic, stylish, cruel, sensual, ultra-Parisian, whatever – she is not, it seems, a writer automatically thought of as great (maybe because there does not exist in her complete works that single, undeniable masterpiece which everyone 'has to have read'). Yet who nowadays could have composed this beautiful defence – from her collection of articles La Jumelle noire *– of the cinema's specifically monochromatic splendour? And who could have coined so miraculously apt a definition of Hollywood – both Hollywood then (1935) and Hollywood now (1999) – as 'a kindergarten of prodigies?'*

For the record, the little boy whose name she forgets, and whose fame she predicts, was Mickey Rooney.

Let them not come too soon, those colors for which cinema is looking and which it calls the colors of life.

We wait for them without impatience, not yet resigned, after the latest experiments, to the indiscreet clarity, the flat springtime, and the monotony they throw over the deep domain of black and white.

Black, white, their combinations, their infinite contrasts, demonstrate to us every day that they adapt very well to the arbitrary, that is, the intervention of human art. What will become of cinema if it is again reduced to the photographic verisimilitude by which it was dominated until it was able to free itself.

What will happen to the gripping contrast of shadow and light, psychological commentaries of incomparable eloquence? The technique of the color film will not rediscover them except by forcing, by playing tricks with, the colors of nature, which rarely superabounds with polychrome excesses. We already see the necessity of creating a cinematographic palette, which is a betrayal of the natural colors that the laboratories are so avidly seeking . . . Before I have even lost this black and white, my premature regrets and my apprehensions are aroused by the film I saw yesterday.

Max Reinhardt's *Midsummer Night's Dream* unrolled its virgin reels, its kilometers of film, for five or six pairs of eyes. It was a spectacle that for me was not without melancholy. Only two years ago Reinhardt planned to put on *The Dream* at the Théâtre Pigalle and asked me to do a French adaptation of the text. We lacked only backers. Bizarre, delicious evening on which we celebrated our agreement! Over our cooling lobster we exchanged ideas with the aid of the kind interpreter whom our rapid talk kept dinnerless. I admired how the director of *Die Fledermaus* was already able to draw in the air the size of Bottom's ass's-head and to replace Titania with a spiral of smoke . . .

'Yes, yes,' he said, 'we'll keep Mendelssohn . . . Shakespeare, Mendelssohn, they've been together such a long time . . . After fifty years of living together, there are no bad marriages . . .'

The spiral of smoke that symbolized Titania I saw again last night. Around a gigantic tree, the veteran of a clearing, it rose, serving as a highway for all the creatures born of our dreaming when it is at its sweetest and most fruitful, when it turns toward childhood and, enchanted, creates. Reinhardt's imagination, a cinematic technique that admits no obstacles, a luxury that consists in taking time, in beginning again, again, and still again, and a conjunction of diverse efforts have all given birth to a translucent people, elfs in spun glass, a Titania through which one can see, as through arborized agate, ferns and little branches of heath. The white of pearls, the white of milk, the whitish-blue of the full moon, the whited gold of the rising sun . . . Tiny white children, pathetic, with hair of frost; white lightning-bolts like a thousand fires, scattered by the somber Oberon; white of fog that swallows up graceful, imponderable bodies, fleshy petal-white of tuberoses on the body of the last adorable daughter of Night . . . They are too rare, in the cinema, these moments when we are touched simply by the perfect and sufficient harmony of lines, of lights, of the opportunity for silence, movement, and immobility.

It is not my function to make premature criticisms of the troupe of actors to whom Reinhardt has entrusted Shakespeare's text. But my astonishment at the actor playing Puck is my excuse for breaking with the usual conventions. He is a child of twelve, perhaps a little younger. Having seen it yesterday and only briefly, I forget his name, which tomorrow will be famous. Of course, all children are remarkable screen actors.

Hollywood is a kindergarten of prodigies, where the blessed parents take their ease while their progeny, between three and seven years old, assume the responsibility for assuring the family's future. Tiny little France has Robert Lynen, Gaby Triquet, Paulette Elambert . . . But now I'm stupefied to learn that Puck really exists. No mechanical training, no hard schooling, could have taught this faun-child the art of enunciating his words, of understanding the difficult old English, of ennobling its phrases. A miracle of rhythm animates him, sets aflame his small body, his masterless and malicious face, which seems unaware that we are spying on him.

His voice will doubtless sound around the world. It is the true voice of Oberon's forest messenger, a voice that has never battered itself against the walls of human habitation, a voice as raucous as a peacock's call, strong and many-toned. But above all one must hear it as it drones out onomatopoeias that the child has perhaps invented for himself, snuffles of a little boar, chattering of a squirrel, and especially a rising laugh, victorious, impossible to describe, and more savage than all his other sounds.

'If my books had been any worse, I should not have been invited to Hollywood, and if they had been any better, I should not have come'

RAYMOND CHANDLER

CLAUDE OLLIER
A King in New York: *King Kong*

Claude Ollier's essay on Ernest B. Schoedsack's and Merian C. Cooper's
King Kong *initially appeared in* Cahiers du Cinéma *in 1965, when that once prestigious journal hadn't yet forfeited its legendary trenchancy and originality. Although there exists no body of criticism on the rather mysterious Schoedsack,* King Kong *being generally regarded as a miracle, a one-off, a sublime fluke of the system (just as no critic has ever expatiated on Mark Sandrich, director of a series of Astaire–Rogers musicals for whose undimmed enchantment he must have been at least a tiny bit responsible), the movie is an absolute masterpiece, number 11 in many critics' Ten Best lists. And no one has ever written as brilliantly as the novelist Ollier on the terrifying pathos of poor, forlorn and lovelorn Kong, that Quasimodo of the Empire State Building.*

In 1925, the captive brontosaurus brought back from *The Lost World* and exhibited as a fairground attraction in London broke loose from its chains, wrought considerable destruction around Piccadilly Circus and headed for London Bridge, where it slipped, sprawled headlong, and brought the bridge tumbling down under its weight. Six years later, Willis O'Brien, creator of the models and techniques used in these special effects, was asked by Merian C. Cooper (co-director with Ernest Beaumont Schoedsack of *Grass, Chang, The Four Feathers, Rango*, and later producer of some of John Ford's best films) to prepare a series of designs illustrating a project for a film about a giant gorilla. Aided by Mario Larrinaga and Byron L. Crabbe, O'Brien duly produced twelve tableaux likely to have clarified Cooper's ideas.

> The very first sketch showed King Kong on top of the Empire State Building, clutching the girl in his hand and being machine-gunned by the planes. The second showed Kong in the jungle, shaking the tree-trunk in order to throw off the sailors. Then in the third, Kong was beating his breast and defying the sun, with the girl this time at his feet. There were

twelve sketches in all. During shooting, eleven of them were meticulously reproduced in live action sequences.

So the adventure of filming *King Kong* in fact started with its closing sequence. It would be interesting to know in what order the screenwriters who ultimately worked out the details of the action – James Creelman and Ruth Rose (Mrs Schoedsack who, contrary to some reports, was never a stripper) – actually elaborated the episodes. It would not really be surprising if they did in fact work backwards: the most fertile fictions are sometimes born this way, since the very fact of proceeding backwards forces the author, on pain of death, to find an absolutely irrefutable chain of causality (usually finding it fairly quickly, since the 'impossible' links eliminate themselves, as it were); whereas if he proceeds in the supposedly more normal forward direction, the possibilities spread out before him like a fan, much too diffuse to ensure a necessarily healthy growth, and the ineluctability of the plot suffers. The retrospective method, on the other hand, stands a good chance of imposing a self-evident truth, indisputable even though it may conflict with everyday logic and likelihood. The hard facts follow abruptly on each other's heels, driven by some obscure subterranean impulse, and one no more feels the need to query them than the scriptwriter, borne back into the fiction's darker reaches, was at liberty to suppress the gifts of divination forced upon him.

It may be that Creelman and Ruth Rose did in fact proceed in the manner most spectators (and readers) imagine to be the way of sensible screenwriters: going clockwise rather than back-tracking an ineffable course of time. The fact remains that the motifs governing the film are all comprised in O'Brien's initial conception, a veritable blueprint synthesizing the fiction: Beauty, a prized jewel wrested from her doomed social milieu, bearing witness to the mortal combat engaged by mechanized civilization and the gorilla-god of primitive nature (she seems distinctly less terrified than at the 'beginning', and not only, it would seem, because fear exhausts itself through its own expression); the furious Beast, who pathetically defends her rather than himself against the flying machines, since he is shot in the back by the daring US air force Spads while momentarily relaxing his vigilance to check on the safety of his protégée; the theme of the omnipotence of public entertainment, of the commercial interests it involves and consumes to the point of exhaustion or catastrophic (but possibly welcome) disaster; as a corollary to this, the extravagant role played by publicity in the star system, with the prehistoric beast promoted to the status of star revealing itself to be a god of love, and therefore of destruction; finally, and most notably, the elaboration – rendered in concrete form by the presence of the monster on top of a skyscraper – of a parallel between the primitive island and the modern metropolis; one might add, for the record, yet another demonstration of the unshakeable faith of those 'explorers' Cooper and Schoedsack in the cinema's capacity – and calling – to make itself a vehicle for any delirium whatsoever.

Product or not of a backwards logic exploding from that grandiose image, the script for *King Kong*, which combines three celebrated tales – *The Sorcerer's Apprentice, Beauty and the Beast* and *The Lost World* – is uncommonly rich in its implications. It is rather disconcerting to see how, in describing this masterpiece of symmetry, even the most laudatory critics of thirty years ago used the term 'infantile' which can still be heard from the mouths of many a favourable spectator today. (In that autumn of 1933, of course, when the Place Clichy was dominated by an enormous pasteboard Kong covering the façade of the Gaumont-Palace, French audiences were deprived of the film's opening reel, happily now restored for their admiration in the current reissue.) At first glance the narrative is doubtless not the most remarkable aspect of this remarkable movie. The power of *King Kong* of course drives primarily from a visual splendour unequalled in the genre, from the brilliance of its oneiric imagery, and from a capacity for erotic suggestion astonishing enough to have caused generations of schoolgirls to fall for the great ape, protective perhaps, but terrifying to say the least.

The workings of this plot nevertheless deserve further examination. What, to begin with, is it about? It's about a compleat *auteur* (backer, producer, scriptwriter, cameraman, director) preparing to set out once more for virgin territories to film another of the never-before-seen spectacles which have made his name. The originality of this *mise en abîme* derives from the fact that it is surrounded with the same atmosphere of secrecy as the story of the actual voyage: to the unforeseen – relatively foreseen – of the film to be shot is added an unforeseen element through the parsimonious details offered concerning the second story. There is of course an obvious motive for this precaution: if the crew knew what awaited them at the end of the voyage, they would probably never sign on. But more particularly, this process of gradual, grudging revelation adds to the overall feeling of an 'adventure movie'.

And in so doing it also offers an opportunity to clarify certain facts or to hint with delightful anticipation at things to come. If, for example, that daredevil of celluloid Carl Denham has involved a girl in one of his productions for the first time, it is because the critics – and therefore the public – have earnestly demanded that he freshen his formula by adding sex to the exoticism. The project in hand is to a large extent, therefore, a response to collective demand. Moreover, the circumstances in which Denham himself comes ashore to pick his female star off the streets are not left to chance: what attracts his attention is a piercing cry, provoked by an act of aggression as the fruit-vendor brutally grabs his victim. Around this voice, potentially a shriek of anguish, the mystery of our dual suspense is polarized; a mystery which Denham does not dissipate until they are lying off the island. Naturally he has a scenario in mind, or rather an outline singularly modern in conception since he envisages, within a set framework and with certain given data – an unexplored land, a primitive people, a young American woman, a legendary creature neither man nor beast and in essence seemingly divine – very sizeable unstable areas in which complete improvisation will reign. The theme chosen is that of Madame Leprince de Beaumont's celebrated tale; in detail, scenes will depend on what happens during shooting. Like some Rouch of prehistory hatching a monstrous psychodrama, Denham puts the time spent at sea to good use by fashioning his Beauty: a costume specially designed for the role, exercises in mime, voice tests in the higher registers, a conditioning to fear. As for the Beast, he will direct it as best he can, backed up by gas grenades. Note the classic mythic nature of the island: the Norwegian sailor who passed on the map had never seen it himself; it was a native, survivor of a shipwreck, who told him about it. The ritual elements of the late nineteenth-century adventure yarn, along with its earnest tone, the sense of leisureliness, the naive and slightly fusty tone, are also scrupulously preserved: a storm to be outrun, a course deviating from normal shipping routes, an uneasy captain, a restive crew, clammy heat, torpor, fogs and reefs. But the island does indeed exist, and so does Kong, whose name echoes in the ears of the sailors like some vague memory rooted in the mists of time.

The first day's shooting exceeds all expectations the heir to the Scandinavian 'discoverer' may have cherished. Very soon overtaken by events more cinematic than he could ever have dared hope (the natives seize his leading lady and take over the *mise en scène*), deprived of the initiative but wrestling it back through strong-arm tactics, Denham substitutes the spectacle itself for an exotic film spectacular, subjugating the monster and shipping it aboard with the intention of exhibiting it in New York along with the heroes who captured it – one of the rare instances in which the spectacle itself is likely to be more impressive than a record of it on film. Like Denham, we have had our fill as far as adventure is concerned. But there is another way of telling the story with equal fidelity: an inveterate speculator, spurred by the unprecedented economic depression that is shaking his country to its foundations, realizes that he must stage an absolutely extraordinary show to stave off the crisis. Leaving the country – where the authorities, faced with a grave, unforeseen peril, have responded with neither a coherent plan nor any effort towards a fundamental revision of the system, leaving the hapless populace trembling before the spectre of poverty – he sails to an unknown, almost entirely virgin island whose primitive inhabitants are similarly exposed to a terrible menace, permanent in this case, indeed virtually eternal, but who have come to terms with it in a form of exchange that seems to have worked hitherto to everybody's satisfaction. Intoxicated by the scent of profit, totally failing to recognize the native wisdom which he treats with the contempt befitting an honest white racist, he manages within a record time – like the foolish merchant of the fairytale who sets too little store by Beauty – not only to bring terrible deaths upon several of his companions, but to destroy the delicate balance set up by the local witch-doctors. Roused and despoiled through his foolish intervention, the monstrous creature shatters the age-old ramparts and lays waste to the village.

Even this is not enough for Denham. Still driven by his contemptible purpose, he mobilizes the resources of technology in order to ship the gigantic, vengeful creature to his own country, thereby unthinkingly placing the life and property of many of his compatriots at risk. Only the very latest weaponry enables him to lay the bogey. So, through the fault of one of its own citizens desperately seeking a constructive solution, the menace hovering over the New World, hitherto on a human scale, is now reinforced and redoubled by a much more terrible threat from nature, superhuman, enigmatic, in defiance of reason, a retaliation by savage forces which inevitably looms as a function: it is contact with a tainted, unjust society, degrading to the individual, that drives Nature in all its 'horror' and long-forgotten bestiality to intervene and try to rescue the only being worth saving from the chaos that threatens her and which it destroys. The element of provocation is vitally important here: it was the white man who broke the pact by taking back the proffered sacrifice. To ignore the laws of Nature – or to animate and violate them – is to unleash a cataclysm.

Setting aside the social and moral implications of a second half in which the themes and their figurations combine and interweave so as to 'reconstitute' the ultimate vision of the gorilla – dominating the city over which it brandishes the threat of sovereign retribution – in all its original simplicity, let us consider two spatial locations equated by a 'puerile' script of remarkable complexity. The topography of the island, for a start: Skull Island seems very similar to all those imaginary islands in the shape of hemispheres, skulls or inverted teacups – like the Back Cup of *Facing the Flag*, admirably animated by Karel Zeman in *The Fabulous World of Jules Verne*, who draws his inspiration from the steel engravings by Roux for the Hetzel collected edition of Verne. Here, a narrow peninsula extends to the foot of a huge mountain, exactly like the tip of Manhattan beneath the skyscrapers. An ingenious native tribe survives as best it can in the lowlands close by the dreaded barrier, just as the civilized population swarms round buildings where the powers-that-be sport with and mysteriously control its destiny. But in both cases the bulwark ensuring security and prosperity eventually gives way; even the razing of the main gateway in the barrier has its symbolic echo in the unthinkable 'contemporary' catastrophe of the Wall Street Crash which blew the financial floodgates wide open. In each case the equilibrium is destroyed, the only difference being that for the people of New York the two dangers are cumulative, while it is a white man who sounds the alarm going to summon help from black natives he has just accused of cowardice and for whose deaths he is responsible. Once stirred up and let loose, King Kong rather unfairly attacks black or white without distinction. The whites admittedly rid the island of his presence, but did not Kong also rid it of giant beasts on occasion? All that is left for the natives to do is to bury their dead and rebuild the gateway before the real monsters, the truly vile and bestial ones with whom no pact is possible, can breach it in their turn.

A parallel is thus drawn between two jungles. Thanks to virtuoso special effects reaching a peak of skill and sumptuousness here, the jungle of Skull Island – created out of models, transparencies, articulated armatures and stop motion photography – transfers its oneiric power of suggestion to that other more modern island, made up largely of very real views of New York. This way in which the fantastic spreads by contamination from one world to the other of course constitutes the film's prime source of power. But there is another, relating to the laws governing each of these worlds, which deserves some attention. Students of market values would certainly find matters worthy of analysis here.

Against her will, the heroine Ann Darrow puts each of them to the test: as a token for barter (initially almost worthless, relatively valuable as soon as Denham hires her), she finds herself promoted to current coinage by the natives of Skull Island. Then another promotion: in King Kong's hand she becomes the object of a love cult. Rescued by Denham, her stock goes down a couple of points but her exchange rate soars vertiginously. By reclaiming her and placing her out of reach of his money-grubbing peers, Kong saves her from a degrading 'fetishization': the wrath of god is explained as much by the theft practised on him as by the disrespectful attitude of the theatre audience to the couple starring in the drama. Ann's turbulent fate is thus closely linked to the conditions of life prevailing in her social group: in triumph as in terror it is exemplary, and this is what the shrill modulations of her scream express throughout. 'Your only hope is to scream,' Denham tells her on the boat. From the very outset this scream predestines her to rape, and the misadventures of Ann in *King Kong* prefigure those of another similarly predestined American heroine, the Melanie Daniels of *The Birds*. The link between individual and collective destinies, through progressive amplification and eventual generalization, is continually established in both films: Melanie conjures the birds to attack, as Ann does with the gorilla; in her wake, first the limited group, then society in general and the entire country become prey to destruction. The famous 'overlong' opening to *The Birds* corresponds exactly to the first part of *King Kong*, where nothing uncanny happens, nothing but progressive tremors of apprehension in the 'chosen one' rapidly communicating themselves to ever widening social circles. In *King Kong*, the retracing of the heroine's past, which served as the object of investigation and analysis in *The Birds*, is elided and condensed into Ann's scream, into that exceptional faculty she possesses for expressing terror which brings her to Denham's attention, just as Mitch is drawn to Melanie on the strength of her 'innocent' little machinations. This said, New York is saved from destruction, Denham pronounces his funeral oration over the body of the vanquished beast, and he has the final word, whereas Hitchcock's screen remained occupied by thousands of winged creatures, menacing, observing a truce between two attacks.

But the prosperous America of 1963 could afford to indulge an ending fraught with uncertainty and danger; the America of 1931, the year in which *King Kong* was conceived, could not dispense with the happy ending. (Not until the year of *The Birds*, 1963, could one see New York obliterated by the US President's own hand: the *ne plus ultra* of a screenwriter's daring in a time of fatted calves.)

But to return to Ann's nightmare. With the lights of New York echoing the torches of Skull Island, all the scenes in which blonde Fay Wray (delightful Mitzi in *The Wedding March*, Eve Trowbridge in *The Most Dangerous Game*) changes masters – one eye licentious, the other apprehensive – take place at night: Denham carrying her off, her seizure by the natives, Kong first taking possession of her from the sacrificial altar, then again as a prelude to his irresistible climb up the skyscraper. The one exception is when Driscoll reclaims her during the fight between Kong and the pterodactyl (or pteranodon?), concluding a non-stop series of clashes which constitute the acute phase of the experience. Interposed at this point are two vertical plunges, perhaps one of the best devices the cinema has seized on to express the phenomenon of temporary relief as nightmare fades: the climb down the providential creeper, then the vertiginous plunge into the water incredibly far below. Terror dissolves, crystallizes, dissolves again in admirably interwoven sequence, resolved in Ann's sinuous flight, her hair flying free and her body relaxed for the first time since the start of this terrible series of convulsions and battles to the death. (The fall from the clifftop is worth comparing to certain perspectives of flight featured in Norman Z. McLeod's *Alice in Wonderland*, made in the same year.)

Another sequence communicates one of the most hallucinatory sensations of incredulity ever seen on the screen. This is the one in which a helpless and terrified Ann, having fallen from the treetop where Kong had placed her for safety, looks on as her protector and the tyrannosaurus fight to the death. Here a slight difference in shading between the foreground shots involving Ann and the middle distance where the monsters are battling away contradicts the impression of proximity sufficiently to cast doubts as to the distance that really separates the two locations. The brutes are indeed close by since they batter several times against the now uprooted tree-trunk, yet their confrontation (in medium long shot) is taking place at a problematic, 'unthinkable' distance. Ann's terror derives equally from the immediate vicinity of the spectacle (and the intense danger that implies) and from a suspicion one senses growing in her as to the reality of what is happening. (If, moreover, there were any 'everyday' logic to the affair, it would surely be quickly snuffed out by the staggeringly terrible punishment the combatants inflict on each other.) But at this point the 'splitting' of the action is obvious. To a large extent Ann is attending her own nightmare. A similar though less evident sense of dislocation hovers almost constantly over the fight scenes: for instance in the overly speeded-up motion of the brontosaurus which emerges from the swamps and pursues the sailors through the jungle. Here several effects of different origin combine as they come into play: the more or less visible ruptures in depth shots achieved by multiple printing, the rupturing transition from long shot to medium shot of Kong (or indeed that extraordinary dolly in to his enraged features), and above all the jerky movements caused in filming frame by frame. One can see how even the defects, certain imperfections or slight lapses in perception of movement, far from destroying or lessening the credibility of what we see, in fact contribute to the sense of overwhelming oneirism, so true is it that the world of dreams is one of spatial effects, optical dislocations, sequential breaks and general discontinuity. Together, the 'dubious' space created by O'Brien's in-depth montages and the need to film in fragmented motion compose a visual universe which perfectly realizes the 'collage' effect basic to any nightmare vision: stippled space and stippled time, gaps, fringes, overlaps and incompatibilities in action, zones of imponderable duration, into which apprehensions of unreality tumble headlong. In the same way, the occasional errors in proportional scale noticeable here and there between Kong and his surroundings also add to the radical compartmentalizations characteristic of dreams, where the relative sizes of people and objects are constantly evolving. (It is a pity that a scene in which the sailors hurled into the precipice were devoured by giant spiders – and which was shot – was not retained in the final cut, apparently at the film-makers' own wish.)

From a purely visual point of view, O'Brien's creations – both on paper and on film – have a strange, sumptuous, pullulating beauty: this jungle, comprising vegetation that is geographically unlikely and animals more legendary than scientifically prehistoric, stems directly from engravings inspired by several centuries of adventure stories. In the scene involving the underground lake, for example, one finds the same chiaroscuro as in many an illustration for Jules Verne or Paul d'Ivoi (a very similar lake, for instance, where the hero, hunted and taking refuge in a grotto, had to tackle a giant octopus single-handed and in total silence since his enemies were prowling nearby). In certain compositions involving rocky escarpments, the affinity with Gustave Doré is obvious. We know, too, that the painting of Skull Island reproduces Arnold Böcklin's celebrated 'Isle of the Dead': a few years earlier, Fritz Lang had similarly used elements from three Böcklin paintings for two sequences in his *Die Nibelungen*. As for the animation of the King of the Jungle, secrecy continues to shroud the various techniques used simultaneously or by turns. The character is so indubitably driven by a vital spark of life – one might almost say of humanity – that it is difficult to disabuse spectators, impressed by his magnificent demeanour and movement, of the notion – totally unfounded – that the role of Kong was played by a human being. Finally, in so far as cruelty is concerned, horror in its whole gamut of dark, basic sensations (suffocation, oppression, vertigo, pulverization, burial, ingestion, sinking, strangulation, dismemberment), the film offers many terrible, matchless displays: witness the image of an enormous paw with hooked claws carefully crushing an unfortunate black into the spongy mire.

King Kong, a masterpiece of the fantastic and certainly one of the finest and most disturbing examples ever made, recalls a period in cinema when every true audacity was permitted and often inscribed on the screen. There can be no doubt that it owes its resounding success to the competence and cohesion of an exceptional team of film-makers. The heart of the matter probably lies less there, however, than in the source of inspiration on which that team chose to draw. Through literature, painting and engraving, O'Brien and his collaborators revived a rich tradition of illustrated myths and legends, and this is certainly the direction to follow in preference to the sort of breathless leap into some pseudo-atomic science fiction instanced most recently at its lowest ebb by the drearily ugly *Goldfinger*. One regret, perhaps: that the scriptwriters did not faithfully follow the story Denham had intended to film to its conclusion. Another possible happy ending would have lifted crucial doubts as to the Beast's other guise, a mystery that remains shrouded. How would Kong have looked if, in those last moments, Ann had loved him?

RENÉ CLAIR
An Inquiry

It is possible to imagine that cinematic special effects might for once be deployed by a genuine auteur, an artist of the first water, to personal, autobiographical and unpopulist ends. And it is possible, too, to imagine one way at least in which they could be so deployed. Think of such an auteur filming himself (or, of course, herself) this year, instigating one half of a conversation (about what? That would be up to him); then waiting another 20 years before filming his older self engaging, across the millennial abyss, in the other half of the same conversation; then invisibly stitching the two halves together. Now that would *be a special effect.*

Here, from René Clair's book Reflections on the Cinema, *published in 1953, is precisely that fantasy. Naturally, as Clair realized, the most appropriate subject for such a tête-à-tête* would *be the cinema itself.*

If you are prepared to believe that it is possible to take a stroll into the past, I should like to go back to the spring of 1923, and to appear as I am now, burdened with a good many superfluous years, in the Champs-Elysées of that period where the magnificent chestnuts have not yet given place to the meagre planes of today.

Making my way along the Avenue Montaigne, among passers-by unmoved by the anachronism of my appearance, I reach the cul-de-sac on the Théâtre des Champs Elysées side. I open a glass-panelled door, walk up some cement steps with an iron rail, and stop on the third floor. There, in a kind of triangular cupboard striving to pass as an office, I find a thin young man busy correcting proofs.

I: I presume you're René Clair?

THE YOUNG MAN: Yes, that's me.

Let us now imagine that the two get into conversation, and I ask the young man what he thinks of the cinema in 1923. The young man, with the grim assurance possible only at that age, replies without a moment's hesitation:

'The cinema is too young and too imperfect to satisfy us if it remains static. As soon as it stops advancing it seems to go backwards.'

RC 1950: What exactly do you mean by 'cinema'? That's a word which in the future will probably be open to many interpretations.

RC 1923: It is words we must get rid of. If things are not improving, it is because we don't make a clean sweep. 'Cinema' is what cannot be told in words. But just try and explain that to people spoilt by thirty centuries of chatter – poetry, novels, plays. You would have to begin by giving them back the eyes of a savage, or of a child watching a Punch and Judy show, who is less interested by the story than by the hail of blows.

RC 1950: Right. But while we're waiting for the unlikely fulfilment of that dream, would you say that there's any cause for despair?

RC 1923: In my optimistic moments I admit that the cinema seems to be endowed with a remarkably healthy constitution. Everything has been done to stifle it from birth, and yet it has grown, and will go on growing. It will eventually grow into something monstrous, a kind of deformed giant, to the astonishment of those who were so anxious to keep it in baby clothes. Of course, when I say 'cinema', I am not speaking of the film industry, which seems to be going from bad to worse, thanks to the parasites and crooks who feed on it (together with a few well-meaning but naïve enthusiasts). I am speaking of the cinema as a means of expression, or, if you like, as a means of teaching us to appreciate silence. Just think of it: we actually began by filming theatre plays, in theatre sets, with theatre actors in their red make-up which turned them into negroes. And then thousands of novels, *written* books, were adapted to the art of moving images. And even in our time we have preaching, moralizing films, we have films with a message, and we are threatened by coloured films and three-dimensional films. As though the things surrounding us and our whole existence were so pretty that we must reproduce them at all costs exactly as they are.

But, for all that, the cinema is not dead. Its vitality is amazing. No doubt, Providence wishes to make up to us for the delights of modern living – five-year wars, destruction by remote control, bankruptcy, taxes, poverty, flu and stock-exchange speculations – and perhaps for an even more delightful future, by giving us a universal toy to play with and taking care that we don't smash it.

RC 1950: Please don't talk about war and destruction through remote control: you might make me believe you're a good prophet. I'd rather you told me what we should do to help the cinema fulfil its destiny.

RC 1923: The public should be sent to a school where nothing is taught. A school of unlearning, or more exactly a vacuum-cleaning establishment. There, my dear millions of friends, your minds would be cleared of all rubbish, of the waste of out-of-date literature, of the artistic sedatives you have absorbed from childhood, which prevent you looking at the world and at a work of art with an individual eye, and crush your primitive sensitivity to such an extent that you are no longer capable of emitting a cry of ecstasy, except in certain familiar and exactly predictable circumstances. Wastes of literature: Michel Zévaco, Stendhal, Mallarmé, *Jeudi de la Jeunesse*, parliamentary speeches, and so on and so forth. Such things (depending on your taste and the education you received) dance before your eyes and blur your vision. What the cinema asks of you is to learn to S E E.

RC 1950: It would be difficult to take this kind of *mystique* of the cinema any further. The tone of your pronouncements, so in keeping with the fashion of your time, is both inspired and provocative – for, surely, your real motive in attacking Stendhal and Mallarmé is merely to show that you will not stop at any sacrifice?

RC 1923 (who prefers not to hear this last remark): If I could teach you to forget I would turn you into fine, simple savages. In front of the screen, at first entirely blank, you would marvel at elementary visions: a leaf, a hand, water, an ear; then a tree, a human body, a river, a face; after that, wind in the leaves, a man walking, a river flowing, simple facial expressions. In the second year, you would solve visual puzzles. You would be taught the rudiments of a provisional syntax. You would learn to guess the meaning of various successions of images, as a child or a foreigner, little by little, finds out the meaning of the sounds he hears. And after several years, or, perhaps, several generations (I'm not a prophet), you would have learned to accept the rules of a visual convention as practical as the verbal one, and no more exacting.

RC 1950: And after that?

RC 1923: After that we'd invent something else. Perhaps a tactile, or an olfactory convention.

RC 1950 (who remembers in time that the young people of 1923 were inclined to be aggressively humorous when they spoke of the things they felt most deeply about): So your intention is to create, through the medium of cinema, a new language, a sort of visual esperanto, and so to escape from the 'old slavery of words'? This hope, I must admit, is not devoid of grandeur, even though one day it may raise a smile. But to come back to the present . . .

RC 1923: Even at present, we should learn to take from every film what we like. Admittedly, the bad taste of the majority of both spectators and film makers necessarily involves both bad literature and gross sentimentality. And as the film industry would not be able to survive if it ignored the majority we must learn, on occasion, to shut our eyes.

RC 1950: Spectators do not demand anything. Sooner or later you will realize that they are children, ready to accept whatever they are shown as long as it is entertaining: sometimes it's rubbish, and sometimes a masterpiece. Are not the great successes of our day Chaplin's and Douglas Fairbank's films?

RC 1923: We should not expect a masterpiece every time. We ought to be content, sometimes, to let ourselves be carried away on a stream of images. Thirty seconds of pure cinema in a film lasting one hour should be sufficient to keep hope alive. If we ignore the absurdity of the plot – which, after all, is only a pretext – and abandon ourselves to the charm of flowing images, we shall be able to enjoy a new pleasure. A moving landscape. A hand. The prow of a boat. A woman's smile. Three trees in the sky . . . Don't tell me what they mean according to the arbitrary laws of your language. It is enough to see them, to enjoy their harmony and their contrasts. Let us learn how to look at what is in front of us. Words have assumed too much importance. We know most word combinations by heart. But we have eyes and still don't see.

CESARE ZAVATTINI
Some Ideas on the Cinema

The principal articles of faith underpinning the ethos of Italian neo-realism ought to be familiar to every cinéphile: the insistence on shooting on actual locations rather than in the studio; the use of non-professional performers; the focus on the (by the cinema) far too often neglected social strata of the working-class poor and the unemployed. The move-ment itself, launched in 1942 by Luchino Visconti's Ossessione *(a free, and unpaid-for, adaptation of James M. Cain's* The Postman Always Rings Twice*), and brought both to artistic fruition and international prominence by Roberto Rossellini's* Roma Città Aperta *in 1945, not only added a cluster of masterpieces to the cinema's history but had an incalculable influence on filmmaking practices around the world – including in Hollywood.*

Cesare Zavattini, one of the founders of neorealism, the screenwriter of Vittorio De Sica's Shoeshine, Bicycle Thieves *and* Umberto D, *was also its most significant theoretician. This article, originally published in* Sight and Sound, *was based on an interview that he granted to the Italian film journal* La Rivista del Cinema Italiano.

No doubt one's first and most superficial reaction to everyday reality is that it is tedious. Until we are able to overcome some moral and intellectual laziness, in fact, this reality will continue to appear uninteresting. One shouldn't be astonished that the cinema has always felt the natural, unavoidable necessity to insert a 'story' in the reality to make it exciting and 'spectacular'. All the same, it is clear that such a method evades a direct approach to everyday reality, and suggests that it cannot be portrayed without the intervention of fantasy or artifice.

The most important characteristic, and the most important innovation, of what is called neo-realism, it seems to me, is to have realised that the necessity of the 'story' was only an unconscious way of disguising a human defeat, and that the kind of imagination it involved was simply a technique of superimposing dead formulas over living social facts.

Now it has been perceived that reality is hugely rich, that to be able to look directly at it is enough; and that the artist's task is not to make people moved or indignant at metaphorical situations, but to make them reflect (and, if you like, to be moved and indignant too) on what they and others are doing, on the real things, exactly as they are.

For me this has been a great victory. I would like to have achieved it many years earlier. But I made the discovery only at the end of the war. It was a moral discovery, an appeal to order. I saw at last what lay in front of me, and I understood that to have evaded reality had been to betray it.

Example: Before this, if one was thinking over the idea of a film on, say, a strike, one was immediately forced to invent a plot. And the strike itself became only the background to the film. Today, our attitude would be one of 'revelation': we would describe the strike itself, try to work out the largest possible number of human, moral, social, economic, poetic values from the bare documentary fact.

We have passed from an unconsciously rooted mistrust of reality, an illusory and equivocal evasion, to an unlimited trust in things, facts and people. Such a position requires us, in effect, to excavate reality, to give it a power, a communication, a series of reflexes, which until recently we had never thought it had. It requires, too, a true and real interest in what is happening, a search for the most deeply hidden human values; which is why we feel that the cinema must recruit not only intelligent people, but, above all, 'living' souls, the morally richest people.

The cinema's overwhelming desire to see, to analyse, its hunger for reality, is an act of concrete homage towards other people, towards what is happening and existing in the world. And, incidentally, it is what distinguishes 'neo-realism' from the American cinema.

In fact, the American position is the antithesis of our own; while we are interested in the reality around us and want to know it directly, reality in American films is unnaturally filtered, 'purified', and comes out at one or two removes. In America, lack of subjects for films causes a crisis, but with us such a crisis is impossible. One cannot be short of themes while there is still plenty of reality. Any hour of the day, any place, any person, is a subject for narrative if the narrator is capable of observing and illuminating all these collective elements by exploring their interior value.

So there is no question of a crisis of subjects, only of their interpretation. This substantial difference was nicely emphasised by a well-known

American producer when he told me: 'This is how *we* would imagine a scene with an aeroplane. The plane passes by . . . a machine-gun fires . . . the plane crashes. . . . And this is how *you* would imagine it. The plane passes by. . . . The plane passes by again . . . the plane passes by once more . . .' He was right. But we have still not gone far enough. It is not enough to make the aeroplane pass by three times: we must make it pass by twenty times.

What effects on narrative, then, and on the portrayal of human character, has the neo-realistic style produced?

To begin with, while the cinema used to make one situation produce another situation, and another, and another, again and again, and each scene was thought out and immediately related to the next (the natural result of a mistrust of reality), today, when we have thought out a scene, we feel the need to 'remain' in it, because the single scene itself can contain so many echoes and reverberations, can even contain all the situations we may need. Today, in fact, we can quietly say: give us whatever 'fact' you like, and we will disembowel it, make it something worth watching.

While the cinema used to portray life in its most visible and external moments – and a film was usually only a series of situations selected and linked together with varying success – today the neo-realistic affirms that each one of these situations, rather than all the external moments, contains in itself enough material for a film.

Example: In most films, the adventures of two people looking for somewhere to live, for a house, would be shown externally in a few moments of action, but for us it could provide the scenario for a whole film, and we would explore all its echoes, all its implications.

Of course, we are still a long way from a true analysis of human situations, and one can speak of analysis only in comparison with the dull synthesis of most current production. We are, rather, still in an 'attitude' of analysis; but in this attitude there is a strong purpose, a desire for understanding, for belonging, for participating – for living together, in fact.

Substantially, then, the question today is, instead of turning imaginary situations into 'reality' and trying to make them look 'true', to make things as they are, almost by themselves, create their own special significance. Life is not what is invented in 'stories'; life is another matter. To understand it involves a minute, unrelenting, and patient search.

Here I must bring in another point of view. I believe that the world goes on getting worse because we are not truly aware of reality. The most authentic position anyone can take up today is to engage himself in tracing the roots of this problem. The keenest necessity of our time is 'social attention'.

Attention, though, to what is there, *directly*: not through an apologue, however well conceived. A starving man, a humiliated man, must be shown by name and surname; no fable for a starving man, because that is something else, less effective and less moral. The true function of the cinema is not to tell fables, and to a true function we must recall it.

Of course, reality can be analysed by ways of fiction. Fictions can be expressive and natural; but neo-realism, if it wants to be worthwhile, must sustain the moral impulse that characterised its beginnings, in an analytical documentary way. No other medium of expression has the cinema's original and innate capacity for showing things, that we believe worth showing, as they happen day by day – in what we might call their 'dailiness', their longest and truest duration. The cinema has everything in front of it, and no other medium has the same possibilities for getting it known quickly to the greatest number of people.

As the cinema's responsibility also comes from its enormous power, it should try to make every frame of film count, by which I mean that it should penetrate more and more into the manifestations and the essence of reality.

The cinema only affirms its moral responsibility when it approaches reality in this way.

The moral, like the artistic, problem lies in being able to observe reality, not to extract fictions from it.

Naturally, some film-makers, although they realise the problem, have still been compelled, for a variety of reasons (some valid, others not) to 'invent' stories in the traditional manner, and to incorporate in these stories some fragments of their real intuition. This, effectively, has served as neo-realism for some film-makers in Italy.

For this reason, the first endeavour was often to reduce the story to its most elementary, simple, and, I would rather say, banal form. It was the beginning of a speech that was later interrupted. *Bicycle Thieves* provides a typical example. The child follows his father along the street; at one moment, the child is nearly run over, but the father does not even notice. This episode was 'invented', but with the intention of communicating an everyday fact about these people's lives, a little fact

– so little that the protagonists don't even care about it – but full of life.

In fact *Paisà, Open City, Sciuscià, Bicycle Thieves, La Terra Trema*, all contain elements of an absolute significance – they reflect the idea that everything can be recounted; but their sense remains metaphorical, because there is still an invented story, not the documentary spirit. In other films, such as *Umberto D*, reality as an analysed fact is much more evident, but the presentation is still traditional.

We have not yet reached the centre of neo-realism. Neo-realism today is an army ready to start; and there are the soldiers – behind Rossellini, De Sica, Visconti. The soldiers have to go into the attack and win the battle.

We must recognise that all of us are still only starting, some farther on, others farther behind. But it is still something. The great danger today is to abandon that position, the moral position implicit in the work of many of us during and immediately after the war.

A woman is going to buy a pair of shoes. Upon this elementary situation it is possible to build a film. All we have to do is to discover and then show all the elements that go to create this adventure, in all their banal 'dailiness', and it will become worthy of attention, it will even become 'spectacular'. But it will become spectacular not through its exceptional, but through its *normal* qualities; it will astonish us by showing so many things that happen every day under our eyes, things we have never noticed before.

The result would not be easy to achieve. It would require an intensity of human vision both from the creator of the film and from the audience. The question is: how to give human life its historical importance at every minute.

In life, in reality today, there are no more empty spaces. Between things, facts, people, exists such an interdependence that a blow struck for the cinema in Rome could have repercussions all over the world. If this is true, it must be worthwhile to take any moment of a human life and show how 'striking' that moment is: to excavate and identify it, to send its echo vibrating into other parts of the world.

This is as valid for poverty as for peace. For peace, too, the human moment should not be a great one, but an ordinary daily happening. Peace is usually the sum of small happenings, all having the same moral implications at their roots.

It is not only a question, however, of creating a film that makes its audience understand a social or a collective situation. People understand themselves better than the social fabric; and to see themselves on the screen, performing their daily actions – remembering that to see oneself gives one the sense of being unlike oneself – like hearing one's own voice on the radio – can help them to fill up a void, a lack of knowledge of reality.

If this love for reality, for human nature directly observed, must still adapt itself to the necessities of the cinema as it is now organised, must yield, suffer and wait, it means that the cinema's capitalist structure still has a tremendous influence over its true function. One can see this in the growing opposition in many places to the fundamental motives of neo-realism, the main results of which are a return to so-called 'original' subjects, as in the past, and the consequent evasion of reality, and a number of bourgeois accusations against neo-realist principles.

The main accusation is: *neo-realism only describes poverty.* But neo-realism can and must face poverty. We have begun with poverty for the simple reason that it is one of the most vital realities of our time, and I challenge anyone to prove the contrary. To believe, or to pretend to believe, that by making half a dozen films on poverty we have finished with the problem, would be a great mistake. As well believe that, if you have to plough up a whole country, you can sit down after the first acre.

The theme of poverty, of rich and poor, is something one can dedicate one's whole life to. We have just begun. We must have the courage to explore all the details. If the rich turn up their noses especially at *Miracolo a Milano*, we can only ask them to be a little patient. *Miracolo a Milano* is only a fable. There is still much more to say. I put myself among the rich, not only because I have some money (which is only the most apparent and immediate aspect of wealth), but because I am also in a position to create oppression and justice. That is the moral (or immoral) position of the so-called rich man.

When anyone (he could be the audience, the director, the critic, the State, or the Church) says, 'Stop the poverty,' i.e. stop the films about poverty, he is committing a moral sin. He is refusing to understand, to learn. And when he refuses to learn, consciously or not, he is evading reality. The evasion springs from lack of courage, from fear. (One should make a film on this subject, showing at what point we begin to evade reality in the face of disquieting facts, at what point we begin to sweeten it.)

If I were not afraid of being thought irreverent, I should say that Christ, had He a camera in His hand, would not shoot fables, however wonderful, but would show us the good ones and the bad ones of this world – in actuality, giving us close-ups of those who make their neighbours' bread too bitter, and of their victims, if the censor allowed it.

To say that we have had 'enough' films about poverty suggests that one can measure reality with a chronometer. In fact, it is not simply a question of choosing the theme of poverty, but of going on to explore and analyse the poverty. What one needs is more and more knowledge, precise and simple, of human needs and the motives governing them. Neo-realism should ignore the chronometer and go forward for as long as is necessary.

Neo-realism, it is also said, *does not offer solutions. The end of a neo-realist film is particularly inconclusive.* I cannot accept this at all. With regard to my own work, the characters and situations in films for which I have written the scenario, they remain unresolved from a practical point of view simply because 'this is reality'. But every moment of the film is, in itself, a continuous answer to some question. It is not the concern of an artist to propound solutions. It is enough, and quite a lot, I should say, to make an audience feel the need, the urgency, for them.

In any case, what films *do* offer solutions? 'Solutions' in this sense, if they are offered, are sentimental ones, resulting from the superficial way in which problems have been faced. At least, in my work I leave the solution to the audience.

The fundamental emotion of *Miracolo a Milano* is not one of escape (the flight at the end), but of indignation, a desire for solidarity with certain people, a refusal of it with others. The film's structure is intended to suggest that there is a great gathering of the humble ones against the others. But the humble ones have no tanks, or they would have been ready to defend their land and their huts.

The true neo-realistic cinema is, of course, less expensive than the cinema at present. Its subjects can be expressed cheaply, and it can dispense with capitalist resources on the present scale. The cinema has not yet found its morality, its necessity, its quality, precisely because it costs too much; being so conditional, it is much less an art than it could be.

The cinema should never turn back. It should accept, unconditionally, what is contemporary. *Today, today, today.*

It must tell reality as if it were a story; there must be no gap between life and what is on the screen. To give an example:

A woman goes to a shop to buy a pair of shoes. The shoes cost 7,000 lire. The woman tries to bargain. The scene lasts, perhaps, two minutes. I must make a 2-hour film. What do I do?

I analyse the fact in all its constituent elements, in its 'before', in its 'after', in its contemporaneity. The fact creates its own fiction, in its own particular sense.

The woman is buying the shoes. What is her son doing at the same moment? What are people doing in India that could have some relation to this fact of the shoes? The shoes cost 7,000 lire. How did the woman happen to have 7,000 lire? How hard did she work for them, what do they represent for her?

And the bargaining shopkeeper, who is he? What relationship has developed between these two human beings? What do they mean, what interests are they defending, as they bargain? The shopkeeper also has two sons, who eat and speak: do you want to know what they are saying? Here they are, in front of you . . .

The question is, to be able to fathom the real correspondences between facts and their process of birth, to discover what lies beneath them.

Thus to analyse 'buying a pair of shoes' in such a way opens to us a vast and complex world, rich in importance and values, in its practical, social, economic, psychological motives. Banality disappears because each moment is really charged with responsibility. Every moment is infinitely rich. Banality never really existed.

Excavate, and every little fact is revealed as a mine. If the gold-diggers come at last to dig in the illimitable mine of reality, the cinema will become socially important.

This can also be done, evidently, with invented characters; but if I use living, real characters with which to sound reality, people in whose life I can directly participate, my emotion becomes more effective, morally stronger, more useful. Art must be expressed through a true name and surname, not a false one.

I am bored to death with heroes more or less imaginary. I want to meet the real protagonist of everyday life, I want to see how he is made, if he has a moustache or not, if he is tall or short, I want to see his eyes, and I want to speak to him.

We can look at him on the screen with the same anxiety, the same curiosity as when, in a square, seeing a crowd of people all hurrying up to the same place, we ask, What is happening? What is happening to a real person? Neo-realism has perceived that the most irreplaceable experience comes from things happening under our own eyes from natural necessity.

I am against 'exceptional' personages. The time has come to tell the audience that they are the true protagonists of life. The result will be a constant appeal to the responsibility and dignity of every human being. Otherwise the frequent habit of identifying oneself with fictional characters will become very dangerous. We must identify ourselves with what we are. The world is composed of millions of people thinking of myths.

The term neo-realism – in a very latin sense – implies, too, elimination of technical-professional apparatus, screen-writer included. Handbooks, formulas, grammars, have no more application. There will be no more technical terms. Everybody has his personal shooting-script. Neo-realism breaks all the rules, rejects all those canons which, in fact, only exist to codify limitations. Reality breaks all the rules, as can be discovered if you walk out with a camera to meet it.

The figure of a screen-writer today is, besides, very equivocal. He is usually considered part of the technical apparatus. I am a screen-writer trying to say certain things, and saying them in my own way. It is clear that certain moral and social ideas are the foundation of my expressive activities, and I can't be satisfied to offer a simple technical contribution. In films which do not touch me directly, also, when I am called in to do a certain amount of work on them, I try to insert as much as possible of my own world, of the moral emergencies within myself.

On the other hand, I don't think the screenplay in itself contains any particular problems; only when subject, screenplay and direction become three distinct phases, as they so often do today, which is abnormal. The screen-writer as such should disappear, and we should arrive at the sole author of a film.

Everything becomes flexible when only one person is making a film, everything continually possible, not only during the shooting, but during the editing, the laying of tracks, the post-synchronisation, to the particular moment when we say, 'Stop.' And it is only then that we put an end to the film.

Of course, it is possible to make films in collaboration, as happens with novels and plays, because there are always numerous bonds of identity between people (for example, millions of men go to war, and are killed, for the same reasons), but no work of art exists on which someone has not set the seal of his own interest, of his own poetic world. There is always somebody to make the decisive creative act, there is always one prevailing intelligence, there is always someone who, at a certain moment, 'chooses', and says, 'This, yes,' and 'This, no,' and then resolves it: reaction shot of the Mother crying Help!

Technique and capitalist method, however, have imposed collaboration on the cinema. It is one thing to adapt ourselves to the imposed exigencies of the cinema's present structure, another to imagine that they are indispensable and necessary. It is obvious that when films cost sixpence and everybody can have a camera, the cinema would become a creative medium as flexible and as free as any other.

It is evident that, with neo-realism, the actor – as a person fictitiously lending his own flesh to another – has no more right to exist than the 'story'. In neo-realism, as I intend it, everyone must be his own actor. To want one person to play another implies the calculated plot, the fable, and not 'things happening'. I attempted such a film with Caterina Rigoglioso; it was called 'the lightning film'. But unfortunately at the last moment everything broke down. Caterina did not seem to 'take' to the cinema. But wasn't she 'Caterina'?

Of course, it will be necessary to choose themes excluding actors. I want, for example, to make a report on children in the world. If I am not allowed to make it, I will limit it to Europe, or to Italy alone. But I will make it. Here is an example of the film not needing actors. I hope the actors' union will not protest.

Neo-realism does not reject psychological exploration. Psychology is one of the many premises of reality. I face it as I face any other. If I want to write a scene of two men quarrelling, I will not do so at my desk. I must leave my den and find them. I take these men and make them talk in front of me for one hour or for twenty, depending on necessity. My creative method is first to call on them, then to listen to them, 'choosing' what they say. But I do all this not with the intention of creating heroes, because I think that a hero is not 'certain men' but 'every man'.

Wanting to give everyone a sense of equality is not levelling him down, but exalting his solidarity. Lack of solidarity is always born from presuming to be different, from a *But*: 'Paul is suffering, it's true, I am suffering, too, *but* my suffering has something that . . . my nature has something that . . .' and so on. The *But* must disappear, and we must be able to say: 'That man is bearing what I myself should bear in the same circumstances.'

Others have observed that the best dialogue in films is always in dialect. Dialect is nearer to reality. In our literary and spoken language, the synthetic constructions and the words themselves are always a little false. When writing a dialogue, I always think of it in dialect, in that of Rome or my own village. Using dialect, I feel it to be more essential, truer. Then I translate it into Italian, thus maintaining the dialect's syntax. I don't, therefore, write dialogue in dialect, but I am interested in what dialects have in common: immediacy, freshness, verisimilitude.

But I take most of all from nature. I go out into the street, catch words, sentences, discussions. My great aids are memory and the short-hand writer.

Afterwards, I do with the words what I do with the images. I choose, I cut the material I have gathered to give it the right rhythm, to capture the essence, the truth. However great a faith I might have in imagination, in solitude, I have a greater one in reality, in people. I am interested in the drama of things we happen to encounter, not those we plan.

In short, to exercise our own poetic talents on location, we must leave our rooms and go, in body and mind, out to meet other people, to see and understand them. This is a genuine moral necessity for me and, if I lose faith in it, so much the worse for me.

I am quite aware that it is possible to make wonderful films, like Charlie Chaplin's, and they are not neo-realistic. I am quite aware that there are Americans, Russians, Frenchmen and others who have made movies. I wonder, too, how many more great works they will again give us, according to their particular genius, with actors and studios and novels. But Italian film-makers, I think, if they are to sustain and deepen their cause and their style, after having courageously half-opened their doors to reality, must (in the sense I have mentioned) open them wide.

'The director is the first spectator of a film'

MARCEL L'HERBIER

ROBERT BRESSON
from *Notes on Cinematography*

As even those who find his films unenjoyably arduous experiences are generally, if a tad grudgingly, ready to acknowledge, Robert Bresson was one of the cinema's supreme artists, his greatest works, constructed, as he himself put it, 'on blankness, silence and immobility', among the medium's unimpeachable masterpieces. When reading this brief extract from Notes sur le cinématographe, *his chilly anthology of aphorisms, it helps to remember that, after his first three films, he never again employed a professional actor or actress. Why were the performances that he obtained from these non-professionals so mesmerizing? Perhaps because they were founded on his sadistic exploitation of 'le trac' – or what we refer to in English as 'stage fright'. His performers were, in short, terrified; and it was that terror which, maintained throughout a three-month shoot, generated the extraordinary intensity of their presence on the screen.*

A film cannot be a stage show, because a stage show requires flesh-and-blood presence. But it can be, as photographed theatre or CINEMA is, the photographic reproduction of a stage show. The photographic reproduction of a stage show is comparable to the photographic reproduction of a painting or of a sculpture. But a photographic reproduction of Donatello's *Saint John the Baptist* or of Vermeer's *Young Woman with Necklace* has not the power, the value or the price of that sculpture or that painting. It does not create it. Does not create anything.

CINEMA films are historical documents whose place is in the archives: how a play was acted in 19— by Mr X, Miss Y.

An actor in cinematography might as well be in a foreign country. He does not speak its language.

The photographed theatre or CINEMA requires a *metteur-en-scène* or director to make some actors perform a play and to photograph these actors performing the play; afterwards he lines up the images. Bastard theatre lacking what makes theatre: material presence of living actors, direct action of the audience on the actors.

. . . without lacking naturalness they lack nature.[1]   Chauteaubriand

Who said: 'A single look lets loose a passion, a murder, a war'?

The ejaculatory force of the eye.

To set up a film is to bind persons to each other and to objects by looks.

Two persons, looking each other in the eye, see not their eyes but their looks. (The reason why we get the colour of a person's eyes wrong?)

On two deaths and three births
My movie is born first in my head, dies on paper; is resuscitated by the living persons and real objects I use, which are killed on film but, placed in a certain order and projected on to a screen, come to life again like flowers in water.[2]

To admit that X may be by turns Attila, Mahomet, a bank clerk, a lumberman, is to admit that the movies in which he acts smack of the stage. Not to admit that X acts is to admit that Attila = Mahomet = a bank clerk = a lumberman, which is absurd.

NOTES

1. . . . *sans manquer de naturel, manquent de nature.*
2. To 'cinematograph' someone is not to give him life. It is because they are living that actors make a stage play alive.

ROLAND BARTHES
The Romans in Films

The late Roland Barthes' most widely read and accessible book, Myth-
ologies, *was originally published in France in 1957 and appeared in a
considerably abridged English language version in 1972. In it were 50
or so brief but densely argued reflections on some of the more tenacious
myths informing the daily life and culture of the period. What preoccu-
pied Barthes, and what he profoundly distrusted, was, on the part of
those media whose role is supposedly to define and disseminate that
culture, the wilful confusion of Nature and History and the reassuring
notion that every 'cultural' manifestation, be it a wrestling bout or a
plate of* steak frites, *could therefore, secure in its single, inalterable,
natural meaning, be* taken *for granted. For Barthes, on the contrary,
culture was 'coded'. That which seemed natural was falsely so. What he
perceived around him was a perpetual bombardment of signs and signals
and messages, all of them requiring to be deciphered,* read, *for all of
them might be guilty of masking some latent ideological abuse. He
regarded himself, in consequence, as not only a semiologist – semiology
is the science of signs and symbols – but as what he termed a 'semioclast'.
Beyond his frequently witty and startling insights lay the ambition, not
exactly to demythify (for he never claimed to be the repository of any
capitalized 'Truth'), but certainly to probe, to expose, to subvert, in the
sense in which these words are commonly applied to investigative
journalists. He was, in short, a master of* idées refusées, *as one refers
to* idées reçues.

*The first of the two essays which follow, 'The Romans in Films', a
brilliant debunking of Joseph L. Mankiewicz's usually rather well-
thought-of film version of* Julius Caesar, *also serves as an ideal introduction to Barthes' own formidable intelligence.*

In Mankiewicz's *Julius Caesar*, all the characters are wearing
fringes. Some have them curly, some straggly, some tufted, some oily,
all have them well combed, and the bald are not admitted, although

there are plenty to be found in Roman history. Those who have little hair have not been let off for all that, and the hairdresser – the king-pin of the film – has still managed to produce one last lock which duly reaches the top of the forehead, one of those Roman foreheads, whose smallness has at all times indicated a specific mixture of self-righteousness, virtue and conquest.

What then is associated with these insistent fringes? Quite simply the label of Roman-ness. We therefore see here the mainspring of the Spectacle – the *sign* – operating in the open. The frontal lock overwhelms one with evidence, no one can doubt that he is in Ancient Rome. And this certainty is permanent: the actors speak, act, torment themselves, debate 'questions of universal import', without losing, thanks to this little flag displayed on their foreheads, any of their historical plausibility. Their general representativeness can even expand in complete safety, cross the ocean and the centuries, and merge into the Yankee mugs of Hollywood extras: no matter, everyone is reassured, installed in the quiet certainty of a universe without duplicity, where Romans are Romans thanks to the most legible of signs: hair on the forehead.

A Frenchman, to whose eyes American faces still have something exotic, finds comical the combination of the morphologies of these gangster-sheriffs with the little Roman fringe: it rather looks like an excellent music-hall gag. This is because for the French the sign in this case overshoots the target and discredits itself by letting its aim appear clearly. But this very fringe, when combed on the only naturally Latin forehead in the film, that of Marlon Brando, impresses us and does not make us laugh; and it is not impossible that part of the success of this actor in Europe is due to the perfect integration of Roman capillary habits with the general morphology of the characters he usually portrays. Conversely, one cannot believe in Julius Caesar, whose physiognomy is that of an Anglo-Saxon lawyer – a face with which one is already acquainted through a thousand bit parts in thrillers or comedies, and a compliant skull on which the hairdresser has raked, with great effort, a lock of hair.

In the category of capillary meanings, here is a sub-sign, that of nocturnal surprises: Portia and Calpurnia, woken up at dead of night, have conspicuously uncombed hair. The former, who is young, expresses disorder by flowing locks: her unreadiness is, so to speak, of the first degree. The latter, who is middle-aged, exhibits a more painstaking vulnerability: a plait winds round her neck and comes to rest on her right shoulder so as to impose the traditional sign of disorder, asymmetry. But these signs are at the same time excessive and ineffectual: they postulate a 'nature' which they have not even the courage to acknowledge fully: they are not 'fair and square'.

Yet another sign in this *Julius Caesar*: all the faces sweat constantly. Labourers, soldiers, conspirators, all have their austere and tense features streaming (with Vaseline). And close-ups are so frequent that evidently sweat here is an attribute with a purpose. Like the Roman fringe or the nocturnal plait, sweat is a sign. Of what? Of moral feeling. Everyone is sweating because everyone is debating something within himself; we are here supposed to be in the locus of a horribly tormented virtue, that is, in the very locus of tragedy, and it is sweat which has the function of conveying this. The populace, upset by the death of Caesar, then by the arguments of Mark Antony, is sweating, and combining economically, in this single sign, the intensity of its emotion and the simplicity of its condition. And the virtuous men, Brutus, Cassius, Casca, are ceaselessly perspiring too, testifying thereby to the enormous physiological labour produced in them by a virtue just about to give birth to a crime. To sweat is to think – which evidently rests on the postulate, appropriate to a nation of businessmen, that thought is a violent, cataclysmic operation, of which sweat is only the most benign symptom. In the whole film, there is but one man who does not sweat and who remains smooth-faced, unperturbed and water-tight: Caesar. Of course Caesar, the *object* of the crime, remains dry since *he* does not know, *he does not think*, and so must keep the firm and polished texture of an exhibit standing isolated in the courtroom.

Here again, the sign is ambiguous: it remains on the surface, yet does not for all that give up the attempt to pass itself off as depth. It aims at making people understand (which is laudable) but at the same time suggests that it is spontaneous (which is cheating); it presents itself at once as intentional and irrepressible, artificial and natural, manufactured and discovered. This can lead us to an ethic of signs. Signs ought to present themselves only in two extreme forms: either openly intellectual and so remote that they are reduced to an algebra, as in the Chinese theatre, where a flag on its own signifies a regiment; or deeply rooted, invented, so to speak, on each occasion, revealing an internal, a hidden facet, and indicative of a moment in time, no longer of a concept (as in the art of Stanislavsky, for instance). But the intermediate sign, the fringe of Roman-ness or the sweating of thought, reveals a degraded spectacle, which is equally afraid of simple reality and of total artifice. For although it is a good thing if a spectacle is created to make the world more explicit, it is both reprehensible and deceitful to confuse the sign with what is signified. And it is a duplicity which is peculiar to bourgeois art: between the intellectual and the visceral sign is hypocritically inserted a hybrid, at once elliptical and pretentious, which is pompously christened '*nature*'.

'The sound film has, above all, invented silence. I find explanatory dialogue marvellous and convenient. But the ideal would be, rather, that the dialogue would accompany the characters, just as a sleigh-bell accompanies a horse, or buzzing accompanies a bee . . .' **ROBERT BRESSON**

ROLAND BARTHES
The Face of Garbo

Gar-bo. Probably the two most famous syllables in the history of the cinema. So famous that Garbo's own celebrity has eclipsed that of the historical and theatrical luminaries she incarnated on the screen, whether Queen Christina or Marie Walewska, Anna Christie or Marguerite Gautier. Nor did her premature retirement and refusal to effect a comeback dent that celebrity. Quite the reverse. She had no need of a comeback, for in reality she never went away. Living as a recluse, dividing her life between a villa in Switzerland and an apartment in New York, occasionally sighted along Fifth Avenue like a rare specimen of some exotic avian species – the seldom-spotted movie star, perhaps – she was as much the cynosure of her seclusion as she had ever been of her public prominence.

Clarence Brown, who directed her in seven films, considered her the very prototype of charisma. Kenneth Tynan remarked that she appeared as desirable to a sober man as another woman to an inebriated one. Her allure, however, defied every attempt to encapsulate it verbally – or even cinematically. Hers was a face that did not rely exclusively on Hollywood's great lighting cameramen to capture its lustre. Unlike Dietrich, a creature of celluloid if ever there was, Garbo would have generated a comparable emotional charge on stage.

There, basically, as it has been handed down from generation to generation of film buffs, is the Garbo of myth, or the myth of Garbo. But even if the ethereality of her onscreen presence – her face, someone said, resembled 'photographed thought' – was near-ineffable, it does merit, and it can support, analysis. Which is what it receives, inimitably, incomparably, from Roland Barthes.

G arbo still belongs to that moment in cinema when capturing the human face still plunged audiences into the deepest ecstasy, when one literally lost oneself in a human image as one would in a philtre, when the face represented a kind of absolute state of the flesh, which could be neither reached nor renounced. A few years earlier the face of Valentino was causing suicides; that of Garbo still partakes of the same rule of Courtly Love, where the flesh gives rise to mystical feelings of perdition.

It is indeed an admirable face-object. In *Queen Christina*, a film which has again been shown in Paris in the last few years, the make-up has the snowy thickness of a mask: it is not a painted face, but one set in plaster, protected by the surface of the colour, not by its lineaments. Amid all this snow at once fragile and compact, the eyes alone, black like strange soft flesh, but not in the least expressive, are two faintly tremulous wounds. In spite of its extreme beauty, this face, not drawn but sculpted in something smooth and friable, that is, at once perfect and ephemeral, comes to resemble the flour-white complexion of Charlie Chaplin, the dark vegetation of his eyes, his totem-like countenance.

Now the temptation of the absolute mask (the mask of antiquity, for instance) perhaps implies less the theme of the secret (as is the case with Italian half mask) than that of an archetype of the human face. Garbo offered to one's gaze a sort of Platonic Idea of the human creature, which explains why her face is almost sexually undefined, without however leaving one in doubt. It is true that this film (in which Queen Christina is by turns a woman and a young cavalier) lends itself to this lack of differentiation; but Garbo does not perform in it any feat of transvestism; she is always herself, and carries without pretence, under her crown or her wide-brimmed hats, the same snowy solitary face. The name given to her, *the Divine*, probably aimed to convey less a superlative state of beauty than the essence of her corporeal person, descended from a heaven where all things are formed and perfected in the clearest light. She herself knew this: how many actresses have consented to let the crowd see the ominous maturing of their beauty. Not she, however; the essence was not to be degraded, her face was not to have any reality except that of its perfection, which was intellectual even more than formal. The Essence became gradually obscured, progressively veiled with dark glasses, broad hats and exiles: but it never deteriorated.

And yet, in this deified face, something sharper than a mask is looming: a kind of voluntary and therefore human relation between the curve of the nostrils and the arch of the eyebrows; a rare, individual function relating two regions of the face. A mask is but a sum of lines; a face, on the contrary, is above all their thematic harmony. Garbo's face represents this fragile moment when the cinema is about to draw an existential from an essential beauty, when the archetype leans towards the fascination of mortal faces, when the clarity of the flesh as essence yields its place to a lyricism of Woman.

Viewed as a transition the face of Garbo reconciles two iconographic ages, it assures the passage from awe to charm. As is well known, we are today at the other pole of this evolution: the face of Audrey Hepburn, for instance, is individualized, not only because of its peculiar thematics (woman as child, woman as kitten) but also because of her person, of an almost unique specification of the face, which has nothing of the essence left in it, but is constituted by an infinite complexity of morphological functions. As a language, Garbo's singularity was of the order of the concept, that of Audrey Hepburn is of the order of the substance. The face of Garbo is an Idea, that of Hepburn, an Event.

CHRIS MARKER
A Free Replay (Notes on *Vertigo*)

Both the author of this essay, the maverick documentarist Chris Marker
(Cuba Si!, Le Joli Mai, Le Fond de l'air est rouge, Sans Soleil), who
travels around the world indefatigably filming other people but refuses
to be as much as photographed himself, and the film which it analyses,
Alfred Hitchcock's Vertigo, regarded by innumerable cinéphiles as one
of the greatest achievements of the American sound cinema, have become
the objects of cults. Readers, naturally, must judge for themselves. But
this encounter of two obsessions, Marker's with Hitchcock's film and
Scottie's with the doomed Madeleine, is a quintessential specimen of
auteurist criticism.

'Power and freedom'. Coupled together, these two words are
repeated three times in *Vertigo*. First, at the 12th minute by Gavin
Elster ('freedom' underlined by a move to close-up) who, looking at a
picture of Old San Francisco, expresses his nostalgia to Scottie ('San
Francisco has changed. The things that spelled San Francisco to me
are disappearing fast'), a nostalgia for a time when men – some men at
least – had 'power and freedom'. Second, at the 35th minute, in the
bookstore, where 'Pop' Liebel explains how Carlotta Valdes's rich lover
threw her out yet kept her child: 'Men could do that in those days. They
had the power and the freedom . . .' And finally at the 125th minute –
and 51st second to be precise – but in reverse order (which is logical,
given we are now in the second part, on the other side of the mirror)
by Scottie himself when, realizing the workings of the trap laid by the
now free and powerful Elster, he says, a few seconds before Judy's fall
– which, for him, will be Madeleine's second death – 'with all his wife's
money and all that freedom and power . . .' Just try telling me these are
coincidences.

Such precise signs must have a meaning. Could it be psychological,
an explanation of the criminal's motives? If so, the effort seems a little
wasted on what is, after all, a secondary character. This strategic triad

gave me the first inkling of a possible reading of *Vertigo*. The vertigo
the film deals with isn't to do with space and falling; it is a clear,
understandable and spectacular metaphor for yet another kind of vertigo,
much more difficult to represent – the vertigo of time. Elster's 'perfect'
crime almost achieves the impossible: reinventing a time when men
and women and San Francisco were different to what they are now.
And its perfection, as with all perfection in Hitchcock, exists in duality.
Scottie will absorb the folly of time with which Elster infuses him through
Madeleine/Judy. But where Elster reduces the fantasy to mediocre
manifestations (wealth, power, etc.), Scottie transmutes it into its most
utopian form: he overcomes the most irreparable damage caused by
time and resurrects a love that is dead. The entire second part of the
film, on the other side of the mirror, is nothing but a mad, maniacal
attempt to deny time, to recreate through trivial yet necessary signs
(like the signs of a liturgy: clothes, make-up, hair) the woman whose
loss he has never been able to accept. His own feelings of responsibility
and guilt for this loss are mere Christian Band-Aids dressing a metaphysical wound of much greater depth. Were one to quote the Scriptures,
Corinthians I (an epistle one of Bergman's characters uses to define
love) would apply: 'Death, where is your victory?'

So Elster infuses Scottie with the madness of time. It's interesting to
see how this is done. As ever with Alfred, stratagems merely serve to
hold up a mirror (and there are many mirrors in this story) to the hero
and bring out his repressed desires. In *Strangers on a Train*, Bruno
offers Guy the crime he doesn't dare desire. In *Vertigo*, Scottie, although
overtly reluctant, is always willing, always the one taking the first step.
Once in Gavin's office and again in front of his own house (the morning
after the fake drowning), the manipulators pretend to give up: Gavin
sits down and apologizes for having asked the impossible; Madeleine
gets back in the car and gets ready to leave. Everything could stop there.
But, on both occasions, Scottie takes the initiative and restarts the
machine. Gavin hardly has to persuade Scottie to undertake his search:
he simply suggests that he see Madeleine, knowing full well that a
glimpse of her will be enough to set the supreme manipulator, Destiny,
in motion. After a shot of Madeleine, glimpsed at Ernie's, there follows
a shot of Scottie beginning his stake-out of the Elster house. Acceptance
(bewitchment) needs no scene of its own; it is contained in the fade to
black between the two scenes. This is the first of three ellipses of
essential moments, all avoided, which another director would have felt

obliged to show. The second ellipse is in the first scene of physical love between Judy and Scottie, which clearly takes place in the hotel room after the last transformation (the hair-do corrected in the bathroom). How is it possible, after such a fabulous, hallucinatory moment, to sustain such intensity?

In this case, the censorship of the time saved Hitchcock from a doubly impossible situation. Such a scene can only exist in the imagination (or in life). But when a film has referred to fantasy only in the highly coded context of dreams and two lovers embrace in the realist set of the hotel room; when one of them, Scottie, thanks to the most magical camera movement in the history of cinema, discovers another set around him, that of the stable at the Dolores Mission where he last kissed a wife whose double he has now created; isn't *that* scene the metaphor for the love scene Hitchcock cannot show? And if love is truly the only victor over time, isn't this scene *per se the* love scene? The third ellipse, which has long been the joy of connoisseurs, I'll mention for the sheer pleasure of it. It occurs much earlier, in the first part. We have just seen Scottie pull Madeleine unconscious out of San Francisco bay (at Fort Point). Fade to black. Scottie is at home, lighting a log fire. As he goes to sit down – the camera follows – he looks straight ahead. The camera follows his look and ends on Madeleine, seen through the open bedroom door, asleep in bed with a sheet up to her neck. But as the camera travels towards her, it also registers her clothes and underclothes hanging on a drier in the kitchen. The telephone rings and wakes her up. Scottie, who's come into the room, leaves, shutting the door. Madeleine reappears dressed in the red dressing-gown he happened to have draped across the bed. Neither of them alludes to the intervening period, apart from the *double entendre* in Scottie's line the next day: 'I enjoyed, er . . . talking to you . . .' Three scenes, therefore, where imagination wins over representation; three moments, three keys which become locks, but which no present-day director would think of leaving out. On the contrary, he'd make them heavily explicit and, of course, banal. As a result of saying it can show anything, cinema has abandoned its power over the imagination. And, like cinema, this century is perhaps starting to pay a high price for this betrayal of the imagination – or, more precisely, those who still have an imagination, albeit a poor one, are being made to pay that price.

Double entendre? All the gestures, looks, phrases in *Vertigo* have a double meaning. Everybody knows that it is probably the only film where a 'double' vision is not only advisable but indispensable for rereading the first part of the film in the light of the second. Cabrera Infante called it 'the first great surrealist film', and if there is a theme present in the surrealistic imagination (and for that matter, in the literary one), then surely it is that of the Double, the *Doppelgänger* (who from Doctor Jekyll to *Kagemusha*, from the *Prisoner of Zenda* to *Persona*, has trod a royal path through the history of the medium). In *Vertigo*, the theme is even reflected in the doubling-up of details: Madeleine's look towards the tower (the first scene of San Juan Bautista, looking right, while Scottie kisses her) and the line 'Too late' which accompanies it have a precise meaning for the naïve spectator, unaware of the stratagem, but another meaning, just as precise, for a watchful spectator seeing it a second time. The look and the line are repeated at the very end, in a shot exactly symmetrical with the first, by Scottie, looking left, 'Too late', just before Judy falls. For as there is an Other of the Other, there is also a Double of the Double. The right profile of the first revelation, when Madeleine momentarily stands still behind Scottie at Ernie's, the moment which decides everything, is repeated at the beginning of the second part, so precisely that it's Scottie who, the second time, is 'in front' of Judy. Thus begins a play of mirrors which can only end in their destruction. We, the audience, discover the stratagem via the letter Judy doesn't send. Scottie discovers it at the end via the necklace. (Note that this moment also has its double: Scottie has just seen the necklace head-on and hasn't reacted. He only reacts when he sees it in the mirror.) In between, Scottie's attraction for Judy, who at first was merely a fourth case of mistaken identity (the constant of a love touched by death; see Proust) Scottie encountered in his search through the places of their past, this attraction has crystallized with her profile in front of the window ('Do I remind you of her?') in that green neon light, for which Hitchcock, it seems, specially chose the Empire Hotel: her left profile. This is the moment when Scottie crosses to the other side of the mirror and his folly is born . . .

. . . If one believes, that is, the apparent intentions of the authors (authors in the plural because the writer, Samuel Taylor, was largely Alfred's accomplice). The ingenious stratagem, the way of making us understand we've been hoodwinked, the stroke of genius of revealing the truth to us well before the hero, the whole thing bathed in the light of an *amour fou*, 'fixed' by what Cabrera (who should know) called the 'decadent *habañeras*' of Bernard Herrman – all that isn't bad. But what if *they* were lying to us as well? Resnais liked to say that nothing forces us to believe the heroine of *Hiroshima*. She could be making up everything she says. The flashbacks aren't the affirmations of the writer, but stories told by a character. All we know about Scottie at the beginning of the second part is that he is in a state of total catatonia, that he is 'somewhere else', that it 'could last a long time' (according to the doctor), that he loved a dead woman 'and still does' (according to Midge). Is it too absurd to imagine that this agonizing, though reasonable, and obstinate soul ('hard-hitting' says Gavin), imagined this totally extravagant scenario, full of unbelievable coincidences and entanglements, yet logical enough to drive one to the one salvatory conclusion: this woman is not dead, I can find her again?

There are many arguments in favour of a dream reading of the second part of *Vertigo*. The disappearance of Barbara Bel Geddes (Midge, his friend and confidante, secretly in love with him) is one of them. I know very well that she married a rich Texan oilman in the meantime, and is preparing a dreadful reappearance as a widow in the Ewing clan; but still, her disappearance from *Vertigo* is probably unparalleled in the serial economy of Hollywood scripts. A character important for half the film disappears without trace – there isn't even an allusion to her in the subsequent dialogue – until the end of the second part. In the dream reading of the film, this absence would only be explained by her last line to Scottie in the hospital: 'You don't even know I'm here . . .'

In this case, the entire second part would be nothing but a fantasy, revealing at last the double of the double. We were tricked into believing that the first part was the truth, then told it was a lie born of a perverse mind, that the second part contained the truth. But what if the first part really were the truth and the second the product of a sick mind? In that case, what one may find overcharged and outrageously expressionistic in the nightmare images preceding the hospital room would be nothing but a trick, yet another red herring, camouflaging the fantasy that will occupy us for another hour in order to lead us even further away from the appearance of realism. The only exception to this is the moment I've already mentioned, the change of set during the kiss. In this light, the scene acquires a new meaning: it's a fleeting concession, a revealing detail, the blink of a madman's eyelids as his eyes glaze over, the kind of gaze which sometimes gives a madman away.

There used to be a special effect in old movies where a character would detach himself from his sleeping or dead body, and his transparent form would float up to the sky or into the land of dreams. In the mirror play of *Vertigo* there is a similar moment, if in a more subtle form: in the clothes store when Judy, realizing that Scottie is transforming her piece by piece into Madeleine (in other words, into the reality he isn't deemed to know, making her repeat what she did for Elster), makes to go, and bumps into a *mirror*. Scottie joins her in front of the mirror and, while he's dictating to an amazed shop assistant the details of one of Madeleine's dresses, a fabulous shot shows us 'all four of them' together: him and his double, her and her double. At that moment, Scottie has truly escaped from his hospital chair; there are two Scotties as well as two Judys. We can therefore add schizophrenia to the illnesses whose symptoms others have already judiciously identified in Scottie's behaviour. Personally, though, I'd leave out necrophilia, so often mentioned, which seems to me more indicative of a critic's neurosis than the character's: Scottie continues to love a truly living Madeleine. In his madness, he looks for proof in her life.

It's all very well reasoning like this, but one must also return to the appearance of the facts, obstinate as they are. There is a crushing argument in favour of a phantasmagoric reading of the second part. When, after the transformation and the hallucination, Madeleine/Judy, with the blitheness of a satisfied body, gets ready for dinner and Scottie asks her what restaurant she'd like to go to, she immediately suggests Ernie's. It's the place where they first met (but Scottie isn't meant to know this yet – Judy's careless 'It's our place' is the first give-away before the necklace). So they go there *without making a reservation*. Just try doing this in San Francisco and you'll understand we're in a dream.

As Gavin says, San Francisco has changed. During a screening at Berkeley in the early eighties, when everyone had forgotten the movie (the old fox had kept the rights in order to sell them at a premium to TV, hence the cuts for commercials and the changed ending) and the word was that it was just another minor thriller, I remember the audience gasping with amazement on seeing the panoramic view of the city which opens the second part. It's another city, without skyscrapers (apart from Coppola's Sentinel Building), a picture as dated as the engraving Scottie looks at when Elster first pronounces those two fateful words. And it was only twenty years ago . . . San Francisco, of course, is nothing but another character in the film. Samuel Taylor wrote to me agreeing that Hitchcock liked the town but only knew 'what he saw from hotels or restaurants or out of the limo window'. He was 'what you might call a sedentary person'. But he still decided to use the Dolores Mission and, strangely, to make the house on Lombard Street Scottie's home 'because of the red door'. Taylor was in love with his city (Alex Coppel, the first writer, was 'a transplanted Englishman') and put all his love into the script; and perhaps even more than that, if I am to believe a rather cryptic phrase at the end of his letter: 'I rewrote the script at the same time that I explored San Francisco and recaptured my past . . .' Words which could apply as much to the characters as to the author, and which afford us another interpretation, like an added flat to a key, of the direction given by Elster to Scottie at the start of the film, when he's describing Madeleine's wanderings; the pillars Scottie gazes at for so long on the other side of Lloyd Lake – the *Portals of the Past*. This personal note would explain many things: the *amour fou*, the dream signs, all the things that make *Vertigo* a film which is both typically and untypically Hitchcockian in relation to the rest of his work, the work of a perfect cynic. Cynical to the point of adding for television – an anxiously moral medium, as we all know – a new ending to the film: Scottie reunited with Midge and the radio reporting Elster's arrest. Crime doesn't pay.

Ten years later, time has continued to work its effect. What used to mean San Francisco for me is disappearing fast. The spiral of time, like Saul Bass's spiral in the credit sequence, the spiral of Madeleine's hair and Carlotta's in the portrait, cannot stop swallowing up the present and enlarging the contours of the past. The Empire Hotel has become the York and lost its green neon lights; the McKittrick Hotel, the Victorian house where Madeleine disappears like a ghost (another inexplicable detail if we ignore the dream-reading: what of the hotel's mysterious janitress? 'A paid accomplice' was Hitchcock's reply to Truffaut. Come on, Alfred!) has been replaced by a school built of concrete. But Ernie's restaurant is still there, as is Podestà Baldocchi's flower-shop with its tiled mosaics where one proudly remembers Kim Novak choosing a bouquet. The cross-section of sequoia is still at the entrance to Muir Woods, on the other side of the bay. The Botanical Gardens were less fortunate: they are now parked underground. (*Vertigo* could almost be shot in the same locations, unlike its remake in Paris.) The Veterans' Museum is still there, as is the cemetery at the Dolores Mission and San Juan Bautista, south of another mission, where Hitchcock added (by an optical effect) a high tower, the real one being so low you'd hardly sprain an ankle falling off it, complete with stable, carriages and stuffed horse used in the film just as they are in life. And of course, there's Fort Point, under the Golden Gate Bridge, which he wanted to cover with birds at the end of *The Birds*. The *Vertigo* tour is now obligatory for lovers of San Francisco. Even the Pope, pretending otherwise, visited two locations: the Golden Gate Bridge and (under the pretext of kissing an AIDS patient) the Dolores Mission. Whether one accepts the dream reading or not, the power of this once-ignored film has become a commonplace, proving that the idea of resurrecting a lost love can touch any human heart, whatever he or she may say. 'You're my second chance!' cries Scottie as he drags Judy up the stairs of the tower. No one now wants to interpret these words in their superficial sense, meaning his vertigo has been conquered. It's about reliving a moment lost in the past, about bringing it back to life only to lose it again. One does not resurrect the dead, one doesn't look back at Eurydice. Scottie experiences the greatest joy a man can imagine, a second life, in exchange for the greatest tragedy, a second death. What do video games, which tell us more about our unconscious than the works of Lacan, offer us? Neither money nor glory, but a new game. The possibility of playing again. 'A second chance.' A free replay. And another thing: Madeleine tells Scottie she managed to find her way back to the house 'by spotting the Coit Tower' – the tower which dominates the surrounding hills and whose name makes visiting French tourists laugh. 'Well, it's the first time I ever had to thank the Coit Tower,' says Scottie, the blasé San Franciscan. Madeleine would never find her way back today. The bushes have grown on Lombard Street, hiding all landmarks. The house itself, number 900, has changed. The new owners have got rid of (or the old owner kept) the cast-iron balcony with its Chinese inscription 'Twin Happiness'. The door is still red, but now blessed with a notice which, in its way, is a tribute to Alfred: 'Warning: Crime Watch.' And, from the steps where Kim Novak and James Stewart are first reunited, no one can see any more the tower 'in the shape of a fire-hose', offered as a posthumous gift to the San Francisco Fire Brigade by a millionairess called Lilli *Hitchcock* Coit . . .

Obviously, this text is addressed to those who know *Vertigo* by heart. But do those who don't deserve anything at all?

WIM WENDERS
Despising What You Sell

Wim Wenders wrote the following angry article in 1969. It was not meant to be 'prophetic' since it patently reflected an already prevalent situation. Yet, in the 30 years which have now elapsed, the situation has become evident not just to cinéphiles as prescient as the young Wenders was. Audiences currently shop for movies: multiplexes have become the medium's malls. And, like the little corner store, the little corner cinema, already under threat in 1969, is now history.

'Movies are made by blind people. But it's only blind people who sell, deal with and distribute them. So films are treated worse than Chiquita bananas or rental-cars'

Karl Marx, in conversation with David W. Griffith

In 1966 I worked half-days for three months as an office assistant in the administrative department of the Düsseldorf branch of United Artists. I don't imagine that the distribution system has changed in the meantime.

When I got out of the lift on the third floor in the morning, I went through a glass swing door beneath a large painted board advertising the film *The Group*. I walked into a wide hall, divided by a long counter, into an office space with several desks and a waiting-room with a few plastic-covered chairs. At my desk in the corner I sat with my back to *633 Squadron*. If I raised my head I looked Yves Montand or Sean Connery straight in the eyes.

I had to carry out simple office chores: transcribe the contracts brought in by the representatives, send memos, ascertain any delays, write in attendance figures, etc.

During this time, I witnessed the closure of around a dozen cinemas; their file cards were crossed out. I listened to the salesman and agents talking about films as if they were new potatoes or meat prices: it was not even appropriate to the film *It's a Mad Mad Mad Mad World*.

I saw cinema-owners being hailed as old friends when they came to the counter: they were the ones who owned the city-centre theatres, usually whole chains of them. They could choose the films they wanted to show, when and for how long. They could reject films and swap them for others as they wished.

I saw cinema-owners quivering with rage or weeping or wringing their hands as they begged. Actually quivering, weeping and begging. They didn't get the films that could have filled their cinemas. Instead they had to book films and carry out contracts that guaranteed bankruptcy. They were the ones who owned the cinemas in the suburbs and in the country, which no longer got three performances in a row on weekdays.

During the period when I was working there, the manager got fired and the head agent was switched to another branch: high-level decisions.

'High-level' meant from the German head office in Frankfurt, or even the European head office in Paris.

'Top-level decision' meant: from New York. The importance of a long-distance letter or telephone call was immediately recognizable from the language it used.

The cinema-owners who had it made were slapping each other on the back. The cinema-owners who had to double as their own ushers ignored each other, some of them giving each other dirty looks.

Once I drove a print of a film eighty kilometres to a place in the mountains. The people who despatched me had made a mistake. The film was only being given for one late-night showing. When I added up the attendance figures later I could see that the takings just about covered my petrol.

During this period I could often go to the cinema for nothing because staff always got free tickets. The films I saw as a result were almost always a continuation of what I had experienced during the day in the distribution office. And vice versa: the distribution system was only an extension of the films that kept it going. From production to distribution, the same violence was at work: the same lack of love in dealing with images, sound and language; the stupidity of German dubbing; the vulgarity of the block and blind booking system; the lack of variety in advertising; the lack of conscience involved in exploiting the cinema-owners; the idiocy involved in cutting films down, etc.

It is sort of understandable that an industry can't afford to be idealistic. But that it despises its goods and its customers – that's just beyond comprehension, it shouldn't be allowed to.

JEAN BAUDRILLARD
Apocalypse Now

Jean Baudrillard, sociologist, philosopher, demented Pope of the post-modern, is a fairly unloveable guru, but it would be churlish not to salute his prescience. In the first of two essays republished here, dating from 1981, what he anticipated was not the 1980s but the 1990s (and beyond?), the decade in which nothing would exist – child abuse, serial killings, presidential sexual misconduct, terminal disease, even the approach of death itself – unless and until the media, the confessional box of the global village, decreed that it existed (and fulfilled its zealously assumed exorcistic and exculpatory functions by granting absolution to the confessor).

Beyond the specifics of Francis Ford Coppola's Apocalypse Now, *a film whose eerie kinship with the war which it depicted (the legendary investments of time and money swallowed up in the jungles of South-East Asia, the invasion of an underdeveloped country by massive Yankee technology, the fuzziness of motivation, the daily battle with the elements, the sense of a journey destined to end no one knew how or where) Baudrillard was by no means alone in remarking, this text remains a template for all subsequent critiques and indictments of what Guy Debord had already – even before Baudrillard – termed 'the society of spectacle'.*

Coppola makes his film like the Americans made war – in this sense, it is the best possible testimonial – with the same immoderation, the same excess of means, the same monstrous candor . . . and the same success. The war as entrenchment, as technological and psychedelic fantasy, the war as a succession of special effects, the war become film even before being filmed. The war abolishes itself in its technological test, and for Americans it was primarily that: a test site, a gigantic territory in which to test their arms, their methods, their power.

Coppola does nothing but that: test cinema's *power of intervention*, test the impact of a cinema that has become an immeasurable machinery of special effects. In this sense, his film is really the extension of the war through other means, the pinnacle of this failed war, and its apotheosis. The war became film, the film becomes war, the two are joined by their common hemorrhage into technology.

The real war is waged by Coppola as it is by Westmoreland: without counting the inspired irony of having forests and Philippine villages napalmed to retrace the hell of South Vietnam. One revisits everything through cinema and one begins again: the Molochian joy of filming, the sacrificial joy of so many millions spent, of such a holocaust of means, of so many misadventures, and the remarkable paranoia that from the beginning conceived of this film as a historical, *global* event, in which, in the mind of the creator, the war in Vietnam would have been nothing other than what it is, would not fundamentally have existed – and it is necessary for us to believe in this: the war in Vietnam 'in itself' perhaps in fact never happened, it is a dream, a baroque dream of napalm and of the tropics, a psychotropic dream that had the goal neither of a victory nor of a policy at stake, but, rather, the sacrificial, excessive deployment of a power already filming itself as it unfolded, perhaps waiting for nothing but consecration by a superfilm, which completes the mass-spectacle effect of this war.

No real distance, no critical sense, no desire for 'raising consciousness' in relation to the war: and in a sense this is the brutal quality of this film – not being rotten with the moral psychology of war. Coppola can certainly deck out his helicopter captain in a ridiculous hat of the light cavalry, and make him crush the Vietnamese village to the sound of Wagner's music – those are not critical, distant signs, they are immersed in the machinery, they are part of the special effect, and he himself makes movies in the same way, with the same retro megalomania, and the same non-signifying furor, with the same clownish effect in overdrive. But there it is, he hits us with that, it is there, it is bewildering, and one can say to oneself: how is such a horror possible (not that of the war, but that of the film strictly speaking)? But there is no answer, there is no possible verdict, and one can even rejoice in this monstrous trick (exactly as with Wagner) – but one can always retrieve a tiny little idea that is not nasty, that is not a value judgment, but that tells you the war in Vietnam and this film are cut from the same cloth, that nothing separates them, that this film is part of the war – if the Americans (seemingly) lost the other one, they certainly won this one. *Apocalypse Now* is a global victory. Cinematographic power equal and superior to that of the industrial and military complexes, equal or superior to that of the Pentagon and of governments.

And all of a sudden, the film is not without interest: it retrospectively illuminates (not even retrospectively, because the film is a phase of this war without end) what was already crazy about this war, irrational in political terms: the Americans and the Vietnamese are already reconciled, right after the end of the hostilities the Americans offered economic aid, exactly as if they had annihilated the jungle and the towns, exactly as they are making their film today. One has understood nothing, neither about the war nor about cinema (at least the latter) if one has not grasped this lack of distinction that is no longer either an ideological or a moral one, one of good and evil, but one of the reversibility of both destruction and production, of the immanence of a thing in its very revolution, of the organic metabolism of all the technologies, of the carpet of bombs in the strip of film . . .

'I've killed more Indians than Custer, Beecher and Chivington put together'   JOHN FORD

JEAN BAUDRILLARD
The China Syndrome

This second essay by Baudrillard deals with a now forgotten movie on the dangers of nuclear power, James Bridges' The China Syndrome. *It became something of a sensation in its day when, very shortly after its release in 1978, there occurred the major and potentially catastrophic Three Mile Island incident.*

The fundamental stake is at the level of television and information. Just as the extermination of the Jews disappeared behind the televised event *Holocaust* – the cold medium of television having been simply substituted for the cold system of extermination one believed to be exorcising through it – so *The China Syndrome* is a great example of the supremacy of the televised event over the nuclear event which, itself, remains improbable and in some sense imaginary.

Besides, the film shows this to be the case (without wanting to): that TV is present precisely where it happens is not coincidental, it is the intrusion of TV into the reactor that seems to give rise to the nuclear incident – because TV is like its anticipation and its model in the everyday universe: telefission of the real and of the real world; because TV and information in general are a form of catastrophe in the formal and topological sense René Thom gives the word: a radical qualitative change of a whole system. Or, rather, TV and the nuclear are of the same nature: behind the 'hot' and negentropic concepts of energy and information, they have the same power of deterrence as cold systems do. TV itself is also a nuclear process of chain reaction, but implosive: it cools and neutralizes the meaning and the energy of events. Thus the nuclear, behind the presumed risks of explosion, that is to say of hot catastrophe, conceals a long, cold catastrophe, the universalization of a system of deterrence.

At the end of the film again comes the second massive intrusion of the press and of TV that instigates the drama – the murder of the technical director by the Special Forces, a drama that substitutes for the nuclear catastrophe that will not occur.

The homology of the nuclear and of television can be read directly in the images: nothing resembles the control and telecommand headquarters of the nuclear power station more than TV studios, and the nuclear consoles are combined with those of the recording and broadcasting studios in the same imaginary. Thus everything takes place between these two poles: of the other 'center', that of the reactor, in principle the veritable heart of the matter, we will know nothing; it, like the real, has vanished and become illegible, and is at bottom unimportant in the film (when one attempts to suggest it to us, in its imminent catastrophe, it does not work on the imaginary plane: the drama unfolds on the screens and nowhere else).

Harrisburg, Watergate, and *Network*: such is the trilogy of *The China Syndrome* – an indissoluble trilogy in which one no longer knows which is the effect and which is the symptom: the ideological argument (Watergate effect), isn't it nothing but the symptom of the nuclear (Harrisburg effect) or of the computer science model (Network effect) – the real (Harrisburg), isn't it nothing but the symptom of the imaginary (Network and China Syndrome) or the opposite? Marvelous indifferentiation, ideal constellation of simulation. Marvelous title, then, this *China Syndrome*, because the reversibility of symptoms and their convergence in the same process constitute precisely what we call a syndrome – that it is Chinese adds the poetic and intellectual quality of a conundrum or supplication.

Obsessive conjunction of *The China Syndrome* and Harrisburg. But is all that so involuntary? Without positing magical links between the simulacrum and the real, it is clear that the Syndrome is not a stranger to the 'real' accident in Harrisburg, not according to a causal logic, but according to the relations of contagion and silent analogy that link the real to models and to simulacra: to television's *induction* of the nuclear into the film corresponds, with a troubling obviousness, the film's *induction* of the nuclear incident in Harrisburg. Strange precession of a film over the real, the most surprising that was given us to witness: the real corresponded point by point to the simulacrum, including the suspended, incomplete character of the catastrophe, which is essential from the point of view of deterrence: the real arranged itself, in the image of the film, to produce a *simulation* of catastrophe.

From there to reverse our logic and to see in *The China Syndrome* the veritable event and in Harrisburg its simulacrum, there is only one step that must be cheerfully taken. Because it is via the same logic that, in the film, nuclear reality arises from the television effect, and that in 'reality' Harrisburg arises from the *China Syndrome* cinema effect.

But *The China Syndrome* is also not the original prototype of Harrisburg, one is not the simulacrum of which the other would be the real: there are only simulacra, and Harrisburg is a sort of second-order simulation. There is certainly a chain reaction somewhere, and we will perhaps die of it, but *this chain reaction is never that of the nuclear, it is that of simulacra* and of the simulation where all the energy of the real is effectively swallowed, no longer in a spectacular nuclear explosion, but in a secret and continuous implosion, and that today perhaps takes a more deathly turn than that of all the explosions that rock us.

Because an explosion is always a promise, it *is* our hope: note how much, in the film as in Harrisburg, the whole world waits for something to blow up, for destruction to announce itself and remove us from this unnameable panic, from this panic of deterrence that it exercises in the invisible form of the nuclear. That the 'heart' of the reactor at last reveals its hot power of destruction, that it reassures us about the presence of energy, albeit catastrophic, and bestows its *spectacle* on us. Because unhappiness is when there is no nuclear spectacle, no spectacle of nuclear energy in itself (Hiroshima is over), and it is for that reason that it is rejected – it would be perfectly accepted if it lent itself to spectacle as previous forms of energy did. Parousia of catastrophe: substantial food for our messianic libido.

But that is precisely what will never happen. What will happen will never again be the explosion, but the implosion. No more energy in its spectacular and pathetic form – all the romanticism of the explosion, which had so much charm, being at the same time that of revolution – but the cold energy of the simulacrum and of its distillation in homeopathic doses in the cold systems of information.

What else do the media dream of besides creating the event simply by their presence? Everyone decries it, but everyone is secretly fascinated by this eventuality. Such is the logic of simulacra, it is no longer that of divine predestination, it is that of the precession of models, but it is just as inexorable. And it is because of this that events no longer have meaning: it is not that they are insignificant in themselves, it is that they were preceded by the model, with which their processes only coincided. Thus it would have been marvelous to repeat the script for *The China Syndrome* at Fessenheim, during the visit offered to the journalists by the E D F (French Electric Company), to repeat on this occasion the accident linked to the magic eye, to the provocative presence of the media. Alas, nothing happened. And on the other hand yes! so powerful is the logic of simulacra: a week after, the unions discovered fissures in the reactors. Miracle of contagions, miracle of analogic chain reactions.

Thus, the essence of the film is not in any respect the Watergate effect in the person of Jane Fonda, not in any respect TV as a means of exposing nuclear vices, but on the contrary TV as the twin orbit and twin chain reaction of the nuclear one. Besides, just at the end – and there the film is unrelenting in regard to its own argument – when Jane Fonda makes the truth explode directly (maximum Watergate effect), her image is juxtaposed with what will inexorably follow it and efface it on the screen: a commercial of some kind. The Network effect goes far beyond the Watergate effect and spreads mysteriously into the Harrisburg effect, that is to say not into the nuclear threat, but into the *simulation* of nuclear catastrophe.

So, it is simulation that is effective, never the real. The simulation of nuclear catastrophe is the strategic result of this generic and universal undertaking of deterrence: accustoming the people to the ideology and the discipline of absolute security to the metaphysics of fission and fissure. To this end the fissure must be a fiction. A real catastrophe would delay things, it would constitute a retrograde incident, of the explosive kind (without changing the course of things: did Hiroshima perceptibly delay, deter, the universal process of deterrence?)

In the film, also, real fusion would be a bad argument: the film would regress to the level of a disaster movie – weak by definition, because it means returning things to their pure event. *The China Syndrome*, itself, finds its strength in filtering catastrophe, in the distillation of the nuclear specter through the omnipresent hertzian relays of information. It teaches us (once again without meaning to) that *nuclear catastrophe does not occur, is not meant to happen*, in the real either, any more than the atomic clash was at the dawning of the cold war. The equilibrium of terror rests on the eternal deferral of the atomic clash. The atom and the nuclear are made to be disseminated for deterrent ends, the power of catastrophe must, instead of stupidly exploding, be disseminated in homeopathic, molecular doses, in the continuous reservoirs of information. Therein lies the true contamination: never biological and radio-active, but, rather, a mental destructuration through a mental strategy of catastrophe.

If one looks carefully, the film introduces us to this mental strategy, and in going further, it even delivers a lesson diametrically opposed to that of Watergate: if every strategy today is that of mental terror and of deterrence tied to the suspension and the eternal simulation of catastrophe, then the only means of mitigating this scenario would be to *make* the catastrophe arrive, to produce or to reproduce a *real* catastrophe. To which Nature is at times given: in its inspired moments, it is God who through his cataclysms unknots the equilibrium of terror in which humans are imprisoned. Closer to us, this is what terrorism is occupied with as well: making real, palpable violence surface in opposition to the invisible violence of security. Besides, therein lies terrorism's ambiguity.

PETER GREENAWAY
Just Place, Preferably Architectural Place

Like all of Peter Greenaway's writings – and, indeed, his films – this brilliant essay can dispense with an editorial preface. (Greenaway himself, after all, is always ready to provide one of his own.) The disquiet induced by a genius loci? *The disquiet induced by, for example, the island of Sark? By the fogs and mists of Kurosawa's films? By the disturbingly long perspective of the Viennese cemetery in the even more disturbingly long closing shot of* The Third Man? *By Tigerlily's pagoda in the* Rupert Bear *comic strip, for Heaven's sake? You either get it or you don't.*

Place in preference to people. I know my enthusiasms to be stronger for a sense of place than for a sense of people. Yet I like crowds. Perhaps that is not so contradictory. Sufficient numbers of people on a flat and empty plane make a place, a *genius loci* with its own shape. And smell. And temperature. And when the crowd disperses, you are left with a pregnant void that's tangible enough.

At the moment, there is a pregnant void at the back of the Wallace Collection in Manchester Square that is causing me some tangible anxiety. Some disquiet. Disquiet is concomitant with a *genius loci*. It's a large and empty well or basement open to the air. There is no way down into it except from above, over the spear-headed railings, and I doubt whether the sun ever reaches the paving-stones at the bottom. More than once, freakishly, I've seen the shadow of an aircraft flick up the brick façade. The space is about six metres by seven and of triangular shape. It's kept clean and swept. Who sweeps it? The Wallace Collection is full of swords. I have some notion that this basement should be coloured brown and black, and heaped high with swords, and the window should be criss-crossed neatly with strips of sticky brown paper to prevent shattering by bomb-blast. I'm sure that there will have to be a film to justify the place.

This disquiet is not an infrequent occurrence. The island of Sark does it for me, and the house in Robbe-Grillet's *Jealousy*, and Tigerlily's pagoda in *Rupert Bear*, and the bridge of San Luis Rey, and Birnam Wood, and e.e. cummings's *Enormous Room*, the stairway in Kitaj's *Smyrna Greek*, and the open, unprotected country roads of *Uccellacci e uccellini*. Is the *genius* of the *loci* reconvertible? Consider working the situation backwards, and attempt to recreate a real location solely on the information given by a book. Or a painting. Or indeed a film. Very rapidly, that real landscape would be full of voids and blanks and grossly ill-fitting, disquieting details. Long practice has accustomed us to this misalignment of real space. Cinema audiences have well learnt to hide their anxieties and conspire in the great 'location-deception'.

Really to impress itself on the imagination, the place undoubtedly has to have been fashioned by humans. At the very least, it has to have been touched – even if briefly – by human hand. And then it preferably has to be 'untouched', released again a little from human grasp. This applies to the country landscape as well as to the city. Little in England has not been fashioned by human touch; there is little in England of what you could call wilderness. And a very long and extended and continuous human presence in a landscape is going to excite particularly. There aren't too many serious films about continually used landscape, about excavations, about serious archaeology, about a serious 'love of ruins'. Indiana Jones is no serious archaeologist.

If the delight in place is strong, if you can drive a car or catch a plane or take a boat to visit it, it is just as strong, if not stronger, if the place is physically unreachable. If it exists solely in words. In a painting. In a film. This way you can add your own disquiet. Are you going to find an audience who want to watch a film solely about the place? There aren't going to be any people in this hypothetical film – no actors, no extras, no crowds – but just the marks they have made, preferably the marks they made a long time ago. Maybe there could be just a few Chirico shadows on a wall in the middle distance. But the film would be full of quotations, like those impressive eighteenth-century *capriccios* which, avoiding the inconvenience of the unobtainable vantage-point and the uncooperative weather, could put your favourite building in a location of your choosing, could mix up chronologies and styles, could build a Utopian city of immaculate perspectives like della Francesca's Ideal Town. Make your ideal city. Put St Paul's on the Grand Canal and Cologne Cathedral in the Black Forest. You could go better, like Hadrian collecting all the great buildings of his empire and putting them together in his garden. More humbly, like Ellis at Portmeirion – though an Italian campanile in North Wales is problematical. Piranesi must be the most pre-eminent exponent, though Desiderio is more mysterious and Boullée more monumental. Delightfully, you can always prefabricate the same architectural deceptions in cinema, in a studio, with an armoury of devices – glass-painting, multiple light-sources, blue-screen backgrounds, *trompe l'oeil* artifices. Architecture built solely for the camera. At noon you can make dawn, and after lunch you can make midnight, with a moon that can be manipulated to shine right into the peristyle and separate out seven separate shadows from seven different pillars.

In this hypothetical *genius loci* film, I would quote the Italian suburbs in *La Strada* – town-edges smelling of burning rubbish and noisy with the echo of sentimental trombones bouncing off bleak tower-blocks. And the long autumn perspective of the cemetery at the end of *The Third Man*. The tree grove in Giovanni Bellini's *Death of St Peter Martyr* – though we would have to clean up the bloodstains. The isolated barns in the background of innumerable Stubbs paintings – new brick, new tiles, the smell of horse urine and the sound of skylarks. The damp ditch in Hunt's *Hireling Shepherd*, a patch of reed and dragonflies in C. S. Lewis's *Out of the Silent Planet*. All wet places are good – as long as there's no fear of drowning. I remember a Po-valley rice drama with Sophia Loren or Gina Lollobrigida – or was it Anna Magnani? I cannot see the actress's face or her bare legs, but I remember the low horizons and the puddled rice. I can hear mosquitoes.

Space with architecture. Is there much true interest in the cinema in architectural space for its own sake? Happily, I would say there is – often. Tisse photographing tenements for Eisenstein's *Strike*, Muller photographing New Orleans for Jarmusch's *Down By Law*, Coutard looking at Godard's Paris, especially (and unexpectedly) the tourist monuments, Fellini looking at Rome. With Fellini at the top of the list, there should certainly be two great directors of place – Resnais and Antonioni, with Vierny and Venanzo as cameramen.

I can think of Bogarde in Resnais' *Providence* taking a drive along a street of bourgeois buildings and middle-class palaces, accompanied by the most proud and celebratory music. Narratively slight, unaccountably disturbing. I have rarely looked at comparable buildings without experiencing an exciting disquiet. I remember the English equivalent all too well; every day I walked past similar ivy-covered domestic mausoleums on my way to school – each of their driveways was like a dual-carriageway main road. Resnais is an excellent placer of architecture. The black-and-white streets of collaborationist Nevers, the sunset casinos in *Muriel*, and the slumbering architectural nightmare-dreams of *Marienbad*. Post-*Marienbad*, I have now seen Atget's Versailles and St Cloud in still, photographic black-and-white. And they link me to Kurosawa's mists and fogs. How can you have a *genius loci* with dense mist and fog? Kurosawa's mists and fogs come with charging cavalrymen enveloped inside them like architectural details to help you find the scale.

To see how best to scale and pitch people, not against fog but against solid, shiny walls and dead brick and melancholic, end-of-the-day street-corners, look at any Antonioni black-and-white movie. Superb, atmospheric architectural montages. Even in Antonioni's London, which I am supposed to know – in *Blow-Up* – why didn't I see the quiet, urban parks in the wind, looking as dangerous as those Magritte houses at lamp-lighting time, and those isolated Carel Willink houses, northern Europe's answer to Hopper? I remember the fuss over the mushroom water-towers in Antonioni's *The Eclipse* – harbingers of the atomic cloud. I like water-towers. And I like beach-houses. In northern Europe, they are both touched and then untouched places, without being archaeology. They are abandoned, not-abandoned places. You never see a water-tower and a person together. And nobody – in England – ever lives in a beach-house. Except us. As children. As a family. My father liked the smell of creosote and methylated spirits – the first to keep out the water and the second to boil it with. For tea. My father liked the damp, and he was a keen appreciator of the *genius loci*.

Hilla and Bernd Becher are for taking pictures of water-towers as Meyerowitz is for taking pictures of beach-houses. I had photographed water-towers along the River Humber in Yorkshire, perverting their purposes, imagining they had been converted into echoic film-vaults, having in their blunt circularity much sympathetic resemblance to a stack of empty film-cans that clanged when kicked. Meyerowitz's white-frame, damp-floored beach-houses, variously photographed in conditions of thunderstorm or bright noon light, inspired a canvas-sailed, pavilioned beach-house from the art department of *Drowning by Numbers*. That beach-house pleased and entertained so much that prints from the film-frame were demanded by German and American viewers, thinking perhaps that they too could build themselves such a country cabin or seaside gazebo. One gentleman from Maine sent us a cheque for five thousand dollars for the plans. But our building was pasteboard to the winds of the North Sea, and it blew right away in October 1987, on the night of the one and only English hurricane of the twentieth century.

The strongest remembrances of a sense of place I have as a child were of beaches – any beaches – the unfamiliar places of summer vacations. If possible, I was the last to leave the shore, shut the beach-house door, close the curtains, pull down the blinds, never certain I would see the world outside again just as I left it.

I was hesitant about travel because of the unlikelihood of being able to repeat my coveted experience of place. As a child, I especially disliked travelling fast in case I failed to understand the connections between places. I slept on trains to avoid consequent misalignment, and I was happy that there were superstitions enough to legitimize my fear of not seeing a place again. I threw coins in every fountain. I begged the use of a cheap camera, but twenty-four black-and-white snaps of the sea and sand in poor focus were not good enough. I still felt uncomfortable in an unknown city until Sacha Vierny encouraged me to carry a compass. He always carries one – it's about the size of a squashed pea. He uses it to be certain from which direction the sun's going to attack him and thwart his control. With a compass at least you can know where north is. A map usually fixes the discomfort. At least a map will offer a spurious sense of capture, and will situate the details and continuity of a place even if you cannot experience every single street. I need to see the back of buildings. Perhaps that's the interest of the basement at the back of the Wallace Collection in London W1.

I am certain now that those early anxieties were not irrelevant to the question of light, because night so often annihilated the problem. I well knew the possibility of change in a location was less likely after dark. Perhaps it is an English preoccupation, since the light changes quickly in England and cannot be relied upon to be repeated. Constable knew this. So did Turner. Constable faced it out and stayed. Turner became exasperated and went to Italy. The value of my anxiety has changed; it has now become professional not personal. I suspect one of the unadvertised reasons for the claustrophobic studio shoots of my past three feature films has to do with anxiety about volatile light-changes outside the film-maker's control.

No architectural excitement of place can be separated from the excitements of light. In *A Zed and Two Noughts*, much of the background

architecture was the Hollywood-Dutch Art Deco of van Ravenstyn. At
night, through the camera, the architecture seemed to be newly minted.
Lion and tiger prowled with beautiful incongruity among the softly
moulded edges. In daylight, all the camera persisted in seeing was
the decay of rusting bars and stucco falling off the rococo concrete.
Architecture of space after dark is almost a genre in itself, with a
particular and curious rule that, for once, the camera can sometimes
see what the human eye cannot – unless, that is, the director uses the
light of a wartime explosion or the flare of a firework display. The
celebrated train-spotter O. Winston Link, setting out to trap fast-moving
locomotives in the blink of a startled eye, also incidentally trapped
small-town railway architecture, throwing the brightest of lights uniquely
into front porches and dead-of-night sitting-rooms. Bergman's moonlit
forests in *The Seventh Seal* should be reprised in this hypothetical film
of place, and it is unsettling and comforting at the same time to know
that these are not rolling broadleaf oak forests that stretched from
Sweden to the Urals in thirteenth-century Europe, but were a thicket
of softwoods on the set backlot in the 1950s. You can cheat the *genius
loci*.

Architectural space on film is stubborn. To film architecture is to
become aware of multiple curiosities of vision and downright retinal
deceptions.

On the film *Belly of an Architect* Sacha Vierny and I paced and
re-paced selected buildings in Rome to find the exact required emphasis
of man and building. We never found it with the impossibly sited
Augusteum, which refused to permit its totality to be seen in any
conceivable wide-shot, but maybe the Pantheon and the Victor
Emmanuel building were more lenient. If your favoured architectural
setting is classical, then you have to fight the frustrating immutability
of verticals that persist in pretending not to be diagonals – not every
film can shoot its architectural verticals on the angle like Reed's *The
Third Man*. You have to accept the disappointment of the refusal of
carefully stage-managed entasis to work for the camera lens. All the
important horizontals sag in wide-shot. A painter can cheat. Canaletto
painting Venice. Saenredam painting Amsterdam churches. Piranesi
drawing Rome. Even Sickert painting Camden Town. The painter easily
invents multiple vanishing-points. He is cavalier with scale. He keeps
an arbitrary palette. His ubiquitous vision is enviable. He can see – with
apparent conviction – both sides of the same wall at once. However, if

a painter cheats within his very agreeable licences, it is not to say that the architect has not cheated before him. I have come to believe that, in terms of classical perfection, the architect, or perhaps it is his builder, has taken just as many liberties, for the camera – which of course never lies – refuses to agree that the spot chosen by the architect as the centre of all things really is the centre of all things: it's five metres to the right, up a bit, and facing south-south-west – not west at all.

I have, on more than one occasion, been accused of wasting actors in the interests of praising architecture: 'Why employ such talent if all you want is an architectural mannikin, a scale figure for a façade, a body to measure off a curving space?' However, I am pleased to know now three actors, self-consciousness permitting, who are happy to sit in front of a fine piece of architecture and clap it if it pleases them, like the architectural enthusiasts applauding the Roman Pantheon in *The Belly of an Architect*. The architecture in these three cases was first, not surprisingly, the Taj Mahal, then more surprisingly the Wrexham gasometer, and then, most disturbingly, anything by Quinlan Terry – you may create the habit, but there is no telling the result.

Why can't we simply applaud the excitements, the drama and the changing light of a sense of place? One day, I'm going to do it. No actors. No dialogue. No plot. No narrative. No extras. No crowds. It was said of the Great Mosque at Córdoba – a place that is truly architecturally astonishing – that 'there is nothing crueller in life than to be blind in Córdoba'. Now that would be some epitaph for a film.

'The living ones want their life fiction, and the fiction ones want their life real'   WOODY ALLEN

Reflecting

BÉLA BALÁZS
Filming Death

The Hungarian Béla Balázs (1884–1949) was many 'ists': journalist, dramatist (a collaborator, notably, of Erwin Piscator and Max Rein-hardt), scenarist (of G. W. Pabst's controversial film version of Brecht and Weill's The Threepenny Opera*), librettist (of Bartók's opera* Bluebeard's Castle*) and, last if certainly not least, the cinema's very first Marxist theorist. In this essay, extracted from his critical study,* The Theory of the Film, *he confronts an important parameter of filmic specificity: the fact that, no matter the genre, no matter the style, no matter the period in which a film is set, or was made, there will always be about its imagery an ineradicable immediacy, what one might call a* hereness *and* nowness.

Not surprisingly, that sense of immediacy is most powerfully felt in newsreel footage, which is why the images described by Balázs, of war, of death, of calamity, of the faceless gueules cassées, *will never date. The images, above all, of the concentration camps will never date – not in a thousand years to come. Indeed, it might even be said that, had it not been for the invention of film, we might never have known what the Holocaust looked like.*

What concerns us here are not open-air photographs of thousands of guns, flying armadas or bursting bombs and shells but what is at the root of it all, the human face, which only the film camera can approach so intimately.

In general war films are as primitive and brutal as is war itself. For this reason only one war film is to be mentioned here. Its artistic and moral message is such that it is worthy of being preserved forever in some Pantheon of greatest human documents.

This film was made after the First World War and its title was *Pour La Paix du Monde*. It was produced by the French organization of the most grievously injured of all war-wounded, the name of which was 'Les Gueules Cassés'. The director who compiled the film from the strips in the archives of the armed forces was Colonel Piquard, chairman of the organization of the 'Faceless Ones', the men who lived like lepers in an isolated, secret community of their own, because the sight of them would have been unbearable for their fellow-men. The film begins by showing these faceless ones in close-up, their mutilations covered by masks. Then they take off their silken masks and with it they tear the mask off the face of war.

Those whom the war has robbed of their faces show the true face of war to those who know nothing of it. And this physiognomy of war is of an emotional power, a force of pathos no artistic feature film about the war had ever attained. For here war is presented by its victims, horror is presented by the horrified, torture by the tortured, deadly peril by those endangered – and it is they who see these things in their true colours. A panning shot glides over a quiet, a now quietened battlefield. The desolation of a lunar landscape. Nowhere a single blade of grass. On the mountainside gunfire has peeled the earth from the naked rock. Shell craters, trenches without end. The camera pans slowly round without stopping. Trenches full of dead bodies, more trenches and more and more and more. An immense space in which nothing moves. Corpses, corpses, only corpses. Panorama. This stolid monotony which takes hold of you and will not let go is like a long-drawn, desperate howling.

Here is another shot: a whole regiment blinded by poison gas is being driven through the streets of burning Bruges. Yes, the herd of blind men is being driven like a herd of sheep, herded with bayonet and butt to keep them from running into the burning ruins in their path. A picture for another Dante.

But there are worse things, although no human beings appear. The gardens of the Champagne after the German retreat. (It was not in the Second World War that the Germans invented some of their methods.) We see a charnel-house of an ancient and lovely orchard culture. Thousands of precious, noble fruit-trees neatly sawed off by power-saw, all exactly at the same height. The creation of centuries of skill and industry destroyed with machine-like accuracy. These pictures, too, have a physiognomy; the distorted faces of the tree-corpses are no less terrible than those of the human dead. But the caption to this, of course silent, shot was not: 'Behold the German barbarian!' It said 'C'est la guerre!' The noble faith of French peace-lovers did not blame the Germans even here, it blamed war. Nevertheless, under the Weimar Republic the showing of this film was banned in Germany.

This French documentary of the First World War was dedicated to the six cameramen who had been killed on active service while shooting it. The Soviet war film showing the conquest of Berlin names in its credits fourteen cameramen killed while shooting it. This fate of the creative artist is also a new phenomenon in cultural history and is specific to film art. Artists in olden days rarely died of their dangerous creative work. And this has not merely a moral or political significance, but is of importance for the psychology of art as well.

This presentation of reality by means of motion pictures differs essentially from all other modes of presentation in that the reality being presented is not yet completed; it is itself still in the making while the presentation is being prepared. The creative artist does not need to dip into his memory and recall what has happened – he is present at the happening itself and participates in it.

When someone tells about past battles, these battles are already over and the greatest perils are no longer perils, once they are past and can be told by word of mouth or print.

The camera image is different. It is not made after the event. The cameraman is himself in the dangerous situation we see in his shot and it is by no means certain that he will survive the birth of his picture. Until the strip has been run to its end we cannot know whether it will be completed at all. It is this tangible being-present that gives the documentary the peculiar tension no other art can produce.

Whoever has listened to a report given over a field telephone, when the noise of battle, the rattle of shots and the screams of the wounded can be heard together with the words spoken into the microphone, will have experienced this tension in the acoustic sphere. Such telephone reports sometimes break off in the middle of a sentence and the silence that follows is as eloquent as a scream of mortal agony.

In the French war film just discussed, a sequence suddenly breaks off. It darkens and the camera wobbles. It is like an eye glazing in death. The director did not cut out this 'spoilt' bit – it shows where the camera was overturned and the cameraman killed, while the automatic mechanism ran on. In another picture we see the cameraman dying for the sake of his picture.

The significance of such shots lies not in the death-despising courage to which they bear witness. We have often heard of men who could look death in the eye. We may even have seen them. What is new and different here is that these cameramen look death in the face through the lens of a movie picture camera. This happens not only on battlefields.

Who could forget Captain Scott's film, which is almost as if he had shot his own death and breathed his last sigh into a microphone?

Who could forget Sir Ernest Shackleton's magnificent pictures of his Antarctic journey or the film taken by the Soviet Polar explorers camping beside the wreck of the ice-breaker *Chelyuskin*?

Yes, it is a new form of human consciousness that was born out of the union of man and camera. For as long as these men do not lose consciousness, their eye looks through the lens and reports and renders conscious their situation. The ice crushes their ship and with it their last hope? They shoot. The ice-floe melts under their feet? They shoot. They shoot the fact that there is scarcely room left for them to set up the camera.

Like the captain on his bridge, like the wireless operator at his set, the cameraman remains at his post to the last instant. The internal processes of presence of mind and observation are here projected outwards into the bodily action of operating the camera. The operator sees clearly and calmly as long as he is shooting in this way; it is this that helps him mechanically to preserve his consciousness, which in other circumstances consists of a sequence of images in the mind. But now it is projected outwards and runs in the camera as a strip of film, which is of advantage because the camera has no nerves and therefore is not easily perturbed. The psychological process is inverted – the cameraman does not shoot as long as he is conscious – he is conscious as long as he is shooting.

ERWIN LEISER
The Wandering Jew

Erwin Leiser was a Berlin-born historian and filmmaker who emigrated to Sweden in 1938 and subsequently settled in Switzerland. His most significant work in the cinema was a trio of documentaries detailing and denouncing the abuses of totalitarianism: Mein Kampf *(1959),* Eichmann und das dritte Reich *(1961) and* Deutschland, erwache! *(or, in English,* Germany Awake!*), a 1967 film on the insidiously 'ordinary Nazism' which, long after the Second World War, continued to fester in his native country. The following text is extracted from his book,* Nazi Cinema, *the English translation of which was published in 1975.*

There were several versions of the 'documentary film' produced by the Reich Propaganda Department of the National Socialist Party under the title *The Wandering Jew* [*Der Ewige Jude*, also known as *The Eternal Jew*]. 'Sensitive souls' were advised to see the shorter version, from which the Jewish ritual slaughter sequences were omitted. The commentary by Eberhard Taubert was dropped in the foreign language versions of the film; its demagogic tone, aimed at German audiences, might have damaged the credibility of the 'document'. The effect of this was to give more prominence to the music, which here, as in other anti-Jewish propaganda films, took on a turgid oriental flavour the moment Jews appeared on the screen. Shots of Nordic people, on the other hand, were accompanied by Bach. The film was mostly shot in the Jewish areas of Poland, though the commentary omits to mention that it was the Nazis themselves who were responsible for the dingy, cramped conditions of these ghettos. The opening sentence immediately sets the tone: 'The civilized Jews such as those we know in Germany provide an incomplete picture of their racial characteristics. This film shows original material shot in the Polish ghettos, shows us the Jews as they really looked before they concealed themselves behind the mask of civilized Europeans.'

The ghetto was 'a breeding ground of epidemics . . . endangering the

health of the Aryan people'. The implication is that here was a menace
which must be 'resisted'. A montage sequence of rats, calculated to leave
an indelible impression on the minds of any audience, is accompanied by
a commentary informing us that rats 'have followed men like parasites
from the very beginning', destroying the country and spreading disease.
'They are cunning, cowardly and fierce, and usually appear in large packs.
In the animal world they represent the element of insidious subterranean
destruction.' 'Not dissimilar from the place Jews have among men,' the
commentary continues, as the rats are followed by shots of Jews crowded
together in the ghetto. It could hardly be stated more clearly: the killing
of one or of many Jews was not a crime but a necessity. Jews, the film
implies, are not human beings but pests which have to be exterminated.

This montage was duly applauded by the critics. The correspondent
from the *Deutsche Allgemeine Zeitung* 'heaved a sign of relief when the
film ended with pictures of Germans and things German'. Apart from
The Wandering Jew, distorted documentary material included several
short exercises which in similar vein compared Jews with cockroaches.

. . . Emmanuel Ringelblum, the historian of the Warsaw ghetto, has
described how the German film cameramen went about their work in
the summer of 1942. Jews were herded together and then the Jewish
security police were ordered to disperse them. Scenes showing very
Jewish-looking men locked together in the ritual baths with young
women were manufactured to create the impression that the Jews
bathed together in the nude. A restaurant owner was forced to lay
his tables to suggest to the audience an abundance of delicacies and
champagne; then Jews were indiscriminately rounded up on the streets
and filmed eating and drinking. Grocery shop windows were filled with
rare delicacies before being filmed. These shots were supposed to
convey to German audiences that the Jews in the ghettos were far too
prosperous. The banquet was meant to incite envy and resentment
among those who could not afford such expensive food. At the same
time film of the miserable conditions in the ghetto was juxtaposed with
doctored images of a fictitious prosperity; some of this material was
used in a series of articles in the *Berliner Illustrierter* entitled 'Jews at
home'. Jews were said to be cruel to each other, while the rich Jews of
the ghetto were indifferent to the poor; and scenes were shot to prove
this cruelty. A member of the Jewish security police is about to strike
a Jew when a German runs up to stop him. A boy is made to steal a loaf
of bread and run off with it to his friends, who are supposed to be hiding

him and his loot. In reality there was hardly any bread in the ghetto, and the guards at the walls stopped any food being taken in. But in the film the little thief is protected from the baker and the police by a German. Beating children is wrong.

According to the commentary of *The Wandering Jew*, the ghetto's poor were not poor at all, but 'through decades of trading had hoarded enough money to make clean and comfortable homes for themselves and their families. Yet they continue to live for generations in the same dirty, flea-ridden holes.' In reality, according to Governor General Frank, the one consolation the Poles themselves had was that 'the Jews are even worse off'. While one of Himmler's aides was proposing that the Poles should be forced to practise birth control and should be allowed only four years of primary school education, the ghettos which the SS set up all over the East were being designated as the first phase in the physical annihilation of all Jews. They were deliberately located near railway lines; it would thus be no trouble to deport those who hadn't died on the spot to one of the extermination camps.

Nazi cameramen recorded every stage in the demoralization process, filming starving people begging on the streets or lying outside their houses too weak to move; children who grew up in the shadow of death, plagued by vermin and disease, unsmiling and with no toys to play with, their eyes already old and accustomed to misery and death; epidemics raging in the ghetto – though there was of course no mention of the fact that these very epidemics were spread by the Nazis under the pretence of fighting them. There is also no reference in these filmed records to the fact that immediately after the defeat of Poland an area of ten square kilometres in Warsaw was transformed into a ghetto. This district had previously housed a population of 240,000 Jews and 80,000 non-Jews. Now the non-Jews had to move out to make room for hundreds of thousands of Jews forcibly transported to the ghetto. There were initially six people to every room in the ghetto, but this soon rose to thirteen to a room. People who only a few weeks before had been living a normal life found themselves forced to live and die like rats in the ghetto. Herein lies the cynicism of a 'document' like *The Wandering Jew*: people confined in a world of dirt like animals in overcrowded cages, and their subsequent degradation presented as though it were completely normal, an existence which these victims of the Nazi terror had supposedly chosen for themselves, a simple demonstration of the theory that Jews are not people like you and me.

The most harrowing sequences from these Nazi films on the hell devised in the Polish ghettos for the victims of the 'final solution' were never used. It was by no means certain that the material would actually induce loathing and resentment in the general public. Preview audiences had in fact been sympathetic. And it was precisely the most vicious of the doctored sequences which produced this unintended effect. Pairs of Jewish men and women had been put in front of the camera to demonstrate social differences which had been contrived for these very shots, but the eyes of those filmed expressed something altogether different from what the cameramen had been trying to register. What was communicated was the silent despair of these humiliated people, who knew that what awaited them after the filming was an unknown and degrading death.

In 1945 representatives of the International Red Cross visited the Jewish 'model camp' at Theresienstadt (Terezin) in Czechoslovakia and were shown part of a film made there in the summer of 1944. Kurt Gerron, a once prominent actor who had emigrated to Holland in 1933, had fallen into the hands of the Gestapo there and was now a prisoner at the camp, was given the responsibility for writing and directing a film called *The Führer Gives the Jews a Town*, which was designed to reveal Theresienstadt as a 'paradise for Jews'. Like all other investigators, when I questioned survivors of Theresienstadt, I found some dispute about Gerron's contribution to the film and his motives for collaborating on it. When the film was completed, Gerron and most of the other leading collaborators were deported to Poland and gassed. At the very moment when the transports to the extermination camps were being got under way, thousands of Theresienstadt inmates were recruited as extras in a film designed to camouflage what was really happening in the camp. The film included a number of scenes with children designed to create the impression that Theresienstadt was a particularly pleasant place for children to be. Since in the autumn of 1944 an estimated 1,600 children were deported from Theresienstadt, and in the Auschwitz selection process no child who looked under fourteen escaped the gas chamber, most of the children in the film must have been murdered soon after it was completed. There were shops in the film which were specially constructed for the cameras and in which there was nothing to buy. A stage was built for an open-air cabaret show at a spot which was normally out of bounds to prisoners. In the film's Theresienstadt, people are happily playing football, well-fed men stand under showers, coquettish girls are busy putting on make-up. In his book *The Hidden Truth*, H. G. Adler quotes as an example of the way in which the Nazis were planning to use film – but which to a large extent was by this time no longer feasible – a newsreel from the autumn of 1944 which juxtaposes a coffee-house scene shot in Theresienstadt with a montage of scenes from the front lines. The commentator remarks: 'While Jews in Theresienstadt sit enjoying coffee and cakes and dance around, our soldiers are bearing the brunt of this terrible war, the suffering and the hardship, to defend their homeland.'

MED HONDO
What is Cinema for Us?

The (filmically speaking) anglophobic François Truffaut once infamously
mused on what he was pleased to call, with a contempt that was all the
more cutting for being held at barge-pole length, 'a certain incompati-
bility between the terms "Britain" and "cinema"'. The British were
naturally outraged by so cavalier a dismissal of an industrious century
of national film production, and even those of us willing to travel some
little way along the road with him on this issue found it difficult to
defend his flagrant manifesto of pure prejudice. Yet what about, say,
Africa? If pressed, wouldn't most British buffs have to admit to har-
bouring a similar prejudice where the incompatibility of the terms
'cinema' and 'Africa' is concerned? How many of them have ever actually
seen, have ever actually cared to see or tried to see an African film, a
film from a single African country – one by, for example, the Egyptian
Youssef Chahine or the Senegalese Ousmane Sembène or the Malian
Souleymane Cissé or the Mauritanian Med Hondo, each of them a finer
artist than all but a tiny cluster of British filmmakers? How pawed over
are the movies! And how little-known is the cinema!

Throughout the world when people use the term 'cinema' all
refer more or less consciously to a single cinema, which for more than
half a century has been created, produced, industrialised, programmed
and then shown on the world's screens: Euro-American cinema. This
cinema has gradually imposed itself on a set of dominated peoples. With
no means of protecting their own cultures, these peoples have been
systematically invaded by diverse, cleverly articulated cinematographic
products. The ideologies of these products never 'represent' their personality, their collective or private way of life, their cultural codes, or,
of course, the least reflection of their specific 'art', their way of thinking,
of communicating – in a word, their own history . . . their civilisation.

The images this cinema offers systematically exclude the African and
the Arab. It would be dangerous (and impossible) to reject this cinema

as simply alien – the damage is done. We must get to know it, the better to analyse it and to understand that this cinema has never really concerned the African and Arab peoples. This seems paradoxical, since it fills all the cinemas, dominates the screens of all African and Arab cities and towns. But do the masses have any other choice? 'Consuming' at least fifty films in a year, how many films does the average African see that really talk to him? Is there a single one which evokes the least resonance, the least reflection of his people's life and history – past, present and future? Is there a single image of the experiences of his forefathers, heroes of African and Arab history? Is there a single film inscribed in the new reality of co-operation, communication, support, and solidarity of Africans and Arabs?

In *Lawrence of Arabia* an image of Lawrence – not of the Arabs – is disseminated. In *Gentleman of Cocodie* a European is the gentleman hero, and not an Ivorian. This may seem exaggerated. Some will say that at least one African country, Egypt, produces some relatively important films each year; that since independence in African countries a number of cinéastes have made a future for themselves. In the whole continent of Africa, Egypt is only one country, one cultural source, one sector of the market – and few African countries buy Egyptian films. They produce too few films, and the market within Egypt is still dominated by foreign films.

African and Arab film-makers have decided to produce their own films. But despite their undoubted quality they have no chance of being distributed normally, at home or in the dominant countries, except in marginalised circuits – the dead-end art cinemas. Even a few dozen more film-makers producing films would only achieve a ratio of one to ten thousand. An everyday creative dynamic is necessary for a radical change in the relationship between the dominant Euro-American production and distribution networks and African and Arab production and distribution, which we must control.

Only in this way, in a spirit of creative and stimulating competition between African and Arab film-makers, can we make artistic progress and become competitive in the world market. We must first control our own markets, satisfy our own peoples' desires to liberate their screens, then establish respectful relations with other peoples, and balanced exchange.

We must change the humiliating relationship between dominating and dominated, between masters and slaves.

Some flee this catastrophic state of affairs, thinking cinema restricted to Western, Christian and capitalist élites, or throwing a cloak of fraternal paternalism over our film-makers, ignoring and discrediting their works, blaming them, in the short term forcing them to comply with a formal and ethical mimesis – imitating precisely those cinemas we denounce – in order to become known and be admitted into international cinema, in the end forcing them into submission, into renouncing their own lives, their creativity and their militancy.

Since the independence of our countries, a sizeable number of our film-makers have proved their abilities as auteurs. They encounter increasing difficulties in surviving and continuing to work, because their films are seldom distributed and no aid is forthcoming. Due to the total lack of a global cultural policy, African and Arab cinema is relegated to being an exotic and episodic subproduct, limited to aesthetic reviews at festivals, which, although not negligible, are undoubtedly insufficient.

Each year millions of dollars are harvested from our continents, taken back to the original countries, then used to produce new films which are again sent out onto our screens. Fifty per cent of the profits of multinational film companies accrue from the screens of the Third World. Thus each of our countries unknowingly contributes substantial finance to the production of films distributed in Paris, New York, London, Rome or Hong Kong. They have no control over them, and reap no financial or moral benefit, being involved in neither the production nor the distribution. In reality, however, they are coerced into being 'co-producers'. Their resources are plundered.

The United States permits a penetration of foreign films in its domestic market of less than 13 percent – and most of these are produced by European subsidiaries controlled by the US majors. They exercise an absolute protectionism.

Most important is the role of the cinema in the construction of peoples' consciousness. Cinema is the mechanism *par excellence* for penetrating the minds of our peoples, influencing their everyday social behaviour, directing them, diverting them from their historic national responsibilities. It imposes alien and insidious models and references, and without apparent constraint enforces the adoption of modes of behaviour and communication of the dominating ideologies. This damages their own cultural development and blocks true communication between Africans and Arabs, brothers and friends who have been historically united for thousands of years.

This alienation disseminated through the image is all the more dangerous for being insidious, uncontroversial, 'accepted', seemingly inoffensive and neutral. It needs no armed forces and no permanent programme of education on the part of those seeking to maintain the division of the African and Arab peoples – to enforce their weakness, submission, servitude, their ignorance of each other and of their own history. They forget their positive heritage, united through their forefathers with all humanity. Above all, they have no say in the progress of world history.

Dominant imperialism seeks to prevent the portrayal of African and Arab values to other nations; were those responsible for this imperialism to appreciate our values and behaviour, they might respond positively to us. We are not proposing isolation, the closing of frontiers to all Western film, nor any protectionism separating us from the rest of the world. We wish to survive, develop, participate as sovereign peoples in our own specific cultural fields, and fulfil our responsibilities in a world from which we are now excluded. The night of colonialism caused many quarrels among us; we have yet to assess the full consequences. It poisoned our potential communications with other peoples; we are forced into relations of colonial domination. We have only preconceived and false ideas of each other imprinted by racism. Those who dominate us believe themselves 'superior'; they are unaware of our peoples' roles in world history.

We have been colonised and then subjected to even more pernicious imperialist domination. Although we are not entirely responsible for this state of affairs, some intellectuals, writers, film-makers, thinkers – our cultural leaders and policy-makers – are responsible for perpetuating this insatiable domination. It has never been enough simply to denounce our dominators, for they dictate the rules of their game to their own advantage. Some African and Arab film-makers realise that the cinema alone cannot change our disadvantaged position, but they know that it is the best means of education and information and thus of solidarity.

It is imperative to organise our forces, to reassert our different creative potentialities, and to fill the void in our national, regional and continental cinemas. We must establish relations of communication and co-operation between our peoples, in a spirit of equality, dignity and justice. We have the will, the means and the talent to undertake this great enterprise. Without organisation of resources we cannot flourish at home, and dozens of African and Arab intellectuals, film-makers, technicians, writers, journalists and leaders have had to leave their countries, often despite themselves, to contribute to the development and overdevelopment of countries that don't need them, and that use their excesses to dominate us. This will continue until we grasp the crucial importance of this cultural and economic strategy, and create our own networks of film production and distribution, liberating ourselves from all foreign monopolies.

Worshipping

BUSTER KEATON

The infant Buster Keaton, born on 4 October 1895, and hence just two months older than the cinema itself. Apparently, he declined to smile even way back then. Yet it's perhaps worth recalling that his fabled impassivity worked both ways – he had the good taste, rare in a clown, never to shed tears.

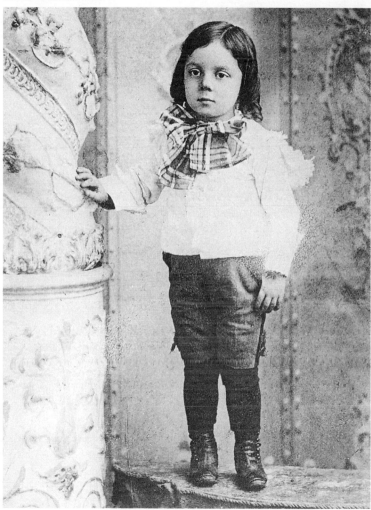

ANDRÉ BAZIN
Entomology of the Pin-up Girl

*Psychologists and neurologists concur in the view that humankind sleeps
in order to dream, not vice-versa, and it may equally be that we go to
the cinema for the same reason. Hollywood, after all, was familiarly
dubbed the 'Dream Factory'.*

*Dreams, we have also been assured, bear an intimate kinship to sex,
and the most potent dreams to roll off Hollywood's production line have
been vehicles for impossible sex objects, women (men as well, of course)
preserved on celluloid, as in amber. Garbo's off-screen anonymity could
not dim the luminosity of her on-screen beauty. Marilyn may have died,
she has not dated. Bardot, no matter how she has aged, is a kitten still.
Film, a medium whose function was defined by Cocteau as revealing
death at work, is also that which has realized the eternal fantasy of
eternal youth.*

*Here is the critic André Bazin, the mentor of the French New Wave,
writing on the phenomenon of the pin-up.*

First, let us not confuse the pin-up girl with the pornographic or
erotic imagery that dates from the dark backward and abysm of time.
The pin-up girl is a specific erotic phenomenon, both as to form and
function.

Definition and Morphology
A wartime product created for the benefit of the American soldiers
swarming to a long exile at the four corners of the world, the pin-up
girl soon became an industrial product, subject to well-fixed norms and
as stable in quality as peanut butter or chewing gum. Rapidly perfected,
like the jeep, among those things specifically stipulated for modern
American military sociology, she is a perfectly harmonized product of
given racial, geographic, social, and religious influences.

Physically, this American Venus is a tall, vigorous girl whose long
streamlined body splendidly represents a tall race. Different from the

Greek ideal, with its shorter legs and torso, she thus differs distinctly from European Venuses. With her narrow hips, the pin-up girl does not evoke motherhood. Instead, let us note particularly the firm opulence of her bosom. American eroticism – and hence cinematic eroticism – seems to have moved in recent years from the leg to the breast.

The parading of Marlene Dietrich and of her legs, with their almost mathematically perfect contours, the success of Rita Hayworth, the success (this time *de scandale*) in Howard Hughes' film *The Outlaw* of Jane Russell, whose twin hemispheres were inflated by an airborne publicity campaign to the size of clouds, are an indication of this sweeping displacement in the geography of sex appeal – or rather, since the term is already out of date, in 'man appeal'. The vanguard of feminine attractiveness stands today at the level of the heart. I offer as proof reports which reach us from Hollywood, and the suit that Paulette Goddard has brought against a journalist who dared to suggest that she wore falsies.

An adequate physique, a young and vigorous body, provokingly firm breasts still do not define the pin-up girl for us. She must also conceal that bosom, which we are not supposed to get a peep at. The clever kind of censorship which clothing can exercise is perhaps more essential than the most unmistakable anatomic affirmation.

The typical garment of the pin-up girl is the two-piece bathing suit – which coincides with the limitations authorized socially by fashion and modesty in recent years. At the same time, however, an infinite variety of suggestive degrees of undress – never exceeding some rigorously defined limits – show off to advantage the charms of the pin-up girl while pretending to hide them. For my part, I am inclined to consider these niceties somewhat decadent: a contamination of the pure pin-up with traditional erotic imagery. At any rate, it is only too obvious that the veils in which the pin-up girl is draped serve a dual purpose: they comply with the social censorship of a Protestant country which otherwise would not have allowed the pin-up girl to develop on an industrial and quasi-official scale; but at the same time make it possible to experiment with the censoring itself and use it as an additional form of sexual stimulus. The precise balance between the requirements of censorship and the maximum benefits one can derive from them without lapsing into an indecency too provocative for public opinion defines the existence of the pin-up girl, and clearly distinguishes her from the salaciously erotic or pornographic postcard.

The science of these forms of provocative undress has been developed to a nicety: today Rita Hayworth need only take off her gloves to draw admiring whistles from a hall full of Americans.

Metamorphosis of the Pin-up Girl
The multiplication and absurdity of today's supporting decors in contrast to the childlike and unsophisticated simplicity of the first pin-ups, can be explained by the need felt by the artist or photographer to vary his presentation. There are several thousand ways to show a pretty girl in a bathing suit, but certainly not hundreds of thousands. But as we see it, this development is a disintegration of the ideal of the pin-up girl.

A wartime product, a weapon of war, with the coming of peace the pin-up has lost her essential *raison d'être*. In the process of its revival this wartime myth is being separated into its two components, eroticism and morality. On the one hand, the pin-up girl tends to revert to the category of sex imagery and all its hypocritical vestiary complications; on the other to post-mobilization domestic virtues. Furthermore, in the United States there are even contests for 'pin-up mothers' and 'pin-up babies'. And finally, the advertisers of tonic waters, chewing gum, and cigarettes are trying to convert the various salvageable surpluses for peacetime purposes.

Philosophy of the Pin-up Girl
In a general history of eroticism, and more specifically in a history of eroticism as it relates to the cinema, the pin-up girl embodies the sexual ideal of the future. In *Brave New World* Aldous Huxley tells us that when children are produced in test-tubes, relations between men and women, sterile henceforth, will have no other purpose than unrestricted pleasure. Huxley neatly sums up the idea of beauty and female sexual attractiveness in an epithet that is at once tactile, muscular, and visual, the adjective 'pneumatic'. Is not the pneumatic girl of Huxley the archetype, projected into the future, of the Varga girl? In a long-drawn-out, distant war of invasion, the feminine ideal necessarily represents imagination, sterility, play. The pin-up girl is the expression of this idea, extended to the pure status and scope of a myth, in a society where Protestantism still maintains a vigilant censorship.

The Pin-up and the Cinema
If I have had little to say of cinema up to this point, it is because the pin-up girl is not originally part of it. The pin-up was not born on the screen but

on magazine covers, on the fold-outs of *Esquire*, on the cut-out pages of *Yank*. Subsequently the cinema adopted this erotic mythology as its own, and soon the American star resembled the drawings of Varga.

The screen already had a solid tradition in this field. The women in clinging bathing suits who people the trick-shot skies of Georges Méliès derived, too, from a naïvely erotic imagery whose glory, at the turn of the century, was the princess of Caraman-Chimay. A little later, in America, Mack Sennett, that astute precursor in the field, foresaw clearly the popularity of the bathing suit, but the performances of his bathing beauties as a group, rather like those of the music hall, gave no hint as yet of the highly individual future of the pin-up girl and the star. Thus the cinema from its beginning was predisposed to the use of the pin-up, and reciprocally to reinforce the feminine ideal she represents in the imagination and taste of the public.

I do not value this kind of cinematic eroticism very highly. Produced by special historical circumstances, the feminine ideal reflected in the pin-up girl is in the last analysis (despite its apparent anatomical vigor) extremely artificial, ambiguous, and shallow. Sprung from the accidental sociological situation of the war, it is nothing more than chewing gum for the imagination. Manufactured on the assembly line, standardized by Varga, sterilized by censorship, the pin-up girl certainly represents a qualitative regression in cinematic eroticism. Lillian Gish in *Broken Blossoms*, Dietrich in *The Blue Angel*, Garbo, now Ingrid Bergman, are after all quite different from Rita Hayworth.

In 1931 the stars were living on grapefruit and hiding their bosoms. At the same time, the tidal wave of the Hays office censorship was breaking over Hollywood. The danger, though seeming to come from the opposite direction, was at bottom the same: phoniness. Cinematic eroticism wasted away in artifice and hypocrisy. Then came Mae West. The Mae West of the future will doubtless not have the generous curves of a Fifi Peachskin. But neither will she have to react against the same artificialities and shams; shocking or chaste, shy or provocative, all the American cinema needs from her is more authenticity.

'I'll have to sacrifice my art and go in the movies'

FELIX THE CAT

BRIGITTE HELM

Brigitte Helm as Antinea in G. W. Pabst's 1932 adaptation of Pierre Benoit's bestselling novel L'Atlantide. *A diamond on fire!*

NORMAN MAILER
Marilyn

Marilyn!

There have been other Marilyns in American show business history (Marilyn Miller, Marilyn Maxwell), and who knows how many beautiful women have borne, and still bear, that same name on either side of the Atlantic? Yet, in the cultural mythology of the ebbing twentieth century, it will always refer to one person. For, although there were many feminine stars of the 1950s whose vital statistics satisfied the obsession of the American (and also, let's not forget, British) male with outlandish mammary equipment, only Marilyn, with her tender, volatile features, her pouting lips and strangely innocent eyes, contrived to distract us from that equipment, contrived to make us forget her breasts. In fact, it is even possible, as Norman Mailer argues, that she was profoundly ill-at-ease inside that fabulous body, even possible that inside the statistically vital star there lurked a perfectly ordinary young woman – flighty, temperamental, no intellectual – screaming to be let out. Unfortunately for her, but to the greater glory of film history, her screams were heard only when it was too late.

So we think of Marilyn who was every man's love affair with America, Marilyn Monroe who was blonde and beautiful and had a sweet little rinky-dink of a voice and all the cleanliness of all the clean American backyards. She was our angel, the sweet angel of sex, and the sugar of sex came up from her like a resonance of sound in the clearest grain of a violin. Across five continents the men who knew the most about love would covet her, and the classical pimples of the adolescent working his first gas pump would also pump for her, since Marilyn was deliverance, a very Stradivarius of sex, so gorgeous, forgiving, humorous, compliant and tender that even the most mediocre musician would relax his lack of art in the dissolving magic of her violin. 'Divine love always has met and always will meet every human need,' was the sentiment she offered from the works of Mary Baker Eddy as 'my prayer for you always' (to the man who may have been her first illicit lover), and if we change *love* to *sex*, we have the subtext in the promise. 'Marilyn Monroe's sex,' said the smile of the young star, 'will meet every human need.' She gave the feeling that if you made love to her, why then how could you not move more easily into sweets and the purchase of the full promise of future sweets, move into tender heavens where your flesh would be restored. She would ask no price. She was not the dark contract of those passionate brunette depths that speak of blood, vows taken for life, and the furies of vengeance if you are untrue to the depth of passion, no, Marilyn suggested sex might be difficult and dangerous with others, but ice cream with her. If your taste combined with her taste, how nice, how sweet would be that tender dream of flesh there to share.

In her early career, in the time of *Asphalt Jungle* when the sexual immanence of her face came up on the screen like a sweet peach bursting before one's eyes, she looked then like a new love ready and waiting between the sheets in the unexpected clean breath of a rare sexy morning, looked like she'd stepped fully clothed out of a chocolate box for Valentine's Day, so desirable as to fulfill each of the letters in that favorite word of the publicity flack, *curvaceous*, so curvaceous and yet without menace as to turn one's fingertips into ten happy prowlers. Sex was, yes, ice cream to her. 'Take me,' said her smile. 'I'm easy. I'm happy. I'm an angel of sex, you bet.'

What a jolt to the dream life of the nation that the angel died of an overdose. Whether calculated suicide by barbiturates or accidental suicide by losing count of how many barbiturates she had already taken, or an end even more sinister, no one was able to say. Her death was covered over with ambiguity even as Hemingway's was exploded into horror, and as the deaths and spiritual disasters of the decade of the Sixties came one by one to American Kings and Queens, as Jack Kennedy was killed, and Bobby, and Martin Luther King, as Jackie Kennedy married Aristotle Onassis and Teddy Kennedy went off the bridge at Chappaquiddick, so the decade that began with Hemingway as the monarch of American arts ended with Andy Warhol as its regent, and the ghost of Marilyn's death gave a lavender edge to that dramatic American design of the Sixties which seemed in retrospect to have done nothing so much as to bring Richard Nixon to the threshold of imperial power. 'Romance is a nonsense bet,' said the jolt in the electric shock, and so began that long decade of the Sixties which ended with television living like an inchworm on the aesthetic gut of the drug-deadened American belly.

In what a light does that leave the last angel of the cinema! She was never for TV. She preferred a theatre and those hundreds of bodies in the dark, those wandering lights on the screen when the luminous life of her face grew ten feet tall. It was possible she knew better than anyone that she was the last of the myths to thrive in the long evening of the American dream – she had been born, after all, in the year Valentino died, and his footprints in the forecourt at Grauman's Chinese Theatre were the only ones that fit her feet. She was one of the last of cinema's aristocrats and may not have wanted to be examined, then *ingested*, in the neighborly reductive dimensions of America's living room. No, she belonged to the occult church of the film, and the last covens of Hollywood. She might be as modest in her voice and as soft in her flesh as the girl next door, but she was nonetheless larger than life up on the screen. Even down in the Eisenhower shank of the early Fifties she was already promising that a time was coming when sex would be easy and sweet, democratic provender for all. Her stomach, untrammeled by girdles or sheaths, popped forward in a full woman's belly, inelegant as hell, an avowal of a womb fairly salivating in seed – that belly which was never to have a child – and her breasts popped buds and burgeons of flesh over many a questing sweating moviegoer's face. She was a cornucopia. She excited dreams of honey for the horn.

Yet she was more. She was a presence. She was ambiguous. She was the angel of sex, and the angel was in her detachment. For she was separated from what she offered. 'None but Marilyn Monroe,' wrote Diana Trilling,

> could suggest such a purity of sexual delight. The boldness with which she could parade herself and yet never be gross, her sexual flamboyance and bravado which yet breathed an air of mystery and even reticence, her voice which carried such ripe overtones of erotic excitement and yet was the voice of a shy child – these complications were integral to her gift. And they described a young woman trapped in some never-never land of unawareness.

Or is it that behind the gift is the tender wistful hint of another mood? For she also seems to say, 'When an absurd presence is perfect, some little god must have made it.' At its best, the echo of her small and perfect creation reached to the horizon of our mind. We heard her speak in that tiny tinkly voice so much like a little dinner bell, and it tolled when she was dead across all that decade of the Sixties she had helped to create, across its promise, its excitement, its ghosts and its center of tragedy.

Since she was also a movie star of the most stubborn secretiveness and flamboyant candor, most conflicting arrogance and on-rushing inferiority; great populist of philosophers – she loved the working man – and most tyrannical of mates, a queen of a castrator who was ready to weep for a dying minnow; a lover of books who did not read, and a proud, inviolate artist who could haunch over to publicity when the heat was upon her faster than a whore could lust over a hot buck; a female spurt of wit and sensitive energy who could hang like a sloth for days in a muddy-mooded coma; a child-girl, yet an actress to loose a riot by dropping her glove at a premiere; a fountain of charm and a dreary bore; an ambulating cyclone of beauty when dressed to show, a dank hunched-up drab at her worst – with a bad smell! – a giant and an emotional pygmy; a lover of life and a cowardly hyena of death who drenched herself in chemical stupors; a sexual oven whose fire may rarely have been lit – she would go to bed with her brassière on – she was certainly more and less than the silver witch of us all. In her ambition, so Faustian, and in her ignorance of culture's dimensions, in her liberation and her tyrannical desires, her noble democratic longings intimately contradicted by the widening pool of her narcissism (where every friend and slave must bathe), we can see the magnified mirror of ourselves, our exaggerated and now all but defeated generation, yes, she ran a reconnaissance through the Fifties, and left a message for us in her death, 'Baby go boom.' Now she is the ghost of the Sixties. The sorrow of her loss is in this passage her friend Norman Rosten would write in *Marilyn – An Untold Story*:

> She was proud of her dishwashing and held up the glasses for inspection. She played badminton with a real flair, occasionally banging someone on the head (no damage). She was just herself, and herself was gay, noisy, giggling, tender. Seven summers before her death . . . She liked her guest room; she'd say, 'Make it dark, and give me air.' She slept late, got her own breakfast and went off for a walk in the woods with only the cat for company.
>
> Marilyn loved animals; she was drawn to all living things. She would

spend hundreds of dollars to try to save a storm-damaged tree and would mourn its death. She welcomed birds, providing tree houses and food for the many species that visited her lawn, she worried about them in bad weather. She worried about dogs and cats. She once had a dog that was by nature contemplative, but she was convinced he was depressed. She did her best to make him play, and that depressed him even more; on the rare occasions when he did an antic pirouette, Marilyn would hug and kiss him, delirious with joy.

They are loving lines. Rosten's book must offer the tenderest portrait available of Monroe, but those who suspect such tender beauty can find other anecdotes in Maurice Zolotow's biography:

> One evening, some of the cast – though not Monroe – were watching the rushes of the yacht sequence. . . . [Tony Curtis] is posing as a rich man's son who suffers from a frigid libido. Girls cannot excite him. Monroe decides to cure him of his ailment by kissing him and making love to him. On the fifth kiss, the treatment succeeds admirably.
>
> In the darkness, someone said to Curtis, 'You seemed to enjoy kissing Marilyn.' And he said loudly, 'It's like kissing Hitler.'
>
> When the lights came on, Paula Strasberg was crying. 'How could you say a terrible thing like that, Tony?' she said. 'You try acting with her, Paula,' he snapped, 'and see how you feel.'
>
> During much of the shooting, Monroe was reading Paine's *Rights of Man*. One day, the second assistant director, Hal Polaire, went to her dressing room. He knocked on the door. He called out, 'We're ready for you, Miss Monroe.'

She replied with a simple obliterative. 'Go fuck yourself,' she said. Did she anticipate how a future generation of women would evaluate the rights of men? Even so consummate a wit as Billy Wilder would yet describe her as the meanest woman in Hollywood, a remark of no spectacular humor that was offered nonetheless in an interview four years after her death, as though to suggest that even remembering Marilyn across the void was still sufficiently irritating to strip his wit. Yet during the filming of *Let's Make Love* she was to write in her dressing room notebook, 'What am I afraid of? Why am I so afraid? Do I think I can't act? I know I can act but I am afraid. I am afraid and I should not be and I must not be.' It is in fear and trembling that she writes. In dread. Nothing less than some intimation of the death of her soul may be in her fear. But then is it not hopeless to comprehend her without some concept of a soul? One might literally have to invent the idea of a soul in order to approach her. 'What am I afraid of?'

It may be fair to quote another woman whose life ended in suicide: 'A biography is considered complete if it merely accounts for six or seven selves, whereas a person may well have as many as one thousand.' The words are by Virginia Woolf. In its wake, the materials of any biographer come begging with his credentials.

But why not assume Marilyn Monroe opens the entire problem of biography? The question is whether a person can be comprehended by the facts of the life, and this does not even begin to take into account that abominable magnetism of facts. They always attract polar facts. Rare is the piece of special evidence in any life that is not quickly contradicted by other witnesses. In a career like Monroe's, where no one can be certain whether she was playing an old role, experimenting with a new one, or even being nothing less than the *true* self (which she had spent her life trying to discover), the establishing of facts dissolves into the deeper enigma of how reality may appear to a truly talented actor. Since the psychological heft of a role has more existential presence than daily life (and in fact the role creates *real* reactions in everyone who sees it), so the twilight between reality and fantasy is obliged to become more predominant for a great actor than for others. Even if a few of the *facts* of Monroe's life can be verified, therefore, or, equally, if we learn the sad fact that Monroe reminiscing about her past at a given moment is not being accurate – to say the least! – how little is established. For an actor lives with the lie as if it were truth. A false truth can offer more reality than the truth that was altered.

Since this is a poor way to establish history, the next question is whether a life like hers is not antipathetic to biographical tools. Certainly, the two histories already published show the limitations of a conventional approach. The first, by Maurice Zolotow, *Marilyn Monroe*, written while she was still alive, is filled with interesting psychoanalytical insights of the sort one can hear at a New York coffee table when two intelligent people are analyzing a third, but much of the conversation is reamed with overstressed anecdotes. For here is a feature writer who has included in his source material the work of other feature writers and so develops a book with facts embellished by factoids (to join the hungry ranks of those who coin a word), that is, facts which have no existence before appearing in a magazine or newspaper, creations which are not so much lies as a product to manipulate emotion in the Silent Majority. (It is possible, for example, that Richard Nixon has spoken in nothing but factoids during his public life.)

So Zolotow's book is able to make another biographer wistful. If a few of his best stories were true, how nice they might be for one's own use; but one cannot depend on them entirely. Some of them were written by Marilyn, which is to say, by Marilyn as told to Ben Hecht, a prodigiously factoidal enterprise printed as Sunday supplement pieces in 1954. Hecht was never a writer to tell the truth when a concoction could put life in his prose, and Marilyn had been polishing her fables for years. No team of authors contributes more to the literary smog that hangs over legend than Marilyn ben Hecht.

The other book, *Norma Jean*, by Fred Lawrence Guiles, seems more accurate, and is certainly more scrupulous, as close to the facts of its subject as Carlos Baker's book may have been for Hemingway, a work of sources and careful chronology, a reporter's job of love since in journalism the labor of cross-checking is equal to love. Therefore it is a biography of much estimable value for verifying the events of her life. Yet her personality remains mysterious. The facts live, but Marilyn is elusive. So the final virtue of *Norma Jean* is that a great biography might be constructed some day upon its foundations, although it might have to contend with the notion that exceptional people (often the most patriotic, artistic, heroic, or prodigious) had a way of living with opposites in themselves that could only be called schizophrenic when it failed. That was a theory developed while studying astronauts, and it seemed suitable for Marilyn, and so most interesting, for what had a movie star like Monroe in common with an astronaut? One has to speak of transcendence. But transcendence was precisely the enigma which faced every psychohistorian, for it was a habit as much as a miracle, yet a mystical habit, not amenable to reason – it assumed that something in the shape of things respected any human who would force an impossible solution up out of the soup, as if the soup itself were sympathetic to the effort. By the logic of transcendence, it was exactly in the secret scheme of things that a man should be able to write about a beautiful woman, or a woman to write about a great novelist – that would be transcendence, indeed! The new candidate for biographer now bought a bottle of Chanel No. 5 – Monroe was famous for having worn it – and thought it was the operative definition of a dime-store stink. But he would never have a real clue to how it smelled on her skin. Not having known her was going to prove, he knew, a recurrent wound in the writing, analogous to the regret, let us say, of not having been alone and in love in Paris when one was young. No matter how much he could learn about her, he could never have the simple invaluable knowledge of knowing that he liked her a little, or did not like her, and so could have a sense that they were working for the same god, or at odds.

If the temptation, then, to undertake such a work of psychohistory was present, he still knew he was not serious. It would consume years, and he was not the type to bed down into the curious hollow of writing about a strange woman whose career had so often passed through places where he had lived at the same time. One of the frustrations of his life was that he had never met her, especially since a few people he knew had been so near to her. Once in Brooklyn, long before anyone had heard of Marilyn Monroe – she had been alive for twenty years but not yet named! – he had lived in the same brownstone house in which Arthur Miller was working on *Death of a Salesman* and this at just the time he was himself doing *The Naked and the Dead*. The authors, meeting occasionally on the stairs, or at the mail box in the hall, would chat with diffidence as they looked for a bit of politics or literary business to mouth upon – each certainly convinced on parting that the other's modest personality would never amount to much. In later years, when Miller was married to Monroe, the playwright and the movie star lived in a farmhouse in Connecticut not five miles away from the younger author, who, not yet aware of what his final relation to Marilyn Monroe would be, waited for the call to visit, which of course never came. The playwright and the novelist had never been close. Nor could the novelist in conscience condemn the playwright for such avoidance of drama. The secret ambition, after all, had been to steal Marilyn; in all his vanity he thought no one was so well suited to bring out the best in her as himself, a conceit which fifty million other men may also have held – he was still too untested to recognize that the foundation of her art might be to speak to each man as if he were all of male existence available to her. It was only a few marriages (which is to say a few failures) later that he could recognize how he would have done no better than Miller and probably have been damaged further in the process. In retrospect, it might be conceded that Miller had been made of the toughest middle-class stuff – which, existentially speaking, is tough as hard synthetic material.

So there would be then no immense job on Monroe by himself, no, rather a study like this, bound to stray toward the borders of magic. For a man with a cabalistic turn of mind, it was fair and engraved coincidence that the letters in Marilyn Monroe (if the 'a' were used twice and the 'o' but once) would spell his own name leaving only the 'y' for excess, a trifling discrepancy, no more calculated to upset the heavens than the most minuscule diffraction of the red shift.

Of course, if he wished to play anagrams, she was also Marlon Y. Normie, and an unlimited use of the letters in *el amor* gave Marolem Mamroe, a forthright Latin sound (considerably better than Mormam Maeler). But let us back off such pleasures. It is possible there is no instrument more ready to capture the elusive quality of her nature than a novel. Set a thief to catch a thief, and put an artist on an artist. Could the solution be nothing less vainglorious than a novel of Marilyn Monroe? Written in the form of biography? Since it would rely in the main on other sources, it could hardly be more than a long biographical article – nonetheless, a *species* of novel ready to play by the rules of biography. No items could be made up and evidence would be provided when facts were moot. Speculation *had* to be underlined. Yet he would never delude himself that he might be telling a story which could possibly be more accurate than a fiction since he would often be quick to imagine the interior of many a closed and silent life, and with the sanction of a novelist was going to look into the unspoken impulses of some of his real characters. At the end, if successful, he would have offered a literary hypothesis of a *possible* Marilyn Monroe who might actually have lived and fit most of the facts available. If his instincts were good, then future facts discovered about her would not have to war with the character he created. A reasonable venture! It satisfied his fundamental idea that acquisition of knowledge for a literary man was best achieved in those imaginative acts of appropriation picked up by the disciplined exercise of one's skill. Let us hasten, then, to the story of her life. Magic is worked by the working.

She was born on June 1, 1926 at 9:30 in the morning, an easy birth, easiest of her mother's three deliveries. As the world knows, it was out of wedlock. At the time of Marilyn's first marriage to James Dougherty, the name of Norma Jean Baker was put on the marriage license (Baker by way of her mother's first husband). On the second marriage to Joe DiMaggio, the last name became Mortenson, taken from the second husband. (Even the middle name, Jean, was originally written as Jeane – a quintessentially prairie spelling like Choreanne for Corinne.) There is no need to look for any purpose behind the use of the names. Uneducated (that familiar woe of a beautiful blonde), she was also cultureless – can we guess she would not care to say whether Rococo was three hundred years before the Renaissance, any more than she would be ready to swear the retreat of Napoleon from Moscow didn't come about because his railroad trains couldn't run in the cold. Historically empty, she was nonetheless sensitive – as sensitive as she was historically empty – and her normal state when not under too much sedation was, by many an account, vibrant to new perception. It is as if she was ready when exhilarated to reach out to the washes of a psychedelic tide. So, talking to one publicity man, it would seem natural in the scheme of things that her last name was Baker – maybe that sounded better as she looked at the man's nose. Another flack with something flaccid in the look of his muscles from the solar plexus to the gut would inspire Mortenson. Since it was all movie publicity, nobody bothered to check. To what end? Who knew the real legal situation? If the mother, Gladys Monroe Baker, had been married to Edward Mortenson, 'an itinerant lover,' he had already disappeared by the time Marilyn was born; some reports even had him dead of a motorcycle accident before Norma Jean was conceived. There may also have been some question whether Gladys Monroe was ever divorced from the first husband, Baker, or merely separated. And the real father, according to Fred Guiles, was C. Stanley Gifford, an employee of Consolidated Film Industries, where Gladys Baker worked. A handsome man. Shown a picture of him by her mother when still a child, Marilyn described him later 'wearing a slouch hat cocked on one side of his head. He had a little mustache and a smile. He looked kind of like Clark Gable, you know, strong and manly.' In her early teens, she kept a picture of Gable on her wall and lied to high school friends that Gable was her secret father. Not too long out of the orphanage where she had just spent twenty-one months, then veteran of numerous foster homes, it is obvious she was looking for a sense of self-importance, but we may as well assume something more extravagant: the demand upon a biographer is to explain why she is exceptional. So, in that part of her adolescent mind where fantasy washes reality as the ego begins to emerge, it is possible she is already (like Richard Nixon) searching for an imperial sense of self-justification. Illegitimate she might be, but still selected for a high destiny – Clark Gable was her secret father. That she would yet come to know Gable while making *The Misfits* (know him toward the end of her life down in the infernal wastes of that psychic state where the brimstone of insomnia and barbiturates is boiled, her marriage to Miller already lost, her lateness a disease more debilitating than palsy), what portents she must have sensed playing love scenes at last with the secret father, what a cacophony of cries in the silence of her head when Gable was dead eleven days after finishing the film. But then omens surrounded her like the relatives she never had at a family dinner. If her footprints fit Valentino's about the time she became a star, so too was a bowl of tomato sauce dropped on her groom's white jacket the day of her first wedding, and down she was turned, down a hall with no exit in City Hall in San Francisco just before she married Joe DiMaggio, little fish of intimation too small for a biographer to fry, but remembered perhaps when a woman reporter was killed chasing after her in a sports car the day she was getting married to Miller. (And Marilyn was having her period that day.) What a vision of blood! – a woman smashed and dead on the day she is joining herself to the one man she may be convinced she does love. It is not sedative for a young woman whose sense of her own sanity can never be secure: she has no roots but illegitimacy on one side and a full pedigree of insanity on the other. Her grandfather Monroe (who would naturally claim to be descended from President Monroe) had spent the last part of his life committed to a state asylum. Monroe's wife, Marilyn's grandmother, Della Monroe Grainger, a beauty with red hair and green-blue eyes, had insane rages on quiet suburban semi-slum streets in environs of Los Angeles like Hawthorne, and was also committed to a mental hospital before she died. So was Marilyn's mother in an asylum for most of Marilyn's life. And the brother of the mother killed himself. When the wings of insanity beat thus near, one pays attention to a feather. The most casual coincidence is obliged to seem another warning from the deep. So must it have been like opening the door to a secret room (and finding that it looks exactly as envisioned) to know that the director of her first starring movie, *Don't Bother to Knock* (about a girl who was mad), should have the name of Baker.

Still, these reinforced roots of insanity, and this absence of clear identity, are not only a weakness but an intense motive to become an actor. In the logic of transcendence, every weakness presupposes the possibility of a future strength. Great actors usually discover they have a talent by first searching in desperation for an identity. It is no ordinary identity that will suit them, and no ordinary desperation can drive them. The force that propels a great actor in his youth is insane ambition. Illegitimacy and insanity are the godparents of the great actor. A child who is missing either parent is a study in the search for identity and quickly becomes a candidate for actor (since the most creative way to discover a new and possible identity is through the close fit of a role). But then the origins of insanity can also be glimpsed in wild and unmanageable ambition. While the appearance of insanity is not ever simple, and two insane people are rarely alike (except when in depression), still the root of insanity is easier to locate than sanity, for it is more single-minded. The root is to be found in frustrated ambition, no more, provided we conceive the true pain of such a state – an undying will existing in conditions of hopeless entombment. To be buried alive is insanity. What creates such complexity in the mad – that labyrinth of interlocking selves with every knotted incapacity to act on simple lines – is the reaction of thwarted will upon every structure of the character. While the cause of insanity is therefore as simple as the process that makes an enlargement (where a focus of light burns in, distorts, dodges, or solarizes the original negative), still the content of the insanity is not simple, for it must remain at least as complex as the content of the negative itself, that is, the complexity of the original character.

While formal psychiatry is a maze of medical disciplines that seek to cure, stupefy, or *pulverize* madness, it is another kind of inquiry to search into the uncontrollable ambition to dominate one's own life, the life of others, or the life of communities not yet conceived, that simple rage to put one's signature upon existence. Let us bow our heads. If we want to comprehend the insane, then we must question the fundamental notion of modern psychiatry – that we have but one life and one death. The concept that no human being has ever existed before or will be reincarnated again is a philosophical rule of thumb which dominates psychiatry; yet all theory built upon this concept has failed – one is tempted to say *systematically* – in every effort to find a consistent method of cure for psychotics. Even the least spectacular processes of reasoning may therefore suggest that to comprehend psychosis, and the psychology of those who are exceptional (like our heroine), it could be time to look upon human behavior as possessed of a double root. While the dominant trunk of our actions has to be influenced by the foreground of our one life here and now and living, the other root may be attached to some karmic virtue or debt some of us (or all of us) acquired by our courage or failure in lives we have already lived. If such theory is certainly supported by no foundation, nonetheless it offers some immediate assistance for comprehending the insane, since it would suggest we are not all conceived in equal happiness or desperation. Any human who begins life with the debt of owing existence somewhat more than others is thereby more likely to generate an ambition huge enough to swallow old debts. (And be less content with modest success.) Of course, the failure of such ambition must double all desperation.

Double-entry bookkeeping on a celestial level! I stub my toe because of a leap taken in another life! Then I fight with my wife because once I disputed in similar circumstances with my fourteenth-century mother. Absurdities eat into the argument with the ferocity of ants. Yet if we are to understand Monroe, and no one has – we have only seen her limned as an angelic and sensitive victim or a murderous emotional cripple – why not assume that in a family of such concentrated insanity as her own, the illegitimate daughter of Gladys Monroe Baker may have been born with a desperate imperative formed out of all those previous debts and failures of her whole family of souls. And the imperative may have been to display herself as a presence to the world, there to leaven the thickening air with the tender, wise and witty flesh of an angel of sex. Conscious of how this presence may have been managed and directed and advanced its insufferably difficult way forward by a harsh and near to maniacal voice of the most inward, concealed and secretive desperation, since the failure of her project was insanity, or some further variety of doom.

We draw back from such a projection. It is too much, and much too soon. She was a dumb and sexy broad, a voice of outraged bitterness is bound to say, a dizzy dish with a flair and a miserable childhood and much good and bad luck, and she took a little talent a long way. You could go to any southern town and find twelve of her. A familiar voice. It is comfortable. Yet facing the phenomenon of her huge appeal to the world – Napoleonic was her capture of the attention of the world – let us at least recognize that the reductive voice speaks with no more authority than the romantic, that it is also an unproved thesis, and does no more than scorn the first-thesis, indeed, it fails to explain her altogether. There are a million dumb and dizzy broads with luck and none come near to Monroe, no. To explain her at all, let us hold to that karmic notion as one more idea to support in our mind while trying to follow the involuted pathways of her life.

GREIL MARCUS
John Wayne Listening

Unlike Humphrey Bogart, whose peculiar brand of cynical idealism made him the (posthumous) idol of a generation of students and middle-class youths, John Wayne was a blue-collar hero, the defender of traditional American values and the sworn enemy of intellectuals, communists and (what may in his mind have amounted to the same thing) perverts. Particularly during the 1960s and 1970s his appeal to educated young people tended to atrophy the moment they enrolled in college – a disaffection nevertheless tempered by regular television exposure to a career that could be considered distinguished by any standard and by a maybe grudging respect for the mythic figure he cut with such easy virile grace and good humour. Many of the student radicals of the 1960s who despised Wayne's politics, his reprehensible political cronies and his often deplorable public pronouncements on the Vietnam War retained a sneaking affection for the guts 'n' glory films which had comprised the staple Saturday matinée fare in the neighbourhood fleapits of their adolescence, the white screen serving as a mammoth security blanket. Even in adulthood, rare was the spectator who was capable of distinguishing actor from role and who, armed with that distinction, could lace his enjoyment with irony, smugly retaining his distance from some more artless fan beside him.

Now that Wayne is dead, now that the man no longer obscures the artist, we can all see him for what he was: one of the American cinema's most indispensable performers. It's that John Wayne to whom Greil Marcus pays tribute.

When a much-loved (and secretly feared) public figure dies or falls gravely ill, the tendency is to sentimentalize his or her career, to smooth it out. John Wayne is getting the treatment now, but in fact it has been underway for some time. In the last decade, John Wayne became so venerated as an American symbol, became so obvious and banal an icon, that he is now safe. Even liberals, some contriving elaborate rationalizations for his mythic stature, have forgiven him his politics. Ultimate professional ('I got paid for it,' Wayne told film critic Jay Cocks, when asked if he wasn't disappointed so few people saw *The Searchers* at the time of its 1956 release), professional American, he wears the mantle of Manifest Destiny easily, happy to represent America to the world, to itself, and to himself. And yet what Wayne represents is not, after all this time, very interesting. Today, forty years of memorable and forgettable films blur into a single, indelible, seemingly inevitable image: a big man, in the big country, in cowboy gear, aging but indomitable, shilling for Great Western Savings on TV.

It's an absurdly incomplete image, but we are vulnerable to it – for it's that image, not Great Western, that Wayne is really selling. He seems to have taken one last opportunity to connect himself and us to a heroically decent America we can neither rationally credit nor emotionally surrender. As we listen to what is by now a kitsch-mythic voice, whatever Wayne might have shown us about the country and ourselves stiffens, as if, as a legend – the man who, on screen or off, stands tall, certain in the knowledge that he is always right, waiting quietly to make his move – he were already the freeze-frame we will get at the close of the tributes that will appear on each network the day after he dies.

Because Wayne's legend has become encrusted with the myths he has acted out (or maybe vice versa), it's no longer satisfying to ask what, as a kind of statue-in-waiting, John Wayne means. We can do better looking for the psychological and historical territory he has explored and others have avoided. This is wild, unsettled, unsettleable territory: almost a blank spot on the map of Wayne's career as the media floats it before our eyes, but also the site of his greatest and most frightening triumphs – triumphs so frightening, in fact, it's as if Wayne's legend has taken shape and been accepted precisely to exclude those moments, to render them invisible.

The Wayne we know best is the Wayne of Howard Hawks's *Rio Bravo* (1959), a perfectly focused version of a persona that consistently develops from *Stagecoach* (1939, directed by John Ford) to *Dark Command* (1940, Raoul Walsh) to *Back to Bataan* (1945, Edward Dmytryk) to *Fort Apache* (1948, Ford) to *The Quiet Man* (1952, Ford) to *The Man Who Shot Liberty Valance* (1961, Ford). This Wayne is not remotely a cartoon. In *Rio Bravo*, as John Chance, a sheriff holding a prisoner against great odds and slowly coming to accept the help he needs, Wayne acts out a toughness that is inseparable from his restraint. When he's arrogant, or even wrong, you're utterly convinced he's earned the right to be so. This is a man who has truly *learned*, and is still learning. He – the sheriff, but also Wayne the actor, Wayne the representative man – has invented and discovered himself out of necessity and out of curiosity about life. His natural superiority, and his unmistakable menace – his readiness to kill his enemies, his honest belief that some people don't deserve to live – is redeemed from cynicism by open humor, which keeps the character alive. This John Wayne is flawed just sufficiently to be wholly admirable, and he leaves behind an overwhelming, almost fated sense of moral symmetry: nothing so hard as justice, more like fairness.

What makes the John Wayne of *Rio Bravo* so convincing is that he does not take his role for granted. Underneath the assurance and experience he must communicate, he is feeling out the role moment to moment – constantly judging himself and others, weighing choices, posing moral alternatives and, once he has acted, sanctifying his actions by agreeing with them.

I don't mean simply that as a mature actor Wayne betrays no distance between himself and his character, or that he loses himself in his role. He doesn't. Rather, the distance between Wayne as an individual and the role he is playing is always present, and, over and over again, you can see him close it.

This is an extraordinarily intense style of performance – and within the basically smooth good guys vs. bad guys matrix of most good John Wayne movies, that intensity is not as threatening as it probably ought to be. The moral uncertainties that push to the surface as Wayne the man sanctions what his character must do are easy to miss, or forget. If Wayne's films dramatize a heroically decent America, then their essence is the story of how the hero achieves decency and passes it on to others, and the ultimate outcome is not in doubt. It's when the same style of performance is brought to bear in much rougher territory that the heroically decent America comes unglued, and Wayne emerges as an actor less easy to track.

If in other movies Sheriff Wayne is, to take a figure from *Moby Dick*, Starbuck armed – the god-fearing man acting forcefully within limits – then in Howard Hawks's *Red River* (1948) and John Ford's *The Searchers* Wayne is plainly Ahab. He is the good American hero driving himself past all known limits and into madness, his commitment to honor and decency burned down to a core of vengeance. This Wayne is better than other men not in a social sense – because someone must do society's dirty work; because he has a stronger idea of right and wrong – but for his own dark reasons. The sin of pride is all mixed up with a bitter, murderous defiance, and before our eyes Wayne changes from a man with whom we are comfortable into a walking Judgment Day, ready to destroy the world to save it from itself.

In both *Red River* and *The Searchers*, the main action gets underway in Texas after the Civil War. In *The Searchers*, Wayne plays Ethan Edwards; still wearing the pants from his Confederate uniform, he returns to his Texas relatives under a cloud so heavy thunder seems to be breaking over his head as he enters their house. The family is soon wiped out by Comanches – except for Edwards's young niece, who is abducted. Edwards sets out with his adopted nephew to find her; five years later, after searching from Canada to Mexico, he does. But by then she is a woman, no longer innocent, defiled by the Comanche chief under whose hand she has lived, and we realize that what Edwards has gained from his long search is the knowledge that he will have to kill her, and the will to do it.

In *Red River*, Wayne plays Tom Dunson, cattleman. His adopted son returns from the war to find the Dunson ranch on the verge of bankruptcy; Dunson decides to risk everything and take his ten thousand head of cattle to the new markets in Missouri. No one has ever made this drive before. The trek begins with exhilaration, but it's not long before Dunson is pushing his men too hard. Discipline begins to crack; Dunson bears down harder. He refuses advice from men he's trusted most of his life, takes to the bottle, sleeps with a gun, and, in a truly staggering coincidence, if that is what it is, slowly and surely begins to look like another Texan – the embattled Lyndon Johnson, fighting off quitters and cowards as he struggled to hold on to his war and his sanity.[1]

The whole camp twitches with fear; finally, after a ruinous stampede, some men desert. Dunson has them brought back. They are prepared to be shot for stealing provisions, but in a horrifyingly determined moment Dunson announces he will hang them instead. Violating the code everyone understands, he will replace justice with sadism.

With this act, Dunson crosses over into territory where none will follow. Faced with rebellion, he goes for his gun, and it's shot out of his hand; his son takes over the drive. Wounded, leaning against his horse like some forsaken god, Dunson is left behind, but not before swearing to chase down his son and kill him.

The grandeur of the settings of these movies – the Red River as the huge herd enters it so gracefully, Monument Valley in *The Searchers* – ennobles their characters even as it dwarfs them. But as Edwards or Dunson, Wayne refuses to be either ennobled or dwarfed. He has other business. As the conflict his characters insist on deepens, as they greet madness as a spell they have cast on themselves, their resistance seems to encompass not only the actions of others, but the natural scale of things. If Ethan Edwards gazed too long on the wonders of the country through which he pursues his niece, he might realize that his quest was, in some essential way, beside the point. And so, like Ahab, who is softened when he contemplates the beauty and the vastness of the sea, and thus turns away from it, Edwards accepts no messages from god.

We are a long way from the prosaic troubles of *Rio Bravo*. We are in a country where final, elemental murders can take place, and Edwards and Dunson have vowed that they will. That Edwards does not kill his niece or Dunson his son takes little if any of the edge off: Wayne's performances are terrifying because he has, as an individual, accepted the choices of his characters.

Shot by shot in *The Searchers* and *Red River*, you understand that Wayne is judging the motives and actions of his characters and finding them correct, necessary – satisfying. With a thousand details of expression, inflection, carriage – the tiredness of Dunson leaning on his horse, Edwards's revulsion when he sees how years of Indian captivity have turned two white women into gibbering lunatics – Wayne conveys to his audience the hard reality that, were he thrown into the situations his characters face, he would act as they do, or hope for the strength to do so. That these situations are horrible – not heroic but a perversion of heroic possibility – lets us see the oddity of Wayne's way of acting them out. Very few actors enter such desperate, psychologically catastrophic crises, and when they do they protect themselves. They overact, distancing themselves and their audience from the action, or they underact and convey reservation. Or, like Robert De Niro in *Taxi Driver* or Al Pacino in the *Godfather* movies, they lose themselves in their roles and thus as individuals really do get lost – they can't be seen. In the imagination of the audience, they aren't culpable for what their characters do.

Wayne watches the action unfold even as he carries it forward; you can feel him thinking as he moves. He doesn't throw himself into his role, he edges into it, step by step, until he comes out the other side.

In *Short Letter, Long Farewell*, Peter Handke describes a scene from

John Ford's *Young Mr Lincoln*. Lincoln, played by Henry Fonda, has agreed to defend two brothers accused of murder; a drunken mob arrives at the jail to lynch them, and Lincoln faces it down. He talks; he captures the drunks 'by softly reminding them of themselves, of what they were, what they could be, and what they had forgotten. This scene – Lincoln on the wooden steps of the jailhouse, with his hand on the mob's battering ram – embodied every possibility of human behavior. In the end, not only the drunks, but also the actors playing the drunks, were listening intently to Lincoln.' The scene is a cinematic miracle, but it is not complete: Henry Fonda does not listen to Lincoln. He simply plays him, and there is the difference. When Ethan Edwards speaks in *The Searchers*, or Tom Dunson in *Red River* – when their vows are made, and then they are taken back – John Wayne is listening to what they say.

NOTE

1. As Lawrence Wright wrote in 1988 in *In the New World*, after being driven from office by antiwar protesters and the North Vietnamese army Johnson 'came home to Texas and let his hair grow down to his shoulders'. The symbolism of that line is bottomless. Was Johnson's long hair the hair of the people who shouted him down? The men who died at the Alamo? George Custer? Regardless of whose it was, it was also that of Wayne's Dunson; once he begins to crack his gray hair seems to lengthen by the day.

'A rock is a rock, and a tree is a tree. Shoot it in Griffith Park'
ABE STERN

Creating

ANDRÉ BAZIN
Charlie Chaplin

André Bazin, arguably the greatest of film critics, on Charlie Chaplin,
arguably the greatest of filmmakers.

Charlie is a Mythical Character

Charlie is a mythical figure who rises above every adventure in
which he becomes involved. For the general public, Charlie exists as a
person before and after *Easy Street* and *The Pilgrim*. For hundreds of
millions of people on this planet he is a hero like Ulysses or Roland in
other civilizations – but with the difference that we know the heroes of
old through literary works that are complete and have defined, once
and for all, their adventures and their various manifestations. Charlie,
on the other hand, is always free to appear in another film. The living
Charlie remains the creator and guarantor of Charlie the character.

But What Makes Charlie Run?

But the continuity and coherence of Charlie's aesthetic existence can
only be experienced by way of the films that he inhabits. The public
recognizes him from his face and especially from his little trapezoidal
moustache and his duck-like waddle rather than from his dress which,
here again, does not make the monk. In *The Pilgrim* we see him dressed
only as a convict and as a clergyman and in a lot of films he wears a
tuxedo or the elegant cutaway coat of a millionaire. These physical
'markings' would be of less than no importance if one did not perceive,
more importantly, the interior constants that are the true constituents
of the character. These are however less easy to define or describe. One
way would be to examine his reaction to a particular event, for example
his complete absence of obstinacy when the world offers too strong an
opposition. In such cases he tries to get round the problem rather than
solve it. A temporary way out is enough for him, just as if for him there
was no such thing as the future. For example in *The Pilgrim* he props

a rolling-pin on a shelf with a bottle of milk that he is going to need in a minute or two. Of course the rolling-pin falls onto his head. While a provisional solution always seems to satisfy him he shows a fabulous ingenuity in the immediate circumstance. He is never at a loss in any situation. There is a solution for everything even though the world (and especially things in it rather than the people) is not made for him.

Charlie and Things

The utilitarian function of things relates to a human order of things itself utilitarian and which in turn has an eye to the future. In our world, things are tools, some more or less efficient, but all directed towards a specific purpose. However, they do not serve Charlie as they serve us. Just as human society never accepts him even provisionally except as a result of a misunderstanding, every time that Charlie wants to use something for the purpose for which it was made, that is to say, within the framework of our society, either he goes about it in an extremely awkward fashion (especially at table) or the things themselves refuse to be used, almost it would seem deliberately. In *A Day's Pleasure* the engine of the old Ford stops every time he opens the door. In *One A.M.* his bed moves around unpredictably so that he cannot lie down. In *The Pawnshop* the works of the alarm clock that he had just taken to pieces start moving around on their own like worms. But, conversely, things which refuse to serve him the way they serve us are in fact used by him to much better purpose because he puts them to multifarious uses according to his need at the moment.

The street lamp in *Easy Street* serves the function of an anaesthetist's mask to asphyxiate the terror of the neighbourhood. A little later a cast-iron stove is used to knock the man flat, whereas the 'functional' truncheon only gives him a slight singing in the ears. In *The Adventurer* a blind transforms him into a lampstand, invisible to the police. In *Sunnyside* a shirt serves as a tablecloth, as sleeves, as a towel, and so on. It looks as if things are only willing to be of use to him in ways that are purely marginal to the uses assigned by society. The most beautiful example of these strange uses is the famous dance of the rolls which contribute to a sudden outburst of highly unusual choreography.

Let us look at another characteristic gag. In *The Adventurer* Charlie thinks he has disposed of the warders pursuing him, by pelting them with stones from the top of a cliff. The warders are actually lying on the ground more or less unconscious. Instead of seizing the opportunity to put daylight between himself and them, he amuses himself by throwing more stones, pebbles this time, by way of refining on the operation. While he is doing this he fails to notice that another warder has arrived behind him and is watching him. As he reaches for another stone his hand touches the warden's shoe. His reaction is something to marvel at. Instead of trying to run away, which would in any case be useless, or having sized up his desperate plight, handing himself over to the officer, Charlie covers the ill-met shoe with a handful of dust. You laugh and your neighbor laughs too. At first it is all the same laughter. But I have 'listened in' to this gag twenty times in different theaters. When the audience, or at least part of it, was made up of intellectuals, students for example, there was a second wave of laughter of a different kind. At that moment the hall was no longer filled with the original laughter but with a series of echoes, a second wave of laughter, reflected off the minds of the spectators as if from the invisible walls of an abyss. These echoed effects are not always audible; first of all they depend on the audience but most of all because Charlie's gags are often of such short duration that they allow just enough time for you to 'get it', nor are they followed by a time lag that gives you a chance to think about them. It is the opposite of the technique called for in the theater by the laughter from the house. Although he was brought up in the school of the music hall, Charlie has refined down its comedy, refusing in any way to pander to the public. This need for simplicity and effectiveness requires of the gag the greatest elliptical clarity, and once he has achieved this he refuses to elaborate on it.

The technique of Charlie's gags naturally calls for a study to itself, which we cannot undertake here. Sufficient perhaps that we have made it clear that they have attained a kind of final perfection, the highest degree of style. It is stupid to treat Charlie as a clown of genius. If there had never been a cinema he would undoubtedly have been a clown of genius, but the cinema has allowed him to raise the comedy of circus and music hall to the highest aesthetic level. Chaplin needed the medium of the cinema to free comedy completely from the limits of space and time imposed by the stage or the circus arena.

Thanks to the camera, the evolution of the comic effect which is being presented, all the while with the greatest clarity, not only does not need boosting so that a whole audience can enjoy it, on the contrary it can now be refined down to the utmost degree; thus the machinery is kept to a minimum, so that it becomes a high-precision mechanism capable of responding instantly to the most delicate of springs.

It is significant, furthermore, that the best Chaplin films can be seen over and over again with no loss of pleasure – indeed the very opposite is the case. It is doubtless a fact that the satisfaction derived from certain gags is inexhaustible, so deep does it lie, but it is furthermore supremely true that comic form and aesthetic value owe nothing to surprise. The latter is exhausted the first time around and is replaced by a much more subtle pleasure, namely the delight of anticipating and recognizing perfection.

Charlie and Time

Whatever the facts, one can clearly see that the gag referred to above opens up under the initial comic shock a spiritual abyss which induces in the spectator, without giving him a chance to analyze it, that delicious vertigo that quickly modifies the tone of the laughter it provokes. The reason is that Charlie carries to absurd lengths his basic principle of never going beyond the actual moment. Having got rid of his two wardens, thanks to his capacity to exploit the terrain and whatever objects are to hand, once the danger is past he immediately stops thinking about building up a reserve store of supplementary prudence. The consequence is not long delayed. But this time it is so serious that Charlie is not able to find an immediate solution – rest assured that he soon will – he cannot go beyond a reflex action and the pretence at improvisation. One second, just time enough for a gesture of dismissal and the threat, in illusion, will have been effaced by the derisory stroke of an eraser. Let no one, however, stupidly confuse Charlie's gesture with that of an ostrich burying its head in the sand. The whole bearing of Charlie refutes this; it is sheer improvisation, unlimited imagination in the face of danger. The swiftness of the threat, however, and above all its brutal nature in contrast to the euphorious condition of the mind in which it takes conscious shape, does not allow him, this time, to escape immediately. Besides who can tell – because of the surprise it gives to the warden who was expecting a gesture of fear – if his action will not in the end allow him that fraction of a second that he needs to make his escape? Instead of solving the problem Charlie has no recourse other than to pretend things are not what they seem.

As a matter of fact this gesture of brushing aside danger is one of a number of gags peculiar to Charlie. Among these should be included the celebrated occasion when he camouflages himself as a tree in *Shoulder Arms*. 'Camouflage' is not really the right term. It is more properly a form of mimicry. One might go so far as to say that the defense reflexes of Charlie end in a reabsorption of time by space. Driven into a corner by a terrible and unavoidable danger, Charlie hides behind appearances like a crab burying itself in the sand. And this is no mere metaphor. At the opening of *The Adventurer* we see the convict emerging from the sand in which he was hiding, and burying himself again when danger returns.

The painted canvas tree in which Charlie is hiding blends in with the trees of the forest in a way that is quite 'hallucinating'. One is reminded of those little stick-like insects that are indiscernible in a clump of twigs or those little Indian insects that can take on the appearance of leaves, even leaves that caterpillars have nibbled. The sudden vegetable-like immobility of Charlie-the-tree is like an insect playing dead, as is his other gag in *The Adventurer* when he pretends to have been killed by a shot from a warden's gun. But what distinguishes Charlie from the insect is the speed with which he returns from his condition of spatial dissolution into the cosmos, to a state of instant readiness for action. Thus, motionless inside his tree he flattens out, one after the other, with swift precise movements of his 'branches', a file of German soldiers as they come within range.

The Swift Kick Characterizes the Man

It is with a simple and yet sublime gesture that Charlie expresses his supreme detachment from that biographical and social world in which we are plunged and which, for us, is a cause for regret and uneasiness, namely that remarkable backward kick which he employs to dispose alike of a banana peel, the head of Goliath and, more ideally still, of every bothersome thought. It is significant that Charlie never kicks straight ahead. Even when he kicks his partners in the pants he manages to do it while looking the other way. A cobbler would explain that this was because of the points of his outsize shoes. However, perhaps I may be allowed to ignore this piece of superficial realism and to see in the style and frequent and very personal use of this backward kick the reflection of a very vital approach to things. On the other hand, Charlie never liked, if I may dare to say so, to approach a problem head on. He prefers to take it by surprise with his back turned. On the other hand, especially when it seems to have no precise purpose, a simple gesture of revenge for example, this back-kick is a perfect expression of his constant determination not to be attached to the past, not to drag anything along behind him. This admirable gesture is furthermore capable of a thousand nuances ranging all the way from peevish revenge to a gay 'I'm free at last', except, that is to say, when he is not shaking off an invisible thread attached to his leg.

The Sin of Repetition

His use of the mechanical is the price he is forced to pay for his nonadherence to the normal sequence of events and to the function of things. Since for him things have no future in the sense of being planned to serve an end, when Charlie is involved with an object for some time he quickly contracts a sort of mechanical cramp, a surface condition in which the original reason for what he is doing is forgotten. This unfortunate inclination always serves him well. It is the basis for the famous gag in *Modern Times* when Charlie, working on the assembly line, continues spasmodically to tighten imaginary bolts; in *Easy Street*, we observe it in a more subtle form. When the big tough is chasing him round the room Charlie shoves the bed between them. There then follows a series of feints in the course of which each moves up and down his side of the bed. After a while, in spite of the continued danger, Charlie becomes used to this temporary defense tactic, and instead of continuing to direct his movements by the movements of his adversary, ends by running up and down on his own side as if the gesture were sufficient of itself to ward off all danger forever. Naturally, no matter how stupid the other man might be, all he has to do is to switch rhythm, to have Charlie run right into his arms. I am confident that in all Charlie's pictures there is not one where this mechanical movement does not end badly for him. In other words, mechanization of movement is in a sense Charlie's original sin, the ceaseless temptation. His independence of things and events can only be projected in time in the shape of something mechanical, like a force of inertia which continues under its initial impetus. The activity of a social being, such as you or me, is planned with foresight and as it develops, its direction is checked by constant reference to the reality that it is concerned to shape. It adheres throughout to the evolution of the event of which it is becoming part. Charlie's activity on the contrary is composed of a succession of separate instants sufficient to each of which is the evil thereof. Then laziness supervenes and Charlie continues thereafter to offer the solution proper to a previous and specific moment. The capital sin of Charlie, and he does not hesitate to make us laugh about it at his own expense, is to project into time a mode of being that is suited to one instant, and that is what is meant by 'repetition'.

I think we should also include in this sin of repetition the category of well-known gags in which we see a joyous Charlie brought to order by reality, for example the famous gag in *Modern Times* when he wants to bathe and dives into a river that is little more than foot deep or again, at the beginning of *Easy Street* when, converted by love, he walks out of a room and falls on his face on the stairway. Subject to a more precise check, I would be willing to suggest that every time Charlie makes us laugh at his own expense and not at that of other people, it is when he has been imprudent enough, one way or another, to presume that the future will resemble the past or to join naively in the game as played by society and to have faith in its elaborate machinery for building the future . . . its moral, religious, social and political machinery.

'I didn't like the doctor I consulted yesterday – he wasn't any good in the role'   **SACHA GUITRY**

OTAR IOSSELIANI
About Boris Barnet

Who is the finest of all Russian filmmakers? There would seem to be a positive embarras de richesse. Eisenstein? Dovzhenko? Dziga Vertov? Pudovkin? Donskoi? I would suggest, heretically, the much less well-known Boris Barnet, whose still growing stature offers conclusive proof that, even a century after its foundation, film history remains in a constant, ebullient state of revision and reinvention. And who, while we're at it, is the finest Russian filmmaker of the current era? Again, I would propose an unexpected candidate, the Georgian-born but Paris-based Otar Iosseliani, the creator of such witty, lyrical, ultimately indescribable masterpieces – halfway between Jacques Tati and René Clair – as Pastorale, Les Favoris de la Lune and La Chasse aux papillons, all of them unknown in English-speaking countries. Now read on.

In order to choose a film-maker whom I respect and to whom I owe my joy and love of film-making, I have to observe certain criteria. He could be cultured, but that's not essential. He could be honest; it's necessary, but not sufficient. I prefer to apply Cauchy's criterion for mathematical analysis which holds that a subject must be both necessary and sufficient. So the film-maker must be humane, good, serious, and not a cheat; he must know what he is talking about, how to communicate his message, and why he is doing so. He must also be, throughout his whole life, the sole owner of his thoughts and the work he has accomplished. In no way can he follow ready-made clichés or waste his energies using methods invented by others. Above all, he must show imagination and a sense of fantasy by refusing, for example, to adapt famous literary works or film the biographies of famous people. That is also a moral position. Faced with a great text, one knows that the author has expressed himself fully. There is no need to translate it into a another, more primitive language than his own.

So for all these reasons, I'd like to talk about Boris Barnet. He was a large man, physically at ease and determinedly generous. Since God had endowed him with enormous gifts, he could be neither mean nor stingy, nor the thief of other people's ideas.

More importantly, he lived in the Soviet Union and behaved as if the state didn't exist, except as a paradox. *Okraina*, for example, dealt with the relationship between a Russian woman and a German, both of whom had lived through the First World War. It was also a film about dressmakers and shoemakers, artisans who, by the very fact of having to work together, cannot be enemies. This was a point of view directly opposed to that of the Communists, who held that only the proletariat, who made nothing, could unite and build a socialist paradise on earth. As a poet, Mayakovsky, also a great talent and a generous man, fell into the trap of believing this Communist dream due to his lack of education. Where Barnet would project himself into the past and knew that all on this earth was vanity and that everything ended badly, Mayakovsky believed that the socialist revolution would be a decisive turning-point. And on that unfortunately mistaken belief, he built his poetic achievement. Barnet did not make such an error. Dovzhenko did because he was a peasant, revelling in having learnt to read and write. He had been accepted into a circle of great men who impressed him deeply: Pudovkin, fellow-believers like Mayakovsky, and the arrogant, cynical and cold Eisenstein, who tossed off paradoxes left and right, manipulated words and images, but who was ideologically empty, believing that art existed merely as form.

When Barnet realized it was no longer possible for him to follow the only profession he knew, he escaped into genre films – adventure movies, police and spy films. Mikhail Romm – a man who deserves our respect – had made *Boule de Suif*, adapted from Maupassant's story, and then was broken by the system because of his weakness, fear or desire to be obedient. He went on to make films about Lenin, but always dreamed of returning to his first love. Barnet, however, stopped practising his art. He spent his time playing practical jokes. His friend Nikolai Chenguelaya recounts how Romm was shooting *The Thirteen* in the Kara-Koum desert. At the time, Barnet was living with the very beautiful Elena Kouzmina, a famous Soviet actress who was playing in the film. A small plane flew over the location, and at the same moment Kouzmina disappeared behind the sand-dunes. A week later, the little plane flew over again, but in the opposite direction. They discovered dozens of empty champagne, vodka and beer bottles behind the dunes. Barnet, who'd been flying the plane, and Kouzmina had spent the entire week

drinking and making love in the desert! And the filming could only start
again when Barnet flew away! Barnet was a charming, honest man, solid
but impecunious. He was much loved by women who were obliged to
live with mediocrities who protected them materially, but whom they
detested.

He later lived with an editor, thirty years his junior, from the Mosfilm
Studios. She told me a great deal about him and said she had never met
anyone quite like him.

Why should we follow Barnet's example? Because he did everything
himself without adapting anyone else's work. He believed one must
never betray oneself, that a film must be clear, precise, articulate and
its subject well-fashioned and identifiable. As far as he was concerned,
it was impossible not to be faithful to one's own project because it was
a 'decree from heaven'. I rediscovered this notion of a 'decree from
heaven' through Dovzhenko, who was my professor at VGIK. He told
me that every act in one's life must be accomplished as if it were one's
last. He'd say that one could be knocked down by a bus in the street
and leave the world having done something badly. One must never
believe that one can repair what one has done badly, for death can come
at any moment.

I particularly like Barnet's *By the Bluest of Seas*. It's a marvel, full of
an admiration for life, for love, desire, and fidelity. All with a *kolkhoz*
for a setting! But Barnet places this *kolkhoz* on an island and cuts it off
from the rest of the world. In fact, it's a fishing community linked to
a beautiful, powerful, glittering sea, ploughed by sailing boats and
overlooked by clouds. Two men fall in love with the same woman, only
to discover she's waiting for a man who is far away. Anything is possible
at any moment of this film. One moment, you think she is falling for
one of the men, then the next moment the other. In the end, it's neither.
The pain which arises out of unrequited love is transformed into beauty.
There is the scene where the two men, unhappy with their lot, eat a
bitter lemon which makes them grimace; or the equally wonderful scene
when, during a storm, a wave throws the woman into the hold of the
boat where people are sitting.

I knew Barnet a little. We met once or twice over a bottle of vodka. We
talked of insignificant things. He showed me how to win at arm-wrestling,
told me stories about the time of the tsars. We were drinking and
suddenly he said, 'By the way, the pleasure of refusing a gift is a privilege
one can get a real kick out of.' And it's noticeable that he never had the

kind of charm which predisposed the Bolsheviks either to kill him or to be taken in by him. For example, Bulgakov, another giant of the period, provoked the authorities to such an extent they killed him. As for Barnet, he was absent from the social stage. He didn't want a flat, or an Order of Lenin, or favours, or any of the things that pushed some Russians to compromise themselves and betray others. Mikhail Romm, who was the only film-maker to confess publicly, as an example to others, the errors he had committed, received a state *dacha* as thanks for the films he made about Lenin. He once asked the forester why the elms had been chopped down around the house, and the forester answered, 'Because they were beautiful.' Romm would go on to say that Barnet was not the kind of tree one could cut down. Barnet was a phenomenon apart, because he asked for nothing.

Nothing Barnet made later can erase the memory of *By the Bluest of Seas*, *Okraina* or *The Girl With the Hatbox*. There are film-makers who are thinkers, but too much thought can deprive a director of the lightness which is vital to his art. One can detect the metaphysical dimension in Barnet's work, but thought never dominates. His art is nonchalant and superficial, like life. At no stage do serious ideas stultify his work, as they sometimes do in Thomas Mann or Tolstoy. Oddly enough, Barnet's method reminds me of Anatole France's, as exemplified by *The Opinions of Monsieur Jérôme Coignard*. That is why, out of all the directors who've influenced me – Clair, Vigo, Tati – I chose to speak about Barnet, less well-known than they but nonetheless belonging to the same family.

JEAN RENOIR
Marcel Pagnol

The modern, millennial cinema is stateless – and also increasingly, if in a highly limited sense, timeless. How else, other than by the public's preference for the ersatz, to explain the vast international popularity of Claude Berri's two bogus Marcel Pagnol films, Jean de Florette *and* Manon des Sources, *and the relative neglect and obscurity in which Pagnol's own body of work languishes? It is, perhaps, a question of rhetoric. What Berri trades in is 'filmed cinema' (as one refers to 'filmed theatre'), and the sickly visuals of his pastiches remind one of nothing so much as the idiom adopted by the sort of spuriously authentic restaurants whose bread is invariably 'oven-browned' and whose tomatoes are obligatorily 'sun-dried'. Pagnol's own wonderful films are just bread, plain loaves of unsliced bread; they are, equally, as juicy and refreshing as ordinary raw tomatoes. Without any smothering of Technicolor sauce, they taste, like the simplest and best kinds of food, of nothing but themselves.*

Here is Jean Renoir, another great filmmaker, writing movingly and sincerely about his friend and colleague.

There exist in this world rare human beings who are possessed of gifts both for commerce and for the art of entertainment. Charlie Chaplin is the outstanding example, and on a more modest financial level one may cite the Swedish director, Ingmar Bergman. The latter has contrived to make films of his own choosing and to survive, thanks to an organization that seems to me in all respects remarkable. He works in collaboration with the Royal Theatre in Stockholm, and in winter, when the weather is not suitable for outdoor photography, he works for the stage. With the return of summer weather he makes films. His actors are paid both by the theatre and by the films in which he casts them. This is a wonderfully economical system of production. Since they are in the Swedish language his films obviously have a limited distribution, which limits the actors' salaries. Only those who speak English can from time to time indulge in the luxury of an American engagement.

In France an author of genius managed to create a perfectly efficient organization for the distribution of his films. This was Marcel Pagnol. Not only did he restrict himself geographically, like Bergman, but he did so also in the historical sense. His company, 'Les Films Marcel Pagnol', operated like a medieval workshop. While I was working on my film *Toni*, I saw him constantly. He used my Vieux Colombier electrical equipment. He collected technicians, actors and workpeople in his country house like a fifteenth-century master-carpenter. I had rented a lodging not far away and I competed with his outfit in thrilling games of *pétanque* or *boules*. We exchanged professional services: I occasionally directed a scene for him and he helped me out with problems of dialogue. He had his own distributing organization and, after the appearance of *Marius* and *Fanny*, he even owned a cinema on the Canebière in Marseilles. The great reputation he had achieved allowed him this degree of independence. Pagnol's commercial success was based on his talent. It worked, and worked very well.

Marcel Pagnol considered that the only purpose of women was to bear children, and that this was approximately where their usefulness ceased. He had made up his mind to have a child, and a fair-haired one, and he was looking round for a blonde mother, whom he proposed to marry. His friend, Léon Voltera, proprietor of the Casino de Paris, the most fashionable post-war music-hall, and also of the Théâtre de Paris, which specialized in serious theatre, advised him to choose one of his English dancing-girls, and every night Pagnol and Voltera looked in at the Casino de Paris, where 'les girls' were performing, and discussed the merits of the unwitting candidates. Sometimes they preferred one and sometimes another, but in the end they made up their minds and Pagnol called upon the winner. She accepted on the spot, delighted at the idea of becoming Madame Marcel Pagnol. I met her a number of times. She was a charming girl, but she wanted more out of life than merely the function of bearing children. In an unconscious protest the child she bore her husband was dark-haired.

Léon Voltera adored Pagnol. It must be said that, thanks to *Marius* and *Fanny*, the Théâtre de Paris, which was only separated by a passage-way from the Casino, was always filled. Voltera was also the owner of Luna Park, the amusement park by the Porte Maillot. He would invite freaks from Luna Park to first nights at the Théâtre de Paris, and thus one was liable to see Parisian celebrities seated next to the 'living skeleton' or the 'bearded lady'. His reason for gathering together this mixed assemblage of people had nothing to do with publicity. It was simply an act of friendliness towards the people who worked for him.

One cannot talk of Marcel Pagnol without conjuring up the powerful figure of Raimu. Although Raimu was perhaps the greatest French actor of the century, he was completely ignorant of some things. All he knew about the cinema was that a close-up showed the details of a face. During shooting he would constantly say to the cameraman, 'Make me big.' I was very fond of him, and I think he had a liking for me. Perhaps he felt that intelligence, that quality so highly esteemed by the world, is often accompanied by a painful lack of simplicity. He played the parts entrusted to him by Pagnol without thinking about them, trusting to his own instinct and the immense talent of the author.

There is a widespread belief in the stupidity of actors, but it is without foundation. Intelligence is as well distributed among actors as among other kinds of human being; but in the case of an actor his talent, or genius, has nothing to do with his intellect. I have known actors with brilliant minds who were lamentable on the stage.

This was not the case with Jouvet, who was bursting with both talent and intelligence. Jouvet analysed his parts word by word. He knew how to extract the deepest sense of a text. His rehearsals were a constant series of discoveries. Giraudoux often re-wrote his own lines after Jouvet had found a new meaning in them.

Pagnol believes in nothing but dialogue, and in his case he is right, this is the medium that serves him best. My own conception is diametrically opposed to this. I believe in dialogue not as a means of explaining the situation but as an integral part of the scene. Let us suppose it is a love-scene. The actress is happy in her part; she is beautiful and talented. The young man is extremely handsome and, what is more, has a pleasing personality. One has to convey to the public their overwhelming emotion. In the theatre there is only one way of involving the audience, and that is by finding language worthy of the occasion. But in a film, thanks to the close-up, so much explicitness is unnecessary. The texture of the skin, the glow in the eyes, the moisture of the mouth – all these can say more than any number of words. Most film dialogue seems to have been interpolated for the sake of clarification. It is a false approach. Dialogue is a part of the theme and reveals character. For the real theme is the person, whom dialogue, picture, situation, setting, temperature and lighting all combine together to depict. The world is one whole.

SERGEI EISENSTEIN
from 'Eisenstein on Disney'

What was the most Eisensteinian of films not directed by Sergei Eisenstein? I propose the 'Sorcerer's Apprentice' sequence from Disney's (otherwise lamentable) Fantasia. *And what was the most Disneyesque of films not produced by Walt Disney? I propose Eisenstein's* Ivan the Terrible. *Sergei Eisenstein, one of the cinema's giants, was also one of its most penetrating critics, as witness this superb text on Disney.*

1

Begin with:

'The work of this master is the greatest contribution of the American people to art.'

Dozens and dozens of newspaper clippings, modifying this sentence in various ways, pour down upon the astonished master. They are all from different statements, in different places, to different newspapers and different journalists. And they all come from one and the same man. A Russian film-maker who had just landed upon the North American continent. However, the same news had already preceded him from England. There for the first time and on the very first day of his arrival on British soil, he had rushed off to see the works of the man upon whom he had showered such passionate praise in all his interviews. Thus long before their meeting in person, friendly relations had been established between praiser and praised. Between a Russian and an American. In short – between Disney and myself. When we met each other in person, we met like old acquaintances. And all the more so since he also knew our pictures.

Young and with a small moustache. Very elegant. The elegance of a dancer, I'd say. There's undeniably something of his own hero in him. Mickey has the same grace, ease of gesture and elegance. Not at all surprising!

As later becomes clear, his method is as follows: Disney himself acts out the 'part' or 'role' of Mickey for this or that film. A dozen or so artists stand around him in a circle, quickly capturing the hilarious expressions of their posing and performing boss. And the extremely lively and lifelike preparations for the cartoon are ready – infectious through the whole hyperbolization of the drawing only because taken from a living person. No less alive are the Wolf, the Bear, the Hound (the coarse partner of the refined Mickey); again not accidentally full of life, he comes from Walt's first cousin who, in contrast to him, is chubby, coarse and clumsy.

We tour his tiny studio, far, far away in those days from the centre of Hollywood vanity and life. We are amazed by the modesty of his equipment, considering the colossal scale of productivity. 52 'Mickeys' a year, plus 12 *Silly Symphonies*, including the unsurpassed *The Skeleton Dance*, with the skeletons who play on their own ribs as xylophones! We are surprised by the harmony of the collective. By the harmony of technique. And especially by the fact that the soundtrack is made in New York, where they send the most precisely marked rolls of the drawings' movements, shot to the most precise music score. Not in the slightest resulting in Impressionism. Disney's plastic visions, echoing the sounds, are captured *a priori*. Placed in a vise of the strictest plastic and temporal calculations. Made real. Coordinated by the dozens of hands of his collective. Shot on irreproachable rolls carrying charm, laughter and amazement at his virtuosity around the entire world.

I'm sometimes frightened when I watch his films. Frightened because of some absolute perfection in what he does. This man seems to know not only the magic of all technical means, but also all the most secret strands of human thought, images, ideas, feelings. Such was probably the effect of Saint Francis of Assisi's sermons. Fra Angelico's paintings bewitch in this way. He creates somewhere in the realm of the very purest and most primal depths. There, where we are all children of nature. He creates on the conceptual level of man not yet shackled by logic, reason, or experience. That's how butterflies fly. That's how flowers grow. That's how brooks marvel at their own course. That's how Andersen and Alice charm in Wonderland. That's how Hoffmann wrote in lighter moments. The same current of interflowing images. The archivist Lindhorst, who is also King of the Elves, etc. One of Disney's most amazing films is his *Merbabies*. What purity and clarity of soul is needed to make such a thing! To what depths of untouched nature is it necessary to dive with bubbles and bubblelike children in order to reach such absolute freedom from all categories, all conventions. In order to be like children.

The very last line written by Gogol's hand was: 'For only as a child may you enter the Holy Kingdom.'

Chaplin, too, is infantile. But his is a constant, agonized and somewhere at its core, an always tragic lament over the lost golden age of childhood. The epos of Chaplin is the *Paradise Lost* of today. The epos of Disney is *Paradise Regained*. Precisely Paradise. Unreachable on Earth. Created only by a drawing. It's not the absurdity of childish conceptions of an eccentric clashing with adult reality. The humour of the incompatibility of one with the other. And the sadness over man's forever lost childhood, and mankind's Golden Age, lost irrevocably to those who want to bring it back from the past, instead of creating it in a better Socialist future. Disney (and it's not accidental that his films are drawn) is a complete return to a world of complete freedom (not accidentally fictitious), freed from the necessity of another primal extinction.

As an unforgettable symbol of his whole creative work, there stands before me a family of octopuses on four legs, with a fifth serving as a tail, and a sixth – a trunk. How much (imaginary!) divine omnipotence there is in this! What magic of reconstructing the world according to one's fantasy and will! A fictitious world. A world of lines and colours which subjugates and alters itself to your command. You tell a mountain: move, and it moves. You tell an octopus: be an elephant, and the octopus becomes an elephant. You tell the sun: 'Stop!' – and it stops.

You're able to see how the image of the hero who stopped the sun arose among those who were powerless to even take cover from it, and whose whole way of life was at the mercy of the sun. And you see how the drawn magic of a reconstructed world had to arise at the very summit of a society that had completely enslaved nature – namely, in America. Where, at the same time, man has become more merciless than in the Stone Age, more doomed than in prehistoric times, more enslaved than during the slave owning era.

Disney is a marvellous lullaby for the suffering and unfortunate, the oppressed and deprived. For those who are shackled by hours of work and regulated moments of rest, by a mathematical precision of time, whose lives are graphed by the cent and dollar. Whose lives are divided up into little squares, like a chess board, with the sole difference that whether you're a knight or a rook, a queen or a bishop – on this board, you can only lose. And also because its black squares don't alternate with white ones, but are all of a protective grey colour, day after day. Grey, grey, grey. From birth to death. Grey squares of city blocks. Grey prison cells of city streets. Grey faces of endless street crowds. The grey, empty eyes of those who are forever at the mercy of a pitiless procession of laws, not of their own making, laws that divide up the soul, feelings, thoughts, just as the carcasses of pigs are dismembered by the conveyor belts of Chicago slaughter houses, and the separate pieces of cars are assembled into mechanical organisms by Ford's conveyor belts. That's why Disney films blaze with colour. Like the patterns in the eyes of people who have been deprived of the colours in nature. That's why the imagination in them is limitless, for Disney's films are a revolt against conditioning and legislating, against spiritual stagnation and greyness. But the revolt is lyrical. The revolt is a daydream. Fruitless and lacking consequences. These aren't those daydreams which, accumulating, give birth to action and give a hand to realize the dream. They are the 'golden dreams' you escape to, like other worlds where everything is different, where you're free from all fetters, where you can clown around just as nature itself seemed to have done in the joyful ages of its coming into being, when she herself invented curiosities worthy of Disney: the ridiculous ostrich next to the logical hen, the absurd giraffe next to the loyal cat, the kangaroo mocking the future Madonna!

Disney's beasts, fish and birds have the habit of stretching and shrinking. Of mocking at their own form, just as the fish-tiger and octopus-elephant of *Merbabies* mock at the categories of zoology. This triumph over the fetters of form is symptomatic. This triumph over all fetters, over everything that binds, resounds throughout, from the plastic trick to the hymn of *The Three Little Pigs*: 'We're not afraid of the big, grey wolf . . .'

With what triumphant joy the millions of hearts join in this chorus, who every moment *are* afraid of the big grey wolf. The 'grey wolf' in America is behind every corner, behind every counter, on the heels of every person. One moment he blows away to the auction block the home and property of a farmer, ruined by the financial crisis. Another moment he blows out of the comfortable house a man who's worked many years for Ford, but who couldn't make his last payment. Frightening, frightening is the 'grey wolf' of unemployment: millions and millions of people are gobbled up by its voracious appetite.

But 'we're not afraid of the big, grey wolf' flies carefreely from the screen. This cry of optimism could only be drawn. For there is no such slant on truthfully shot capitalist reality which, without lying, could possibly sound like optimistic reassurance! But, fortunately, there are lines and colours. Music and cartoons. The talent of Disney and the 'great consoler' – the cinema.

There exists a touching legend from the Middle Ages about 'The Juggler of the Holy Mother'. A pilgrimage was made to bring gifts to the Madonna. He alone had nothing to take her. And so he spread out his mat before her statue and honoured her with his art. This didn't please the fat monks and greedy priest: they preferred fat and candles, silver coins and wine. But even so, the legend of the juggler was preserved with reverence, even by them.

This is how Americans, once they start to undertake the realization of the Golden Age of the future, will recall with warmth and gratitude the man who cheered them up with 'golden dreams' during their period of oppression.

Who, for an instant, allowed them to forget, to not feel the chilling horror before the grey wolf who, while you were at the movies, pitilessly turned off your gas and water for non-payment. Who gave a feeling of warmth and closeness with grasshoppers and birds, beasts and flowers to those whose dungeons of the streets of New York were always cut off from everything happy and live.

Among the strange characteristics of the tribes who populate this continent, North America, is the one by which its inhabitants choose specific stars for themselves and live their lives in worship of them.

These are not stars of heaven, but of the movies, but that doesn't change matters. It even provides a way of strengthening the financial resources of the Postal Service through an unending flood of letters addressed to beloved stars.

The American magazine, *The New Yorker*, once ran a cartoon making fun of this strangeness and passion of its fellow-tribesmen. An elderly lady from the very highest society, with a diamond diadem in her grey hair and a discreet butler bowing in the background, is busy at the same activity as any young shopgirl or officeboy: she is writing to her favourite star . . .

But the point is not in the act of writing itself.

The point is the addressee.

The letter begins with the greeting: 'Dear Mickey Mouse'.

That is the point.

The huge, all-embracing, international popularity among all ages which is possessed by this small, drawn hero of the great artist and master. Walt Disney, who exceeds in popularity that other American by the name of Walt – Walt Whitman.

Truly, all ages – from children to the elderly, all nationalities, all races and all types of social systems are intoxicated by him with the same delight, surrender with the same fervour to his charm, with the same ecstasy allow themselves to be carried away by Disney's living drawings (animated cartoons).

How is this achieved?

First of all, one could say that Disney's works seem to contain all the faultlessly active features by which a work of art influences – seemingly in the greatest possible quantity and the greatest possible purity.

In terms of the faultlessness of its influence, Disney's work statistically scores the greatest possible number of points, considering the viewers won over by it.

And our supposition, therefore, is entirely legitimate.

We shall try to enumerate the peculiarities and characteristic features which distinguish Disney's work. And we shall try to generalize these features. They shall prove to be decisive features in any art form, but only in Disney, presented in their very purest form.

2

Childhood recollections have deposited three scenes in my memory.

The first was from a reader. Some poem about an Arab in the desert and his crazed camel. About a mad camel who chases his master. About how the Arab, fleeing from the camel, falls into a precipice, but catches hold of a bush hanging over the bottomless abyss.

And about how, in the middle of this hopeless situation – with the infuriated camel above him and the bottomless precipice below – the Arab suddenly notices two or three red berries on the bush and, forgetting about everything, reaches for them.

The next recollection is vaguer. It must be earlier. In it, some sort of odd, sentimental angels are allowed to descend into Hell to lay their refreshing hands for an instant upon the heads of sinners boiling in pitch. Or, perhaps, to let a drop of moisture fall upon their thirst-tortured lips . . .

The third recollection is more concrete. It has an author – Victor Hugo, a precise place of action – Paris, and specific names of characters. His name is Quasimodo. Hers is Esmeralda. Accompanied by an elegant little goat, Esmeralda goes up to Quasimodo, who has been cruelly whipped and chained to a scaffold; to Quasimodo, suffering and tormented by thirst and the crowd's mockery. She lets him drink and gently presses her lips against his hideous, tortured, suffering face.

While watching Disney's *Snow White*, I recall these three scenes.

But not because Snow White kisses the funny and ugly gnomes one by one on their bald heads; not because a flock of no less elegant deer and wild goats follows behind her; and not because she is surrounded by fairy tale terrors and horrors.

But because Disney's works themselves strike me as the same kind of drop of comfort, an instant of relief, a fleeting touch of lips in the hell of social burdens, injustices and torments, in which the circle of his American viewers is forever trapped.

Beyond the framework of the poem, the Arab, of course, will fall into the precipice or will be trampled to death by the camel. The sinners will go on suffering in the cauldrons of boiling pitch. The angels' caress, the two or three refreshing berries, Esmeralda's cup and goat will in no way change their fate. But for an instant, for a fraction of a second, they give them the most precious thing in their situation – obliviousness.

And Disney, like all of them, through the magic of his works and more intensely, perhaps, than anyone else, bestows precisely this upon his viewer, precisely obliviousness, an instant of complete and total release from everything connected with the suffering caused by the social conditions of the social order of the largest capitalist government.

Disney neither brands, nor exposes.

We are used to the beasts in fables. The beasts there provide no comfort.

They don't bite the reader, don't scratch, don't growl at him and don't kick.

But they do something a lot less pleasant: they hold a distorting mirror up to their bigger brother – man.

This is how he thinks, the bigger brother, man. His own . . . snout is actually warped.

And this disturbing exposure is further aided by his smaller brothers – goats and sheep, foxes and lions, eagles and snakes, frogs and monkeys.

Disney's don't expose anyone, don't blame and don't preach.

And if most of them didn't flash by us so quickly in one or two short little reels, we could be made angry by the moral uselessness of their existence on the screen.

But because of the fleeting ephemerality of their existence, you can't reproach them for their mindlessness.

Even the string of a bow can't be strained forever.

The same for the nerves.

And instants of this 'releasing' – an expression which unsuccessfully conveys the sense of the untranslatable [into Russian] word, 'relax', – are just as prophylactically necessary as the daily dose of carefree laughter in the well-known American saying: 'A laugh a day keeps the doctor away.'

The triumphant proletariat of a future America will erect no monument to Disney as a fighter either in their hearts, or on street squares.

Memory won't crown his brow with the glory of a fabulist or a lampoonist, if you can even call a 'brow' the merry, moustached, mocking and ironically affable face of the creator of Mickey Mouse.

But everyone will recall him with warm gratitude for those instants of respite amid the torrential, desperate struggle for life and existence which he gave to the viewer in the troubled years of the social paradise of democratic America.

We know many workers in the cinema who also lead the viewer to an obliviousness of the truth of life and to the golden dreams of a lie.

We know the concealed purpose of this. We've seen the fluffy dramatizations of similar spectacles off the screen as well.

With the same goal – to distract the attention of 'the man on the street' from the genuine and serious problems of the interrelation of labour and capital to such absurd pseudo-problems as the struggle around the 'Dry Law'.

And here too, as in the corresponding works, obliviousness is evil.

Obliviousness as a means of lulling to sleep; obliviousness as a way of distracting thought from the real to the fantastic; obliviousness as a tool for disarming the struggle.

This is not what Disney gives us.

Not a pile of 'happy ends' – happy only on the screen; not a gilded lie about the fast-paced, honest careers and generosity of capitalist magnates; not a base sermon, slurring over social contradictions, is delivered by the small screen of Disney's cartoons – in contrast to the 'big' American screen. Without encouraging to fight against this evil, neither does he neutrally serve the cause of this evil by hiding behind a hypocritical: 'I'm not responsible for what I create.'

Disney is simply 'beyond good and evil'. Like the sun, like trees, like birds, like the ducks and mice, deer and pigeons that run across his screen. To an even greater degree than Chaplin. Than Chaplin, who sermonizes and often gets lost in Quakerizing.

Disney's films, while not exposing sunspots, themselves act like reflections of sunrays and spots across the screen of the earth.

They flash by, burn briefly and are gone.

In a certain French song, a cat stole a round piece of cheese, but the obliging moon placed on the empty dish a little white round reflection of the lunar disc.

He who takes it into his head to bite hold of Disney by the usual analysis and yardstick, the ordinary requirements, the standard norms, inquiries and demands of 'high' genres of art – will gnash his teeth on empty air. And still, this is a joyful and beautiful art that sparkles with a refinement of form and dazzling purity.

As much a paradox in the community of the 'serious' arts, as the unprincipled but eternal circus, as the singing of a bird – lacking any content, but infinitely exciting in its warbling.

And, perhaps, precisely in this lies the especially curious nature of the method and means of Disney's art, as the purest model of *inviolably-natural* elements, characteristic of any art and here presented in a chemically pure form.

Here it's like an aroma given without a flower; a taste extracted from a fruit; sound as such; affect freed from any purpose.

How is this amazing phenomenon achieved?

To a certain extent, of course, it only seems to be so.

For at the centre of Disney, as well, stands man. But man brought back, as it were, to those pre-stages that were traced out by . . . Darwin.

In *Merbabies*, a striped fish in a cage is transformed into a tiger and roars with the voice of a lion or panther. Octopuses turn into elephants. A fish – into a donkey. A departure from one's self. From once and forever prescribed norms of nomenclature, form and behaviour. Here it's overt. In the open. And, of course, in comic form. Seriously, as in life – and especially in American life – there's no such thing, it doesn't occur and cannot.

Is this a motif in Disney's works, or chance?

Let's look at other films.

Let's examine the characteristics of the pre-colour *Mickey Mouses*.

What do you remember from them? A lot. There's the steamboat that folds logs like pastries; there are the hotdogs whose skins are pulled down and are spanked; there are the piano keys which bite the pianist like teeth, and much, much more.

And here too, of course, are the same traits of a transformed world, a world going out of itself. The world around the author – an inhuman world, and probably for that very reason inciting Disney to humanize Wilbur the grasshopper, Goofy the dog, Donald Duck, and first and foremost, Mickey and Minnie.

But one eternal trait especially sticks in the mind – a purely formal one, it would seem.

Mickey starts to sing, his hands folded together. The hands echo the music as only the movements of Disney's characters are capable of echoing a melody. And then reaching for a high note, the arms shoot up far beyond the limits of their normal representation. In tone to the music, they stretch far beyond the length allotted them. The necks of his surprised horses stretch the same way, or their legs become extended when running.

This is repeated by the necks of ostriches, the tails of cows, not to mention all the attributes of the beasts and plants in the *Silly Symphonies*, shot so as to meticulously coil to the tone and melody of the music.

And here too, as we see, there seems to be the same playing at 'something else', 'the impossible'.

But here it's deeper and broader.

In this aspect, is it characteristic only of Disney?

To solve the secret meaning of this phenomenon, let's look for examples beyond Disney's works.

Disney has become on the screen what in the world of books in the 'seventies was *Alice in Wonderland* by Lewis Carroll.

The same rabbits with vest pockets, rats and mice, turtles and walruses live in its pages.

And . . . in the very first two chapters of her adventures, we find what we're looking for.

Alice is in a desperate situation: in Carroll's method, this is presented literally – there are no ways out from the place she has landed in, having fallen through a rabbit hole.

That is, there are some doors, but they're all locked.

And moreover, the doors are so small that at best her head could get through, but certainly not her shoulders. 'Drink me' – is written on a little bottle on a little table next to a little golden key to the door.

'". . . – What a curious feeling!" said Alice. "I must be shutting up like a telescope."'

(She had drunk the contents of the little bottle.)

'. . . And so it was indeed: she was now only ten inches high, and her face brightened up at the thought that she was now the right size for going through the little door into that lovely garden. First, however, she waited for a few minutes to see if she was going to shrink any further: she felt a little nervous about this; "for it might end, you know," said Alice to herself, "in my going out altogether, like a candle. I wonder what I should be like then?" And she tried to fancy what the flame of a candle looks like after the candle is blown out, for she could not remember ever having seen such a thing.'

But Alice doesn't manage to go out into the garden. She forgot the little key to the door on the table, and now her small height prevents her from reaching it. And her attempts to scramble onto the table along its legs are useless – it proves to be too slippery . . .

Alice starts to cry.

'Eat me' – is the beautiful writing on a little cake.

'Curiouser and curiouser!' – cries Alice who ate it:

'"Now I'm opening out like the largest telescope that ever was! Goodbye, feet!" (for when she looked down at her feet, they seemed to be almost out of sight, they were getting so far off). "Oh, my poor little feet, I wonder who will put on your shoes and stockings for you now, dears? I'm sure I shan't be able! I shall be a great deal too far off to trouble myself about you . . ."'

Alice is now so huge that again she can't pass through the doors of the underground room.

In a new fit of despair, she starts to shed tears, but suddenly she notices that she's quickly started to shrink again: the reason for this is the fan she's been waving back and forth. She just barely manages to throw it away before she disappears completely, and then suddenly falls in a lake of tears – her own tears she had shed when she was huge. 'I wish I hadn't cried so much!' says Alice, swimming about the salty waves. But we'll leave her here, for the episode of expanding and shrinking height which interests us is over.

Is there a borrowing here by Disney? Or is this image of elasticity of shapes generally widespread?

I find it in the drawings of the German caricaturist, Trier. The adventures of a little boy with a super-long arm.

But this same image I also find among eighteenth-century Japanese etchings. The many-metred arms of geishas reaching out after frightened customers through the gratings of Yoshiwara's teahouses.

More ancient are patterns with an abstract interplay of infinitely stretching necks, legs and noses. Stretched noses are the property of even an entire breed of mythological beings – the Tengu, etc. Moreover, I recall the circus arena and the entirely incomprehensible interest which has compelled hundreds of thousands of people over the centuries to follow with bated breath this same thing which the stage and variety artist is capable of doing within the limits of human possibilities: before the viewer is a 'human snake' – a spineless, elastic creature, for some reason most often dressed as Mephistopheles, if it's not by chance the 'Snake Dancer' of New York Negro nightclubs, where the same kind of creature writhes in abstract, silk robes . . .

The attractiveness of this process is obvious. I purposely cited it as the first example in the very purest and even abstract and storyless form. This doesn't mean it cannot be used as a working model for loftier, moralizing and philosophical purposes. And without losing any of its 'attractionness', as I called a similar attraction in my youth, which imparts a warm lifelikeness and vital imagery to the most morally ethical thesis. For aren't there echoes of the attractiveness of this very phenomenon in the fate of the shrinking skin which serves as the central image of . . . Balzac's *La Peau de Chagrin*? An image which is profound in thought and irresistibly attractive and exciting in form?

What's strange is not the fact that it exists.

What's strange is that it attracts!

And you can't help but arrive at the conclusion that a single, common prerequisite of attractiveness shows through in all these examples: a rejection of once-and-forever allotted form, freedom from ossification, the ability to dynamically assume any form.

An ability that I'd call 'plasmaticness', for here we have a being represented in drawing, a being of a definite form, a being which has attained a definite appearance, and which behaves like the primal protoplasm, not yet possessing a 'stable' form, but capable of assuming any form and which, skipping along the rungs of the evolutionary ladder, attaches itself to any and all forms of animal existence.

Why is the sight of this so attractive?

It's difficult to assume in the viewer a 'memory' of his own existence at a similar stage – the origin of the foetus or further back down the evolutionary scale (even if one measures the depth of the 'base' of memory not just as it resides in the brain, but in all its predecessors, right down to the cellular tissue!).

But it's easier to accept that this picture is inescapably attractive through its trait of all-possible diversity of form. In a country and social order with such a mercilessly standardized and mechanically measured existence, which is difficult to call life, the sight of such 'omnipotence' (that is, the ability to become 'whatever you wish'), cannot but hold a sharp degree of attractiveness. This is as true for the United States as it is for the petrified canons of world-outlook, art and philosophy of eighteenth-century Japan. This is also true for the starch-bound and tuxedoed habitué of nightclubs who feasts his eyes upon the boneless elastic figures, who know nothing of the rigid spine and stiff corset of high society.

A lost changeability, fluidity, suddenness of formations – that's the 'subtext' brought to the viewer who lacks all this by these seemingly strange traits which permeate folktales, cartoons, the spineless circus performer and the seemingly groundless scattering of extremities in Disney's drawings.

It's natural to expect that such a strong tendency of the transformation of stable forms into forms of mobility could not be confined solely to means of form: this tendency exceeds the boundaries of form and extends to subject and theme. An unstable character becomes a film hero; that is, the kind of character for whom a changeable appearance is . . . natural. Here, changeability of form is no longer a paradoxical expressiveness, as in the case of stretching necks, tails and legs: here, God Himself commanded the character to be fluid.

Such a picture is about ghosts. Here, Mickey and his friends are members of a company that exterminates ghosts. And the whole film draws peripeteias of a heated hunt for ghosts throughout a deserted house. There's no limit here to the outburst of transformations of a greenish cloud with the appearance of red-nosed mischievous ghosts. But the film is further remarkable in that the basic theme here appears distinctly in the whole solution of the thing.

This film, if you will, is not only nostalgia and daydreaming about the liberation of forms from the laws of logic and forever established stability, as it was in *Merbabies*. This film, if you will, is a challenge, and its 'moral'

– an appeal to the fact that, only having loosened the fetters of stability is the attainment of life possible. Indeed, we will look upon this opus not as a work rolling gaily along beside us, but as a document that has 'come down to us' of certain eras and tendencies, like folktales of antiquity or myths. And its tendencies will become completely clear. The 'Ghost Exterminating Company' – isn't this actually a symbol of formal logic which drives out everything living, mobile, fantastical? Its failures and losses in the war with a handful of ghosts, with the fantastic which lurks in the nature of every night table, in every soup bowl, behind every door and in every wall! And the victory over ghosts? It's provided by a charming scene: the frightened 'agents' of the war with ghosts, after a thousand and one adventures where they are duped by the ghosts, fall into a mass of dough. Just like Max and Moritz. But here they don't become gingerbread men, but run around as terrifying white shadows, dragging their tails of dough. Their appearance is fantastic, ghostly. They themselves become like ghosts. And then what? The ghosts themselves, frightened by them, take off like a bullet from the 'haunted' house! A stroke of pure Disney charm. In essence – a unique morality-play on the theme that, only having joined in the fantastical, alogical and sensuous order is it possible to achieve a mastery and supremacy in the realm of freedom from the shackles of logic, from shackles in general.

This . . . is a fictitious freedom. For an instant. A momentary, imaginary, comical liberation from the timelock mechanism of American life. A five-minute 'break' for the psyche, but during which the viewer himself remains chained to the winch of the machine.

But at the same time, this situation is also a symbol of Disney's method. For through his whole system of devices, themes and subjects, Disney constantly gives us prescriptions for folkloric, mythological, prelogical thought – but always rejecting, pushing aside logic, brushing aside logistics, formal logic, the logical 'case'.

Let's take another example. Who else is in a silly situation in a film about prescriptions for self-control? Who masters himself, who instead of giving free reign to his impulses, obediently repeats the prescription broadcast on the radio, and meekly counts off 1, 2, 3 . . . up to ten.

And with what delight Donald Duck smashes this machine of self-discipline and self-control – the radio, after having suffered over the course of the picture a thousand and one misfortunes, in which he had inhibited his own spontaneity and consciously tried to fetter and enslave it to please the hypocritically sanctimonious voice from the radio, which appealed to the purely Christian virtue of the enslavement of one's own individuality. In what a flood of treacle flows the same kind of sermon throughout the United States – the innumerable churches, brotherhoods, sermons, leaflets, societies! How powerful in America is this Christmas-time appeal of the Salvation Army and the followers of Mary Baker Eddy ('Christian Science') and Aimee McPherson: to make the shackles imposed by the social order on the life and existence of its free people glow as virtues!

Disney doesn't go into the roots. But has fun and entertains, mocks and amuses – jumping like a squirrel from branch to branch somewhere along the very surface of the phenomenon, without looking beneath to the origins, at the reasons and causes, at the conditions and preconditions.

But the unstable hero with purely protean greed seeks ever newer and newer forms of embodiment.

Mobility of contour is not enough for him. The play of waters, moving like a giant, living, formless amoeba in *Hawaiian Holiday* with Goofy and his surfboard, are not enough for him. (In one of his black-and-white films, the waves, thus playing, tousle a steamship, gathering into puffs of foam, puffs which suddenly become . . . fists in boxing gloves, delivering punches to the poor sides of the steamships.) The collapsible steamship which arises from a system of bolls to scatter suddenly again into nothing, is not enough for him. (Elastic necks of contours are stretched here to the gigantic proportions of a whole ship arising from nothing and again dissolving into nothing.) The interplay of storm clouds in the sky and the greenish cloud of endlessly changing ghosts inside the deserted house, is not enough for him. The ghostly mask which prophesies to the witch in *Snow White*, appears in . . . fire. And what, if not fire, is capable of most fully conveying the dream of a flowing diversity of forms?!

'A good actor is one who says "I love you!" more convincingly to an actress he doesn't love than to the actress he does'   **SACHA GUITRY**

HENRY MILLER
The Golden Age

Luis Buñuel, the creator of Un chien andalou, L'Age d'or, El, Los Olvidados, Viridiana, Belle de Jour, Tristana *and* Le Charme discret de la bourgeoisie, *was one of those filmmakers for whom it might be said the cinema is for.* Henry Miller's essay, however, extracted from a collection of texts entitled The World of Luis Buñuel, edited by Joan Mellon, is about more than Buñuel himself, about more than L'Age d'or. It is, rather, about the whole vexed concept of avant-garde cinema to which Buñuel's name has immemorially been attached. For Miller, even as he was writing his essay, the cinema as a jubilantly subversive form was already in its death throes. And, indeed, so regularly has it been lamented that the avant-garde is no more, it might make better sense to adopt this permanent proximity to extinction as perhaps its primary defining property. The avant-garde is therefore, in the cinema as elsewhere, that area of creative endeavour which, at any given stage of the contemporary history of culture and ideas, is closer than all others to its own obsolescence. Long may it continue to be so!*

At present the cinema is the great popular art form, which is to say it is not an art at all. Ever since its birth we have been hearing that at last an art has been born which will reach the masses and perhaps liberate them. People profess to see in the cinema possibilities which are denied the other arts. So much the worse for the cinema!

There is not one art called the Cinema but there is, as in every art, a form of production for the many and another for the few. Since the death of avant-garde films – *Le Sang d'un Poète*, by Cocteau, was I believe the last – there remains only the mass production of Hollywood.

The few films which might justify the category of 'art' that have appeared since the birth of the cinema (a matter of forty years or so) died almost at their inception. This is one of the lamentable and amazing facts in connection with the development of a new art form. Despite all effort the cinema seems incapable of establishing itself as art. Perhaps it is due to the fact that the cinema more than any other art form has become a controlled industry, a dictatorship in which the artist is dominated and silenced.

Immediately an astonishing fact asserts itself, namely, that the greatest films were produced at little expense! It does not require millions to produce an artistic film; in fact, it is almost axiomatic that the more money a film costs the worse it is apt to be. Why then does the real cinema not come into being? Why does the cinema remain in the hands of the mob or its dictators? Is it purely an economic question?

The other arts, it should be remembered, are fostered in us. Nay, they are forced upon us almost from birth. Our taste is conditioned by centuries of inoculation. Nowadays one is almost ashamed to admit that one does not like this or that book, this or that painting, this or that piece of music. One may be bored to tears, but one dare not admit it. We have been educated to pretend to like and admire the great works of art with which, alas, we have no longer any connection.

The cinema is born and it is an art, another art – but it is born too late. The cinema is born out of a great feeling of lassitude. Indeed lassitude is too mild a word. The cinema is born just as we are dying. The cinema, like some ugly duckling, imagines that it is related in some way to the theater, that it was born perhaps to replace the theater, which is already dead. Born into a world devoid of enthusiasm, devoid of taste, the cinema functions like a eunuch: it waves a peacock-feathered fan before our drowsy eyes. The cinema believes that what we want of it is to be put to sleep. It does not know *that we are dying*. Therefore, let us not blame the cinema. Let us ask ourselves why it is that this truly marvelous art form should be allowed to perish before our every eyes. Let us ask why it is that when it makes the most heroic efforts to appeal to us its gestures are unheeded.

I am talking about the cinema as an *actuality*, a something which exists, which has validity, just as music or painting or literature. I am strenuously opposed to those who look upon the cinema as a medium to exploit the other arts or even to synthetize them. The cinema is not another form of this or that, nor is it a synthetic product of all the other this-and-thats. The cinema is the cinema and nothing but. And it is quite enough. In fact, it is magnificent.

Like any other art the cinema has in it all the possibilities for creating antagonisms, for stirring up revolt. The cinema can do for man what the other arts have done, possibly even more, but the first condition, the prerequisite in fact, is – *take it out of the hands of the mob!* I understand full well that it is not the mob which creates the films we see – not technically, at any rate. But in a deeper sense it *is* the mob which *actually* creates the films. For the first time in the history of art the mob has dictated what the artist should do. For the first time in the history of man an art is born which caters exclusively to the masses. Perhaps it is some dim comprehension of this unique and deplorable fact which accounts for the tenacity with which 'the dear public' clings to its art. The silent screen! Shadow images! Absence of color! Spectral, phantasmal beginnings. The dumb masses visualizing themselves in those stinking coffins which served as the first movie houses. An abysmal curiosity to see themselves reflected in the magic mirror of the machine age. Out of what tremendous fear and longing was this 'popular' art born?

I can well imagine the cinema never having been born. I can imagine a race of men for whom the cinema would have been thoroughly unnecessary. But I cannot imagine the robots of this age being without a cinema, *some kind of cinema*. Our starved instincts have been clamoring for centuries for more and more substitutes. And as substitute for living the cinema is ideal. Does one ever remark the look of these cinema hounds as they leave the theater? That dreamy air of vacuity, that washed-out look of the pervert who masturbates in the dark! One can hardly distinguish them from the drug addicts: they walk out of the cinema like somnambulists.

This of course is what they want, our worn-out, harassed beasts of toil. Not more terror and strife, not more mystery, not more wonder and hallucination, but peace, surcease from care, the unreality of the dream. But *pleasant* dreams! *Soothing* dreams! And here it is difficult not to restrain a word of consolation for the poor devils who are put to it to quench this unslakable thirst of the mob. It is the fashion among the intelligentsia to ridicule and condemn the efforts, the truly herculean efforts, of the film directors, the Hollywood dopesters particularly. Little do they realize the invention it requires to create each day a drug that will counteract the insomnia of the mob. There is no use condemning the directors, nor is there any use deploring the public's lack of taste. These are stubborn facts, and irremediable. The panderer and the pandered must be eliminated – *both at once!* There is no other solution.

How speak about an art which no one recognizes as *art*? I know that a great deal has already been written about the 'art of the cinema'. One can read about it most every day in the newspapers and the magazines. But it is not the *art* of the cinema which you will find discussed therein – it is rather the dire, botched embryo as it now stands revealed before our eyes, the stillbirth which was mangled in the womb by the obstetricians of art.

For forty years now the cinema has been struggling to get properly born. Imagine the chances of a creature that has wasted forty years of its life in being born! Can it hope to be anything but a monster, an idiot?

I will admit nevertheless that I expect of this monster-idiot the most tremendous things! I expect of this monster that it will devour its own mother and father, that it will run amuck and destroy the world, that it will drive man to frenzy and desperation. I cannot see it otherwise. There is a law of compensation and this law decrees that even the monster must justify himself.

Five or six years ago I had the rare good fortune to see *L'Age d'Or*, the film made by Luis Buñuel and Salvador Dali, which created a riot at Studio 28. For the first time in my life I had the impression that I was watching a film which was pure cinema and nothing but cinema. Since then I am convinced that *L'Age d'Or* is unique and unparalleled. Before going on I should like to remark that I have been going to the cinema regularly for almost forty years; in that time I have seen several thousand films. It should be understood, therefore, that in glorifying the Buñuel/Dali film I am not unmindful of having seen such remarkable films as:

The Last Laugh (Emil Jannings)
Berlin
Un Chapeau de Paille d'Italie (René Clair)
Le Chemin de la Vie
La Souriante Madame Beudet (Germaine Dulac)
Mann Braucht Kein Geld
La Mélodie du Monde (Walter Ruttmann)
Le Ballet Mécanique
Of What Are the Young Films Dreaming? (Comte de Beaumont)
Rocambolesque
Three Comrades and One Invention
Ivan the Terrible
The Cabinet of Dr Caligari
The Crowd (King Vidor)

La Maternelle
Othello (Krause and Jannings)
Extase (Machaty)
Grass
Eskimo
M
Lilliane (Barbara Stanwyck)
A Nous la Liberté (René Clair)
La Tendre Ennemie (Max Ophuls)
The Trackwalker
Potemkin
Les Marins de Cronstadt
Greed (Eric von Stroheim)
Thunder over Mexico (Eisenstein)
The Beggar's Opera
Mädchen in Uniform (Dorothea Wieck)
Midsummer Night's Dream (Reinhardt)
Crime and Punishment (Pierre Blanchar)
The Student of Prague (Conrad Veidt)
Poil de Carotte
Banquier Pichler
The Informer (Victor McLaglen)
The Blue Angel (Marlene Dietrich)
L'Homme à la Barbiche
L'Affaire est dans le Sac (Prévert)
Moana (Flaherty)
Mayerling (Charles Boyer and Danielle Darrieux)
Kriss
Variety (Krause and Jannings)
Chang
Sunrise (Murnau)

                    nor

three Japanese films (ancient, medieval and modern Japan) the
titles of which I have forgotten;

                    nor

a documentary on India

                    nor

a documentary on Tasmania

                    nor

a documentary on the death rites in Mexico, by Eisenstein
> nor

a psychoanalytic dream picture, in the days of the silent film, with Werner Krause
> nor

certain films of Lon Chaney, particularly one based on a novel of Selma Lagerlöf in which he played with Norma Shearer
> nor

The Great Ziegfeld, nor *Mr Deeds Goes to Town*
> nor

The Lost Horizon (Frank Capra), the first *significant* film out of Hollywood
> nor

the very first movie I ever saw, which was a newsreel showing the Brooklyn Bridge and a Chinese with a pigtail walking over the bridge in the rain! I was only seven or eight years of age when I saw this film in the basement of the old South Third Street Presbyterian Church in Brooklyn. Subsequently I saw hundreds of pictures in which it always seemed to be raining and in which there were always nightmarish pursuits in which houses collapsed and people disappeared through trap doors and pies were thrown and human life was cheap and human dignity was nil. And after thousands of slapstick, pie-throwing Mack Sennett films, after Charlie Chaplin had exhausted his bag of tricks, after Fatty Arbuckle, Harold Lloyd, Harry Langdon, Buster Keaton, each with his own special brand of monkeyshines, came the chef-d'oeuvre of all the slapstick, pie-throwing festivals, a film the title of which I forget, but it was among the very first films starring Laurel and Hardy. This, in my opinion, is the greatest comic film ever made – because it brought the pie throwing to apotheosis. There was nothing but pie throwing in it, nothing but pies, thousands and thousands of pies and everybody throwing them right and left. It was the ultimate in burlesque, and it is already forgotten.

In every art the ultimate is achieved only when the artist passes beyond the bounds of the art he employs. This is as true of Lewis Carroll's work as of Dante's *Divine Comedy*, as true of Lao-tse as of Buddha or Christ. The world must be turned upside down, ransacked, confounded in order that the miracle may be proclaimed. In *L'Age d'Or* we stand again at a miraculous frontier which opens up before us a dazzling new world which no one has explored. '*Mon idée générale,*' wrote Salvador Dali, 'en écrivant avec Buñuel le scénario de L'Age d'Or, a été de présenter la ligne droite et pure de conduite d'un être qui poursuit l'amour à travers les ignorables idéaux humanitaires, patriotiques et autres misérables mécanismes de la réalité.' I am not unaware of the part which Dali played in the creation of this great film, and yet I cannot refrain from thinking of it as the peculiar product of his collaborator, the man who directed the film: Luis Buñuel. Dali's name is now familiar to the world, even to Americans and Englishmen, as the most successful of all the surrealists today. He is enjoying a temporal vogue, largely because he is not understood, largely because his work is sensational. Buñuel, on the other hand, appears to have dropped out of sight. Rumor has it that he is in Spain, that he is quietly amassing a collection of documentary films on the revolution. What these will be, if Buñuel retains any of his old vigor, promises to be nothing short of staggering. For Buñuel, like the miners of the Asturias, is a man who flings dynamite. Buñuel is obsessed by the cruelty, ignorance and superstition which prevail among men. He realizes that there is no hope for man anywhere on this earth unless a clean slate be made of it. He appears on the scene at the moment when civilization is at its nadir.

There can be no doubt about it: the plight of civilized man is a foul plight. He is singing his swan song without the joy of having been a swan. He has been sold out by his intellect, manacled, strangled and mangled by his own symbology. He is mired in his art, suffocated by his religions, paralyzed by his knowledge. That which he glorifies is not life, since he had lost the rhythm of life, but death. What he worships is decay and putrefaction. He is diseased and the whole organism of society is infected.

They have called Buñuel everything – traitor, anarchist, pervert, defamer, iconoclast. But lunatic they dare not call him. True, it is lunacy he portrays in his film, but it is not of his making. This stinking chaos which for a brief hour or so is amalgamated under his magic wand, this is the lunacy of man's achievements after ten thousand years of civilization. Buñuel, to show his reverence and gratitude, puts a cow in the bed and drives a garbage truck through the salon. The film is composed of a succession of images without sequence, the significance of which must be sought below the threshold of consciousness. Those who were disappointed because they could not find order or meaning in it will find order and meaning nowhere except perhaps in the world of the bees or the ants.

I am reminded at this point of the charming little documentary which preceded the Buñuel film the night it was shown at Studio 28. A charming little study of the abattoir it was, altogether fitting *and* significant for the weak-stomached sisters of culture who had come to hiss the big film. Here everything was familiar and comprehensible, though perhaps in bad taste. But there was order and meaning in it, as there is order and meaning in a cannibalistic rite. And finally there was even a touch of aestheticism, for when the slaughter was finished and the decapitated bodies had gone their separate ways each little pig's head was carefully blown up by compressed air until it looked so monstrously lifelike and savory and succulent that the saliva flowed willy-nilly. (Not forgetting the shamrocks that were plugged up the assholes of each and every pig!) As I say, this was a perfectly comprehensible piece of butchery, and indeed, so well was it performed that from some of the more elegant spectators in the audience it brought forth a burst of applause.

It is five years or so ago since I saw the Buñuel film and therefore I cannot be absolutely sure, but I am almost certain that there were in this film no scenes of organized butchery between man and man, no wars, no revolutions, no inquisitions, no lynchings, no third-degree scenes. There was, to be sure, a blind man who was mistreated, there was a dog which was kicked in the stomach, there was a boy who was wantonly shot by his father, there was an old dowager who was slapped in the face at a garden party and there were scorpions who fought to the death among the rocks near the sea. Isolated little cruelties which, because they were not woven into a comprehensible little pattern, seemed to shock the spectators even more than the sight of wholesale trench slaughter. There was something which shocked their delicate sensibilities even more and that was the effect of Wagner's *Tristan and Isolde* upon one of the protagonists. Was it possible that the divine music of Wagner could so arouse the sensual appetites of a man and a woman as to make them roll in the graveled path and bite and chew one another until the blood came? Was it possible that this music could so take possession of the young woman as to make her suck the toe of a statued foot with perverted lasciviousness? Does music bring on orgasms, does it entrain perverse acts, does it drive people truly mad? Does this great legendary theme which Wagner immortalized have to do with such a plain vulgar physiological fact as sexual love? The film seems to suggest that it does. It seems to suggest more, for through the ramifications of the Golden Age Buñuel, like an entomologist, has studied what we call love in order to expose beneath the ideology, the mythology, the platitudes, and phraseologies the complete and bloody machinery of sex. He has distinguished for us the blind metabolisms, the secret poisons, the mechanistic reflexes, the distillations of the glands, the entire plexus of forces which unite love and death in life.

Is it necessary to add that there are scenes in this film which have never been dreamed of before? The scene in the water closet, for example. I quote from the program notes:

> Il est inutile d'ajouter qu'un des points culminants de la pureté de ce film nous semble cristallisé dans la vision de l'héroïne dans les cabinets, où la puissance de l'esprit arrive à sublimer une situation généralement baroque en un élément poétique de la plus pure noblesse et solitude.

A *situation usually baroque*! Perhaps it is the baroque element in human life, or rather in the life of civilized man, which gives to Buñuel's works the aspect of cruelty and sadism. Isolated cruelty and sadism, for it is the great virtue of Buñuel that he refuses to be enmeshed in the glittering web of logic and idealism which seeks to mask us from the real nature of man. Perhaps, like Lawrence, Buñuel is only an inverted idealist. Perhaps it is his great tenderness, the great purity and poetry of his vision which forces him to reveal the abominable, the malicious, the ugly and the hypocritical falsities of man. Like his precursors he seems animated by a tremendous hatred for the lie. Being normal, instinctive, healthy, gay, unpretentious he finds himself alone in the crazy drift of social forces. Being thoroughly normal and honest he finds himself regarded as bizarre. Like Lawrence again his work divides the world into two opposite camps – those who are for him and those who are against him. There is no straddling the issue. Either you are crazy, like the rest of civilized humanity, or you are sane and healthy like Buñuel. And if you are sane and healthy you are an anarchist and you throw bombs. The great honor which was conferred upon Luis Buñuel at the showing of his film was that the citizens of France recognized him as a true anarchist. The theater was taken by assault and the street was cleared by the police. The film has never been shown again, to my knowledge, except at private performances, and then but rarely. It was brought to America, shown to a special audience, and created no impression whatever, except perplexity. Meanwhile Salvador Dali, Buñuel's collaborator, has been to America several times and created a furor there. Dali, whose work is unhealthy, though highly spec-

tacular, highly provocative, is acclaimed as a genius. Dali makes the
American public conscious of surrealism and creates a fad. Dali returns
with his pockets full of dough. Dali is accepted – as another world freak.
Freak for freak: there is a divine justice at work. The world which is
crazy recognizes its master's voice. The yolk of the egg has split: Dali
takes America, Buñuel takes the leavings.

I want to repeat: *L'Age d'Or* is the only film I know of which reveals
the possibilities of the cinema! It makes its appeal neither to the intellect
nor to the heart; it strikes at the solar plexus. It is like kicking a mad
dog in the guts. And though it was a valiant kick in the guts and well
aimed it was not enough! There will have to be other films, films even
more violent than Luis Buñuel's. For the world is in a coma and the
cinema is still waving a peacock-fathered plume before our eyes.

Wondering sometimes where he may be and what he may be doing,
wondering what he *could* do if he were permitted, I get to thinking now
and then of all that is left out of the films. Has anybody ever shown us
the birth of a child, or even the birth of an animal? Insects yes, because
the sexual element is weak, because there are no taboos. But even in
the world of the insects have they shown us the praying mantis, the love
feast which is the acme of sexual voracity? Have they shown us how our
heroes won the war – and died for us? Have they shown us the gaping
wounds, have they shown us the faces that have been shot away? Are
they showing us now what happens in Spain every day when the bombs
rain down on Madrid? Almost every week there is another newsreel
theater opened up, but there is no news. Once a year we have a repertoire
of the outstanding events of the world given us by the news getters. It
is nothing but a series of catastrophes: railroad wrecks, explosions,
floods, earthquakes, automobile accidents, airplane disasters, collisions
of trains and ships, epidemics, lynchings, gangster killings, riots, strikes,
incipient revolutions, *putsches,* assassinations. The world seems like a
madhouse, and the world is a madhouse, but nobody dares dwell on it.
When an appalling piece of insanity, already properly castrated, is about
to be presented, a warning is issued to the spectators not to indulge in
demonstrations. Rest impartial! – that is the edict. Don't budge from
your sleep! We command you in the name of lunacy – *keep cool!* And
for the most part the injunctions are heeded. They are heeded willy-nilly,
for by the time the spectacle is concluded everybody has been bathed
in the innocuous drama of a sentimental couple, plain honest folks like
ourselves, who are doing exactly what we are doing, with the sole

difference that they are being well paid for it. This nullity and vacuity is dished up to us as the main event of the evening. The hors d'oeuvre is the newsreel, which is spiced with death and ignorance and superstition. Between these two phases of life there is absolutely no relation unless it be the link made by the animated cartoon. For the animated cartoon is the censor which permits us to dream the most horrible nightmares, to rape and kill and bugger and plunder, without waking up. Daily life is as we see it in the big film: The newsreel is the eye of God; the animated cartoon is the soul tossing in its anguish. But none of these three is the reality which is common to all of us who think and feel. Somehow they have worked a camouflage on us, and though it is our own camouflage we accept the illusion for reality. And the reason for it is that life as we know it to be has become absolutely unbearable. We flee from it in terror and disgust. The men who come after us will read the truth beneath the camouflage. May they pity us as we who are alive and real pity those about us.

Some people think of the Golden Age as a dream of the past; others think of it as the millennium to come. But the Golden Age is the immanent reality to which all of us, by our daily living, are either contributing or failing to contribute. The world is what we make it each day, or what we fail to make it. If it is lunacy that we have on our hands today, then it is we who are the lunatics. If you accept the fact that it is a crazy world you may perhaps succeed in adapting yourself to it. But those who have a sense of creation are not keen about adapting themselves. We affect one another, whether we wish to or not. Even negatively we affect one another. In writing about Buñuel instead of writing about something else I am aware that I am going to create a certain effect – for most people an unpleasant one, I suspect. But I can no more refrain from writing this way about Buñuel than I can from washing my face tomorrow morning. My past experience of life leads up to this moment and rules it despotically. In asserting the value of Buñuel I am asserting my own values, my own faith in life. In singling out this one man I do what I am constantly doing in every realm of life – selecting and evaluating. Tomorrow is no hazardous affair, a day like any other day; tomorrow is the result of many yesterdays and comes with a potent, cumulative effect. I am tomorrow what I chose to be yesterday and the day before. It is not possible that tomorrow I may negate and nullify everything that led me to this present moment.

In the same way I wish to point out that the film *L'Age d'Or* is no

accident, nor is its dismissal from the screen an accident. The world
has condemned Luis Buñuel and judged him as unfit. Not the whole
world, because, as I said before, the film is scarcely known outside of
France – outside of Paris, in fact. Judging from the trend of affairs since
this momentous event took place I cannot say that I am optimistic about
the revival of this film today. Perhaps the next Buñuel film will be even
more of a bombshell than was *L'Age d'Or*. I fervently hope so. But
meanwhile – and here I must add that this is the first opportunity, apart
from a little review which I wrote for *The New Review*, I have had to
write about Buñuel publicly – meanwhile, I say, this belated tribute to
Buñuel may serve to arouse the curiosity of those who have never heard
the name before. Buñuel's name is not unknown to Hollywood, that I
know. Indeed, like many another man of genius whom the Americans
have got wind of, Luis Buñuel was invited to come to Hollywood and
give of his talent. In short, he was invited to do nothing and draw his
breath. So much for Hollywood.

No, it is not from that quarter that the wind will blow. But things are
curiously arranged in this world. Men who have been dishonored and
driven from their country sometimes return to be crowned as king.
Some return as a scourge. Some leave only their name behind them,
or the remembrance of their deeds, but in the name of this one and
that whole epochs have been revitalized and recreated. I for one believe
that, despite everything I have said against the cinema as we now know
it, something wondrous and vital may yet come of it. Whether this
happens or not depends entirely on us, on you who read this now. What
I say is only a drop in the bucket, but it may have its consequences.
The important thing is that the bucket should not have a hole in it.
Well, I believe that such a bucket can be found. I believe that it is just
as possible to rally men around a vital reality as it is around the false
and the illusory. Luis Bunuel's effect upon me was not lost. And perhaps
my words will not be lost either.

FRANÇOIS TRUFFAUT
The Rogues are Weary

Jacques Becker, about whom Truffaut, his admirer and to some extent his disciple, writes in this Cahiers du Cinéma *article from 1954, is a classic example of the type of director who, outside his native country, has been all but forgotten. Or, in his case, remembered for a single film,* Casque d'or *– although as much for the beauty of its star, Simone Signoret, as for the beauty of its* mise en scène. *It was Becker's misfortune, perhaps,* vis-à-vis *the now prevailing standards and criteria of filmic greatness, to have been active in the 1940s and 1950s, a period when it was possible to make a movie without fretting in advance whether it would be a masterpiece, a period of black-and-white, modestly proportioned films by Bergman and Fellini, Lattuada and De Santis, Bardem and Berlanga, Chukhrai and Kalatozov, films graced by pretty but not supernaturally glamorous young actresses in flouncy 1950s skirts and by personable but not supernaturally good-looking young actors in bright chequered shirts. As it happens, few of these movies, not excluding Becker's, were imperishable masterpieces, but they were touching and poignant, and contrived to tell their stories simply and legibly – just the sort of qualities, alas, that interest no one today.*

There are no theories in circulation about Jacques Becker, no scholarly analyses, no theses. Neither he nor his work encourages commentary, and so much the better for that.

The truth is that Becker has no intention of mystifying or demystifying anyone; his films are neither statements nor indictments, which means that his work is outside the parameters of current fashion, and we could even place him at the opposite pole to every tendency in French cinema.

Every one of Jacques Becker's films is a Jacques Becker film. This is only a small point, but an important one. There is, in fact, little to tell us that the recent *Thérèse Raquin* was not made by Feyder, *Les Orgueilleux* by Pagliero, *Les Amants de Brasmort* by Yves Allégret and *Mam'zelle Nitouche* by Duvivier. Yet we could not conceive of *Edouard et Caroline, Casque d'or* and *Grisbi* being signed by Autant-Lara, Grémillon or Delannoy.

While there is unanimous acknowledgment that it is preferable for the writer and director to be one and the same, the reasons given for this opinion are banal, and no less an admiration continues to be expressed for partnerships and collaborative enterprises – admiration that to my mind is wasted. The fact that Renoir, Bresson, Cocteau and Becker are involved in the writing of a script and sign their names to it not only gives them greater freedom on the studio floor, but more radically it means that they replace scenes and dialogue typical of what scriptwriters produce with scenes and dialogue that a scriptwriter could never dream up. Specificity, dear to Claude Mauriac, is nothing more. And are examples required? For that scene in *Edouard et Caroline* where Elina Labourdette plays at making 'doe eyes' to be filmable, it had first to have been witnessed in real life, then *thought through* in terms of *mise en scène*. I do not know whether we owe this scene to Annette Wademant or to Jacques Becker, but I am sure of one thing – any other director would have cut it from the shooting script: it advances the plot not one jot and is there most of all to give a touch, not of realism, but of reality; it is also there out of love for doing things the hard way.

This search for an ever more exact tone is particularly marked in the dialogue. In *Casque d'or* Raymond (Bussières) comes into Manda's (Reggiani) carpentry workshop and says, '*Alors, boulot boulot, menuise menuise?*' ('Work work, scrape scrape, eh?'). Not only could a scriptwriter never have written this line, but it is also the kind of line which is only improvised on the set. None the less, this '*boulot boulot, menuise menuise*' still has an *intelligence* (in the sense of complicity between friends) which confounds me every time I see it.

It is not so much the choice of subject which characterizes Becker as how he chooses to treat this subject and the scenes to illustrate it. While he will keep only what is essential in the dialogue, or the essential part of what is superfluous (sometimes even onomatopoeias), he will readily make short work of something anyone else would handle with extreme care, so that he can take longer over characters having breakfast, buttering their toast, brushing their teeth, etc. There is a convention whereby lovers are only allowed to kiss in a dissolve. If in a French film you show a couple undressing and walking around in nightclothes in the bedroom, it would be meant as a joke. You could suppose that these unspoken rules are dictated by a concern for elegance. What does Becker do in a situation like this? That taste for doing things the hard way which I have already mentioned will make him handle the scene in a way that breaks the rules. In *Casque d'or* he shows us Reggiani in a nightshirt and Simone Signoret in a nightdress, in *Grisbi* Gabin in pyjamas.

This kind of work is a perpetual challenge to vulgarity, a challenge where Becker is always the winner, for his films are the most elegant I know, and his characters the most dignified.

What happens to Becker's characters is of less importance than the way it happens to them. The plot, no more than a pretext, gets thinner with every film. *Edouard et Caroline* is just the story of an evening, with a telephone and a waistcoat as accessories. *Touchez pas au grisbi* is about nothing more than a demand for the handover of 96 kilos of gold. 'What most interests me is the characters,' Becker tells us; as a matter of fact the real subject of *Grisbi* is growing old and friendship. This is clearly an underlying theme in Simonin's book, but few scriptwriters would have known how to bring it out and foreground it, relegating violent action, along with the picturesque, to the background. Simonin is forty-nine, Becker forty-eight: *Grisbi* is a film about reaching fifty. At the end of the film Max – like Becker – puts on his spectacles 'to read'. Growing old and friendship, we said: when Angelo kidnaps Riton to force Max to hand over the fifty million, he comments on Max's legendary friendship for Riton but also, unwittingly, on Max growing old, for he is allowed to imagine that Max, ten years earlier, would have got things moving to get back both his friend and the money, and settle his score with Angelo too. Simonin and Becker have kept from the book only what would have done very well for the *Nouvelle Revue Française*.

The beauty of the *Grisbi* characters, even more than those in *Casque d'or*, comes from their muteness, the economy of their gestures. They only speak or act to say or do the essential. Like Monsieur Teste, Becker kills the puppet in them. These killers become no more than tom-cats facing one another. I see *Grisbi* as a kind of settling of scores between big cats – but high-class cats – tired and, if I dare say it, used up.

There is a moment when every true creator makes such a leap forward that his audience is left behind. For Renoir, *La Règle du jeu* was the sign of maturity, a film so new that it looks confusingly as if it might be a failure; one of those failures that leaves you, the morning after, counting your friends on the fingers of one hand.

Today, if *La Règle du jeu* is understood, *Le Carrosse d'or* is not. I like this kind of complicated calculation where criticism certainly has nothing to gain, but they are none the less calculations with something to reveal to those who approach them with some friendship: Becker filmed *Casque d'or* at the very same age at which Renoir was making *La Règle du jeu*. With *Casque d'or* Becker shed the less perspicacious among his admirers (I am tempted to write: got rid of them); now he is taking off in an entirely new direction, and *Grisbi* follows in the footsteps of *Swamp Water*.

The clearest thing about the admiration I bring to *Grisbi* comes from my certainty that, as it exists now, this film was unfilmable four years ago. *Casque d'or* had to come first. I am not saying that *Grisbi* is better than *Casque d'or*, but it is an even more difficult film. It is no mean thing to make films in 1954 that were inconceivable in 1950; and that is already the first advantage *Grisbi* has over *Thérèse Raquin*, *Le Blé en herbe*, *L'Amour d'une femme*, those three films of a distant pre-war era.

For those of us who are twenty or not much older, Becker's example is both a lesson and an encouragement. We have known Renoir only as a genius, but we discovered cinema when Becker was just beginning. We have watched him finding his way, trying things out: we have seen a body of work *in progress*. And the success of Jacques Becker is the success of a young man who could conceive of no other way than the one he has chosen, and whose love for the cinema has been repaid.

'The cinema is like sex. When it's good, it's wonderful. But even when it isn't good, it's still pretty wonderful anyway!'   **STANLEY DONEN**

ALFRED HITCHCOCK
from *The Wrong Man*

It was René Clair who, in the early twenties, made the whimsical observation that, whatever else it might be up to, the cinema had offered us a new means of appreciating silence. (In much the same spirit, one might add that, since the thirties, it has become a novel method of appreciating sound.) Yet, for many of the period's directors and critics, the advent of the talkies in 1927 was a disaster for a medium that had just attained an unsurpassable apogee of poetic bravura and sophistication. Indeed, a cluster of its greatest geniuses (F. W. Murnau with Der Letze Mann, *Carl Dreyer with* La Passion de Jeanne d'Arc*) had begun to conceive of films as purely visual experiences, contriving to dispense even with the seen sound, as it were, of intertitles. (His title said . . . and her title replied . . . and so forth.) Even more significantly, there continued to exist, well into the forties and fifties, kindred filmmakers whose sensibility remained rooted in the silent – which is to say, the visual – tradition. One such was Alfred Hitchcock.*

Consider these three stills from Hitchcock's The Wrong Man. *Henry Fonda is a nightclub musician unjustly accused of theft, Vera Miles is Fonda's wife and Anthony Quayle his lawyer. Note how the gradual glazing of Miles's eyes forebodes the mental agony that will end in her complete breakdown. Everything, in short, is there. Although* The Wrong Man *has of course a soundtrack, this sequence of photographs does not: it is, as all films used to be, silent. Yet so hallucinatorily powerful is Hitchcock's* mise en scène *that these images, mere fragments as they are, already succeed in communicating, subtly, disquietingly and above all legibly, the quintessence of his art.*

FRANÇOIS TRUFFAUT
'*La Tour de Nesle*'

Before becoming, if not necessarily the best, then certainly the most
universally beloved of the young Turks, as it were, of the French nouvelle
vague, *François Truffaut was perhaps the finest film critic of his genera-*
tion, with an unmatched capacity for mining his way to those great,
usually breathtakingly simple truths that constitute, or should constitute,
the primary vocation and raison d'être *of all critics, whatever their*
chosen medium. In this 1955 essay, on La Tour de Nesle, *a late, pretty*
undistinguished costume drama by Abel Gance, he expounds his theory
(although Truffaut never 'theorizes' as such) of what he describes, in
the original French, as 'les grands films malades'. *As criticism, it may*
not be exactly scientific, but, as almost invariably with Truffaut the
critic, it cuts to the heart of the matter.

There is nothing very original left to say about *La Tour de Nesle*.
Everyone knows it is a film that was made to order on an absurd budget,
the best part of which remained in the distributor's till. *La Tour de
Nesle* is, if you will, the least good of Abel Gance's films. But, since
Gance is a genius, it is also a film of genius. Gance does not *possess*
genius, he *is possessed* by genius. If you gave him a portable camera
and set him in the midst of twenty other newsreel makers outside the
Palais Bourbon or at the entrance to the Parc des Princes, he alone
would deliver a masterpiece, a few hundred inches of film in which
each shot, each image, each sixteenth or twenty-fourth of a second
would bear the mark of genius, invisible and present, visible and omnipresent. How would it have been done? Only he would know. To tell
the truth, I think that even he would not know how he did it.

I observed Abel Gance during the making of *La Tour de Nesle*. He
gave it eight hours of work a day. There is no doubt that the films on
which he spent twenty-four hours a day are better. Still eight hours is
eight hours. I remember the closeup of Pampanini gazing at herself in
the mirror, at first talking to herself, then silent. Seven inches separated

the mirror from the face, the face from the lens. Seven inches from the mirror and the face and the lens, off camera, stood Abel Gance. Leaning toward the motionless woman, Gance mouthed the words that a French substitute would dub for the Italian actress: 'Look at yourself, Marguerite of Burgundy, look at yourself in the mirror; what have you turned into? You are nothing but a slut!' (I paraphrase from memory.) Gance read this absurd monologue in a kind of lyrical whisper. This was no longer direction, it was hypnotism! As I watched the film later, I waited for this scene. The result was magnificent – her face distorted, her eyes bulging, her mouth open in a gaping scar, the lines of nightly dissipation etched on her face, she was the greatest actress in the world, like Sylvie Gance in *Napoléon*, Micheline Presle in *Paradis Perdu*, Ivy Close in *La Roue*, Line Noro in *Mater Dolorosa*, Jany Holt in *Beethoven*, Viviane Romance in *Vénus aveugle*, and Assia Noris in *Fracasse*. Go and see Pampanini in *La Tour de Nesle* and then go see her in something else and if you don't see immediately that Gance was a genius, you and I do not have the same notion of cinema (mine, obviously, is the correct one). People have said to me, 'Pampanini? All I see is grimaces?' I will permit Jean Renoir to reply, 'A well-done grimace can be magnificent.'

When a great director has been without work for twelve years and is forced to make a movie based on such a scenario, there are two possible solutions: either parody or melodrama. Gance chose the second – a more difficult solution but also the more daring and, in the last analysis, more intelligent and profitable. 'I wanted to make a cloak-and-dagger Western,' the director admitted.

That aside, the film is extraordinarily sound and youthful. Gance moves *La Tour de Nesle* with hell-for-leather speed. There is a steady pace, sustained first of all within scenes and then from one scene to the other, thanks to very skillful editing. The shots that were made with the help of a pictograph are very beautiful, and recall the miniatures in Laurence Olivier's *Henry V*.

The Centrale Catholique, which takes upon itself the duty of rating the morality of films, was in a complete uproar. Erotically, *La Tour de Nesle* went far beyond what people were used to seeing. They had to invent a new code to warn parents whose children might wander in by accident. Recently, answering a question on eroticism, Gance said, 'If we had had a free hand in terms of eroticism, we would have made the most beautiful films in the world.' It is regrettable that once again censorship showed itself so stringent. The film does not fulfill the promises of the photos posted at the entrance to the movie theater. Our expectations are frustrated, we are deceived in our hopes. Surely cinema is *also* eroticism.

Gance has been spoken of as 'failed', and recently even as a 'failed genius'. But we know that 'failed' (*raté*) means 'bitten and spoiled by rats'. The rats swarmed around Gance but they were as unable to absorb his genius as they were to destroy it. The question now is whether one can be both a genius and a failure. I believe, to the contrary, that failure is talent. To succeed is to fail. I wish to defend the proposition that Abel Gance is the failed *auteur* of failed films. I am convinced that there is no great filmmaker who does not sacrifice something. Renoir will sacrifice anything – plot, dialogue, technique – to get a better performance from an actor. Hitchcock sacrifices believability in order to present an extreme situation that he has chosen in advance. Rossellini sacrifices the connection between movement and light to achieve greater warmth in his interpreters. Murnau, Hawks, Lang sacrifice realism in their settings and atmosphere. Nicholas Ray and Griffith sacrifice sobriety. But a film that succeeds, according to the common wisdom, is one in which all the elements are equally balanced in a whole that merits the adjective 'perfect'. Still, I assert that perfection and success are mean, indecent, immoral, and obscene. In this regard, the most hateful film is unarguably *La Kermesse héroique* because everything in it is incomplete, its boldness is attenuated; it is reasonable, measured, its doors are half-open, the paths are sketched and only sketched; everything in it is pleasant and perfect. All great films are 'failed'. They were called so at the time, and some are still so labeled: *Zéro de Conduite, L'Atalante, Faust, Le Pauvre amour, Intolerance, La Chienne, Metropolis, Liliom, Sunrise, Queen Kelly, Beethoven, Abraham Lincoln, La Vénus aveugle, La Règle du Jeu, Le Carrosse d'Or, I Confess, Stromboli* – I cite them in no particular order and I'm sure I'm leaving out others that are just as good. Compare these with a list of successful films and you will have before your eyes an example of the perennial argument about official art.

It's good to go back and again see Abel Gance's *Napoléon* upstairs in Studio 28. Each shot is like a bolt of lightning that illuminates everything around it. The spoken scenes are marvelous and not – as is still being said today in 1955 – unworthy of the original silent scenes. 'Sir Abel Gance', as Jacques Becker says! We won't find again very soon in the world of cinema a man of his breadth, ready to take on the whole world, to mold it like clay, to fashion his own witnesses out of sky, sea, clouds, earth, and hold all in the hollow of his own hand. To put an Abel Gance to work, you have to look for a backer in the class of Louis XIV.

FEDERICO FELLINI
from *Cinecittà*

Critical cliché as it has now become, it's impossible to refer to the work of Federico Fellini, who might be described as the very last of the Italian Futurists, without equally referring to his ultimate source of inspiration: the circus. The circus, however, not merely as a live spectacle but as a truly communal experience. Part of what makes Fellini's films so pleasurable is surely our vivid sense, when watching them, of what it must have been like to have been involved in their creation. It's not too fanciful to suggest that we actually feel transported to the vast, draught-haunted sound stages of Cinecittà, with actors, extras, freaks, sycophants and hangers-on, the by-now familiar fauna and flora of Felliniana, appearing to enjoy absolutely equal status with one another; with the relaxed and negligent, on occasion infelicitious but always festive and carnivalesque mise en scène of the completed work tendering the spectator what he or she suspects is a fairly transparent mirror image of the noisy, fractious, exuberant caravanserai that was the shoot that both preceded and engendered it; above all, with the cast's and crew's faith (in the film's future, in the virtues of collective achievement, in the Maestro's own genially tyrannical presence) exuding from every pore of the screen.

Sometimes I feel as though I do not know Cinecittà at all. In my mind it is really only a few pieces of scenery and one or two areas of the actual site. The first is the entrance, which has an aura of mystery to it that gives one the sensation of crossing a unique and enchanted threshold. More than most other thresholds or entrances, the gate at Cinecittà is a symbol. For me, it has represented a beginning. When I went in there for the first time, the gate-keeper was a real Guardian of the Threshold, a giant of a man well over six feet tall called Pappalardo who wore a great yellow robe which came down to his feet, trimmed with military epaulettes, pockets and insignia, and a hat with a brim bearing the word Cinecittà in raised letters.

Nowadays the gate is guarded by a private police team in light blue uniforms, with pistol holsters and bullet-proof waistcoats, who sit inside a guard post full of closed-circuit television screens and protected by bullet-proof glass. The gate is operated by barriers which can only be lifted electronically. Vigilantes at the entrance to a dream factory, an amusement park, they add the dramatic touch which is typical of present-day society. They are also quick to advise that access to Cinecittà is not open to all, but only to those who belong within its walls.

Another part of Cineccità on which I can speak with some authority is the bar. Again I cannot help making a comparison with images of prison canteens or station buffets, or psychiatric hospitals where patients hang around with no idea of time or purpose. Perhaps the bar at Cinecittà, when I think about it, could be most accurately compared to an old lunatic asylum, where mental illness is in the company of its own illusions. And in fact you can see cardinals, revolutionaries, SS men, troglodytes, green lizards more than six feet long, and concubines, all drinking cups of coffee and eating slices of pizza. They buy rolls and sandwiches and take them out in plastic bags; I have even seen such snacks being stuffed into the pouch of a large kangaroo with the help of Richard Burton who explained affectionately to Elizabeth Taylor, who was more lost in wonder than alarmed by the huge animal, that this particular kangaroo was all wrong because its ears were too far forward on its head. She, in her magnificent Cleopatra costume, a mass of jewels and feathers, looked around her with those incredible violet-coloured eyes as though searching for the perpetrator of such a blunder.

When I worked as a scriptwriter, I used to spend hours on end in a corner of that bar which would not have looked out of place in a nightmare painting by Hieronymus Bosch, trying frantically to re-write the dialogue for the scene which the director was waiting on set to shoot. The actor and leading lady of the film in question had decided that the things they were being asked to say to each other were 'unspeakable'. Those characters would never have expressed themselves as I had made them do in my screenplay; and so with melodramatic urgency, I was collected, or perhaps more accurately snatched, from home and brought in to Cinnecittà to put matters right.

With my portable typewriter on my knees, sitting at a little table littered with left-overs of all kinds, amid the bawling and shouting of people issuing orders and the yells of the crew leaders coming in to collect up groups of extras sprawled over the seats and the bar, I would make up new lines, trying them out to myself in a subdued voice, while surrounded by four or five pests making the usual complaints and asking me to throw in a line for them too and get the director to let them say it.

'But he'll listen to you,' they would insist, pandering to me. 'Without your talent, how would he ever earn a crust? He owes his success to you! Can I get you a cappuccino?'

My director's office is another of the places which represents a microcosm of the whole of Cinecittá for me. It is on the upper floor of Studio 5 where I have worked for so many years. It consists of one large room, dominated by a notice board which hangs above my desk and is covered in green billiard-table baize. Here, while hoping to give the impression that I have a thousand things to do, I stick pieces of paper with names, addresses and ideas on them, even suggestions and instructions to myself which are half an attempt at organization and half just clowning about: like the one reminding me that making a film involves dangers and uncertainties. But there is a time, at the beginning of a project, when that notice board begins to act as an assembly point for photographs of faces: smiles and grimaces gaze at the back of my head, forerunners of the features, types and characters which already tentatively belong to the new film, and which plague me until I finally have to include them.

At the start of a film, my office is like the enquiry desk at police headquarters, as my assistants make telephone calls to London and New York, making enquiries, searching for people about whom they know next to nothing; the file of photographs is continually being leafed through, and then it is discovered that of the possible candidates for a part, one is on the run in Latin America, another has had a sex change, and yet another, once an unimpressive twelve-year-old, has turned into a hirsute, sweaty youth doing military service. I want to see every face on earth: I am never satisfied, and if I see a face I do like, then I want to compare it with still more faces, with every available face. It is an obsession.

ABBAS KIAROSTAMI
from *And Life Continues*

The child hopes to conceal himself, just as a grown-up would. There's only this puny little tree. So the child isn't concealed at all; he is, in a sense, exposed by the tree's spindly trunk. And thus does the cinema, too, expose itself, in all its artifice of narration, its artifice of décor.

Abbas Kiarostami, the Iranian director of the magnificent trilogy, Where Is the Friend's Home? *(one of the very greatest films of the past quarter century),* And Life Continues *and* Through the Olive Trees, *is an artist as widely acclaimed throughout Europe and elsewhere as he is (mostly) unknown in Britain – an artist whose work, in France, for example, is not just esteemed and easily available, as might be expected of that cinéphilic country, but, since interviews with him have turned up in newspapers and even rock magazines, actually* fashionable. *And, pace the Anglo-American film-critical establishment, rightly so. Spielberg is nothing beside Kiarostami. Campion is nothing. Tarantino is nothing.*

The illustration is a still from And Life Continues *and the short text which accompanies it, by Jean-Luc Nancy, was originally published in* Cahiers du Cinéma. *Yes, it's just an image of a little boy endeavouring to conceal himself behind a tree while peeing, but I know of few as affecting in the medium's history.*

Dreaming

CHAS ADDAMS

DELMORE SCHWARTZ
In Dreams Begin Responsibilities

A poet, dramatist and translator (famously, of Rimbaud), Delmore Schwartz was born in 1913 and died, a depressive alcoholic, in 1966. This, his most celebrated short story, was originally published in the Partisan Review, *in whose very first issue (in 1937) it was the very first item of fiction to appear. It must, and it can, speak for itself. Suffice to say that no anthology of film-related texts from which it has been omitted deserves to be taken seriously.*

1

I think it is the year 1909. I feel as if I were in a motion picture theatre, the long arm of light crossing the darkness and spinning, my eyes fixed on the screen. This is a silent picture as if an old Biograph one, in which the actors are dressed in ridiculously old-fashioned clothes, and one flash succeeds another with sudden jumps. The actors too seem to jump about and walk too fast. The shots themselves are full of dots and rays, as if it were raining when the picture was photographed. The light is bad.

It is Sunday afternoon, June 12th, 1909, and my father is walking down the quiet streets of Brooklyn on his way to visit my mother. His clothes are newly pressed and his tie is too tight in his high collar. He jingles the coins in his pockets, thinking of the witty things he will say. I feel as if I had by now relaxed entirely in the soft darkness of the theatre; the organist peals out the obvious and approximate emotions on which the audience rocks unknowingly. I am anonymous, and I have forgotten myself. It is always so when one goes to the movies, it is, as they say, a drug.

My father walks from street to street of trees, lawns and houses, once in a while coming to an avenue on which a street-car skates and gnaws, slowly progressing. The conductor, who has a handle-bar mustache, helps a young lady wearing a hat like a bowl with feathers on to the car. She lifts her long skirts slightly as she mounts the steps. He leisurely makes change and rings his bell. It is obviously Sunday, for everyone is wearing Sunday clothes, and the street-car's noises emphasize the quiet of the holiday. Is not Brooklyn the City of Churches? The shops are closed and their shades drawn, but for an occasional stationery store or drug-store with great green balls in the window.

My father has chosen to take this long walk because he likes to walk and think. He thinks about himself in the future and so arrives at the place he is to visit in a state of mild exaltation. He pays no attention to the houses he is passing, in which the Sunday dinner is being eaten, nor to the many trees which patrol each street, now coming to their full leafage and the time when they will room the whole street in cool shadow. An occasional carriage passes, the horse's hooves falling like stones in the quiet afternoon, and once in a while an automobile, looking like an enormous upholstered sofa, puffs and passes.

My father thinks of my mother, of how nice it will be to introduce her to his family. But he is not yet sure that he wants to marry her, and once in a while he becomes panicky about the bond already established. He reassures himself by thinking of the big men he admires who are married. William Randolph Hearst, and William Howard Taft, who has just become President of the United States.

My father arrives at my mother's house. He has come too early and so is suddenly embarrassed. My aunt, my mother's sister, answers the loud bell with her napkin in her hand, for the family is still at dinner. As my father enters, my grandfather rises from the table and shakes hands with him. My mother has run upstairs to tidy herself. My grandmother asks my father if he has had dinner, and tells him that Rose will be downstairs soon. My grandfather opens the conversation by remarking on the mild June weather. My father sits uncomfortably near the table, holding his hat in his hand. My grandmother tells my aunt to take my father's hat. My uncle, twelve years old, runs into the house, his hair tousled. He shouts a greeting to my father, who has often given him a nickel, and then runs upstairs. It is evident that the respect in which my father is held in this household is tempered by a good deal of mirth. He is impressive, yet he is very awkward.

2

Finally my mother comes downstairs, all dressed up, and my father being engaged in conversation with my grandfather becomes uneasy, not knowing whether to greet my mother or continue the conversation.

He gets up from the chair clumsily and says 'hello' gruffly. My grand-father watches, examining their congruence, such as it is, with a critical eye, and meanwhile rubbing his bearded cheek roughly, as he always does when he reflects. He is worried; he is afraid that my father will not make a good husband for his oldest daughter. At this point something happens to the film, just as my father is saying something funny to my mother; I am awakened to myself and my unhappiness just as my interest was rising. The audience begins to clap impatiently. Then the trouble is cared for but the film has been returned to a portion just shown, and once more I see my grandfather rubbing his bearded cheek and pondering my father's character. It is difficult to get back into the picture once more and forget myself, but as my mother giggles at my father's words, the darkness drowns me.

My father and mother depart from the house, my father shaking hands with my mother once more, out of some unknown uneasiness. I stir uneasily also, slouched in the hard chair of the theatre. Where is the older uncle, my mother's older brother? He is studying in his bedroom upstairs, studying for his final examination at the College of the City of New York, having been dead of rapid pneumonia for the last twenty-one years. My mother and father walk down the same quiet streets once more. My mother is holding my father's arm and telling him of the novel which she has been reading; and my father utters judgments of the characters as the plot is made clear to him. This is a habit which he very much enjoys, for he feels the utmost superiority and confidence when he approves and condemns the behavior of other people. At times he feels moved to utter a brief 'Ugh' – whenever the story becomes what he would call sugary. This tribute is paid to his manliness. My mother feels satisfied by the interest which she has awakened; she is showing my father how intelligent she is, and how interesting.

They reach the avenue, and the street-car leisurely arrives. They are going to Coney Island this afternoon, although my mother considers that such pleasures are inferior. She has made up her mind to indulge only in a walk on the boardwalk and a pleasant dinner, avoiding the riotous amusements as being beneath the dignity of so dignified a couple.

My father tells my mother how much money he has made in the past week, exaggerating an amount which need not have been exaggerated. But my father has always felt that actualities somehow fall short. Suddenly I begin to weep. The determined old lady who sits next to me in the theatre is annoyed and looks at me with an angry face, and being intimidated, I stop. I drag out my handkerchief and dry my face, licking the drop which has fallen near my lips. Meanwhile I have missed something, for here are my mother and father alighting at the last stop, Coney Island.

3

They walk toward the boardwalk, and my father commands my mother to inhale the pungent air from the sea. They both breathe in deeply, both of them laughing as they do so. They have in common a great interest in health, although my father is strong and husky, my mother frail. Their minds are full of theories of what is good to eat and not good to eat, and sometimes they engage in heated discussions of the subject, the whole matter ending in my father's announcement, made with a scornful bluster, that you have to die sooner or later anyway. On the boardwalk's flagpole, the American flag is pulsing in an intermittent wind from the sea.

My father and mother go to the rail of the boardwalk and look down on the beach where a good many bathers are casually walking about. A few are in the surf. A peanut whistle pierces the air with its pleasant and active whine, and my father goes to buy peanuts. My mother remains at the rail and stares at the ocean. The ocean seems merry to her; it pointedly sparkles and again and again the pony waves are released. She notices the children digging in the wet sand, and the bathing costumes of the girls who are her own age. My father returns with the peanuts. Overhead the sun's lightning strikes and strikes, but neither of them are at all aware of it. The boardwalk is full of people dressed in their Sunday clothes and idly strolling. The tide does not reach as far as the boardwalk, and the strollers would feel no danger if it did. My mother and father lean on the rail of the boardwalk and absently stare at the ocean. The ocean is becoming rough; the waves come in slowly, tugging strength from far back. The moment before they somersault, the moment when they arch their backs so beautifully, showing green and white veins amid the black, that moment is intolerable. They finally crack, dashing fiercely upon the sand, actually driving, full force downward, against the sand, bouncing upward and forward, and at last petering out into a small stream which races up the beach and then is recalled. My parents gaze absentmindedly at the ocean, scarcely interested in its harshness. The sun overhead does not disturb them. But I stare at the terrible sun which breaks up sight, and the fatal, merciless, passionate ocean, I forget my parents. I stare fascinated and finally, shocked by the indifference of my father and mother, I burst out weeping once more. The old lady next to me pats me on the shoulder and says: 'There, there, all of this is only a movie, young man, only a movie,' but I look up once more at the terrifying sun and the terrifying ocean, and being unable to control my tears, I get up and go to the men's room, stumbling over the feet of the other people seated in my row.

4

When I return, feeling as if I had awakened in the morning sick for lack of sleep, several hours have apparently passed and my parents are riding on the merry-go-round. My father is on a black horse, my mother on a white one, and they seem to be making an eternal circuit for the single purpose of snatching the nickel rings which are attached to the arm of one of the posts. A hand-organ is playing; it is one with the ceaseless circling of the merry-go-round.

For a moment it seems that they will never get off the merry-go-round because it will never stop. I feel like one who looks down on the avenue from the 50th story of a building. But at length they do get off; even the music of the hand-organ has ceased for a moment. My father has acquired ten rings, my mother only two, although it was my mother who really wanted them.

They walk on along the boardwalk as the afternoon descends by imperceptible degrees into the incredible violet of dusk. Everything fades into a relaxed glow, even the ceaseless murmuring from the beach, and the revolutions of the merry-go-round. They look for a place to have dinner. My father suggests the best one on the boardwalk and my mother demurs, in accordance with her principles.

However, they do go to the best place, asking for a table near the window, so that they can look out on the boardwalk and the mobile ocean. My father feels omnipotent as he places a quarter in the waiter's hand as he asks for a table. The place is crowded and here too there is music, this time from a kind of string trio. My father orders dinner with a fine confidence.

As the dinner is eaten, my father tells of his plans for the future, and my mother shows with expressive face how interested she is, and how impressed. My father becomes exultant. He is lifted up by the waltz that is being played, and his own future begins to intoxicate him. My father tells my mother that he is going to expand his business, for there is a great deal of money to be made. He wants to settle down. After all, he is twenty-nine, he has lived by himself since he was thirteen, he is making more and more money, and he is envious of his married friends when he visits them in the cozy security of their homes, surrounded, it seems, by the calm domestic pleasures, and by delightful children, and then, as the waltz reaches the moment when all the dancers swing madly, then, then with awful daring, then he asks my mother to marry him, although awkwardly enough and puzzled, even in his excitement, at how he had arrived at the proposal, and she, to make the whole business worse, begins to cry, and my father looks nervously about, not knowing at all what to do now, and my mother says: 'It's all I've wanted from the moment I saw you,' sobbing, and he finds all of this very difficult, scarcely to his taste, scarcely as he had thought it would be, on his long walks over Brooklyn Bridge in the revery of a fine cigar, and it was then that I stood up in the theatre and shouted: 'Don't do it. It's not too late to change your minds, both of you. Nothing good will come of it, only remorse, hatred, scandal, and two children whose characters are monstrous.' The whole audience turned to look at me, annoyed, the usher came hurrying down the aisle flashing his searchlight, and the old lady next to me tugged me down into my seat, saying: 'Be quiet. You'll be put out, and you paid thirty-five cents to come in.' And so I shut my eyes because I could not bear to see what was happening. I sat there quietly.

5

But after awhile I begin to take brief glimpses, and at length I watch again with thirsty interest, like a child who wants to maintain his sulk although offered the bribe of candy. My parents are now having their picture taken in a photographer's booth along the boardwalk. The place is shadowed in the mauve light which is apparently necessary. The camera is set to the side on its tripod and looks like a Martian man. The photographer is instructing my parents in how to pose. My father has his arm over my mother's shoulder, and both of them smile emphatically. The photographer brings my mother a bouquet of flowers to hold in her hand but she holds it at the wrong angle. Then the photographer covers himself with the black cloth which drapes the camera and all that one sees of him is one protruding arm and his hand which clutches the rubber ball which he will squeeze when the picture is finally taken. But he is not satisfied with their appearance. He feels with certainty that somehow there is something wrong in their pose. Again and again he issues from his hidden place with new directions. Each suggestion merely makes matters worse. My father is becoming impatient. They try a seated pose. The photographer explains that he has pride, he is not interested in all of this for the money, he wants to make beautiful pictures. My father says: 'Hurry up, will you? We haven't got all night.' But the photographer only scurries about apologetically, and issues new directions. The photographer charms me. I approve of him with all my heart, for I know just how he feels, and as he criticizes each revised pose according to some unknown idea of rightness, I become quite hopeful. But then my father says angrily: 'Come on, you've had enough time, we've not going to wait any longer.' And the photographer, sighing unhappily, goes back under his black covering, holds out his hand, says: 'One, two, three, Now!', and the picture is taken, with my father's smile turned to a grimace and my mother's bright and false. It takes a few minutes for the picture to be developed and as my parents sit in the curious light they become quite depressed.

6

They have passed a fortune-teller's booth, and my mother wishes to go in, but my father does not. They begin to argue about it. My mother becomes stubborn, my father once more impatient, and then they begin to quarrel, and what my father would like to do is walk off and leave my mother there, but he knows that that would never do. My mother refuses to budge. She is near to tears, but she feels an uncontrollable desire to hear what the palm-reader will say. My father consents angrily, and they both go into a booth which is in a way like the photographer's, since it is draped in black cloth and its light is shadowed. The place is too warm, and my father keeps saying this is all nonsense, pointing to the crystal ball on the table. The fortune-teller, a fat, short woman, garbed in what is supposed to be Oriental robes, comes into the room from the back and greets them, speaking with an accent. But suddenly my father feels that the whole thing is intolerable; he tugs at my mother's arm, but my mother refuses to budge. And then, in terrible anger, my father lets go of my mother's arm and strides out, leaving my mother stunned. She moves to go after my father, but the fortune-teller holds her arm tightly and begs her not to do so, and I in my seat am shocked more than can ever be said, for I feel as if I were walking a tight-rope a hundred feet over a circus-audience and suddenly the rope is showing signs of breaking, and I get up from my seat and begin to shout once more the first words I can think of to communicate my terrible fear and once more the usher comes hurrying down the aisle flashing his searchlight, and the old lady pleads with me, and the shocked audience has turned to stare at me, and I keep shouting: 'What are they doing? Don't they know what they are doing? Why doesn't my mother go after my father? If she does not do that, what will she do? Doesn't my father know what he is doing?' – But the usher has seized my arm and is dragging me away, and as he does so, he says: 'What are you doing? Don't you know that you can't do whatever you want to do? Why should a young man like you, with your whole life before you, get hysterical like this? Why don't you *think* of what you're doing? You can't act like this even if other people aren't around! You will be sorry if you do not do what you should do, you can't carry on like this, it is not right, you will find that out soon enough, everything you do matters too much,' and he said that dragging me through the lobby of the theatre into the cold light, and I woke up into the bleak winter morning of my 21st birthday, the windowsill shining with its lip of snow, and the morning already begun.

'An actor is a sculptor in snow'   PIERRE FRESNAY

RUDYARD KIPLING
Naaman's Song

According to the annotations of Philip French and Ken Wlaschin, who included this Kipling poem in their wonderful collection The Faber Book of Movie Verse, *the novelist and poet wrote it during the 1920s 'to accompany and comment on his discursive shaggy-dog story "Aunt Ellen", published in 1932 in his final collection,* Limits and Renewals'. *Since the poem is more than a little convoluted, and since it would be difficult to explicate its meaning with greater concision than do French and Wlaschin themselves, I leave it to them, with gratitude, to prepare the ground again for the reader of this anthology.*

Thus they continue: 'The poem's subject matter is the production of large-scale biblical epics in Hollywood (Kipling was invited to work in the movie industry and had visited the film colony). The Israelites are clearly both the biblical tribe and the Jewish film-makers who created Hollywood. The Old Testament Naaman of the title is the Syrian general (2 Kings, 5) who suffered from leprosy and after somewhat reluctantly seeking the advice of the Israelite enemy was advised by the prophet Elisha to bathe in the River Jordan. This led to a cure and he became a worshipper of Yahweh while retaining a formal attachment to his national temples.'

'Go, wash thyself in Jordan – go, wash thee and be clean!'
Nay, not for any Prophet will I plunge a toe therein!
For the banks of curious Jordan are parcelled into sites,
Commanded and embellished and patrolled by Israelites.

There rise her timeless capitals of Empires daily born,
Whose plinths are laid at midnight, and whose streets are packed
    at morn;
And here come hired youths and maids that feign to love or sin
In tones like rusty razor-blades to tunes like smitten tin.

And here be merry murtherings, and steeds with fiery hooves;
And furious hordes with guns and swords, and clamberings over
    rooves;
And horrid tumblings down from Heaven, and fights with wheels
    and wings;
And always one weak virgin who is chased through all these things.

And here is mock of faith and truth, for children to behold;
And every door of ancient dirt reopened to the old;
With every word that taints the speech, and show that weakens
    thought;
And Israel watcheth over each, and – doth not watch for nought . . .

But Pharpar – but Abana – which Hermon launcheth down –
They perish fighting desert-sands beyond Damascus-town.
But yet their pulse is of the snows – their strength is from on
    high –
And, if they cannot cure my woes, a leper will I die!

THE MARX BROTHERS
from *A Night at the Opera*

Robert Altman's The Player *(1992) immortalized the 'pitch', the exploit whereby a filmmaker wins over his backers by encapsulating the commercial appeal of some putative movie project in a single sentence. Six decades earlier, Sam Wood's* A Night at the Opera *(1935) immortalized another crucial ingredient of the Hollywood deal, the contract. Groucho Marx is Driftwood, Chico is Forelo, the dialogue is by George S. Kaufman and Morrie Ryskind and, when one comes right down to it, the contract could almost pass for the real McCoy.*

Chico claims to be the manager for a tenor whom Groucho would like to sign as singer with the New York Opera Company. Now that they have found each other all that is necessary to complete their little deal is a simple contract.

FORELO: What's the matter, mister?

DRIFTWOOD: Oh, we had an argument and he pulled a knife on me, so I shot him.

FORELO: Do you mind if I –

DRIFTWOOD: No, no, go right ahead. Plenty of room.

DRIFTWOOD: Two beers, bartender.

FORELO: I'll take two beers, too.

DRIFTWOOD: Well, things seem to be getting better around the country.

FORELO: I don't know. I'm a stranger here myself.

DRIFTWOOD: Say, I just remembered. I came back here looking for somebody. You don't know who it is, do you?

FORELO: It's a funny thing. It just slipped my mind.

DRIFTWOOD: Oh, I know – I know. The greatest tenor in the world – that's what I'm after.

FORELO: Well, I'm his manager.

DRIFTWOOD: Whose manager?

FORELO: The greatest tenor in the world.

DRIFTWOOD: The fellow that sings at the opera here?

FORELO: Sure.

DRIFTWOOD: What's his name?

FORELO: What do you care? I can't pronounce it. What do you want with him?

DRIFTWOOD: Well – uh – I want to sign him up for the New York Opera Company. Do you know that America is waiting to hear him sing?

FORELO: Well, he can sing loud, but he can't sing that loud.

DRIFTWOOD: Well, I think I can get America to meet him halfway. Could he sail tomorrow?

FORELO: You pay him enough money he could sail yesterday. How much you pay him?

DRIFTWOOD: Well, I don't know.

DRIFTWOOD: Let's see – a thousand dollars a night. I'm entitled to a small profit. How about ten dollars a night?

FORELO: Ten – ten dollars! I'll take it.

DRIFTWOOD: All right, but remember, I get ten per cent for negotiating the deal.

FORELO: Yes, and I get ten per cent for being the manager. How much does that leave?

DRIFTWOOD: Well, that leaves him – uh – eight dollars.

FORELO: Eight dollars, eh? Well, he send a five dollars home to his mother.

DRIFTWOOD: Well, that leaves three dollars.

FORELO: Three dollars. Can he live in New York on three dollars?

DRIFTWOOD: Like a prince. Of course, he won't be able to eat, but he can live like a prince. However, out of that three dollars, you know, he'll have to pay income tax.

FORELO: Oh, his income tax, eh?

DRIFTWOOD: Yes. You know, there's a Federal tax and a State tax and a city tax and a street tax and a sewer tax.

FORELO: How much does this come to?

DRIFTWOOD: Well, I figure if he doesn't sing too often he can break even.

FORELO: All right, we take it.

DRIFTWOOD: All right, fine. Now – uh, here are the contracts. You just put his name at the top and – uh – and you sign at the bottom. There's no need of you reading that because these are duplicates.

FORELO: Yes, duplicates. Duplicates, eh?

DRIFTWOOD: I say, they're – they're duplicates.

FORELO: Oh, sure, it's a duplicate. Certainly.

DRIFTWOOD: Don't you know what duplicates are?

FORELO: Sure. Those five kids up in Canada.

DRIFTWOOD: Well, I wouldn't know about that. I haven't been in Canada in years. Well, go ahead and read it.

FORELO: What does it say?

DRIFTWOOD: Well, go on and read it.

FORELO: All right – you read it.

DRIFTWOOD: All right, I'll read it to you.

DRIFTWOOD: Can you hear?

FORELO: I haven't heard anything yet.

FORELO: Did you say anything?

DRIFTWOOD: Well, I haven't said anything worth hearing.

FORELO: Well, that's why I didn't hear anything.

DRIFTWOOD: Well, that's why I didn't say anything.

FORELO: Can you read?

DRIFTWOOD: I can read but I can't see it. I don't seem . . . to have it in focus here. If my arms were a little longer, I could read it. You haven't got a baboon in your pocket have you? Here – here – here we are. Now, I've got it. Now, pay particular attention to this first clause because it's most important. Says the – uh – the party of the first part shall be known in this contract as the party of the first part. How do you like that? That's pretty neat, eh?

FORELO: No, that's no good.

DRIFTWOOD: What's the matter with it?

FORELO: I don't know. Let's hear it again.

DRIFTWOOD: Says the – uh – the party of the first part should be known in this contract as the party of the first part.

FORELO: That sounds a little better this time.

DRIFTWOOD: Well, it grows on you. Would you like to hear it once more?

FORELO: Uh – just the first part.

DRIFTWOOD: What do you mean? The – the party of the first part?

FORELO: No, the first part of the party of the first part.

DRIFTWOOD: All right. It says the – uh – the first part of the party of the first part, should be known in this contract as the first part of the party of the first part, should be known in this contract – look. Why should we quarrel about a thing like this? We'll take it right out, eh?

FORELO: Yeah. It's too long anyhow. Now, what have we got left?

DRIFTWOOD: Well, I've got about a foot and a half. Now, it says – uh
– the party of the second part shall be known in this contract as the
party of the second part.

FORELO: Well, I don't know about that.

DRIFTWOOD: Now, what's the matter?

FORELO: I no like the second party either.

DRIFTWOOD: Well, you should have come to the first party. We didn't
get home till around four in the morning. I was blind for three days.

FORELO: Hey, look! Why can't the first part of the second party be
the second part of the first party? Then you've got something.

DRIFTWOOD: Well, look – uh – rather than go through all that again,
what do you say?

FORELO: Fine.

DRIFTWOOD: Now – uh – now, I've got something here you're bound
to like. You'll be crazy about it.

FORELO: No, I don't like it.

DRIFTWOOD: You don't like what?

FORELO: Whatever it is – I don't like it.

DRIFTWOOD: Well, don't let's break up an old friendship over a thing
like that. Ready?

FORELO: Okay. Now, the next part, I don't think you're going to like.

DRIFTWOOD: Well, your word's good enough for me. Now, then, is
my word good enough for you?

FORELO: I should say not.

DRIFTWOOD: Well, that takes out two more clauses.

DRIFTWOOD: Now the party of the eighth part –

FORELO: No.

DRIFTWOOD: No?

FORELO: No. That's no good. No.

DRIFTWOOD: The party of the ninth –

FORELO: No, that's no good too.

FORELO: Hey, how is it my contract is skinnier than yours?

DRIFTWOOD: Well, I don't know. You must have been out on a tear
last night. But, anyhow, we're all set now, aren't we?

DRIFTWOOD: Now, just – uh – just you put your name right down
there and then the deal is – is – uh – legal.

FORELO: I forgot to tell you. I can't write.

DRIFTWOOD: Well, that's all right. There's no ink in the pen anyhow. But, listen, it's a contract, isn't it?

FORELO: Oh, sure.

DRIFTWOOD: You've got a contract?

FORELO: You bet –

DRIFTWOOD: No matter how small it is.

FORELO: Hey, wait – wait! What does this say here? This thing here?

DRIFTWOOD: Oh, that? Oh, that's the usual clause. That's in every contract. That just says – uh – it says – uh – if any of the parties participating in this contract is shown not to be in their right mind, the entire agreement is automatically nullified.

FORELO: Well, I don't know.

DRIFTWOOD: It's all right. That's – that's in every contract. That's – that's what they call a sanity clause.

FORELO: Oh, no. You can't fool me. There ain't on Sanity Clause!

DRIFTWOOD: Well, you win the white – carnation. Sanity Claus.

OGDEN NASH
Shaggy Doggerel

Here, on the cinema's conception of eternal womanhood, are two characteristically delightful examples of shaggy doggerel from the American poet-humourist Ogden Nash.

VIVA VAMP, VALE VAMP

Oh for the days when vamps were vamps,
Not just a bevy of bulbous scamps.
The vintage vamp was serpentine,
Was madder music and stronger wine.
She ate her bedazzled victims whole,
Body and bank account and soul;
Yet, to lure a bishop from his crosier
She needed no pectoral exposure,
But trapped the prelate passing by
With her melting mouth and harem eye.
A gob of lipstick and mascara
Was weapon enough for Theda Bara;
Pola Negri and Lya de Putti
And sister vampires, when on duty,
Carnivorous night-blooming lilies,
They flaunted neither falsies nor realies.
Oh, whither have the vampires drifted?
All are endowed, but few are gifted.
Tape measures now select the talent
To stimulate the loutish gallant
Who has wits enough, but only just,
To stamp and whistle at a bust.
O modern vamp, I quit my seat,
Throw down my cards and call you cheat;

You could not take a trick, in fact,
Unless the deck were brazenly stacked.

MAE WEST

Westward the course of vampire moves its way;
The concave bosom sinks into eclipse;
Everywhere happy endings flatter Mae,
And ape the pace that launched a thousand hips.

RAYMOND CHANDLER
Oscar Night in Hollywood

Raymond Chandler's involvement with film was an uneasy one. On the one hand, he was more fortunate than most so far as screen versions of his novels were concerned. No one whose work was adapted as well as his was – by, notably, Edward Dmytryk with Farewell My Lovely, *Howard Hawks with* The Big Sleep *and (if posthumously) Robert Altman with* The Long Goodbye *– has too much cause for complaint. On the other hand, his own experience as a screenwriter, on Billy Wilder's* Double Indemnity *and Alfred Hitchcock's* Strangers on a Train, *left him ever after with a distrust and even contempt for Hollywood's Byzantine thought processes and whorish commercial appetites.*

That distrust and contempt are perceptible in the following essay. There can indeed be detected at the heart of all prize-awarding ceremonies, supposedly designed to reward excellence, an odd paradox. To wit, an undeserving recipient can win such a prize without at the same time gaining the prestige attached to it because, precisely by virtue of his having won it, that prestige has been irrevocably compromised. And if, over the years, as has certainly been the case with the Oscars, the awarding of undeserving recipients has been the general rule rather than the exception, then the prize must end by forfeiting altogether whatever claim it once had to be taken seriously.

Five or six years ago a distinguished writer-director (if I may be permitted the epithet in connection with a Hollywood personage) was co-author of a screen play nominated for an Academy Award. He was too nervous to attend the proceedings on the big night, so he was listening to a broadcast at home, pacing the floor tensely, chewing his fingers, taking long breaths, scowling and debating with himself in hoarse whispers whether to stick it out until the Oscars were announced, or turn the damned radio off and read about it in the papers the next morning. Getting a little tired of all this artistic temperament in the home, his wife suddenly came up with one of those awful remarks which achieve a wry immortality in Hollywood: 'For Pete's sake, don't take it so seriously, darling. After all, Luise Rainer won it twice.'

To those who did not see the famous telephone scene in *The Great Ziegfeld*, or any of the subsequent versions of it which Miss Rainer played in other pictures, with and without telephone, this remark will lack punch. To others it will serve as well as anything to express that cynical despair with which Hollywood people regard their own highest distinction. It isn't so much that the awards never go to the fine achievements as that those fine achievements are not rewarded as such. They are rewarded as fine achievements in box office hits. You can't be an All-American on a losing team. Technically, they are voted, but actually they are not decided by the use of whatever artistic and critical wisdom Hollywood may happen to possess. They are ballyhooed, pushed, yelled, screamed, and in every way propagandised into the consciousness of the voters so incessantly, in the weeks before the final balloting, that everything except the golden aura of the box office is forgotten.

The Motion Picture Academy, at considerable expense and with great efficiency, runs all the nominated pictures at its own theatre, showing each picture twice, once in the afternoon and once in the evening. A nominated picture is one in connection with which any kind of work is nominated for an award, not necessarily acting, directing, or writing; it may be a purely technical matter such as set-dressing or sound work. This running of pictures has the object of permitting voters to look at films which they may happen to have missed or to have partly forgotten. It is an attempt to make them realise that pictures released early in the year and since overlaid with several thicknesses of battered celluloid, are still in the running and that consideration of only those released a short time before the end of the year is not quite just.

The effort is largely a waste. The people with the votes don't go to these showings. They send their relatives, friends, or servants. They have had enough of looking at pictures, and the voices of destiny are by no means inaudible in the Hollywood air. They have a brassy tone, but they are more than distinct.

All this is good democracy of a sort. We elect Congressmen and Presidents in much the same way, so why not actors, cameramen, writers, and all the rest of the people who have to do with the making of pictures? If we permit noise, ballyhoo, and bad theatre to influence us in the selection of the people who are to run the country, why should we object to the same methods in the selection of meritorious achievement in the film business? If we can huckster a President into the White House, why cannot we huckster the agonised Miss Joan Crawford or the hard and beautiful Miss Olivia de Havilland into possession of one of those golden statuettes which express the motion picture industry's frantic desire to kiss itself on the back of the neck? The only answer I can think of is that the motion picture is an art. I say this with a very small voice. It is an inconsiderable statement and has a hard time not sounding a little ludicrous. Nevertheless, it is a fact, not in the least diminished by the further fact that its ethos is so far pretty low and that its techniques are dominated by some pretty awful people.

If you think most motion pictures are bad, which they are (including the foreign), find out from some initiate how they are made, and you will be astonished that any of them could be good. Making a fine motion picture is like painting 'The Laughing Cavalier' in Macy's basement, with a floorwalker to mix your colours for you. Of course, most motion pictures are bad. Why wouldn't they be? Apart from its own intrinsic handicaps of excessive cost, hypercritical bluenosed censorship, and the lack of any single-minded controlling force in the making, the motion picture is bad because 90 per cent is a little too virile and plain-spoken for the putty-minded clerics, the elderly ingenues of the women's clubs, and the tender guardians of that godawful mixture of boredom and bad manners known more eloquently as the Impressionable Age.

The point is not whether there are bad motion pictures or even whether the average motion picture is bad, but whether the motion picture is an artistic medium of sufficient dignity and accomplishment to be treated with respect by the people who control its destinies. Those who deride the motion picture usually are satisfied that they have thrown the book at it by declaring it to be a form of mass entertainment. As if that meant anything. Greek drama, which is still considered quite respectable by most intellectuals, was mass entertainment to the Athenian freeman. So, within its economic and topographical limits, was the Elizabethan drama. The great cathedrals of Europe, although not exactly built to while away an afternoon, certainly had an aesthetic and spiritual effect on the ordinary man. Today, if not always, the fugues and chorales of Bach, the symphonies of Mozart, Borodin, and Brahms, the violin concertos of Vivaldi, the piano sonatas of Scarlatti, and a great deal of what was once rather recondite music are mass entertainment by virtue of radio. Not all fools love it, but not all fools love anything more literate than a comic-strip. It might reasonably be said that all art at some time and in some manner becomes mass entertainment, and that if it does not it dies and is forgotten.

The motion picture admittedly is faced with too large a mass; it must please too many people and offend too few, the second of these restrictions being infinitely more damaging to it artistically than the first. The people who sneer at the motion picture as an art form are furthermore seldom willing to consider it at its best. They insist upon judging it by the picture they saw last week or yesterday; which is even more absurd (in view of the sheer quantity of production) than to judge literature by last week's ten best sellers, or the dramatic art by even the best of the current Broadway hits. In a novel you can still say what you like, and the stage is free almost to the point of obscenity, but the motion picture made in Hollywood, if it is to create art at all, must do so within such strangling limitations of subject and treatment that it is a blind wonder it ever achieves any distinction beyond the purely mechanical slickness of a glass and chromium bathroom. If it were merely a transplanted literary or dramatic art, it certainly would not. The hucksters and the bluenoses between them would see to that.

But the motion picture is *not* a transplanted literary or dramatic art, any more than it is a plastic art. It has elements of all these, but in its essential structure it is much closer to music, in the sense that its finest effects can be independent of precise meaning, that its transitions can be more eloquent than its high-lit scenes, and that its dissolves and camera movements, which cannot be censored, are often far more emotionally effective than its plots, which can. Not only is the motion picture an art, but it is the one entirely new art that has been evolved on this planet for hundreds of years. It is the only art at which we of this generation have any possible chance to greatly excel.

In painting, music, and architecture we are not even second-rate by comparison with the best work of the past. In sculpture we are just funny. In prose literature we not only lack style but we lack the educational and historical background to know what style is. Our fiction and drama are adept, empty, often intriguing, and so mechanical that in another fifty years at most they will be produced by machines with rows of push buttons. We have no popular poetry in the grand style, merely delicate or witty or bitter or obscure verses. Our novels are transient propaganda when they are what is called 'significant', and bedtime reading when they are not.

But in the motion picture we possess an art medium whose glories are not all behind us. It has already produced great work, and if, comparatively and proportionately, far too little of that great work has been achieved in Hollywood, I think that is all the more reason why in its annual tribal dance of the stars and the big-shot producers Hollywood should contrive a little quiet awareness of the fact. Of course it won't. I'm just daydreaming.

Show business has always been a little overnoisy, overdressed, over-brash. Actors are threatened people. Before films came along to make them rich they often had need of a desperate gaiety. Some of these qualities prolonged beyond a strict necessity have passed into the Holly-wood mores and produced that very exhausting thing, the Hollywood manner, which is a chronic case of spurious excitement over absolutely nothing. Nevertheless, and for once in a lifetime, I have to admit that Academy Awards night is a good show and quite funny in spots, although I'll admire you if you can laugh at all of it.

If you can go past those awful idiot faces on the bleachers outside the theatre without a sense of the collapse of the human intelligence; if you can stand the hailstorm of flash bulbs popping at the poor patient actors who, like kings and queens, have never the right to look bored; if you can glance out over the gathered assemblage of what is supposed to be the elite of Hollywood and say to yourself without a sinking feeling, 'In these hands lie the destinies of the only original art the modern world has conceived'; if you can laugh, and you probably will, at the cast-off jokes from the comedians on the stage, stuff that wasn't good enough to use on their radio shows; if you can stand the fake sentimen-tality and the platitudes of the officials and the mincing elocution of the glamour queens (you ought to hear them with four martinis down the hatch); if you can do all these things with grace and pleasure, and not have a wild and forsaken horror at the thought that most of these people actually take this shoddy performance seriously; and if you can then go out into the night to see half the police force of Los Angeles gathered to protect the golden ones from the mob in the free seats but not from that awful moaning sound they give out, like destiny whistling through a hollow shell; if you can do all these things and still feel next morning that the picture business is worth the attention of one single intelligent, artistic mind, then in the picture business you certainly belong, because this sort of vulgarity is part of its inevitable price.

Glancing over the programme of the Awards before the show starts, one is apt to forget that this is really an actors', directors', and big-shot producers' rodeo. It is for the people who *make* pictures (they think), not just for the people who work on them. But these gaudy characters are a kindly bunch at heart: they know that a lot of small-fry characters in minor technical jobs, such as cameramen, musicians, cutters, writers, soundmen, and the inventors of new equipment, have to be given something to amuse them and make them feel mildly elated. So the performance was formerly divided into two parts, with an intermission. On the occasion I attended, however, one of the Masters of Ceremony (I forget which – there was a steady stream of them, like bus passengers) announced that there would be no intermission this year and that they would proceed immediately to the *important* part of the programme.

Let me repeat, the *important part of the programme.*

Perverse fellow that I am, I found myself intrigued by the unimportant part of the programme also. I found my sympathies engaged by the lesser ingredients of picture-making, some of which have been enumerated above. I was intrigued by the efficiently quick on-and-off that was given to these minnows of the picture business; by their nervous attempts via the microphone to give most of the credit for their work to some stuffed shirt in a corner office; by the fact that technical developments which may mean millions of dollars to the industry, and may on occasion influence the whole procedure of picture-making, are just not worth explaining to the audience at all; by the casual, cavalier treatment given to film-editing and to camera work, two of the essential arts of film-making, almost and sometimes quite equal to direction, and much more important than all but the very best acting; intrigued most of all, perhaps, by the formal tribute which is invariably made to the importance of the writer, without whom, my dear, dear friends, nothing could be done at all, but who is for all that merely the climax of the *unimportant* part of the programme.

I am also intrigued by the voting. It was formerly done by all the members of all the various guilds, including the extras and the bit players. Then it was realised that this gave too much voting power to rather unimportant groups, so the voting on various classes of awards was restricted to the guilds which were presumed to have some critical intelligence on the subject. Evidently this did not work either, and the next change was to have the nominating done by the specialist guilds, and the final voting only by the members of the Academy of Motion Picture Arts and Sciences.

It doesn't really seem to make much difference how the voting is done.

The quality of the work is still only recognised in the context of success. A superb job in a flop picture would get you nothing, a routine job in a winner will be voted in. It is against this background of success-worship that the voting is done, with the incidental music supplied by a stream of advertising in the trade papers (which even intelligent people read in Hollywood) designed to put all other pictures than those advertised out of your head at balloting time. The psychological effect is very great on minds conditioned to thinking of merit solely in terms of box office and ballyhoo. The members of the Academy live in this atmosphere, and they are enormously suggestible people, as are all workers in Hollywood. If they are contracted to studios, they are made to feel that it is a matter of group patriotism to vote for the products of their own lot. They are informally advised not to waste their votes, not to plump for something that can't win, especially something made on another lot.

I do not feel any profound conviction, for example, as to whether *The Best Years of Our Lives* was even the best Hollywood motion picture of 1946. It depends what you mean by best. It had a first-class director, some fine actors, and the most appealing sympathy gag in years. It probably had as much all-round distinction as Hollywood is presently capable of. That it had the kind of clean and simple art possessed by *Open City* or the stalwart and magnificent impact of *Henry V* only an idiot would claim. In a sense it did not have art at all. It had that kind of sentimentality which is almost but not quite humanity, and that kind of adeptness which is almost but not quite style. And it had them in large doses, which always helps.

The governing board of the Academy is at great pains to protect the honesty and secrecy of the voting. It is done by anonymous numbered ballots, and the ballots are sent, not to any agency of the motion picture industry, but to a well-known firm of public accountants. The results, in sealed envelopes, are borne by an emissary of the firm right on to the stage of the theatre where the Awards are to be made, and there for the first time, they are made known. Surely precaution could go no further. No one could possibly have known in advance any of these results, not even in Hollywood where every agent learns the closely guarded secrets of the studios with no apparent trouble. If there are secrets in Hollywood, which I sometimes doubt, this voting ought to be one of them.

As for a deeper kind of honesty, I think it is about time for the Academy of Motion Picture Arts and Sciences to use a little of it up by declaring in a forthright manner that foreign pictures are outside competition and will remain so until they face the same economic situation and the same strangling censorship that Hollywood faces. It is all very well to say how clever and artistic the French are, how true to life, what subtle actors they have, what an honest sense of the earth, what forthrightness in dealing with the bawdy side of life. The French can afford these things, we cannot. To the Italians they are permitted, to us they are denied. Even the English possess a freedom we lack. How much did *Brief Encounter* cost? It would have cost at least a million and a half in Hollywood; in order to get that money back, and the distribution costs on top of the negative costs, it would have had to contain innumerable crowd-pleasing ingredients, the very lack of which is what makes it a good picture.

Since the Academy is not an international tribunal of film art it should stop pretending to be one. If foreign pictures have no practical chance whatsoever of winning a major award they should not be nominated. At the very beginning of the performance in 1947 a special Oscar was awarded to Laurence Olivier for *Henry V*, although it was among those nominated as the best picture of the year. There could be no more obvious way of saying that it was not going to win. A couple of minor technical awards and a couple of minor writing awards were also given to foreign pictures, but nothing that ran into important coin, just side meat. Whether these awards were deserved is beside the point, which is that they were minor awards and were intended to be minor awards, and that there was no possibility whatsoever of any foreign-made picture winning a major award.

To outsiders it might appear that something devious went on here. To those who know Hollywood, all that went on was the secure knowledge and awareness that the Oscars exist for and by Hollywood, their standards and problems are the standards and problems of Hollywood, their purpose is to maintain the supremacy of Hollywood, and their phoniness is the phoniness of Hollywood. But the Academy cannot, without appearing ridiculous, maintain the pose of internationalism by tossing a few minor baubles to the foreigners while carefully keeping all the top drawer jewellery for itself. As a writer I resent that writing awards should be among the baubles, and as a member of the Motion Picture Academy I resent its trying to put itself in a position which its annual performance before the public shows it is quite unfit to occupy.

If the actors and actresses like the silly show, and I'm not sure at all the best of them do, they at least know how to look elegant in a strong light, and how to make with the wide-eyed and oh, so humble little speeches as if they believed them. If the big producers like it, and I'm quite sure they do because it contains the only ingredients they really understand – promotion values and the additional grosses that go with them – the producers at least know what they are fighting for. But if the quiet, earnest, and slightly cynical people who really make motion pictures like it, and I'm quite sure they don't, well, after all, it comes only once a year, and it's no worse than a lot of the sleazy vaudeville they have to push out of the way to get their work done.

Of course, that's not quite the point either. The head of a large studio once said privately that in his candid opinion the motion picture business was 25 per cent honest business and the other 75 per cent pure conniving. He didn't say anything about art, although he may have heard of it. But that *is* the real point, isn't it? – whether these annual Awards, regardless of the grotesque ritual that accompanies them, really represent anything at all of artistic importance to the motion picture medium, anything clear and honest that remains after the lights are dimmed, the minks put away, and the aspirin is swallowed? I don't think they do. I think they are just theatre and not even good theatre. As for the personal prestige that goes with winning an Oscar, it may with luck last long enough for your agent to get your contract re-written and your price jacked up another notch. But over the years and in the hearts of men of good will? I hardly think so.

Once upon a time a once very successful Hollywood lady decided (or was forced) to sell her lovely furnishings at auction, together with her lovely home. On the day before she moved out she was showing a party of her friends through the house for a private view. One of them noticed that the lady was using her two golden Oscars as doorstops. It seemed they were just about the right weight, and she had sort of forgotten they were gold.

'But is Mickey a mouse? Well, I am hard put to it at moments certainly, and have had to do some thinking back. Certainly, one would not recognize him in a trap'   **E. M. FORSTER**

JOHN UPDIKE
More Shaggy Doggerel

In 1955 the 27-year-old Eddie Fisher (a now forgotten crooner) married the 22-year-old Debbie Reynolds (a now almost forgotten singer and actress) in, as they say, a blaze of publicity. Just four years later, however, in a matching blaze, Eddie abandoned Debbie for Liz – Debbie's dear friend Elizabeth Taylor. Four turbulent years after that, it was Eddie's turn to be abandoned, for by now Liz had met Richard Burton on the set of Cleopatra. *Who cares? Way back then, everyone did, including John Updike.*

His second squib reflects the fact that home movies, after all, are also movies.

THE NEWLYWEDS

After a one-day honeymoon, the Fishers rushed off to a soft drink bottlers' convention, then on to a ball game, a TV rehearsal and a movie preview.

Life

'**W**e're married,' said Eddie.
Said Debbie, 'Incredi-

ble! When is our honey-
moon?' 'Over and done,' he

replied. 'Feeling logy?
Drink Coke.' 'Look at Yogi

go!' Debbie cried. 'Groovy!'
'Rehearsal?' 'The movie.'

'Some weddie,' said Debbie.
Said Eddie, 'Yeah, mebbe.'

HOME MOVIES

How the children have changed! Rapt we stare
　At flickering lost Edens
　Pale infants, squinting, seem to hark
To their older selves laughing in the dark.

And then, by the trellis in some old Spring –
　The seasons are unaltering –
　We gather, smoother and less bald,
Innocently clowning, having been called

By the coolly invisible cameraman.
　How silently time ran!
　We cannot climb back, nor can our friends,
To that calm light. The brief film ends.

ORSON WELLES
Character

Orson Welles on character – from, as no buff will need to be informed,
his manic 1955 masterpiece, Mr Arkadin. *So many interesting and even*
on occasion plausible hypotheses have been proposed to explain Welles's
chronic inability – after Citizen Kane *– to complete any of his films,*
one wonders why no one ever thought to interrogate the films themselves.
Could this famous little parable be a self-portrait?

Now I am going to tell you about a scorpion. This scorpion
wanted to cross a river, so he asked the frog to carry him. 'No,' said the
frog. 'No, thank you. If I let you on my back you may sting me, and the
sting of the scorpion is death.' 'Now, where,' asked the scorpion, 'is the
logic of that?' (for scorpions always try to be logical). 'If I sting you, you
will die, and I will drown.' So the frog was convinced, and allowed the
scorpion on his back. But just in the middle of the river he felt a terrible
pain and realized that, after all, the scorpion *had* stung him. 'Logic!'
cried the dying frog as he started under, bearing the scorpion down
with him. 'There is no logic in this!' 'I know,' said the scorpion, 'but I
can't help it – it's my character.' Let's *drink* to character . . .

REYNER BANHAM

from *Los Angeles: The Architecture of Four Ecologies*

Disneyland is to Hollywood what Hollywood is to Los Angeles. Hollywood is to Los Angeles what Los Angeles is to California. Los Angeles is to California what California is to America. California is to America what America is to the world.

That, at least, is what the ever more tentacular Disney organization wishes us all to think: that if Hollywood is the projectionist's cabin of America (and, by extension, of the world), then the Disneyland theme parks constitute the ultimate concentration and distillation of Hollywood's dream culture.

One may beg to differ. Disneyland, however, is unignorable. And in Los Angeles: The Architecture of Four Ecologies – *the cutest and acutest book to have been written on what might be termed Shangri LA, that screwy metropolis which has shed so many of its glossy skins over the years that, were it ever to remain for an instant exactly as it was the instant before, it would become utterly unrecognizable – Reyner Banham has this to say about it.*

Until Las Vegas became unashamedly middle-aged and the boring Beaux-Arts Caesars' Palace was built, its architecture was an extreme suburban variant of Los Angeles – Douglas Honnold, now a respected doyen of the architectural profession in Los Angeles, worked for Bugsy Siegel in the design of the Flamingo, the pioneer casino-hotel on the Strip. Las Vegas has been as much a marginal gloss on Los Angeles as was Brighton Pavilion on Regency London. More important, Los Angeles has seen in this century the greatest concentration of fantasy-production, as an industry and as an institution, in the history of Western man. In the guise of Hollywood, Los Angeles gave us the movies as we know them and stamped an image on the infant television industry. And stemming from the impetus given by Hollywood as well as other causes, Los Angeles is also the home of the most extravagant myths of private gratification and self-realization, institutionalized now in the doctrine of 'doing your own thing'.

Both Hollywood's marketable commercial fantasies, and those private ones which are above or below calculable monetary value, have left their marks on the Angel City, but Hollywood brought something that all other fantasists needed – technical skill and resources in converting fantastic ideas into physical realities. Since living flesh-and-blood actors and dancers had to walk through or prance upon Hollywood's fantasies, there was much that could not be accomplished with painted back-cloths or back-projections; much of Shangri-la had to be built in three dimensions, the spiral ramps of the production numbers of Busby Berkeley musical spectaculars had to support the weight of a hundred girls in silver top hats, and so on . . .

The movies were thus a peerless school for building fantasy as fact, and the facts often survived one movie to live again in another, and another and others still to come. Economy in using increasingly valuable acreage on studio-lots caused these fantastic façades and ancient architectures reproduced in plaster to be huddled together into what have become equally fantastic townscapes which not only survive as cities of romantic illusion, but have been elevated to the status of a kind of cultural monuments, which now form the basis for tourist excursions more flourishing than the traditional tours of film-stars' homes.

This business of showing the plant to visitors as a tourist attraction has spread beyond the movie industry, into such monuments of public relations as the Busch Gardens in the San Fernando Valley, where the real-life brewery is only one of the features shown, and back into the movie industry with Disneyland – the set for a film that was never ever going to be made except in the mind of the visitor. In creating this compact sequence of habitable fantasies, WED Enterprises seem to have transcended Hollywood, Los Angeles, Walt Disney's original talents and all other identifiable ingredients of this environmental phantasmagoria.

In terms of an experience one can walk or ride through, inhabit and enjoy, it is done with such consummate skill and such base cunning that one can only compare it to something completely outrageous, like the brothel in Genet's *Le Balcon*. It is an almost faultless organization for delivering, against cash, almost any type at all of environmental experience that human fancy, however inflamed, could ever devise. Here are pedestrian piazzas, seas, jungles, castles, outer space, Main

Street, the old West, mountains, more than can be experienced in a single day's visit . . . and all embraced within some obvious ironies, as all institutionalized fantasies must be.

The greatest of these ironies has to do with transportation, and this underlies the brothel comparison. Set in the middle of a city obsessed with mobility, a city whose most characteristic festival is the Rose Parade in Pasadena, fantastically sculptured Pop inventions entirely surfaced with live flowers rolling slowly down Colorado Boulevard every New Year's Day – in this city Disneyland offers illicit pleasures of mobility. Ensconced in a sea of giant parking-lots in a city devoted to the automobile, it provides transportation that does not exist outside – steam trains, monorails, people-movers, tram-trains, travelators, ropeways, not to mention pure transport fantasies such as simulated space-trips and submarine rides. Under-age children, too young for driver's licences, enjoy the licence of driving on their own freeway system and adults can step off the pavement and mingle with the buses and trams on Main Street in a manner that would lead to sudden death or prosecution outside.

But more than this, the sheer concentration of different forms of mechanical movement means that Disneyland is almost the only place where East Coast town-planning snobs, determined that their cities shall never suffer the automotive 'fate' of Los Angeles, can bring their students or their city councillors to see how the alternative might work in the flesh and metal – to this blatantly commercial fun-fair in the city they hate. And seeing how well it all worked, I began to understand the wisdom of Ray Bradbury in proposing that Walt Disney was the only man who could make rapid transit a success in Los Angeles. All the skill, cunning, salesmanship, and technical proficiency are there.

DAVID THOMSON
from *Suspects*

David Thomson's Suspects *represents a unique approach to cinema criticism: a fictional jigsaw puzzle whose pieces are the interlinking biographies – the back-stories, as they are called in the screenwriting trade – of characters from scores of Hollywood movies. What follows, for example, is the imaginary back-story of Norma Desmond, the deranged diva of Billy Wilder's* Sunset Boulevard *(played by Gloria Swanson in a performance whose epically masochistic self-laceration never ceases to dumbfound). Later in the book Thomson conjectures that she and Joe Gillis, her toyboy writer from the same film (played by William Holden), might in fact (or, rather, in fiction) have been the parents of Julian Kay, the dandified hustler (played by Richard Gere) of Paul Schrader's* American Gigolo.*

For once, though, Thomson has perhaps missed a trick. For if there's any film bathed in the same gangrenous atmosphere as Sunset Boulevard, *it's surely Hitchcock's* Psycho. *A handful of startling parallels can even be drawn between the two. In both, after all, a character pursued by the forces of order, (by a pair of repossession agents in Wilder's film, by the police in Hitchcock's) seeks refuge in an isolated dwelling (a creepy old mansion in Wilder's film, a motel in Hitchcock's) and ends by being slain, respectively in a swimming pool and a shower, by a certifiably demented occupant whose life is irretrievably stuck in the groove of the past. These occupants' forenames are, in addition, Norma and Norman (both of which cry out for the prefix 'ab'); and, given that Norman Bates's psyche has been entirely usurped by his mother's, his name too could be thought of as Norma.*

Norma Desmond as Norman Bates's mother, her skeleton still rocking in its rocking chair in the cellar of the Bates Motel! Such stuff as a film buff's dreams are made on!

You can look at movie magazines from the early 1920s, amazed at the faces of beautiful young actresses, stars then, but so little known now that their euphonious names sound concocted – Barbara La Marr, Lupe Velez, Agnes Ayres, Alexandra Laguna, Leatrice Joy, Norma Desmond, and so on. All brunettes, with black lips, curls stuck on their brows and eyes like bulletholes: they seem to cherish the pain of sexual exploitation by men. There is implacability in the faces, like a ship's figurehead battling into the elements. It comes from signaling feelings; those silent women are stranded in the impossibility of utterance. A few years later, after sound, women's faces softened. The loveliness grew quiet and intriguing. Words were put out, like bait on the threshold of their being. They smiled, where silent faces had had trumpeting frowns.

It must have been maddening. Not many of them lasted more than a few years; the business was exhausting, and that kind of beauty is our endless American resource. It was only will that made any of them famous, or put forbidding strength in their faces. Somehow, they all seemed overdone; no matter how hard they tried, they must have known the shame of feeling coarse or clumsy. You can imagine them killing, even, at the end of their tether, laughing if the gun went off and there was only a small puff of light to show explosion. But the man aimed at was staggering, stupefied, his hands clutched to the hole where life was leaking out. The ladies could make you believe.

So many of their names were false. Norma Desmond was born May Svensson in Milwaukee in 1899. She was the daughter of Swedish immigrants, the youngest of five children. Years later, some version of Miss Desmond told *Photoplay*: 'I had picked a good time and place to be born. The automobile was not much older than I was, so there weren't many of them. Trolleys and wagons were pulled by horses, and none of them went too fast. It was a safe, clean time. When you were thirsty in the summer, your mother made a pitcher of lemonade. And everyone did the family wash on Monday and hung it out in the fresh air to dry.'

Charming, don't you think? But actresses are in love with such crystal-clear happiness. May Svensson's early life was not a pitcher of homemade lemonade or the bouquet of fresh laundry. Instead, she was taken by her father on his tours of Wisconsin and Minnesota, selling Bibles and being driven by penury into increasingly reckless confidence tricks in which the daughter was often the decoy. They lived in cheap hotels, or on the run: there were a few nights in town jails, the child in a cot next to the sheriff's desk waiting for her father to be released.

And so it was, in 1911, that May saw her father shot down by a man named Gregson, the victim of a small enough fraud, a God-fearing but choleric man who had pursued Svensson for seven months. May was holding her father's hand, and talking to him, coming out of a diner in Kenosha, when a pistol blast met them. She felt the pressure in the air and was dragged sideways by her father's fall, his dead grip on her growing tighter.

She had her picture in the Chicago papers, wide-eyed, floridly becurled and stricken. A manager at the Essanay studios noticed it, and his flabby head was so touched by her plight that he saw a way of making money. He found her and devised a series of one-reelers about a waif, 'Sweedie' she was called, an orphan and an outcast who got into sentimental scrapes and comic adventures. The films were poorly made, but the child bloomed in them. The camera breathed in time with the rising beat of puberty; in a year of those short movies she became an object of furtive lust, her picture pinned in lockers. The movies learned early how to fashion an arousing innocence that inspires its own spoiling.

'Norma Desmond', as Essanay had called her, was married at fifteen to Wallace Beery, twice her age and the robust exponent of his own ugliness. It was like a virgin princess being taken by a barbarian. The public was thrilled with alarm. In reality, Norma scolded him incessantly, until he left her with the beach house, all but one of their cars and the vases filled with his cash. This was 1917.

She had an extraordinary career in silent pictures, earning as much as $15,000 a week, to say nothing of bonuses. She worked for Marshall Neilan, Cecil B. De Mille, Harry D'Abbadie D'Arrast and Allan Dwan. Her burning gaze played on audiences like the light of the screen. The industry romanticized her and her 'enchanted' life. Perhaps she believed those stories herself – her image was overpowering. She had gone so swiftly from the sordid to the luxurious, from being abused to being worshipped. She was a Cinderella who became a tyrant queen, without time to clean the coal dust from her fingernails. An aura of transformation surrounded her. There was a famous portrait of her face staring through an embroidered veil, a celebration of beauty as a fatal delusion. She met the tycoon Noah Cross and he mounted a play with her as Salome, discarding hundreds of veils, while he sat on a stool in the wings to see her body emerge through the misty gauze.

Perhaps her conviction was too intense for the naturalism of sound pictures? Or were her demands for money more than the industry could endure? *Princess of the Micks*, her film for Max von Mayerling, her husband, was a disaster in which she sank one million dollars of her own money. And so she went to France, marrying a marquis whose name she never learned to spell. She made a film there, *Une Jeune Fille de campagne*, about Charlotte Corday, in which the character will not speak – to protect her excessive expressiveness or the actress's lack of French.

While in Europe, she married the German Baron von Rauffenstein. Mayerling had never really been given up during these other marriages. He simply went from being husband to personal manager; it meant he dressed earlier in the day. There was consternation in the press, but the three figures handled the 'ménage' without dismay. Moreover, in 1931–2, Norma Desmond had an affair with Serge Alexandre, also known as Stavisky. To this day there is a rumor in France that she had a child by the swindler, a daughter, who was passed on to a simple farming couple on the estate of Baron Raoul, a friend of Alexandre's. (An unexpectedly striking face in an out-of-the-way place will often inspire such fancies. But suppose real foundlings are not especially pretty, what then?)

In 1934, she returned to the mansion on Sunset Boulevard (bought for her by Noah Cross), where she would remain until her removal, at the hands of the police, in 1950. Mayerling came back to America in 1939 and became her butler. Norma Desmond slipped from glory to oblivion, unaware in her retreat of any change in her power or her looks. She was so removed from public contact now, she may have thought herself divine.

She had only a monkey as an intimate until Joe Gillis strayed into her life. He seemed to offer the means of a comeback, but he was also a lover and a slave. When he thought to leave her, she shot him, in the belly, as yet unaware that her own body nurtured his child. In the asylum hospital, she never deigned to notice her swelling or the birth of the boy. She was officially insane, lecturing the other inmates and shooting them with imaginary guns when they ignored her. She died in 1959, still firing.

'The more emotional the material, the less emotional the treatment'   JEAN RENOIR

DUSAN MAKAVEJEV
Life as a Remake of Movies

The now forgotten anarcho-surrealist Yugoslavian filmmaker Dusan Makavejev – auteur of such emblematic works of post-1968 cinematic modernity as W. R. the Mysteries of the Organism *(WR was the just-as-forgotten Wilhelm Reich),* Innocence Unprotected *and* Sweet Movie *– writes here of a sensation that should be familiar to any lover of the American cinema who has finally had an opportunity of personally visiting the United States: the sensation that virtually every Hollywood movie is a remake, a remake of America.*

During my first extended visit to America, we were somewhere in the countryside, passing by beautiful detached houses in green spaces, with nicely-cut grass, no fences between the neighbours, bushes here and there, and patches of well-groomed flowers. A strange and pleasant (but slightly uneasy) feeling began to overwhelm me. I felt enveloped by unreality. The landscape I was observing with enjoyment was as painfully clear as a hyper-realist painting, but it was as if I were seeing double. I was experiencing a psychological phenomenon that I realized I knew about from my school-days. It was called *déjà vu*. I was recognizing places where I had never been!

Then the appearance of someone with a lawn mower triggered my memory. I had only seen this kind of machine in Walt Disney comics. Mickey!

Later on, in California, in glorious houses with interiors 'like a movie set' and picture windows unifying interiors and exteriors, again there was that same sweet, itching *déjà vu* feeling, like when you are falling in love. Sweet haze: where am I?

Most of America's interiors (and exteriors) were built after similar ones – or even the same ones – had first appeared on film. American landscapes look as glorious as their pictures in *National Geographic*; they often seem as if they are 3-D projections from some Kodak photo on slide.

Is it partly because Americans document themselves so thoroughly, have so much of their daily lives captured on film, tapes, slide or photograph? In many ways, because Americans are so much freer, as well as having a much larger margin of tolerance for deviant behaviour, you sometimes simply cannot say who copies whom: Silver Screen copies life, or vice versa?

I have a similar real/unreal feeling these days as I watch the ex-Yugoslavia/Bosnia war, which in so many ways is more horrible than any other war because there is no foreign army or invader here; it's all 'our guys'. This time, the *déjà vu* comes from horror and sci-fi B-movies: *The Island of Doctor Moreau* and similar monstrous inventions, such as *The Night of the Living Dead*, etc. The banality of evil.

Boys in paramilitary units dress and behave as if they were acting in a remake of *The Deer Hunter* or *Platoon*, with Sly Stallone's bandanna from *Rambo*. And they *do* remake these films in their own and other people's lives.

Before Disney went into feature production, he did a lot of stories for daily newspapers and syndication.

In these stories, Mickey and his entourage tracked down secret treasure, published a newspaper, started a detective agency, served in the Foreign Legion. Lots of fantastic moments from Spielberg's movies or *Romancing the Stone* seem to me as if I have already seen them in comics with good old Mickey Mouse, hero of my childhood. Stories with social content, about fighting gangsters, about fighting corruption in local politics, etc., remind me as well of Frank Capra films.

Trying to decide who did it first will not work with American culture. From the famous radio programmes of the forties to the movies and now to television, and of course all the time through an extraordinary and powerful tradition of photography, it is actually life, and the precise registering of it, that makes this country, the USA, so unique: a constant, dream-like flow from images to life and back into image . . .

FRANÇOIS TRUFFAUT
Letter to Jean-Luc Godard

A little remarked upon axiom of film history is that, wherever and whenever at least one great filmmaker emerges, there, too, other, lesser but not negligible figures will spontaneously spring forth around him or her. Contrariwise, in any country devoid, for whatever reason, of even one great filmmaker, they will not. Thus, in the prewar Soviet Union, when Eisenstein was the practising genius-in-residence, such comparably major directors as Barnet, Dziga-Vertov, Dovjenko, Pudovkin, etc., were equally active. Thus, too, in Sweden, during the long postwar heyday of Ingmar Bergman, an impressive number of other interesting directors – Widerberg, Sjöman, Donner, Troell – contributed to the international lustre of that country's national cinema.

Undoubtedly, the most striking instance of such creative simultaneity was the French cinema of the early 1960s, the cinema of the New Wave, the cinema of Godard, Truffaut, Demy, Varda, Marker, Chabrol and that quintet of brilliant Rs, Rohmer, Rivette, Resnais, Rozier and Rouch. Most of these directors were close friends. They viewed rough cuts of one another's films and even made larky cameo appearances in them. Above all, they shamelessly, indefatigably, promoted their fellow New Wavers in what Truffaut himself called, with a wink at the politique des auteurs *(or 'auteur theory'), the* politique des copains *(or 'mutual backscratching theory'). Then, alas, by the end of the same decade, the close-knit New Wave had more or less disintegrated and, as may be inferred from Truffaut's superbly vitriolic letter to Godard, the backscratching degenerated into outright scratching. As Sacha Guitry, charting the inexorable decline of one of his own professional relationships, pithily put it: at first we were shoulder to shoulder; then face to face; then back to back.*

Jean-Luc. So you won't be obliged to read this unpleasant letter right to the end, I'm starting with the essential point: I will not co-produce your film.

Secondly, I'm sending back to you the letter you wrote to Jean-Pierre Léaud: I read it and I think it's obnoxious. And because of that letter I feel the time has come to tell you, at length, that in my opinion you've been acting like a shit.

As regards Jean-Pierre, who's been so badly treated since the business with Marie and more recently in his work, I think it's obnoxious of you to kick him when he's down, obnoxious to extort money by intimidation from someone who is fifteen years younger than you are and whom you used to pay less than a million when he was the lead in films that were earning you thirty times as much.

Yes, Jean-Pierre has changed since *Les 400 Coups*, but I can tell you that it was in *Masculin–Féminin* that I noticed for the first time how he could be filled with anxiety rather than pleasure at the notion of finding himself in front of a camera. The film was good and he was good in the film, but that first scene, in the café, was a painful experience for anyone looking at him with affection and not with an entomologist's eye.

I never expressed the slightest reservation about you to Jean-Pierre, who admired you so much, but I know that you were bad-mouthing me behind my back, in the way that a guy might say to a kid, 'And your father, is he still pissed out of his mind?'

Jean-Pierre is not the only one to have changed in 14 years and if *À bout de souffle* and *Tout va bien* were to be screened one after the other, we'd all be dismayed and saddened to see how cynical and unadventurous the latter is by comparison.

I don't give a shit what you think of *La Nuit américaine*, what I find deplorable on your part is the fact that, even now, you continue to go and see such films, films whose subject-matter you know in advance will not correspond to either your conception of the cinema or your conception of life. Would Jean-Édern Hallier write to Daninos to take issue with him on his latest book?

You've changed your way of life, your way of thinking, yet, even so, you continue to waste hour after hour ruining your eyesight at the cinema. Why? In the hope of finding something that will fuel your contempt for the rest of us, that will reinforce all your new prejudices?

Now it's my turn to call you a liar. At the beginning of *Tout va bien* there is this phrase: 'To make a film one needs stars.' A lie. Everyone knows how determined you were to get J. Fonda who was beginning to lose interest, when all your backers were telling you to take just anyone. You brought together those two stars of yours the way Clouzot used to do: since it's their good fortune to be working with me, they ought to be content with a tenth of their normal salary, etc. Karmitz and Bernard Paul need stars, but not you, so it's a lie. And then we read in the newspapers: he had stars 'imposed' on him ... Another lie, concerning your new film: you don't mention the very substantial subsidy you solicited, and obtained, from the state, and which ought to have been enough even if Ferreri, as you absurdly accuse him, spent the money that was 'reserved' for you. So, he thinks he can get away with anything, this wop who wants to take the bread out of our mouths, this immigrant worker, have him deported, via Cannes!

That's always been one of your gifts, setting yourself up as the eternal victim, like Cayatte, like Boisset, like Michel Drach; the victim of Pompidou, of Marcellin, of the censors and the distributors with their eager little scissors, whereas in reality you've always contrived to have things work out just the way you want them to and when you want them to and above all you've always contrived to uphold your pure, incorruptible image, even if it should be to the detriment of someone as defenceless as, for example, Janine Bazin. Six months after the Kiejman business, Janine had two of her programmes cancelled, an act of vengeance that was very cunningly deferred. Since Kiejman would not have contemplated talking about the cinema and politics without interviewing you, your role in this affair – and a role is what it was – consisted yet again in promoting your own subversive image, which explains the well-chosen little comment. The comment is made: either it's kept in and it's sufficiently sharp for no one to suspect you've gone soft or else it's cut out and everyone is over the moon: yes, decidedly, they say, Godard is Godard, he'll never change, etc.

Everything goes off like clockwork, the programme is cancelled and you remain on your pedestal. No one happens to notice that the comment is just another of your lies. If Pompidou is, as you claim, the 'director' of France, then it's the Communist Party and the unions that you abuse – by means (means too subtle for the 'masses') of periphrasis, antiphrasis and derision – in *Tout va bien*, a film originally intended for the widest possible public.

If I withdrew from the debate on *Fahrenheit 451* at the same period, it was in an attempt to help Janine, not out of solidarity with you, which is why I didn't return your telephone call.

The fact remains that Janine was in hospital last month, she was knocked down by a car while making her last programme, she had to have an operation on her knee (she's had a limp since adolescence, etc.), so there she finds herself in hospital without any work and without any money and naturally without any word from Godard who will only step down from his pedestal to amuse Rassam every so often. And I can tell you: the more you love the masses, the more I love Jean-Pierre Léaud, Janine Bazin, Patricia Finaly (and she's out of a nursing-home and has had to pester the Cinémathèque over and over again for her six months' back salary) and Helen Scott whom you meet in an airport and cut dead, why, because she's an American or because she's a friend of mine? The behaviour of a shit. A girl from the BBC rings you up to ask if you'll say a few words on cinema and politics for a programme about me, I warn her in advance that you'll refuse, but that's not good enough for you, you hang up on her before she's even finished her sentence, the behaviour of an élitist, the behaviour of a shit, as when you agree to go to Geneva or London or Milan and you don't go, to startle people, to astonish them, like Sinatra, like Brando, you're nothing but a piece of shit on a pedestal.

For a while, following May '68, no more was heard of you or else it was all very mysterious: it seems he's working in a factory, he's formed a group, etc., and then, one Saturday, there's an announcement that you're going to speak on the radio with Monod. I stay in the office to listen to it, in a sense just to know what you've been doing; your voice trembles, you seem very nervous, you declare that you're going to make a film called *La Mort de mon frère*, about a black worker who was ill and had been left to die in the basement of a TV factory and, listening to you, and despite the fact that your voice is trembling, I know: 1. that the story isn't true, or at any rate it didn't quite happen like that; 2. that you would <u>never</u> make such a film. And I say to myself: what if the poor guy has a family and his family is now going to live in the hope of the film being made? There wasn't a part for Montand in that film or Jane Fonda, but for a ¼ of an hour you gave the impression of 'doing the right thing', like Messmer when he gives the vote to nineteen-year-olds. Phony. Poseur. You've always been a poseur, as when you sent a telegram to de Gaulle about his prostate, when you called Braunberger a filthy Jew over the telephone, when you said that Chauvet was corrupt (because he was the last and only one to resist you), a poseur when you lump together Renoir and Verneuil as though they were the same thing, a poseur even now when you claim you're going to show the truth about the cinema, those who work in the background, who are badly paid, etc.

When you had a location, a garage or shop set up by your crew, and then you would arrive and say 'I don't have any ideas today, we won't shoot' and the crew would have to take it all back down again, did it never occur to you that the workers might feel completely useless and rejected, like the sound crew that spent a whole day in the empty studio at Pinewood waiting in vain for Brando?

Now, why am I telling you all this today instead of three, five or ten years ago?

For six years, like everyone else, I saw how you were suffering on account of (or for) Anna and everything that was odious about you we forgave because of that suffering.

I knew you had seduced Liliane Dreyfus (ex-David) by telling her 'François doesn't love you any more, he's in love with Marie Dubois who's in his new film,' and I found that pitiful but touching, yes, why not, even touching! I knew you had gone to see Braunberger and said to him, 'Let me make the sketch that Rouch is supposed to shoot' and I found that . . . shall we say, pathetic. I was strolling along the Champs-Élysées with you and you said to me, 'It seems *Bébert et l'Omnibus* isn't doing well, serve it right' and I said 'Oh, come on now . . .'

In Rome, I quarrelled with Moravia because he suggested that I film *Le Mépris*; I had gone there with Jeanne to present *Jules et Jim*, your latest film wasn't doing too well and Moravia was hoping to change horses in midstream.

It was also out of solidarity with you that I had a row with Melville who couldn't forgive you for having helped him make *Léon Morin prêtre* and was looking to do you down. You, meanwhile, deliberately humiliated Jeanne and, to please Anna (after the business of *Eva*) you made a ludicrous attempt to blackmail Marie-France Pisier (Hossein, Yugoslavia . . . over and over again . . . 'the wedding-ring'), etc. You cast Catherine Ribeiro, whom I had sent to you, in *Les Carabiniers*, and then threw yourself on her the way Chaplin throws himself on his secretary in *The Great Dictator* (it wasn't I who made the comparison) – I list all of that just to remind you not to forget anything in this film of yours that's going to be telling the truth about cinema and sex. Instead of showing X—'s arse and Anne Wiazemsky's pretty hands on the window-pane, you might try it the other way around now you know that not only all men but all women are equal, including actresses. With every shot of X— in *Week-End* it was as though you were tipping a wink at your pals: this whore wants to make a film with me, take a good look at how I treat her: there are whores and there are poetic young women.

I'm telling you all of this because, as I have to admit, even though one could still detect, in certain statements you made, that selfsame posturing, now slightly tinged with bitterness, I really thought you had changed, at least that's what I thought until I read the letter you addressed to Jean-Pierre Léaud. If you had sealed it, I would have given it to him without reading it and I would have regretted it, perhaps you wanted to give me the opportunity not to deliver it to him . . . ?

Today you're unassailable, everyone thinks you're unassailable, you're no longer the long-suffering swain, like everyone else you think you're better than everyone else and you know you think you're better than everyone else, you regard yourself as a repository of truth on life, politics, commitment, the cinema and love, it's all an open book to you and anyone who has a different opinion from yours is a creep, even if the opinion you hold in June is not the same one you held in April. In 1973, your prestige is intact, which is to say, when you walk into an office, everyone studies your face to see if you are in a good mood or whether it would be better to stay put in one's own little corner; on occasion you're prepared to laugh or smile; you call people *tu* now instead of *vous*, but the intimidation is still there, as well as the easy insult and the terrorism (that gift of yours for the backhanded compliment). What I mean is that I need have no worries on your account, in Paris there are still enough wealthy young men, with a chip on their shoulder because they had their first car at 18, who will be delighted to pay their dues by announcing: 'I'm the producer of Godard's next film.'

When you wrote to me at the end of '68, demanding 8 or 900 thousand francs which in fact I didn't owe you (even Dussart was shocked!) and you added, 'In any case, we've nothing more to say to each other,' I took it in its absolutely literal sense: I sent you the dough and, apart from a couple of moments when we softened (you when I was unhappy in love, me when you were in hospital), I've felt nothing but contempt for you ever since – as when I saw the scene in *Vent d'est* showing how to make a Molotov cocktail and, a year later, you got cold feet the first time we were asked to distribute *La Cause du peuple* in the street . . .

The notion that all men are equal is theoretical with you, it isn't deeply felt, which is why you have never succeeded in loving anyone or in helping anyone, other than by shoving a few banknotes at them. Someone, maybe Cavanna, once wrote: 'One should despise money, especially small change' and I've never forgotten how you used to get rid of centimes by slipping them down the backs of chairs in cafés. By contrast with you, I've never said a negative word about you, partly because I've always hated feuds between writers or painters, dubious scores being settled by means of open letters to the press, and finally because I've always felt you were both jealous and envious, even when things were going well for you – you're hyper-competitive, I'm almost not at all – and there was also on my part a certain admiration, I find it easy to admire, as you know, and a real desire to remain friends with you ever since you were upset by that remark I made to Claire Fischer about the way our relationship had changed after the army (for me) and Jamaica (for you). There are many things I don't state outright because I'm never completely sure that the contrary isn't just as true, but, if I now state outright that you are a shit, it's because, when I see Janine Bazin in hospital and read your letter to Jean-Pierre, there can no longer be any room for doubt. I'm not raving, I don't say that you are to blame for Janine being in hospital, but the fact that she is out of work, after ten years in television, is directly linked to you and you don't give a shit. Here you are, in 1973, as fond as ever of making grand gestures and spectacular announcements, as arrogant and dogmatic as ever, secure on your pedestal, indifferent to others, incapable of simply and unselfishly giving up a few hours of your time to help someone. Between your interest in the masses and your own narcissism there's no room for anything or anyone else. After all, those who called you a genius, no matter what you did, all belonged to that famous trendy Left that runs the gamut from Susan Sontag to Bertolucci via Richard Roud, Alain Jouffroy, Bourseiller and Cournot, and even if you sought to appear impervious to flattery, because of them you began to ape the world's great men, de Gaulle, Malraux, Clouzot, Langlois, you fostered the myth, you accentuated that side of you that was mysterious, inaccessible and temperamental (as Scott would say), all for the slavish admiration of those around you. You need to play a role and the role needs to be a prestigious one; I've always had the impression that real militants are like cleaning women, doing a thankless, daily but necessary job. But you, you're the Ursula Andress of militancy, you make a brief appearance, just enough time for the cameras to flash, you make two or three duly startling remarks and then you disappear again, trailing clouds of self-serving mystery. Opposed to you are the small men, from Bazin to Edmond Maire and taking in Sartre, Buñuel, Queneau, Mendès-France, Rohmer and Audiberti, who ask others how they're getting on, who help them fill out a social security form, who reply to their letters –

what they have in common is the capacity to think of others rather than themselves and above all to be more interested in what they do than in what they are and in what they appear to be.

Now, anything that can be written can also be said, which is why I conclude as you did: if you want to talk it over, fine,

françois

'If I had, like you, failed to keep the promises of my ordination, I would prefer it to have been for a woman's love rather than for what you call your intellectual development.' *Le Journal d'un curé de campagne.*

JEAN-LUC GODARD
Les 400 Coups

Now, a flashback to 1959 – cruel, like all flashbacks.

With *Les 400 Coups*, François Truffaut enters both modern cinema and the classrooms of our childhood. Bernanos's humiliated children. Vitrac's children in power. Melville–Cocteau's *enfants terribles*. Vigo's children, Rossellini's children, in a word, Truffaut's children – a phrase which will become common usage as soon as the film comes out. Soon people will say Truffaut's children as they say Bengal Lancers, spoil-sports, Mafia chiefs, road-hogs, or again in a word, cinema-addicts. In *Les 400 Coups*, the director of *Les Mistons* will again have his camera, not up there with the men like Old Man Hawks, but down among the children. If a certain arrogance is implied in talking about 'up there' for the over-thirties, 'down there' should also be taken as implying pride in the under-sixteens: *Les 400 Coups* will be the proudest, stubbornest, most obstinate, in other words most free, film in the world. Morally speaking. Aesthetically, too. Henri Decae's Dyaliscope images will dazzle us like those of *Tarnished Angels*. The scenario will be fresh and airy like that of *Juvenile Passion*. The dialogue and gestures as caustic as those in *Baby Face Nelson*. The editing as delicate as that of *The Goddess*. Precocity will reveal its cloven hoof as in *The Left-handed Gun*. These titles do not spring at random from the keys of my electric typewriter. They come from François Truffaut's list of the ten best films of 1958. A charming and handsome family into which *Les 400 Coups* fits beautifully. To sum up, what shall I say? This: *Les 400 Coups* will be a film signed Frankness. Rapidity. Art. Novelty. Cinematograph. Originality. Impertinence. Seriousness. Tragedy. Renovation. Ubu-Roi. Fantasy. Ferocity. Affection. Universality. Tenderness.

MILAN KUNDERA
Slowness

What, in the cinema, is the last taboo with which the ethos of postmodernism has remained obstinately unreconciled? Evidently, not sex. The medium now routinely tackles themes that would have been proscribed just a few years ago. Not death, either. Death is an extra, more frequently a star, in well-nigh every Hollywood film. No, the correct answer, I propose, is slowness.

We postmoderns abominate whatever is deemed to be slow. When applied to a cultural manifestation, the adjective has become unequivocally pejorative. If, questioned about a film which he or she has just seen, an acquaintance replies that it is 'slow', we unanimously interpret that word as a criticism. Ensconced in what might be termed the heaven of polarities, those binary dichotomies by which our apprehension of the world is regulated – black and white, hot and cold, north and south – God surely declines to give preference to any one of His creations over the other. But we humans, unable to accept that without the one the other could not exist, have always felt compelled to construct hierarchies, and where 'fast' and 'slow' are concerned there can be little doubt where our preference lies. One of the most successful films of 1996 was Jan de Bont's Speed, *in which Keanu Reeves found himself in charge of a bus which, if its speed dropped below 50 miles an hour, was primed to blow up. Can one imagine the same actor starring in a film called* Slowness, *about a bus also wired to explode – only this time if it* exceeded, *let's say, a 50 mile an hour speed limit?*

Yet, around the same time as the release of Speed, *Milan Kundera published a novel entitled* Slowness. Speed *or* Slowness? *A film which – predicated as it was on the notion that speed, that emblematic symbol and symptom of modernity, was in itself an unequivocally good thing – careened towards its dénouement with the inflexible single-mindedness of an arrow? Or a novel which celebrated the Epicurean delights of taking one's own sweet time?*

Why has the pleasure of slowness disappeared? Ah, where have they gone, the amblers of yesteryear? Where have they gone, those loafing heroes of folk song, those vagabonds who roam from one mill to another and bed down under the stars? Have they vanished along with footpaths, with grasslands and clearings, with nature? There is a Czech proverb that describes their easy indolence by a metaphor: 'They are gazing at God's windows.' A person gazing at God's windows is not bored; he is happy. In our world, indolence has turned into having nothing to do, which is a completely different thing: a person with nothing to do is frustrated, bored, is constantly searching for the activity he lacks.

RICHARD WILBUR
Last Shaggy Doggerel

'Please let them have it both ways, *the audience prays.*'

   Could it be better said? The Prisoner of Zenda *in question, the fourth (out of five to date) since the cinema's invention, is Richard Thorpe's of 1952, of which Richard Wilbur's drolly miraculous little verse – a miracle that 'Granger' rhymes with both 'danger' and 'stranger', that 'Kerr' rhymes with 'co-star', even that 'Zenda' rhymes, sort of, with 'end a' – constitutes the most compact and perceptive review of the film imaginable.*

THE PRISONER OF ZENDA

At the end a
The Prisoner of Zenda,
The King being out of danger,
Stewart Granger
(As Rudolph Rassendyll)
Must swallow a bitter pill
By renouncing his co-star,
Deborah Kerr.

It would be poor behavia
In him and in Princess Flavia
Were they to put their own
Concerns before those of the Throne.
Deborah Kerr must wed
The King instead.

Rassendyll turns to go.
Must it be so?
Why can't they have their cake
And eat it, for heaven's sake?

Please let them have it both ways,
The audience prays.
And yet it is hard to quarrel
With a plot so moral.

One redeeming factor,
However, is that the actor
Who plays the once-dissolute King
(Who has learned through suffering
Not to drink or be mean
To his future Queen),
Far from being a stranger,
Is *also* Stewart Granger.

Criticizing

G. CABRERA INFANTE
from *A Twentieth Century Job*

From 1954 to 1960, before quitting his native island for what has turned out to be permanent exile in London, the Cuban novelist G. Cabrera Infante wrote film criticism under the nom de plume *of Guillermo Cain and eventually published it within hard covers as* A Twentieth Century Job. *Like, however, those actors who, while temporarily 'resting', are willing to earn a livelihood serving in some greasy short-order diner but would not be seen dead actually eating there, he appears to have had no very exalted opinion of the critic's vocation.*

The Absurd Eating the Absurd

These abhorrent pages seem no more to me than a symptom of the perversion of jobs. If the French Revolution brought us the end of artisanry, the revolutions of this century of revolutions will see the end of jobs. (But not of Job.) Now there is a science to study this anomaly called cybernetics. It is not for fun that I chose the epigraph by François Truffaut to begin the book. It's possible that some boy may still want to be a fireman when he grows up. Even if the fireproof asbestos and the *faiblesse* of matches have practically finished off fires, boys will be boyish and there will be those who want to substitute for lead soldiers facsimiles of flesh and blood: they want to be generals when they grow up. There may even be others who intend to be surgeons or butchers, depending on their skill in disembowelling birds. Or perhaps, to enumerate majordomos or

aviators
bootblacks
divers
spies
undertakers
nuclear physicists

pawnbrokers
proofreaders
gymnasts
pimps
pirates (and the references come together because these pro-
    fessions pertain to the turgid legend of humankind) or even
Nobel laureates
surrealists
café operators
percolators
postmen who ring only once
pilots
co-pilots
Pilates
abstract panthers
ambassadors to the U N
secretaries general
secretaries
undersecretaries
secretary birds
abstract panters
s. j. perelmans
sotto voces
sostenuti
saties
apostles
apostates
opeds
cashiers
muralists
assassins in uniform
confidence men
and even mayors
mythomaniacs
functionaries
receptionists
Poes
poets laureate
poets

poetasters
unpublished poets
popes, a.
sons of popes
vice-presidents
aspirants
minotaurs
devoted spouses
bonapartists
d.j.s.
bongo players
bookbinders
palmists
moonshiners
contrabassoonists
go-betweens
picassos
Jehovah's witnesses
brickmasons
writers
radio writers
sitcom writers
screen writers
CIA agents
rhinoceroses
hippopotami
monks lewis
adolphes saxes
panhandlers
major keys
heavy breathers
adoptive fathers
sons and lovers
buffaloes
buffalo bills
bills
illuminati
american express cards
cards

abstract pinters
trappists
rapists
aerialists
marsupials
moby dicks
peeping toms
bureaucrats
ticket takers
lapps
second lapps
box-office poisoners
valentinos
neonazis
cymbal players
pencil sharpeners
reflexologists
conductors (of trains)
conductors (of orchestras)
alexanders
ragtime bandits
romans-à-clef
negro spirituals
record players
hot jazzists
eunuchs
and of course the oldest profession

But it's doubtful that there's a kid who dreams of being a cinema critic: the absurd never ends up absurd.

'The cinema isn't Latin – it's American'

SACHA GUITRY

WILLIAM PLOMER

'NOT WHERE WE CAME IN'

'This is not where we came in,
The story has all gone wrong.
Don't you remember, we saw
Terraces, vistas, marble urns,
Magnolias of human skin, a tall
Carved door, and that low superb
Smooth car? Between the two
The perfect girl was poised, to lead
With the scent of her physical pride
A millionaire playboy wolf
And a polished, lecherous duke.
It was what we had paid to see –
An epic of processed tripe.

'But the story has all gone wrong,
Her castle was pastry, her diamonds dew,
Her glossy hair is withered,
Her shoe-heels are abraded.
Just look at the girl, would you know her?
A refugee drab, she's lugging
A suitcase full of grudges
That nobody wants to buy.
Look at her now, she's pointing
Straight at us. She's armed. She's speaking.
"It's *you*, and *you*, and *you*
To blame. Take *that*! and *that*! and *that*!"
My God, she's real! I'm shot! It's blood!'

Acknowledgements

I would like personally to acknowledge the help and support given me by the following:
Geoff Andrew, Walter Donohue, Clare Downs, Clive Hirschhorn, David Thompson and David Thomson, as also my two editors Anna South and Paul Keegan. Thank you.
Gilbert Adair

For permission to publish copyright material in this book grateful acknowledgement is made to the following:
Jean Baudrillard: 'Apocalypse Now' and 'The China Syndrome' from *Simulacra and Simulation* (University of Michigan Press, 1994), permission of the publisher; André Bazin: from 'Charlie Chaplin' from *What is Cinema?: Volume 1*, edited and translated by Hugh Gray (University of California Press, 1967) and 'Entomology of the Pin-up Girl' from *What is Cinema?: Volume 2*, edited and translated by Hugh Gray (University of California Press, 1972), by permission of the publisher; Joe Brainard: from *I Remember* (Viking, 1995), © 1975 by Joe Brainard, by permission of Viking Penguin, a division of Penguin Putnam Inc.; Robert Bresson: from *Notes on the Cinematographer* (Quartet Books, 1986), by permission of the publisher; Louise Brooks: 'Pabst and Lulu' from *Lulu in Hollywood* (1974), © 1974, 1982 by Louise Brooks, by permission of Alfred A. Knopf Inc; Karl Brown: from *Adventures with D. W. Griffith*, edited by Kevin Brownlow (Da Capo Press, 1976), by permission of Kevin Brownlow; Raymond Chandler: 'One Night in Hollywood' from *Atlantic Monthly* (1950), © Raymond Chandler 1948, by kind permission of the Estate of Robert Chandler in association with Ed Victor Ltd, Colette: 'Black and White' and 'Backstage at the Studio' from *Colette at the Movies*, translated by Sarah W. R. Smith (Frederick Ungar, 1980), by permission of the Continuum Publishing Company; Sergei Eisenstein: from *Eisenstein on Disney* (Methuen, 1988), by permission of the publisher; Abel Gance: 'The Era of the Image Has Arrived', originally published in 'L'Art Cinématographique' (1927), reprinted in *Regards Neufs sur le Cinéma*, edited by Jacques Chevailler, © 1953 Editions du Seuil, by permission of the publisher; Jean-Luc Godard: 'Les 400 Coups', translated by Tom Milne, from *Cahiers du Cinema, Volume 1: 1950s*, edited by J. Hillier (Routledge, 1985), by permission of the British Film Institute; Maxim Gorky: A review of the Lumière programme at the Nizhni-Novgorod Fair, as printed in the *Nizhegorodski listok*

newspaper, 4 July 1896, translated by Leda Swan, from *Kino* by Jay Leyda (George Allen & Unwin, 1960), by permission of HarperCollins Publishers; Peter Greenaway: 'Just place, preferably architectural place' from *Projections, 4 1/2*, edited by John Boorman and Walter Donohue (Faber & Faber, 1995), by permission of the publisher; J. Hoberman: 'Bad movies' from *Film Comment* (July, 1980), © 1980 by J. Hoberman, by permission of Georges Borchardt, Inc. for the author; G. Cabrera Infante: 'The absurd eating the absurd' from *A Twentieth Century Job*, translated by Kenneth E. Hall (Faber & Faber, 1991), by permission of the publisher; Otar Iosseliani: 'About Boris Barnet' from *Projections, 4 1/2*, edited by John Boorman and Walter Donohue (Faber & Faber, 1995), by permission of the publisher; Rudyard Kipling: 'Naaman's Song' from *Rudyard Kipling's Verse: Definitive Edition* (Hodder & Stoughton, 1940), by permission of A. P. Watt Ltd on behalf of The National Trust for Places of Historic Interest or Natural Beauty; Akira Kurosawa: from *Something Like an Autobiography*, translated by Audie E. Bock (1982), © 1982 by Akira Kurosawa, by permission of Alfred A. Knopf; Erwin Leiser: from 'The Wandering Jew', taken from *Nazi Cinema* (Macmillan, 1975), by permission of Tanja Howarth Literary Agency on behalf of the Estate of Erwin Leiser; Dusan Makavejev: 'Life as a remake of movies' from *Projections, 4 1/2*, edited by John Boorman and Walter Donohue (Faber & Faber, 1995), by permission of the publisher; Greil Marcus: 'John Wayne Listening' from *The Dustbin of History* (Picador, 1996), by permission of David Higham Associates; Jonas Mekas: 'Warhol's Sleep' from *The Village Voice* (July, 1964), © 1964 by Jonas Mekas, by permission of Georges Borchardt, Inc. for the author; Henry Miller: 'The Golden Age' from *The Cosmological Eye* (New Directions Publishing Corporation, 1939), © 1939 by New Directions Publishing Corporation; copyright the Literary Executors of the Estate of Henry Miller, by permission of Curtis Brown Ltd, London, on behalf of the Estate of Henry Miller; Vladimir Nabokov: from *Speak, Memory: An Autobiography* (Weidenfeld & Nicolson, 1967), by permission of The Orion Publishing Group Ltd; Claude Ollier: 'A King in New York: *King Kong*', translated by Tom Milne, from *Cahiers du Cinéma, Volume 2: 1960–1968*, edited by J. Hillier (Routledge, 1990), by permission of The British Film Institute; William Plomer: 'Not Where We Came In' from *Collected Poems* (Jonathan Cape, 1973), by permission of Sir Rupert Hart-Davis; Delmore Schwartz: 'In Dreams Begin Responsibilities' from *In Dreams Begin Responsibilities*, © 1961 by Delmore Schwartz, by permission of Laurence Pollinger Ltd and New Directions Publishing Corporation; François Truffaut: 'The Rogues are Weary', translated by Liz Heron, from *Cahiers du Cinéma, Volume 1: 1950s*, edited by J. Hillier (Routledge, 1985), by permission of The British Film Institute; 'La Tour de nesle', translated by Leonard Mayhew, from *The Films in My Life* (Simon & Schuster, 1978), © 1975 by Flammarion, by permission of Simon & Schuster Inc.; John Updike: 'Home Movies' from *Collected Poems 1953–1993* (Hamish Hamilton, 1993), © 1993 by John Updike, by permission of Alfred A. Knopf Inc.; 'The Newlyweds' from *Collected Poems 1953–1993* (Hamish Hamilton,

1993), © 1993 by John Updike, by permission of Victor Gollancz Ltd and Alfred A. Knopf Inc.; Wim Wenders: 'Despising What You Sell' and 'Re: Bad Day at Black Rock' from *Emotion Pictures: Reflections on the Cinema* (Faber & Faber, 1991), by permission of the publisher; Richard Wilbur: 'The Prisoner of Zenda' from *New and Collected Poems* (Faber & Faber, 1989), by permission of the publisher; Cesare Zavattini: 'Some Ideas on the Cinema' from *Sight and Sound*, Volume 23 (New Quarterly Series) No. 2 (October–December, 1953), by permission of the publisher.

Every effort has been made to trace all copyright holders. The publishers would be pleased to rectify any omissions brought to their notice at the earliest opportunity.

Illustrations

Louis Lumière, *L'Arrivée d'un train à La Ciotat, France* (1987)
(Courtesy: Faber & Faber Ltd and Association frères Lumière)

D. W. Griffith, *Intolerance* (1916)
(Courtesy: The Museum of Modern Art, New York)

Jean Vigo, *À Propos de Nice* (1930). Photograph by Boris Kaufman. In Kevin Macdonald and Mark Cousins (eds.), *Imagining Reality: The Faber Book of Documentary* (Faber, 1996)
(Courtesy: Cahiers du Cinéma)

Buston Keaton (as a child)
(Courtesy: Photofest, New York)

Brigitte Helm, *L'Atlantide* (1932)
(Courtesy: Cahiers du Cinéma)

Alfred Hitchcock, *The Wrong Man* (1957). In François Truffaut, *Hitchcock* (Secker & Warburg, 1968)

Abbas Kiarostami, *And Life Continues*
(Courtesy: Cahiers du Cinéma)

Charles Addams, © The New Yorker Collection, 1947
(Courtesy: The Cartoon Bank, New York. All Rights Reserved)

READ MORE IN PENGUIN

In every corner of the world, on every subject under the sun, Penguin represents quality and variety – the very best in publishing today.

For complete information about books available from Penguin – including Puffins, Penguin Classics and Arkana – and how to order them, write to us at the appropriate address below. Please note that for copyright reasons the selection of books varies from country to country.

In the United Kingdom: Please write to *Dept. EP, Penguin Books Ltd, Bath Road, Harmondsworth, West Drayton, Middlesex UB7 ODA*

In the United States: Please write to *Consumer Sales, Penguin Putnam Inc., P.O. Box 12289 Dept. B, Newark, New Jersey 07101-5289.* VISA and MasterCard holders call 1-800-788-6262 to order Penguin titles

In Canada: Please write to *Penguin Books Canada Ltd, 10 Alcorn Avenue, Suite 300, Toronto, Ontario M4V 3B2*

In Australia: Please write to *Penguin Books Australia Ltd, P.O. Box 257, Ringwood, Victoria 3134*

In New Zealand: Please write to *Penguin Books (NZ) Ltd, Private Bag 102902, North Shore Mail Centre, Auckland 10*

In India: Please write to *Penguin Books India Pvt Ltd, 11 Community Centre, Panchsheel Park, New Delhi 110017*

In the Netherlands: Please write to *Penguin Books Netherlands bv, Postbus 3507, NL-1001 AH Amsterdam*

In Germany: Please write to *Penguin Books Deutschland GmbH, Metzlerstrasse 26, 60594 Frankfurt am Main*

In Spain: Please write to *Penguin Books S. A., Bravo Murillo 19, 1° B, 28015 Madrid*

In Italy: Please write to *Penguin Italia s.r.l., Via Benedetto Croce 2, 20094 Corsico, Milano*

In France: Please write to *Penguin France, Le Carré Wilson, 62 rue Benjamin Baillaud, 31500 Toulouse*

In Japan: Please write to *Penguin Books Japan Ltd, Kaneko Building, 2-3-25 Koraku, Bunkyo-Ku, Tokyo 112*

In South Africa: Please write to *Penguin Books South Africa (Pty) Ltd, Private Bag X14, Parkview, 2122 Johannesburg*

READ MORE IN PENGUIN

READ MORE IN PENGUIN

Published or forthcoming:

Artificial Paradises Edited by Mike Jay

Taking Baudelaire's now famous title as its own, this anthology reveals the diverse roles mind-altering drugs have played throughout history. It brings together a multiplicity of voices to explore the presence – both secret and public – of drugs in the overlapping dialogues of science and religion, pleasure and madness, individualism and social control. From Apuleius's *Golden Ass* to Hunter S. Thompson's frenzied *Fear and Loathing in Las Vegas*, via Sartre's nightmarish experiences with mescaline and Walter Benjamin's ecstatic wanderings on hashish, *Artificial Paradises* is packed full of the weird, the wonderful and the shocking.

'This is a superb anthology – scholarly, penetrative, mind-expanding. It's probably the best of its kind' Ian McEwan

'Excellent . . . shows how drugs permeate the very fabric of our history and culture' Irvine Welsh

READ MORE IN PENGUIN

Published or forthcoming:

Titanic Edited by John Wilson Foster

RMS *Titanic* sank to the bottom of the Atlantic during a night of rare calm, but the tragedy caused shock waves on both sides of the ocean and has continued to haunt our imaginations ever since.

The human drama of the disaster still has much of the power to excite and appal that it had in 1912, inspiring novels, films, plays, paintings and music. This anthology draws from more than eight decades of literature about the great ship, combining journalism, essays, fiction, poems, letters, songs and transcripts of hearings. It relives the event through the accounts of survivors, witnesses and commentators, with contributions from major writers of the time such as Joseph Conrad, H. G. Wells, Thomas Hardy, George Bernard Shaw and Sir Arthur Conan Doyle.

But beyond that it also shows how the sinking of *Titanic* was a cultural phenomenon which fulfilled the anxieties of its time – the frictions of class, race and gender, the hunger for progress and machine efficiency, and the arrogant assumptions of the Mechanical Age.